STUDENT'S ATLAS

OF

AMERICAN PRESIDENTIAL ELECTIONS 1789–1996

Fred L. Israel

Congressional Quarterly Inc.
Washington, D.C.

Copyright © 1997 Congressional Quarterly Inc.
1414 22nd Street N.W., Washington, D.C. 20037

Printed in the United States of America

First Printing

Library of Congress Cataloging-in-Publication Data
Israel, Fred L.
Student's atlas of American presidential elections 1789–1996/Fred L. Israel.
     p.   cm.
     Includes bibliographical references and index.
     ISBN 1-56802-377-4
     1. Presidents – United States – Election – History   I. Title
JK524.I85   1997   97-10233
324.973'009 – dc21   CIP

TABLE OF CONTENTS

INTRODUCTION

The Founding Fathers rejected a hereditary ruler and feared a strong head of state. They established an elected chief executive with a specific term of office. Article II, Section 1 of the Constitution explains: "The executive Power shall be vested in a President of the United States of America. He shall hold his Office during the Term of four Years." The article delegated the choice of president neither to the Congress nor to the people but to a group of "electors" designated in each state for this single, specific, and temporary purpose.

The Founding Fathers assumed that George Washington would be the first president. They did not fix the number of terms because the incentive to be reelected would give the president what Gouverneur Morris of Pennsylvania called "the great motive to good behavior, the hope of being rewarded with a re-appointment." Morris also noted the danger of not allowing the president to stand for reelection: "Shut the Civil road to glory & he may be compelled to seek it by the sword."

Washington left the presidency after eight years because he longed for "the shade of retirement." Thomas Jefferson, who was U.S. minister to France during the Constitutional Convention, had always opposed unrestricted service for any officeholder. In 1807, as his second term neared completion, Jefferson invoked Washington's precedent by emphatically stating that no president should serve more than two terms.

In 1840, the Whig National Convention took the examples of Washington and Jefferson one step further. The Whigs agreed that a president should serve only one four-year term. From 1840 to 1860, no president was renominated. Lincoln restored the two-term tradition in 1864. Of the first 31 presidents from Washington to Herbert Hoover, 20 served one term of four years or less, and none served more than two terms. Franklin D. Roosevelt broke this tradition in 1941 when he was inaugurated to a third term, and public opinion polls found voters deeply divided over Roosevelt's decision. In 1944, as World War II drew to an end, Roosevelt won a fourth term. (He died in office on 12 April 1945.) In February 1951, rejecting the advice offered by Gouverneur Morris in 1787, the Twenty-second Amendment was passed. It said: "No person shall be elected to the office of the President more than twice, and no person who has held the office of President, or acted as President, for more than two years of a term to which some other person was elected President shall be elected to the office of the President more than once."

The Founders expected each state to vote for a "favorite son" for president so that one candidate would seldom obtain a majority of electoral votes necessary for election. That is why they provided for a final election of the president by the U.S. House of Representatives, where the voting would be by states, with a majority necessary to elect. Thus, the large states would nominate popular leaders, but the small states would still have a major share in electing the president. James Madison thought this would happen "nineteen times out of twenty." The emergence of political parties, however, allowed the electoral system envisioned by the Federal Convention to operate only twice, in 1801 and 1825.

In October 1787, Alexander Hamilton asked John Jay and James Madison to join him in writing a series of essays to explain, defend, and promote the ratification of the Constitution. In *Federalist 65*, Hamilton stressed the importance of affording "as little opportunity as possible to tumult and disorder" in the election of the chief magistrate. Selection of the president by Congress, he argued, would invite "cabal, intrigue, and corruption." Direct election by the people would expose the process to "heats and ferments" arising from mass emotion. The election of the president should be made by "a small number of persons, selected by their fellow-citizens . . . [This] body of electors, will be much less apt to convulse the community with any extraordinary and violent movements." In his *Farewell Address* (1796), Washington reiterated Hamilton's views. The President warned against political parties where factions dominate other factions, which could lead to the demise of popular government and to despotism. He urged "uniform vigilance" to prevent divisive political parties from forming. But after the 1796 election, the electors stopped exercising independent judgment and began casting their votes along party lines.

For the next 30 years, a party's membership in Congress—the congressional caucus—chose presidential nominees. Sometimes state and local officials also put forward candidates. The first national nominating convention was held in 1831 by the Anti-Mason Party; the Republican and Democratic parties held their first conventions the next year. Delegates were selected by various state procedures, some more democratic than others. Custom dictated that the convention sought the candidate. Potential nominees tried to appear disinterested, and they rarely attended a nominating convention.

By the first decade of the twentieth century, political reformers considered the convention presidential nominating system most undemocratic because it was dominated by party bosses seeking patronage. The primary system began as a way to increase voter participation in selecting the party's nominees. Candidates now had to seek the support of convention delegates. Most twentieth-century political conventions have seen a combination of delegates chosen by political machines and delegates elected in primaries. In the elections of 1992 and 1996, success in the primaries determined the nominees of both major parties.

Television and public opinion polls have had a dramatic impact on the presidential nominating process in recent years. Both have contributed to reorganizing the traditional political structure. Whereas the boss-dominated machine once held the party together, television now presents the candidates directly to the voter. Public opinion polls present the voters' views directly to the politicians. Political bosses, so important in nineteenth-century America, have gradually lost their influence.

What do the presidents of the United States have in common? First and above all, they were elected by the voters. Article II of the Constitution required that they be natural born citizens and at least 35 years of age. The Constitution left voting qualifications to the states. At first, the states limited voting to White and very few African American men who owned a certain amount of property. After the Civil War (1861–1865), the Fourteenth (1868) and Fifteenth (1870) Amendments guaranteed the vote to all men over the age of 21. The guarantee was only in theory. The Nineteenth Amendment (1920) extended the right to vote to women. In 1964, the Twenty-fourth Amendment abolished the poll tax—a fee paid before a citizen was allowed to vote. This tax had kept many poor people, both Black and White, from voting in several southern states. And the Twenty-sixth Amendment (1971) lowered the voting age to 18. Felons in prison are prohibited from voting in 46 states; only Maine, Massachusetts, Utah, and Vermont allow prison inmates to vote. Thirteen states permanently deprive virtually all felons from voting, and 31 states do not allow felons to vote while they are on probation or parole.

It seems that the presidents have little else in common except that, to date, the voters have elected them to high office. Some presidents were surprisingly strong-willed men, while others were simply miscast. Although Abraham Lincoln prevented the permanent break-up of the Union and Woodrow Wilson and Franklin D. Roosevelt each confronted a world war, most presidents were average men doing the best they could in a complicated job. Sometimes the election process brought forward nominees who seemed poorly qualified for the office but who grew mightily once in power. Likewise, there does not seem to be a pattern in the kind of person whom the voters have chosen to be their president. They have been as young as John F. Kennedy (43) and as old as Ronald Reagan (69). They have come from states across the country, from Vermont to California. They have come from the U.S. Congress and from governor's mansions. Six generals (George Washington, William Henry Harrison, Andrew Jackson, Benjamin Harrison, Ulysses S. Grant, and Dwight D. Eisenhower) have been elected to the presidency.

The awkward nature of the vice presidency has provided material for many jokes. John Adams, the nation's first vice president, found the office "too inactive and insignificant." John Nance Garner, vice president during Franklin D. Roosevelt's first two terms, said that the vice presidency was not "worth a pitcher of warm spit." Usually, the president's running mate has been chosen for partisan considerations to provide sectional balance rather than for his own merit. Many had few credentials for the office. The vice presidential position has often been used to unify a party by the selection of a candidate who had disagreed with the standard-bearer on important issues. For example, George Bush, before being selected by Ronald Reagan as his running mate in 1980, had called Reagan's economic programs "voodoo economics." Some vice presidents who were chosen for purely political reasons, such as Theodore Roosevelt and Harry S. Truman, became genuinely first-rate presidents.

Except for the tragic Civil War which followed the 1860 election of Lincoln, the electorate has accepted the peaceful transfer of power without the "tumult and disorder," the "extraordinary and violent movements," feared by Alexander Hamilton. We probably will never be able to explain why individuals continue to seek the presidency; why they plead and plan their way to a presidential nomination. I assume that since someone has to occupy the highest office the nation can bestow, there are those who sincerely believe that they are the best qualified for the job—that they are the most capable of dealing wisely with the varied problems facing the nation, and that by their leadership, they can guide a great nation to secure and maintain peace and prosperity.

Student's Atlas of American Presidential Elections 1789–1996 is intended to be an introduction to the subject. It attempts to tell the story, graphically and verbally, of each of the 53 presidential elections in the history of the United States. The first 9 elections are covered by one map showing the electoral vote and one page of text. The Electoral College tables for the elections of 1789, 1792, 1796, and 1800 show *all* electoral votes cast. The charts for 1804 and thereafter show electoral votes cast only for president. Starting with 1824, each election is covered by one page showing the electoral vote for president, and also one page giving the popular vote by state, and two pages of text. The Democratic vote in the District of Columbia is not shown for the elections of 1972, 1984, and 1988 because the area is too small to show in a separate color. I have tried to capture the essence of the elections, giving information about the candidates, the issues, the campaign, and the election itself.

ACKNOWLEDGMENTS

I have incurred many debts of gratitude in writing this manuscript. My first is to Charles E. Smith, President, Charles E. Smith Books, Inc. Mr. Smith conceived of this project. He meticulously read and critiqued each essay, and his suggestions were invaluable. I am indebted to Maribeth A. Corona, Editor, Charles E. Smith Books, Inc. She patiently transcribed my script to the typed page, copyedited, and proofread. Her effort was indeed Herculean. I would like to thank M. E. Aslett Corporation, which carried out the electronic preparation of this volume—especially Elizabeth Geary and Robert Bovasso, who designed and compiled the pages, and Jacqueline Flamm, who prepared the index.

Fred L. Israel
The City College of New York

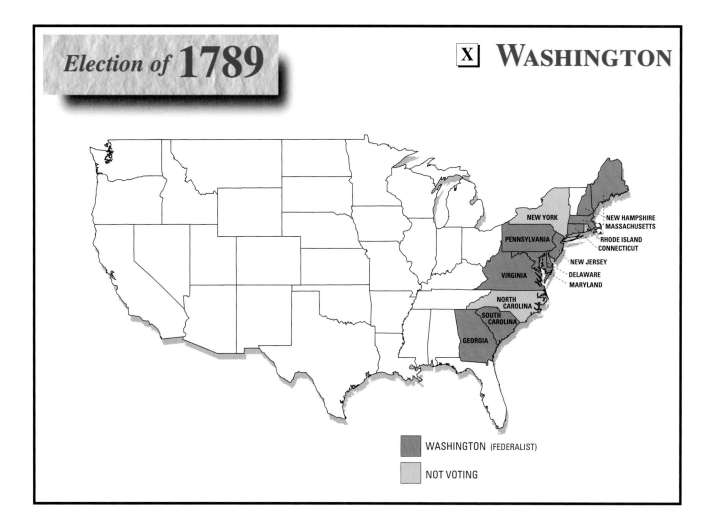

WASHINGTON (FEDERALIST)

NOT VOTING

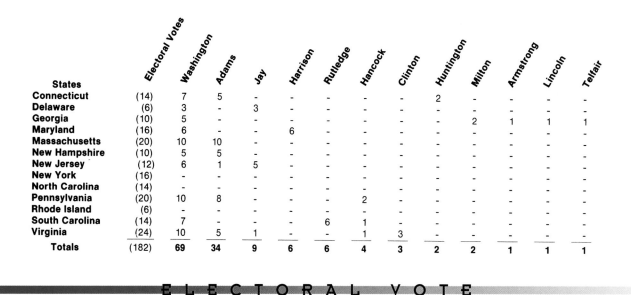

States	Electoral Votes	Washington	Adams	Jay	Harrison	Rutledge	Hancock	Clinton	Huntington	Milton	Armstrong	Lincoln	Telfair
Connecticut	(14)	7	5	-	-	-	-	-	2	-	-	-	-
Delaware	(6)	3	-	3	-	-	-	-	-	-	-	-	-
Georgia	(10)	5	-	-	-	-	-	-	-	2	1	1	1
Maryland	(16)	6	-	-	6	-	-	-	-	-	-	-	-
Massachusetts	(20)	10	10	-	-	-	-	-	-	-	-	-	-
New Hampshire	(10)	5	5	-	-	-	-	-	-	-	-	-	-
New Jersey	(12)	6	1	5	-	-	-	-	-	-	-	-	-
New York	(16)	-	-	-	-	-	-	-	-	-	-	-	-
North Carolina	(14)	-	-	-	-	-	-	-	-	-	-	-	-
Pennsylvania	(20)	10	8	-	-	-	2	-	-	-	-	-	-
Rhode Island	(6)	-	-	-	-	-	-	-	-	-	-	-	-
South Carolina	(14)	7	-	-	-	6	1	-	-	-	-	-	-
Virginia	(24)	10	5	1	-	-	1	3	-	-	-	-	-
Totals	(182)	69	34	9	6	6	4	3	2	2	1	1	1

E L E C T O R A L   V O T E

The inauguration of George Washington as the first president of the United States also marked the beginning of a national republican government. The United States possessed territory equal to all of western Europe plus Great Britain. It stretched from the Atlantic Ocean to the Mississippi River and from the Great Lakes to Spanish-owned Florida. The 1790 census listed the population as just under 4 million, including some 700,000 slaves. Ninety percent of these overwhelmingly rural people lived east of the Appalachian Mountains. Philadelphia, the largest city, had about 42,000 inhabitants, followed by New York with 33,000, and Boston with 18,000.

The question of who the first president of the United States would be never arose during the Constitutional Convention (1787) and the state ratifying conventions. One man towered over all his contemporaries. In the words of Henry Lee of Virginia, George Washington was "first in war, first in peace, first in the hearts of his countrymen." When the Continental Congress chose Washington to command the Continental army (1775), he was already a leader in the movement for independence from Great Britain. By sheer force of character, he held the army together for the eight years it took to win independence. Washington presided over the Constitutional Convention which met in Philadelphia (1787). His widely publicized attendance at the Convention was critical to its success. Washington's personal prestige was needed once again in 1788, this time to launch the new government.

The old Continental Congress, which still met at irregular intervals, passed a resolution on 13 September 1788 which put the Constitution into operation. The first Wednesday of January 1789 was fixed as the day for choosing presidential electors; the first Wednesday of February for their meeting in their several states to cast two ballots, one of which would have to be for a person from another state; and the first Wednesday of March for the opening session of the new Congress in New York City, the nation's temporary capital. Because of various delays, mainly caused by poor roads and bad weather, only one-third of the senators and less than a quarter of the representatives reached New York by the appointed day. "The people will forget the new government before it is born," lamented a senator from Massachusetts.

The first part of the process, choosing the presidential electors, proceeded without difficulty except in New York. The legislatures of Connecticut, New Jersey, Delaware, South Carolina, and Georgia chose the electors. In Pennsylvania, Maryland, and Virginia, the eligible voters chose them from lists proposed by meetings of leading supporters of the Constitution in those states. In New Hampshire, the voters nominated electors but the actual appointment was left to the legislature. In Massachusetts, 2 electors were selected by the voters and the legislature picked 8 others from a list of 24 names recommended by meetings held in each of the state's congressional districts. The details of New York's difficulties are unimportant but since its legislature would not compromise, New York deprived itself of voting in the first presidential election. North Carolina and Rhode Island had not yet ratified the Constitution.

The 69 electors had met in February, cast their votes and sent them to Congress to count them. While all knew the results, it was not until 6 April 1789 that Congress finally had a quorum. Washington received the votes of all 69 electors and was chosen president. John Adams of Massachusetts received the second highest number of votes (34) and, therefore, became the vice president. A messenger reached Adams at his Braintree, Massachusetts home on 12 April and another messenger formally informed Washington of his election at Mount Vernon on 14 April. Washington immediately wrote Congress of his acceptance. He started out for New York two days later and reached it on 23 April.

Washington wrote that he foresaw only "an ocean of difficulties, without that competency of political skill, abilities, and inclination, which are necessary to manage the helm. . . . Integrity and firmness are all I can promise." Robert R. Livingston, chancellor of the State of New York, administered the oath of office to Washington on a balcony of Federal Hall overlooking Wall Street on 30 April 1789. Then, turning toward the people, Livingston proclaimed in a loud voice: "Long live George Washington, President of the United States." The crowd took up the cry and roared its approval.

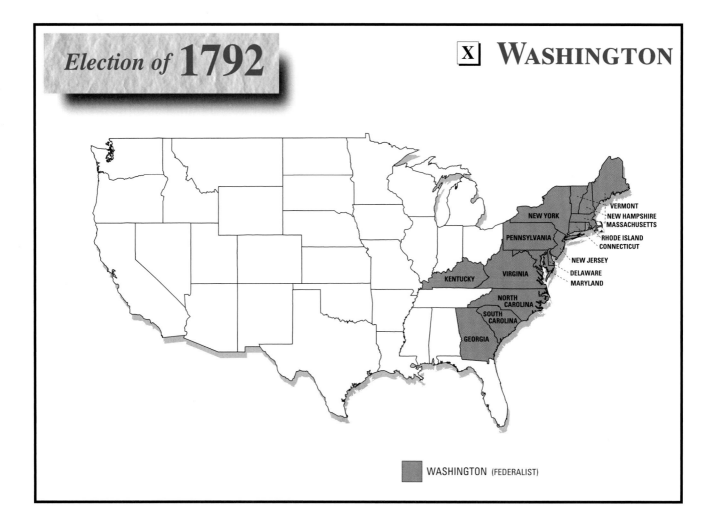

Election of **1792**

X **WASHINGTON**

WASHINGTON (FEDERALIST)

States	Electoral Votes	Washington	Adams	Clinton	Jefferson	Burr
Connecticut	(18)	9	9	-	-	-
Delaware	(6)	3	3	-	-	-
Georgia	(8)	4	-	4	-	-
Kentucky	(8)	4	-	-	4	-
Maryland	(20)	8	8	-	-	-
Massachusetts	(32)	16	16	-	-	-
New Hampshire	(12)	6	6	-	-	-
New Jersey	(14)	7	7	-	-	-
New York	(24)	12	-	12	-	-
North Carolina	(24)	12	-	12	-	-
Pennsylvania	(30)	15	14	1	-	-
Rhode Island	(8)	4	4	-	-	-
South Carolina	(16)	8	7	-	-	1
Vermont	(8)	3	3	-	-	-
Virginia	(42)	21	-	21	-	-
Totals	**(270)**	**132**	**77**	**50**	**4**	**1**

E L E C T O R A L   V O T E

On 5 May 1792, President George Washington confidentially told James Madison that he would retire at the end of his term. Madison wrote in his personal notes that Washington thought himself a poor administrator, inexperienced "in the forms of public business," and insecure in interpreting the Constitution. Now 60 years old, Washington said he was "in the decline of life." Above all, he was disgusted with the political factionalism tearing apart his administration. He longed for the peace of Mount Vernon, his beloved Virginia plantation.

No specific dates can be given for the beginning of political parties in the United States, but they began to solidify between 1789 and 1792. Political groups, whether they be called factions, cliques, or cabals, certainly were not new. They existed throughout eighteenth-century American politics. However, the office of the president of the United States, a democratically elected head of state, was a new element. Washington disliked political parties and considered them unpatriotic. He believed that the president had to stand above such quarrels and focus on the welfare of the nation. Washington was convinced that his proper role was to be the head of the nation, avoiding taking sides in the debates over public policy.

Washington's key advisers were his protégés as well as his trusted friends. They were sharply divided by different visions of the new nation. Alexander Hamilton envisioned a powerful nation with a strong national economy. He supported federal assistance to encourage banking and the country's developing factory system. Hamilton believed in a highly centralized government as a means of keeping public order. This meant making the federal government stronger by reducing the power of the states. It also meant a strong national judicial system and an army maintained on a permanent basis, even in times of peace. An elitist by temperament, Hamilton distrusted "the people" as selfish and unreasonable. Thomas Jefferson, on the other hand, thought farmers were the eternal guardians of public virtue. He distrusted large cities, commerce, and bankers—and Alexander Hamilton. As a slaveholding Virginia country squire, Jefferson had a deep attachment to the land and to those who farmed it. He favored local over national government. He preferred Congress over the other branches of the federal government because he thought Congress best reflected the will of the people. Jefferson and James Madison, friends and neighbors, were opposed to standing armies, fearing that a military leader might seize control of the government. Jefferson believed that all jurisdiction belonging to the federal government was listed in the Constitution and that all other authority was reserved to the states. Hamilton, on the other hand, believed that the general clauses of the Constitution implied vast power for the federal government.

Supporters of Jefferson and Madison were called Democratic-Republicans, usually shortened to Republicans. Their party is the root of today's Democratic Party. Hamilton's allies and supporters were called Federalists. A majority of newspaper editors supported Hamilton's national program, as did persons of wealth. Jefferson drew his support from small farmers and mechanics (workers).

As the 1792 presidential election neared, neither the Republicans nor the Federalists were organized well enough to run a candidate for president. Hamilton and Jefferson each pleaded with Washington to rethink his retirement plans. They feared that the Union would break apart. Reluctantly, Washington agreed to serve again. Jefferson's supporters, however, backed New York Governor George Clinton rather than John Adams for vice president. Washington and Adams were both reelected by electors chosen in almost the same manner as in the first election four years earlier. The electors, now from 15 states, cast 132 of their 135 ballots for Washington; 3 electors did not vote. Vice President John Adams received 77 votes to Clinton's 50.

Neither Adams nor Clinton campaigned but, instead, depended upon the efforts of their friends to influence the electors. However, such influence was minimal, even in states that chose the electors by popular vote. Newspapers supported different candidates, but there was very little excitement prior to the election.

What was most important about the first two presidential elections was that the electoral system worked, despite its awkwardness. The new Republic had shown the world that a national leader could be peacefully elected.

Washington rode alone from his home on Market Street in Philadelphia to the Senate Chamber. He took the oath of office on 4 March 1793 and delivered the shortest inaugural address in U.S. history—135 words.

Election of 1796

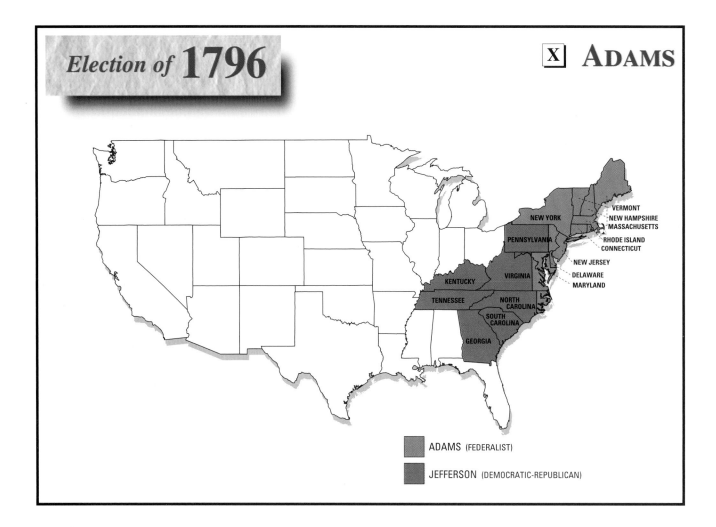

X **ADAMS**

ADAMS (FEDERALIST)

JEFFERSON (DEMOCRATIC-REPUBLICAN)

States	Electoral Votes	J. Adams	Jefferson	T. Pinckney	Burr	S. Adams	Ellsworth	Clinton	Jay	Iredell	Henry	Johnston	Washington	C. Pinckney
Connecticut	(18)	9	-	4	-	-	-	-	5	-	-	-	-	-
Delaware	(6)	3	-	3	-	-	-	-	-	-	-	-	-	-
Georgia	(8)	-	4	-	-	-	-	4	-	-	-	-	-	-
Kentucky	(8)	-	4	-	4	-	-	-	-	-	-	-	-	-
Maryland	(20)	7	4	4	3	-	-	-	-	-	2	-	-	-
Massachusetts	(32)	16	-	13	-	-	1	-	-	-	-	2	-	-
New Hampshire	(12)	6	-	-	-	-	6	-	-	-	-	-	-	-
New Jersey	(14)	7	-	7	-	-	-	-	-	-	-	-	-	-
New York	(24)	12	-	12	-	-	-	-	-	-	-	-	-	-
North Carolina	(24)	1	11	1	6	-	-	-	-	3	-	-	1	1
Pennsylvania	(30)	1	14	2	13	-	-	-	-	-	-	-	-	-
Rhode Island	(8)	4	-	-	-	-	4	-	-	-	-	-	-	-
South Carolina	(16)	-	8	8	-	-	-	-	-	-	-	-	-	-
Tennessee	(6)	-	3	-	3	-	-	-	-	-	-	-	-	-
Vermont	(8)	4	-	4	-	-	-	-	-	-	-	-	-	-
Virginia	(42)	1	20	1	1	15	-	3	-	-	-	-	1	-
Totals	(276)	71	68	59	30	15	11	7	5	3	2	2	2	1

ELECTORAL VOTE

The central issue in the 1796 election was whether the United States could survive without George Washington. Washington, no doubt, could have held the presidency for life had he wished but he was weary of politics. In his *Farewell Address,* the retiring President deplored political conflict and warned Americans against disunity, whether sectional or political. He cautioned against permanent alliances with foreign nations, recommending that the country be guided by its own interests and not become tied to the grander designs of European powers.

By 1796, the fierce differences between the Federalists and the Republicans had spread to state and local elections. The parties had not yet established procedures for selecting candidates. There were no national nominating conventions as we now know them. Instead, the leaders agreed among themselves on who should run.

Federalist members of Congress chose John Adams as their candidate for president. Adams feared that the "common people," if allowed to dominate government, would attack and impoverish the wealthy. He believed that those who owned property were the natural leaders. Unlike Alexander Hamilton, however, he distrusted banks and bankers. He agreed with Thomas Jefferson's views that excessive commercial activities could produce corruption and destroy the nation. Fearful of social strife, and opposed to any threat to wealth, Adams regarded the French Revolution as the unleashing of the most dangerous and hateful forces in history.

The Republicans turned to Thomas Jefferson. Jefferson thought that the British had too much influence in the U.S. government and that Hamilton helped them too much. Jefferson perceived the French Revolution as part of a grand crusade for human rights. Republican newspapers attacked Adams as being a monarchist while the Federalist press accused Jefferson of being a servant of the French.

Each party began a political practice, known as "balancing the ticket," that has been followed ever since. The Federalists chose Thomas Pinckney of South Carolina to run for vice president with Adams who came from Massachusetts and who had strong support in the New England region. The Republicans chose Aaron Burr of New York to balance Jefferson who came from Virginia.

The two presidential candidates did not campaign. This was left to their supporters. Jefferson's supporters directed their efforts at ordinary citizens while Adams's supporters focused on the electors themselves. Republican pamphlets and leaflets accused Adams of supporting a class of American royalty. Handbills were nailed to doors and men were hired to distribute anti-Adams broadsides (posters). The Republican message was that Jefferson was a friend of the rights of man and a champion of democracy while Adams was a monarchist who would ruin the infant Republic.

Sixteen states took part in the 1796 election. The legislature chose the electors in eight states: Vermont, Connecticut, New York, New Jersey, Delaware, South Carolina, Georgia, and Tennessee. The other eight states—New Hampshire, Massachusetts, Rhode Island, Pennsylvania, Maryland, Virginia, North Carolina, and Kentucky—held some sort of popular election for the electors but the method varied. In Rhode Island, for example, town meetings selected the state's four electors. In Kentucky, four special districts were created, each naming one elector. In Pennsylvania, voters chose electors from a statewide ticket. Each party constructed a carefully balanced list of popular persons representing different parts of the state and different ethnic groups. The results showed that many had voted a "straight ticket" for all 15 Federalist or Republican electors.

On the first Wednesday of February 1797, the ballots of 138 electors were counted in the presence of Congress; each elector had 2 votes. John Adams won the election, receiving a majority of 71 electoral votes to Jefferson's 68. At this time, prior to the passage of the Twelfth Amendment (1804), the person with the second highest number of electoral votes became vice president. Jefferson, therefore, became the second vice president of the United States. Adams's strength came from New England and the Middle Atlantic states. Jefferson's support mainly came from the South, the frontier states of Kentucky and Tennessee, and Pennsylvania, where he did extremely well among the working class.

The 1796 election is important because it was the first time in modern history that the elected chief executive of an independent nation had voluntarily surrendered office and his successor was chosen in accordance with a plan detailed in a written constitution. Also, for the first and only time in U.S. history, the United States had a president and a vice president each the nominal head of a rival political party.

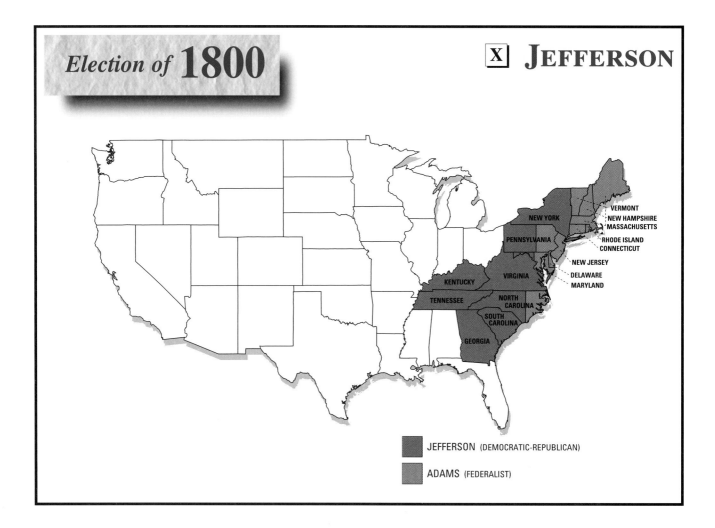

JEFFERSON (DEMOCRATIC-REPUBLICAN)

ADAMS (FEDERALIST)

States	Electoral Votes	Jefferson	Burr	Adams	Pinckney	Jay
Connecticut	(18)	-	-	9	9	-
Delaware	(6)	-	-	3	3	-
Georgia	(8)	4	4	-	-	-
Kentucky	(8)	4	4	-	-	-
Maryland	(20)	5	5	5	5	-
Massachusetts	(32)	-	-	16	16	-
New Hampshire	(12)	-	-	6	6	-
New Jersey	(14)	-	-	7	7	-
New York	(24)	12	12	-	-	-
North Carolina	(24)	8	8	4	4	-
Pennsylvania	(30)	8	8	7	7	-
Rhode Island	(8)	-	-	4	3	1
South Carolina	(16)	8	8	-	-	-
Tennessee	(6)	3	3	-	-	-
Vermont	(8)	-	-	4	4	-
Virginia	(42)	21	21	-	-	-
Totals	(276)	73	73	65	64	1

ELECTORAL VOTE

The election of 1800 demonstrated that political parties had become a permanent part of the American political process. Two issues divided the new parties—the foreign policy of the Adams administration and the Alien and Sedition Acts.

French leaders assumed that most Americans sympathized with the more radical phases of their Revolution. This made them bold enough to embarrass President John Adams by trying to frustrate his pro-British foreign policy. Their actions had the opposite effect; there was an outpouring of patriotic support for the President. The United States began an undeclared naval war against France (1798–1800). The U.S. Navy cooperated with the British against France, the country which had assisted the American revolutionaries. Thomas Jefferson and his Republican associates were shocked at the foreign policy of the Federalist Party.

As the election of 1800 approached, newspaper attacks against Federalist officials reached an unparalleled level of criticism. To counter this, the Federalist-dominated Congress passed the Alien and Sedition Acts (1798). The Alien Act (actually three different acts) authorized the President to deport any immigrant he thought to be a danger to the nation. While the Alien Act was never enforced, the Sedition Act was. Federalist judges strictly enforced this law which called for fines or prison sentences for any person convicted of publishing "false, scandalous or malicious writing" about the United States government, Congress, or the President. Within two years, 10 Republican editors and writers were either fined or jailed. Jefferson, Madison, and their fellow Republicans attacked the Alien and Sedition Acts as unconstitutional. Jefferson and Madison wrote the Kentucky and Virginia Resolutions, adopted by those states in 1798 and 1799 respectively. These resolutions bluntly declared that the federal government was a voluntary compact of sovereign states. If Congress enacted a law which a state legislature considered unconstitutional, that legislature had the right to nullify it, that is, to refuse to obey it. The Acts expired in 1801 and nothing came of this challenge to federal supremacy. However, a dangerous doctrine of nullification had been unleashed. These resolutions were repeatedly cited from the 1820s on by the southern states as a justification for nullification and eventual secession.

Congressional party caucuses selected candidates for president and vice president in 1800. The Republicans chose Jefferson and Aaron Burr and the Federalists chose Adams and Charles Cotesworth Pinckney of South Carolina. A long and nasty campaign was waged through letter writing, newspaper articles, and political pamphlets. Federalist literature portrayed Jefferson as an enemy of religion who would bring the bloody excesses of the French Revolution to the United States. Each side mobilized its forces, marking the stirrings of a modern political campaign.

Most issues were debated in the various state elections for legislatures because only 5 of the 16 states chose presidential electors by popular vote. In the 11 states where the legislature selected the electors, the presidential election was decided gradually as states chose new legislatures on varying dates during the fall of 1800. The Republicans made limited government and constitutional liberties their main issues, while the Federalists described Jefferson as a madman who would bring on a reign of terror. With the exception of one Rhode Island elector, party discipline held and all electors cast their votes for either the Republican ticket of Jefferson and Burr or the Federalist ticket of Adams and Pinckney. This was another sign of emerging political parties. The final vote was 65 for Adams and 64 for Pinckney, his running mate. Jefferson and Burr tied; each received 73 votes.

The Constitution mandated that the choice between the tied candidates—Jefferson and Burr—was up to the U.S. House of Representatives, with each state casting one vote. To win, Jefferson or Burr had to carry a majority of the 16 states then in the Union. The House began voting on 11 February 1801. On the first ballot, 8 states supported Jefferson, 6 supported Burr, and 2 states were divided. On the thirty-sixth ballot, Jefferson won 10 states and became the third president of the United States. Alexander Hamilton, who disliked Jefferson but feared Burr, had convinced Federalist representatives from 2 equally divided states to cast blank ballots allowing Jefferson's supporters to carry these states. A tie between the presidential and vice presidential candidates can never happen again. The Twelfth Amendment (1804), added to the Constitution before the next election, requires electors to vote separately for president and vice president.

In the election of 1800, political power peacefully passed from one political party to another. It was a major and significant accomplishment for the new nation.

Election of 1804

☒ **JEFFERSON**

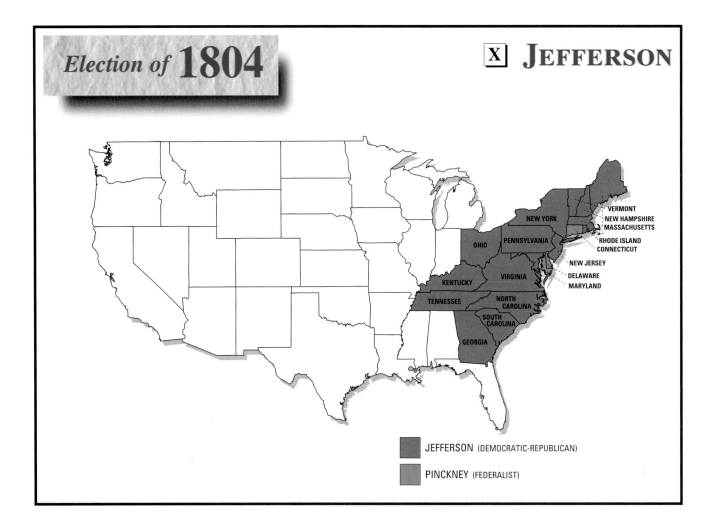

JEFFERSON (DEMOCRATIC-REPUBLICAN)

PINCKNEY (FEDERALIST)

States	Electoral Votes	Jefferson	Pinckney
Connecticut	(9)	-	9
Delaware	(3)	-	3
Georgia	(6)	6	-
Kentucky	(8)	8	-
Maryland	(11)	9	2
Massachusetts	(19)	19	-
New Hampshire	(7)	7	-
New Jersey	(8)	8	-
New York	(19)	19	-
North Carolina	(14)	14	-
Ohio	(3)	3	-
Pennsylvania	(20)	20	-
Rhode Island	(4)	4	-
South Carolina	(10)	10	-
Tennessee	(5)	5	-
Vermont	(6)	6	-
Virginia	(24)	24	-
Totals	**(176)**	**162**	**14**

ELECTORAL VOTE

[10]

In the 1804 election, Thomas Jefferson and his vice presidential running mate George Clinton won a landslide victory, carrying 15 of the now 17 states. Their Federalist opponents, Charles Cotesworth Pinckney and Rufus King, won only 2 states (Connecticut and Delaware) and two electoral votes in Maryland. Why were the results so close in 1800 and so one-sided in 1804? The answer is that Jefferson had built up a great deal of popular support during his first term.

Jefferson's greatest triumph was the Louisiana Purchase (1803). Napoleon had acquired this vast territory from Spain, France's ally. The United States was apprehensive about Napoleon's plan to establish a new empire in the Mississippi Valley. It feared that the mouth of the Mississippi River would be closed to U.S. commerce if a strong power permanently occupied New Orleans. "There is on the globe one single spot, the possessor of which is our natural enemy," Jefferson wrote to Robert R. Livingston, the U.S. minister to France. "It is New Orleans, through which the produce of three-eighths of our territory must pass to market." Jefferson's fears seemed confirmed when, in 1802, Spain, still in authority, suspended America's "right of deposit" at New Orleans—that is, the privilege of safely leaving freight or cargo. Jefferson then sent James Monroe to join Livingston in Paris with instructions to purchase the city of New Orleans or, failing this, to obtain an irrevocable guarantee of the "right of deposit." To their complete surprise, Napoleon offered to sell the entire Louisiana Territory. For $15 million, the United States obtained some 828,000 square miles between the Mississippi River and the Rocky Mountains.

For years, Jefferson and his supporters had criticized the Federalists for their broad interpretation of the Constitution. Some now questioned whether the President had the right to purchase foreign territory. At first, Jefferson suggested a constitutional amendment to authorize such agreements with foreign powers. Realizing that a delay might cause Napoleon to change his mind, the flexible Jefferson interpreted his powers under the Constitution broadly and approved the sale. On 20 December 1803, the United States formally took possession of Louisiana.

In 1804, 6 state legislatures chose the presidential electors and 11 states provided for a popular vote. Political parties continued to grow in structure and in organization. For example, a national Republican campaign committee was formed, made up of one congressman from each state. In some states, committees coordinated the campaign and, in several, one could find committees at the county and even ward levels. These state and local Republican officials often organized groups of associations of mechanics (workers) for completely partisan reasons. Jefferson's supporters also ingratiated themselves with fraternal organizations such as the St. Patrick and the United German Benefit societies.

The party press an important feature of Republican campaigning in 1804. Jefferson's friend Samuel Harrison Smith established the *National Intelligencer,* a Washington based newspaper which published numerous articles praising Jefferson and his administration. Republican newspapers throughout the nation reprinted them. The *National Intelligencer* was written in a more popular style than the Federalist newspapers, which focused on shipping and business news. Republicans stressed that Jefferson stood for greater opportunities to obtain land, to receive an education, and to have the right to vote. National support for canals and roads to help develop the nation were also part of the Republican program. The Louisiana Purchase had doubled the size of the nation and, above all, there was peace.

The Federalists failed at party organization and lost considerable strength in Congress. Their fear of popular rule and distrust of democracy brought about their party's decline as new states gained admission, and their aristocratic leaders failed to attract supporters in these frontier areas. Alexander Hamilton wanted to follow the Republican lead by appealing to a broad spectrum of voters. Other Federalists, however, had a narrow vision of the United States. When Hamilton was killed in a duel with Aaron Burr in July 1804, party leadership passed to a Massachusetts group called the Essex Junto, wealthy commercial leaders who considered the future of the Union as hopeless. Some even urged that New England secede. The Federalists failed to run an effective campaign against Jefferson. Except for two Maryland electors, Jefferson won the 11 states which held popular elections. He also carried 4 of the 6 states where state legislatures did the electoral selection. "The people in mass have joined us," Jefferson boasted.

Election of 1808

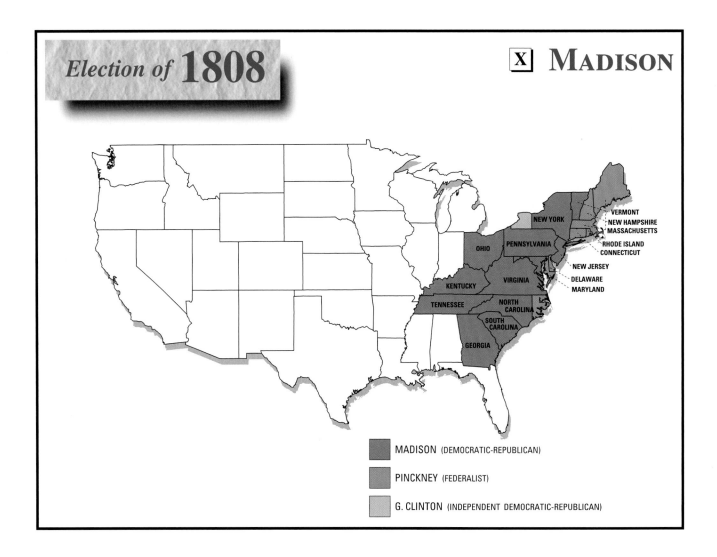

MADISON (DEMOCRATIC-REPUBLICAN)

PINCKNEY (FEDERALIST)

G. CLINTON (INDEPENDENT DEMOCRATIC-REPUBLICAN)

States	Electoral Votes	Madison	Pinckney	Clinton
Connecticut	(9)	-	9	-
Delaware	(3)	-	3	-
Georgia	(6)	6	-	-
Kentucky	(8)	7	-	-
Maryland	(11)	9	2	-
Massachusetts	(19)	-	19	-
New Hampshire	(7)	-	7	-
New Jersey	(8)	8	-	-
New York	(19)	13	-	6
North Carolina	(14)	11	3	-
Ohio	(3)	3	-	-
Pennsylvania	(20)	20	-	-
Rhode Island	(4)	-	4	-
South Carolina	(10)	10	-	-
Tennessee	(5)	5	-	-
Vermont	(6)	6	-	-
Virginia	(24)	24	-	-
Totals	**(176)**	**122**	**47**	**6**

ELECTORAL VOTE

Jefferson's first administration (1801–1805) roughly coincided with the first peaceful years Europe had enjoyed since the start of the French Revolution (1789). His second administration, however, began with renewed hostilities between Great Britain and France. Each nation now threatened to use military force to prevent its opponent from obtaining an advantage through trade with the United States. Diplomatic attempts to ease these threats failed.

Confronted with a drastic shortage of sailors, British naval commanders boarded U.S. ships and removed men whom they accused of desertion (impressment). On 22 June 1807, the British warship *Leopard* stopped the United States frigate *Chesapeake* off the Virginia coast and demanded the surrender of alleged deserters. When Captain James Barron refused, the *Leopard* fired at point-blank range, killing 3 and wounding 18 U.S. seamen. The British boarded the *Chesapeake* and removed 4 men, including 2 African Americans. President Jefferson demanded that they be returned immediately, and he ordered all British ships out of U.S. ports. As impressments and the seizure of U.S. ships increased, an angry nation called for war with Great Britain.

Jefferson decided to try commercial pressure as an alternative to going to war. On 22 December 1807, Congress passed the Embargo Act (eventually five different acts) which prohibited all foreign commerce. Jefferson believed that thousands of British laborers would be thrown out of work as the import of U.S. goods stopped. Unfortunately, this unilateral attempt to prevent the United States from becoming involved in a European war created an economic depression at home within one year. Commercial areas of New England talked of secession, blaming Jefferson and his embargo. Annual U.S. exports fell from $108 million in 1807 to $22 million in 1808. On 1 March 1809, three days before the end of his second term, Jefferson signed a congressional resolution repealing his failed attempt at economic coercion. "The embargo act ," admitted Jefferson, "is certainly the most embarrassing we ever had to execute."

When congressional Republicans informally caucused on 23 January 1808, they knew that Jefferson wanted James Madison, his secretary of state, to succeed him. Vice President George Clinton and James Monroe, who had been U.S. minister to Great Britain, also sought the Republican nomination. A majority of 93 Republican senators and representatives out of 150 chose Madison as the party's presidential nominee.

The embargo and the lack of Republican unity behind Madison's candidacy aroused the Federalists from their inactivity. At a September meeting of Federalist representatives and senators, they again chose Charles Cotesworth Pinckney of South Carolina and Rufus King of New York as their candidates for president and vice president respectively. Federalist newspapers seized upon a story that Madison had become a French citizen. They claimed that Madison would allow "Beast" Napoleon to devour the United States if he became president. "In politics, Mr. Madison is a Frenchman," declared the Federalist *North American.* In 1792, the National Assembly conferred French citizenship on 18 world figures, including George Washington, Alexander Hamilton, and Madison. Madison gratefully accepted this "honorable adoption." His letter was addressed to French Interior Minister Jean-Marie Roland, who escaped the guillotine by committing suicide after his wife was beheaded. Nevertheless, Madison's opponents distorted the truth. Madison remained silent and gave no explanation.

Between 1790 and 1800, newspapers in the United States doubled to nearly 200. In the next decade, another 100 came into being. While the more prominent papers supported Madison, the Federalist press called for an end to the embargo and a revival of trade with Great Britain, even if it meant war with France. They linked Madison to Jefferson—both were Virginians and slaveholders who did not care about shipping or trade, the economic lifeblood of New England. The *Commercial Advertiser* charged that the troubles of the United States "originated in the jealous Virginia spirit, which pines at the prosperity of the North" and wreaks havoc on "the commerce of the Union" like a "pestilent flock of insects."

James Madison's election was never in serious trouble. He had been Jefferson's closest friend and adviser for many years, dating back to the Continental Congress (1774). Throughout the campaign, Madison's strongest weapons were his own words and deeds as secretary of state. In that position, he defended U.S. rights and interests against both English and French actions.

Madison won a total of 122 electoral votes to Pinckney's 47. The slanderous campaign against Madison represented politics at its worst, but his victory was a vote of confidence for his outstanding service to the nation.

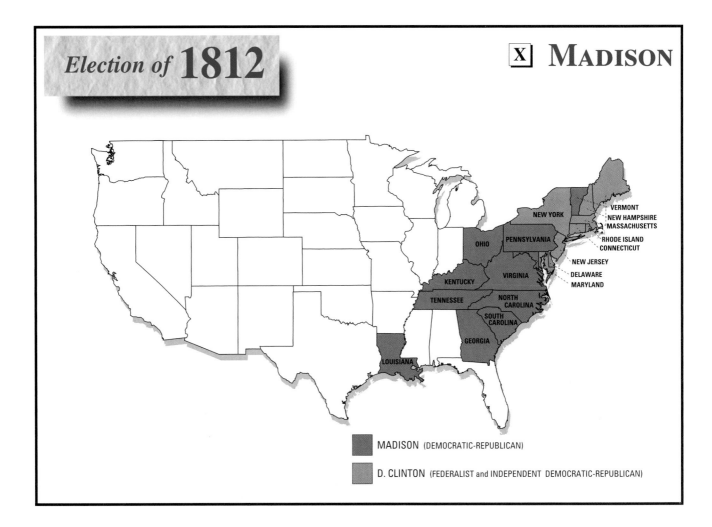

Election of **1812**

X **MADISON**

MADISON (DEMOCRATIC-REPUBLICAN)

D. CLINTON (FEDERALIST and INDEPENDENT DEMOCRATIC-REPUBLICAN)

States	Electoral Votes	Madison	Clinton
Connecticut	(9)	–	9
Delaware	(4)	–	4
Georgia	(8)	8	–
Kentucky	(12)	12	–
Louisiana	(3)	3	–
Maryland	(11)	6	5
Massachusetts	(22)	–	22
New Hampshire	(8)	–	8
New Jersey	(8)	–	8
New York	(29)	–	29
North Carolina	(15)	15	–
Ohio	(8)	7	–
Pennsylvania	(25)	25	–
Rhode Island	(4)	–	4
South Carolina	(11)	11	–
Tennessee	(8)	8	–
Vermont	(8)	8	–
Virginia	(25)	25	–
Totals	(218)	128	89

ELECTORAL VOTE

The presidential election of 1812 was the first that occurred during wartime. It took place five months after the United States declared war on Great Britain. James Madison's confusion in conducting the war and his decision to continue fighting Great Britain, the world's strongest military power, were the principle issues raised during the campaign.

On 1 June 1812, Madison reluctantly asked Congress for a declaration of war against Great Britain. Historians differ on the causes of the War of 1812, which, like those of most wars, appear varied and complex. Madison cited the impressment of seamen and the repeated violation of the rights of the United States as a neutral country as the major causes. But this war, which ended in 1814, revealed severe sectional divisions within the young nation as well as complicated issues which had not been resolved by the American Revolution (1775–1783).

Spokesmen for the western states, for example, held Great Britain responsible for encouraging attacks by Native Americans because they supplied them with powder and guns. They felt that Great Britain had to be driven from Canada to make the frontier safe. Land speculators coveted the fertile plains of Canada. One opponent of the war called these men "war hawks" with "one eternal monotonous tone—Canada! Canada! Canada!" Even Jefferson thought that it would be an easy task to defeat the British and annex Canada. Slaveholders in the South, especially in Georgia and Louisiana, eagerly sought Florida from Spain, Great Britain's ally, to end this haven for runaway slaves. Plantation owners also believed that war would raise prices for their tobacco and cotton crops. Ironically, opposition to war came from the Federalist strongholds in the maritime sections of New England which had suffered the most from impressment of sailors and the seizure of ships. As a whole, the merchant class in the United States always made money, even when the British seized their ships.

Many Americans supported the war, while others thought it such a disaster that they urged secession from the United States. Campaign rhetoric focused exclusively on the wisdom of the war. Both the Federalists and the Republicans had developed party organizations which summoned the faithful to county meetings. They nominated legislative candidates and elected delegates to state conferences. These state meetings chose congressional candidates and nominated slates of presidential electors. The process varied from state to state, but the theme of inclusiveness, extending the right to vote, and the right to hold political office is a constant in U.S. history.

Madison's supporters dominated the Republican Party congressional caucus and it renominated him unanimously. Elbridge Gerry, the governor of Massachusetts, was chosen as his running mate. DeWitt Clinton, the lieutenant governor of New York, nevertheless, challenged Madison in state elections for electors. Clinton, who had opposed the war, hoped to shorten it through firm military measures which would force Great Britain to the peace table. The Federalists nominated Clinton because they realized that they could not defeat Madison without the assistance of dissident Republicans.

Federalist leaders decided to call a convention to discuss how to defeat Madison. On 15 September 1812, 64 delegates form 11 states assembled in New York City to denounce the war and to recommend that Federalist electors throughout the country support Clinton, a Republican. This meeting was the closest event to a party convention prior to the 1830s.

Neither Madison nor Clinton campaigned. The campaign was waged principally in newspapers. The "war hawks," generally young and extremely nationalistic, wrote about "the injuries and indignities" heaped on their nation by an arrogant Great Britain. New Englanders, on the other hand, urged an immediate end to hostilities after a three-pronged invasion of Canada failed in the summer of 1812. The governor of Massachusetts declared a public fast to oppose the war "against the nation from which we are descended." The General Assembly of Connecticut condemned the war and the governor refused to furnish militia to the federal government.

Balloting began on 30 October in Pennsylvania and it went on for several weeks as each state had set its own election day. In the end, Clinton and the Federalists carried every northern state except Pennsylvania and Vermont, still a frontier state. He also won Delaware, and he received some votes in Maryland. Madison, however, was reelected in a decidedly sectional election with the support of the South and the West. The electoral count was 128 votes for Madison and 89 for Clinton. The nation peacefully completed its first wartime election. Although the war faction won, the election demonstrated that powerful opposition existed.

Election of 1816

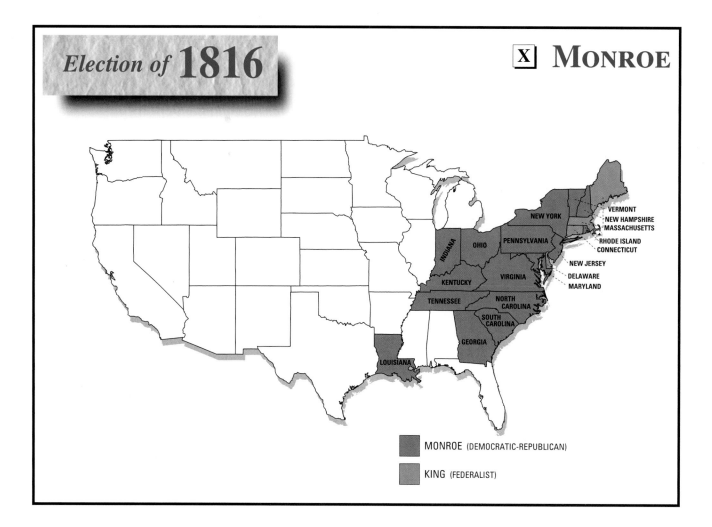

X MONROE

MONROE (DEMOCRATIC-REPUBLICAN)

KING (FEDERALIST)

States	Electoral Votes	Monroe	King
Connecticut	(9)	-	9
Delaware	(4)	-	3
Georgia	(8)	8	-
Indiana	(3)	3	-
Kentucky	(12)	12	-
Louisiana	(3)	3	-
Maryland	(11)	8	-
Massachusetts	(22)	-	22
New Hampshire	(8)	8	-
New Jersey	(8)	8	-
New York	(29)	29	-
North Carolina	(15)	15	-
Ohio	(8)	8	-
Pennsylvania	(25)	25	-
Rhode Island	(4)	4	-
South Carolina	(11)	11	-
Tennessee	(8)	8	-
Vermont	(8)	8	-
Virginia	(25)	25	-
Totals	**(221)**	**183**	**34**

ELECTORAL VOTE

The Federalist Party virtually disappeared during the election of 1816. Federalist delegates from five New England states met in Hartford, Connecticut in December 1814 and January 1815 to protest the war with Great Britain. The major changes in the federal government which they proposed would doom them as a serious political force. The Federalist Party of Washington, Adams, and Hamilton always had favored a strong central government while encouraging the nation's commerce and banking interests. Their heirs, now meeting in Hartford, saw power slipping away from them in New York and New England to the southern agrarian and western frontier states. In an effort to stop this trend, the convention endorsed several changes to the Constitution. They wanted to take away the South's advantage by appointing congressional seats on the basis of the White population alone, thus ending the calculating of the three-fifths of the South's slaves who were then counted in the census. Another suggested change was a constitutional amendment requiring a two-thirds vote in Congress to admit a new state. The convention proposed prohibiting the successive election of presidents from the same state because of the many presidents from Virginia. Above all, the delegates spoke about a state's right to nullify a federal law "in case of deliberate and palpable infractions of the Constitution affecting the sovereignty of a state and the liberties of the people."

When news of Andrew Jackson's victory at New Orleans and of the Treaty of Ghent (24 December 1814), which ended the War of 1812, reached the United States, the Hartford Convention became the butt of ridicule. The opponents of the Convention now accused the Federalists of sedition and treason. The work of the Hartford Convention would come back to haunt the nation during the secession crisis of 1860–1861.

A spirit of nationalism swept the country. "The war," wrote Secretary of the Treasury Albert Gallatin, "had renewed and reinstated the national feeling and character which the Revolution had given, and which were daily lessening . . . The people are more American; they feel and act more as a nation." The discredited Federalists did not formally nominate a presidential candidate in the 1816 election. Their Republican opponents had become the party of nationalism and centralization while the remaining Federalists favored sectionalism. John Adams described the political scene:

"Our two great parties have crossed over the valley and taken possession of each other's mountain." The Republican Party of Jefferson abandoned his reliance upon a citizen militia and now endorsed a strong, permanent army and navy. It also embraced Hamiltonian programs for a national bank, a protective tariff, and a variety of federally financed internal improvements, including roads and canals. Jefferson's successors ignored the constitutionality of these startling new programs.

In 1811, President Madison appointed James Monroe as secretary of state. Many assumed that Monroe, because of his close relationships with both Jefferson and Madison, would be unopposed for the Republican presidential nomination in 1816. Secretary of War William Crawford of Georgia, however, also sought the nomination. Monroe's supporters worried about the traditional congressional caucus method of choosing the nominee because Crawford was very popular with members of Congress. While regional and local newspapers did not attack Monroe, they did praise younger men such as Daniel D. Tompkins of New York and John C. Calhoun of South Carolina. After much political maneuvering, the Republican congressional caucus finally selected Monroe as their presidential candidate and Tompkins as the vice presidential nominee. These complicated political dealings doomed the system of nominating by caucus and paved the way for enlarging the process through party conventions.

Just prior to the formal meeting of the Electoral College, Federalist electors decided to cast their votes for Rufus King of New York. King, a U.S. senator from 1813 to 1825, was the last Federalist candidate for president. Resigned to defeat, the Federalist press attacked Monroe for decisions made while he was U.S. minister to France during Washington's administration. Republican newspapers praised Monroe as a revolutionary hero and as a dedicated patriot. Monroe and Tompkins won an overwhelming victory, receiving 183 electoral votes. King won three states (Connecticut, Delaware, and Massachusetts) with 34 electoral votes.

The fifth president of the United States was not quite 59 years of age when he took his oath of office. He wore knee breeches, long white stockings, and a powdered wig. This fashion long had gone out of style but Monroe was a product of the American Revolution—one of the last still in public life.

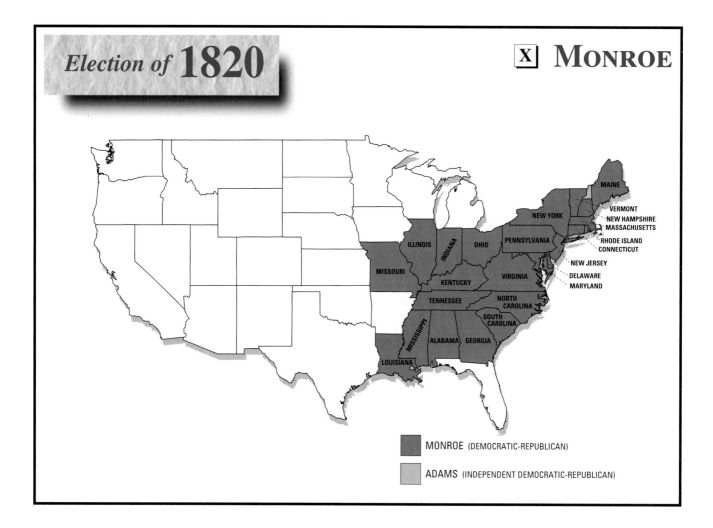

Election of **1820**

X **MONROE**

MONROE (DEMOCRATIC-REPUBLICAN)

ADAMS (INDEPENDENT DEMOCRATIC-REPUBLICAN)

States	Electoral Votes	Monroe	Adams
Alabama	(3)	3	-
Connecticut	(9)	9	-
Delaware	(4)	4	-
Georgia	(8)	8	-
Illinois	(3)	3	-
Indiana	(3)	3	-
Kentucky	(12)	12	-
Louisiana	(3)	3	-
Maine	(9)	9	-
Maryland	(11)	11	-
Massachusetts	(15)	15	-
Mississippi	(3)	2	-
Missouri	(3)	3	-
New Hampshire	(8)	7	1
New Jersey	(8)	8	-
New York	(29)	29	-
North Carolina	(15)	15	-
Ohio	(8)	8	-
Pennsylvania	(25)	24	-
Rhode Island	(4)	4	-
South Carolina	(11)	11	-
Tennessee	(8)	7	-
Vermont	(8)	8	-
Virginia	(25)	25	-
Totals	**(235)**	**231**	**1**

ELECTORAL VOTE

The Federalist Party did not nominate a presidential candidate in 1820. The two party system in the United States had ended, at least temporarily. James Monroe was not formally renominated because not enough members of the Republican congressional caucus attended to form a quorum. Party officials assumed that Monroe was the candidate. The 24 states now in the Union chose their presidential electors using a variety of methods—more than a majority used direct election by those eligible to vote. The election generated very little interest and less than 1 percent of the male population went to the polls. Monroe received all but 1 of the 232 electoral votes cast. Three electors had died before they had the chance to vote. William Plumer of New Hampshire cast his ballot for John Quincy Adams. Over the years, a legend developed that Plumer wanted no one but Washington to receive a unanimous electoral vote. However, Plumer could not possibly have known at the time he voted how the electors outside his own state were voting.

President Monroe made a tour of the New England states during the summer of 1817. Enthusiastic crowds greeted him in Boston, the stronghold of Federalism. The Federalist newspaper *Columbian Sentinel* hailed the event as the "Era of Good Feelings," a phrase still used to describe the United States during the administration of James Monroe.

The United States was still an agricultural country in 1820. Manufacturing took place mainly in the home or in small workshops. Most people made their living not only as farmers but also through a trade or working as a craftsman: blacksmith, shoemaker, weaver, butcher, etc. The nation's primary exports were raw materials: cotton, wheat, and tobacco. Business life centered around the major ports of Boston, New York, and Philadelphia. About 5 percent of the population lived in cities, and most Americans were native-born. However, the country was changing rapidly; the development of the American West had begun.

In 1790, 94 percent of the roughly 4 million inhabitants lived in the original 13 states. By 1820, the population had grown to 9.5 million people. Fifteen percent of the people were slaves. Approximately one-quarter of the total population lived beyond the western limits of the eastern seaboard states. The great westward movement, a constant in the history of the United States, was underway. The National Road began at Cumberland, Maryland in 1811 and soon reached Wheeling, in present-day West Virginia, where much of the traffic transferred to steamboats on the Ohio River. From 1815 on, the National Road was crowded with families headed west, their wagons filled with household goods. It was later crowded with wagons bringing the produce of western farms to eastern markets.

New York, Philadelphia, Boston, and other eastern seaports used canals to link them with the great waterways of the interior of the United States. Construction on the Erie Canal began in 1817. In 1825 it reached Buffalo, connecting New York City, via the Hudson River, with Lake Erie and the West. It made New York City the most important seaport of the United States. Travel time from Albany to Buffalo dropped from 20 days to 8 days, even though the canal barges moved only at the walking pace of the mules that pulled them.

A notable feature of the constitutional and economic growth of the nation had been the orderly admission of new states to the Union. This process was suddenly interrupted by a controversy over the admission of Missouri, which reopened the issue of extension of slavery into the territories—land owned by the United States but not yet admitted as a state. Three states (Alabama, Illinois, and Mississippi) had entered the Union since the election of 1816, a total of 11 free states and 11 slave states. The Missouri Compromise (1820) called for the admission of Missouri as a slave state and Maine as a free state. This would maintain the free-slave balance. In addition, slavery would be prohibited in the remainder of the Louisiana Territory north of Missouri's southern border.

The Missouri Compromise was the most significant event of Monroe's administration. It settled the issue of the spread of slavery for the moment. However, sectional feelings had been aroused that would continue to divide the North and the South. "I take it for granted," wrote John Quincy Adams, "that the present question is a mere preamble—a title page to a great, tragic volume."

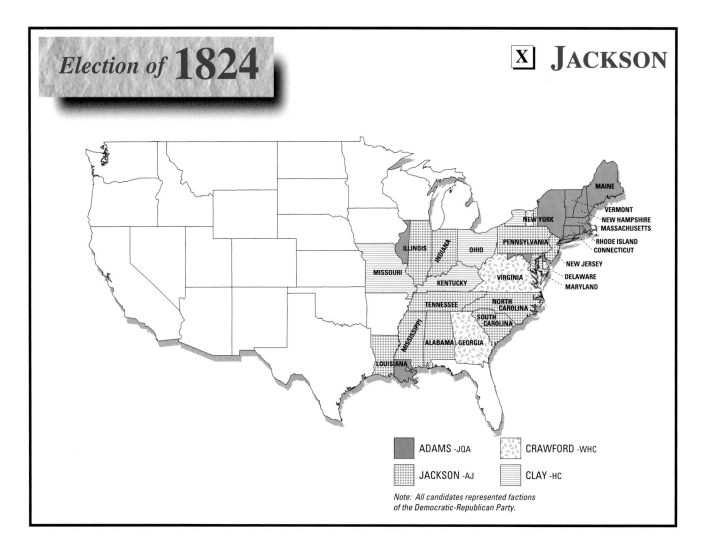

ADAMS -JQA   CRAWFORD -WHC

JACKSON -AJ   CLAY -HC

Note: All candidates represented factions
of the Democratic-Republican Party.

States	Votes	Jackson	Adams	Crawford	Clay
Alabama	(5)	5	-	-	-
Connecticut	(8)	-	8	-	-
Delaware	(3)	-	1	2	-
Georgia	(9)	-	-	9	-
Illinois	(3)	2	1	-	-
Indiana	(5)	5	-	-	-
Kentucky	(14)	-	-	-	14
Louisiana	(5)	3	2	-	-
Maine	(9)	-	9	-	-
Maryland	(11)	7	3	1	-
Massachusetts	(15)	-	15	-	-
Mississippi	(3)	3	-	-	-
Missouri	(3)	-	-	-	3
New Hampshire	(8)	-	8	-	-
New Jersey	(8)	8	-	-	-
New York	(36)	1	26	5	4
North Carolina	(15)	15	-	-	-
Ohio	(16)	-	-	-	16
Pennsylvania	(28)	28	-	-	-
Rhode Island	(4)	-	4	-	-
South Carolina	(11)	11	-	-	-
Tennessee	(11)	11	-	-	-
Vermont	(7)	-	7	-	-
Virginia	(24)	-	-	24	-
Totals	**(261)**	**99**	**84**	**41**	**37**

E L E C T O R A L   V O T E

Election of 1824

STATE	TOTAL VOTE	JOHN Q. ADAMS (Democratic-Republican)		ANDREW JACKSON (Democratic-Republican)		HENRY CLAY (Democratic-Republican)		WILLIAM H. CRAWFORD (Democratic-Republican)		OTHER		PLURALITY	
		Votes	%	Votes	%	Votes	%	Votes	%	Votes	%		
Alabama	13,603	2,422	17.8	9,429	69.3	96	0.7	1,656	12.2	—		7,007	AJ
Connecticut	10,647	7,494	70.4	—		—		1,965	18.5	1,188	11.2	5,529	JQA
Illinois	4,671	1,516	32.5	1,272	27.2	1,036	22.2	847	18.1	—		244	JQA
Indiana	15,838	3,071	19.4	7,444	47.0	5,316	33.6	—		7		2,128	AJ
Kentucky	23,338	—		6,356	27.2	16,982	72.8	—		—		10,626	HC
Maine	12,625	10,289	81.5	—		—		2,336	18.5	—		7,953	JQA
Maryland	33,214	14,632	44.1	14,523	43.7	695	2.1	3,364	10.1	—		109	JQA
Massachusetts	42,056	30,687	73.0	—		—		—		11,369	27.0	24,071	JQA
Mississippi	4,894	1,654	33.8	3,121	63.8			119	2.4	—		1,467	AJ
Missouri	3,432	159	4.6	1,166	34.0	2,042	59.5	32	0.9	33	1.0	876	HC
New Hampshire	10,032	9,389	93.6	—		—		643	6.4	—		8,746	JQA
New Jersey	19,837	8,309	41.9	10,332	52.1	—		1,196	6.0	—		2,023	AJ
North Carolina	36,109	—		20,231	56.0	—		15,622	43.3	256	0.7	4,609	AJ
Ohio	50,024	12,280	24.5	18,489	37.0	19,255	38.5	—		—		766	HC
Pennsylvania	47,073	5,441	11.6	35,736	75.9	1,690	3.6	4,206	8.9	—		30,295	AJ
Rhode Island	2,344	2,144	91.5	—		—		—		200	8.5	1,944	JQA
Tennessee	20,725	216	1.0	20,197	97.5	—		312	1.5	—		19,885	AJ
Virginia	15,371	3,419	22.2	2,975	19.4	419	2.7	8,558	55.7	—		5,139	WHC
Totals	365,833	113,122	30.9	151,271	41.3	47,531	13.0	40,856	11.2	13,053	3.6	38,149	AJ

93382

POPULAR VOTE

James Monroe, president from 1817 to 1825, represented the last of the Revolutionary statesmen. The generation that had controlled the United States since the battles of Bunker Hill and Yorktown now was practically extinct. New issues and new leaders emerged. Unfortunately, these issues involved the growth of sectionalism and the leaders reflected this sectionalism.

The presidential election of 1824 was one of the most complicated in U.S. history. It involved four strong personalities: Andrew Jackson, John Quincy Adams, Henry Clay, and William H. Crawford. All four candidates were Democratic-Republicans. A constitutional provision, used for the first and only time, determined the final result.

In 1824, as was the custom, each state chose presidential electors on different days and even in different months, and in a variety of ways. Of the 24 states then in the Union, 6 states still delegated this authority to the legislature. Elsewhere, the electors were chosen by popular vote, either by districts or by statewide tickets. The 1824 election, therefore, was a drawn out process. Jackson's supporters in Tennessee had elected him to the U.S. Senate in 1822. They planned to nominate the somewhat reluctant Jackson for president two years later as a favorite son, that is, a candidate of a state or region. Voters in the southwest (Alabama, Mississippi, and Louisiana), where memory of the brutal Indian wars was still fresh, were very enthusiastic in their support of Jackson. His strength was due to the work of local politicians and the image of him they portrayed rather than any personal appeal that he made to voters. The election of 1824 brought Andrew Jackson into national political prominence. He became one of the United States's dominant political leaders for at least the next 12 years.

Andrew Jackson was born in a backwoods settlement in South Carolina in 1767. His life was filled with drama, adventure, controversy, and sadness. He came to symbolize the brash self-made frontiersman. Although he accumulated great wealth, he never forgot his humble origins. He was the first of the log cabin presidents, the first to reap the rewards of America's respect and admiration for self-made men.

In the 1824 election, Jackson received the highest popular vote (41.3 percent) and the highest electoral count of 99 votes (38 percent) in a four-way race. However, Jackson's electoral vote was only a plurality, not a majority. He and his followers always believed that victory was stolen from him through a dishonest deal.

John Quincy Adams had been in the service of his country since his youth. His father, John Adams, had been president of the United States and John Quincy was brought up to believe that someday he would also become president. In 1794, when not quite 27 years old, President George Washington appointed him U.S. minister to the Netherlands. He later served as U.S. minister to Prussia, Russia, and Great Britain. In 1817, President James Monroe appointed him secretary of state, a position he held for eight years. He obtained the cession of Florida from Spain (1819) and shared credit with Monroe for formulating the Monroe Doctrine (1823). It was assumed—in the steppingstone tradition of Thomas Jefferson, James Madison, and Monroe—that Secretary of State Adams would succeed to the presidency in 1824. Adams was too independent to be a partisan politician and campaigning struck him as repulsive. His support was also sectional; it came from his native Massachusetts and from the rest of New England and New York. Since Federalists still active in local politics in parts of New England did not have a presidential candidate of their own, they either voted for Adams or stayed at home. He received 30.9 percent of the popular vote and 84 electoral votes (32 percent). That is, he came in second in both categories.

Henry Clay was Kentucky's favorite son in the 1824 election. First elected to the U.S. Congress at age 29, he won fame as one of the most belligerent of the "war hawks" who helped push President Madison into the War of 1812. Madison named Clay to represent the "war hawk" faction at the 1814 peace talks in Ghent, Belgium. His public career was intertwined with Congress, having served as a representative, a senator, and a Speaker of the House for 14 years. His involvement with the Missouri Compromise earned him the title of "The Great Compromiser."

Clay advocated the "American System"—basically, a Hamiltonian nationalist plan which would integrate the economies of the North, South, and West. He believed that high protective tariffs would help eastern manufacturers. Revenues from the tariff would assist in building roads and canals for the benefit of the West and for the dredging of rivers in the South. Eastern textile mills would provide a domestic market for southern cotton and western wool. Eastern cities would provide a market for western food. A national bank would supply a national currency. Clay received 37 electoral votes (14 percent), the lowest of the four candidates, and 13 percent of the popular vote in the 1824 election.

William H. Crawford, a very popular Georgia politician, was the fourth candidate. He had served in Congress and was the U.S. minister to France during the War of 1812. President James Madison appointed him secretary of war, and he later headed the Treasury Department. He led the states' rights group of the party. Most congressional Republicans planned to support his presidential candidacy in 1824, and his prospects to win the caucus continued to grow until he suffered a stroke in the fall of 1823. Crawford's friends still insisted on having him nominated even though he was blind and paralyzed. Crawford was determined to continue his campaign as his condition slowly improved. He did obtain the official Republican nomination on 14 February 1824 but only a minority of those eligible attended the congressional caucus.

This complete failure of the congressional caucus as a presidential nominating body marked the end of that system. Crawford received the electoral votes of Georgia and Virginia plus scattered others for a total of 41 electoral votes (16 percent) and only 11.2 percent of the popular vote. He placed third in the electoral vote although he had the fewest popular votes of the four men running for president.

The Twelfth Amendment to the Constitution (1804) provides that, if no presidential candidate receives a majority of the electoral vote, the U.S. House of Representatives shall choose the president from those with the three highest electors. Jackson fell short of the required electoral majority, but he had the highest number of both popular and electoral votes.

The electors met according to the law in their respective states in early December 1823. Their ballots were forwarded to Congress. On 9 February 1824, the House made its choice. They were not bound by the popular vote nor by the electoral vote which had been cast. The House delegation from each state, regardless of its size, had 1 vote. Thus, the 1 representative from Illinois or the 1 from Delaware,

exercised as much power as the 34 representatives from New York or the 26 from Pennsylvania.

Henry Clay, having received the fewest electoral votes of the four, was eliminated. However, he was Speaker of the House and one of its most powerful members so he obviously would influence the vote. He felt that Crawford was too ill to be seriously considered, so the contest was between Jackson and Adams. Clay disliked Jackson. "I cannot believe," he wrote, "that killing 2,500 Englishmen at New Orleans qualified [him] for the various and complicated duties of the Chief Magistracy." After a confidential meeting with Adams, Clay swung his supporters to him. Adams was elected president on the first ballot by the House of Representatives.

Thirteen states constituted a majority, and 13 voted for Adams, 7 for Jackson, and 4 for Crawford. At noon the next day, a committee of the House of Representatives, chaired by Daniel Webster, called upon Adams at his home to give him formal notice of his election. The group found him very agitated from the strain of the electoral process. Citing the procedure adopted by Thomas Jefferson on "the only preceding occasion since the establishment of the Constitution of the United States upon which a similar notification had been made from the House of Representatives," he unfolded a written acceptance, which he read and handed to Webster.

One of Adams's first acts as president was to choose Clay as secretary of state, a decision equal to designating him as his successor. Jackson's supporters cried that a "corrupt bargain" had been made. Clay strongly denied these charges. He demanded an investigation to clear his name but none was ever held. Jackson was very reluctant in accepting the decision of the House of Representatives as constitutionally legitimate. He called Clay the "Judas of the West," and vowed political revenge. Before 1825 ended, the Tennessee legislature nominated Jackson for president. Determined to run against Adams again and defeat him, he resigned his U.S. Senate seat to begin a three-year campaign.

Election of 1828

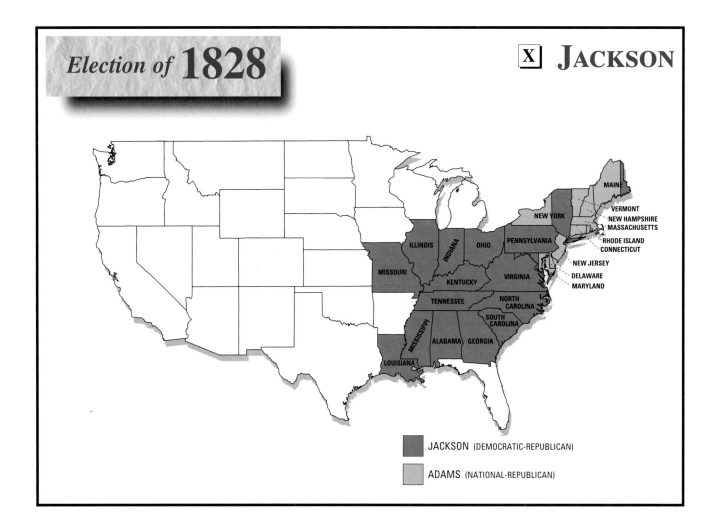

JACKSON (DEMOCRATIC-REPUBLICAN)

ADAMS (NATIONAL-REPUBLICAN)

States	Votes	Jackson	Adams
Alabama	(5)	5	-
Connecticut	(8)	-	8
Delaware	(3)	-	3
Georgia	(9)	9	-
Illinois	(3)	3	-
Indiana	(5)	5	-
Kentucky	(14)	14	-
Louisiana	(5)	5	-
Maine	(9)	1	8
Maryland	(11)	5	6
Massachusetts	(15)	-	15
Mississippi	(3)	3	-
Missouri	(3)	3	-
New Hampshire	(8)	-	8
New Jersey	(8)	-	8
New York	(36)	20	16
North Carolina	(15)	15	-
Ohio	(16)	16	-
Pennsylvania	(28)	28	-
Rhode Island	(4)	-	4
South Carolina	(11)	11	-
Tennessee	(11)	11	-
Vermont	(7)	-	7
Virginia	(24)	24	-
Totals	**(261)**	**178**	**83**

ELECTORAL VOTE

Election of 1828

STATE	TOTAL VOTE	ANDREW JACKSON (Democratic-Republican)		JOHN Q. ADAMS (National-Republican)		OTHER		PLURALITY	
		Votes	%	Votes	%	Votes	%		
Alabama	18,618	16,736	89.9	1,878	10.1	4		14,858	DR
Connecticut	19,378	4,448	23.0	13,829	71.4	1,101	5.7	9,381	NR
Georgia	20,004	19,362	96.8	642	3.2	—		18,720	DR
Illinois	14,222	9,560	67.2	4,662	32.8	—		4,898	DR
Indiana	39,210	22,201	56.6	17,009	43.4	—		5,192	DR
Kentucky	70,776	39,308	55.5	31,468	44.5	—		7,840	DR
Louisiana	8,687	4,605	53.0	4,082	47.0	—		523	DR
Maine	34,789	13,927	40.0	20,773	59.7	89	0.3	6,846	NR
Maryland	45,796	22,782	49.7	23,014	50.3	—		232	NR
Massachusetts	39,074	6,012	15.4	29,836	76.4	3,226	8.3	23,824	NR
Mississippi	8,344	6,763	81.1	1,581	18.9	—		5,182	DR
Missouri	11,654	8,232	70.6	3,422	29.4	—		4,810	DR
New Hampshire	44,035	20,212	45.9	23,823	54.1	—		3,611	NR
New Jersey	45,570	21,809	47.9	23,753	52.1	8		1,944	NR
New York	270,975	139,412	51.4	131,563	48.6	—		7,849	DR
North Carolina	51,747	37,814	73.1	13,918	26.9	15		23,896	DR
Ohio	131,049	67,596	51.6	63,453	48.4	—		4,143	DR
Pennsylvania	152,220	101,457	66.7	50,763	33.3	—		50,694	DR
Rhode Island	3,580	820	22.9	2,755	77.0	5	0.1	1,935	NR
Tennessee	46,533	44,293	95.2	2,240	4.8	—		42,053	DR
Vermont	32,833	8,350	25.4	24,363	74.2	120	0.4	16,013	NR
Virginia	38,924	26,854	69.0	12,070	31.0	—		14,784	DR
Totals	1,148,018	642,553	56.0	500,897	43.6	4,568	0.4	141,656	DR

POPULAR VOTE

The 1828 election is significant because of the rise of Andrew Jackson, who would serve two terms as president of the United States. Jackson embraced and capitalized on the democratic movement in politics. He was by far the most popular and politically successful public figure in the Age of the Common Man—and for a long time thereafter.

During his four years as president, John Quincy Adams's opponents used every opportunity to discredit him and his programs, regardless of their merit. They depicted Adams as a usurper and an elitist, who wasted money purchasing elegant furniture and fine European wines. At one point, the President was accused of buying a table for billiards, then considered a game played by aristocrats. Adams, provoked by this bitter hostility, wrote in his diary: "The skunks of party slander have been squirting around the House of Representatives, thence to issue and perfume the atmosphere of the Union."

The sectional supporters of Vice President John C. Calhoun (South Carolina), William Crawford (Georgia), Martin Van Buren (New York), and Jackson gradually joined together to form a new political coalition. The planters of the South and the Republicans of the North pledged a return to the original principles of the old Republican Party—a states' rights element had joined forces with a nationalist group. This new coalition won a majority of House seats in the 1826 congressional election. At first they were called the Opposition, but they later assumed the name Democratic-Republican Party or, more simply, the Democratic Party. These midterm elections gave a large majority in the House of Representatives to the opponents of an incumbent administration for the first time in the history of the government.

Jackson believed that deceitful politicians had deprived him of the presidency in the previous election. He returned to the Hermitage, his vast Tennessee plantation, and spent the next years pouring out his anger in letters to political figures throughout the nation. The charges of "corrupt bargain, cheating, and corruption, and bribery too" and Jackson's impassioned cry that the "will of the people" had been denied dominated the 1828 campaign. No amount of denials by Henry Clay or the National Republicans, the supporters of Adams, could quiet the passions which Jackson had inflamed. He repeated the charges over and over to virtually every politician who visited him. Once he added

to the charges, saying that he had received damaging details of corruption from "a congressman of high respectability." The congressman turned out to be James Buchanan, then a representative from Pennsylvania. Buchanan, when pressed, could not produce any evidence. Issues were not discussed and mudslinging, at its worst, prevailed.

Between 1824 and 1828, most states removed the qualification that only property owners could vote. The number of free men eligible to vote soared, another major step forward in the move to political equality. By 1828, only two states—South Carolina and Delaware—did not allow the direct election of presidential electors. This growth of democracy required involving more people in the political process. In order to interest them in elections and to get them to vote, it became necessary to build political parties with grass-roots support.

The supporters of Andrew Jackson became masters at political organization. From the local to the state level, the Jacksonians raised money, sponsored parades, listened to grievances, and got the people out to vote. Jackson became the first presidential candidate to have a popular nickname: "Old Hickory." During 1828, his followers formed Hickory Clubs, which held rallies, barbecues, songfests, and other kinds of entertainment. Hickory poles were tied on houses, wagons, and steamboats. These activities were intended to excite the voter to support Jacksonians at every level: ward, city, state, and national. The goal was to defeat John Quincy Adams and replace him in the White House with Andrew Jackson.

In addition to the hickory symbol, Democrats used Jackson's likeness on an endless variety of material objects— snuff boxes, song sheets, ceramic pitchers, whiskey flasks, bandannas, pewter medals, and silk ribbons. Pewter goblets with a log cabin design identified Jackson with the common man. Campaign biographies, which glorified his military achievements, were widely circulated. Very little mention was made of the problems of the day as supporters of each candidate ignored the tariff, internal improvements, and foreign policy.

While supporters often claimed that Jackson would attend a rally, a parade, or a meeting in order to whip up excitement, he never actually did attend because it was considered improper at this time for a candidate to appear to participate in his own campaign. There was one exception.

Jackson attended a ceremony in New Orleans on 8 January 1828 to commemorate the thirteenth anniversary of his victory over the British in 1815. Presumably, this was a national celebration and not a political rally. Supporters jammed the city. Widely reported in Democratic newspapers, one observer described it as "the most stupendous thing of the kind that has ever occurred in the United States." Jackson arrived by steamboat and the thousands waiting for him celebrated for four days. The speeches, parades, and dinners reminded the American people again of the great debt they owed to General Jackson, their military hero.

Adams remained above the hue and cry which swirled around his administration. He did nothing to assist his reelection. If the voters chose him, he would serve again. "I am a man of reserved, cold, austere and forbidding manners," he recorded in his diary. "My political adversaries say, a gloomy misanthrope, and my personal enemies an unsocial savage. With the knowledge of the actual defects of my character, I have not the pliability to reform it." Adams did not remove anyone from office for his political opinions or even for political activity against him. He refrained from using patronage, that is, appointments to reward his friends. Refusing to be president as political leader, Adams instead focused on his broad plans for internal improvements, his ideas of directing government powers to promote the arts and sciences, a national university, astronomical observatories—in short, whatever would help the people and promote knowledge. Northern strict constructionists, former Federalists who had voted for him, were astonished at his proposals that would empower the federal government to introduce expensive programs. Alarmed Southerners feared that slavery might be abolished.

Adams supporters were not as kind as he. They lashed out at the Jacksonians with smear and scandal that was rare for even the dirtiest of political campaigns. Henry Clay and Daniel Webster of Massachusetts raised money to subsidize newspapers supporting Adams. Like the Democrats, the National Republicans held local rallies, country meetings, and state conventions. However, their organizational skills could not compare with those of their Democratic rivals. Adams's strength was with partisan newspaper editors who printed offensive stories about Jackson. They accused Jackson's mother of being a prostitute who married a mulatto. They said that Rachel, his wife, was a bigamist. They claimed that Jackson was a common bully, a gambler, a slavetrader, a drunk, and a cruel military commander. Several broadsides took issue with Jackson's "noble" military record. Holding him accountable for excessive executions of his own men who disobeyed him during the Creek War (1813–1814), John Binns, editor of the Philadelphia Democratic Press, conceived of the so called "Coffin Hand Bill." This leaflet, which was widely distributed, described how six militiamen were put to death during the Creek War because they tried to return home after completing their service. The handbill, bordered in black, had a coffin drawn under the name of each militiaman. "Gentle reader," said the handbill, "it is for you to say whether this man who carries a sword cane, and is willing to run it through the body of any one who may presume to stand in his way, is a fit person to be our President." Of all the negative campaign items, this proved the most effective in conveying the image that Jackson was a wild barbaric man who could not be trusted.

Nevertheless, Jackson won an outstanding victory. He received 56 percent of the more than 1.1 million votes cast, a percentage unequaled in any presidential election during the nineteenth century. His support came from all sections of the nation, including New England. He received 178 electoral votes to 83 for Adams. Jackson won 15 of the 24 states then in the Union. This included every state south of the Potomac River and west of New Jersey. The so-called common man—farmers, workers, frontiersmen—had seized the opportunity to vote for their hero. Jackson's supporters believed that his leadership would provide essential services and protection for the less fortunate and opportunities for all.

As Inauguration Day drew closer, towns and cities along the way from Tennessee to Washington planned elaborate welcoming ceremonies. But the death of Mrs. Jackson on 22 December 1828 changed the joy to mourning. Jackson arrived in the capital after a quiet and uneventful trip. On 4 March 1829, surrounded by "gigs, wood wagons, vehicles of every sort crowded with women eager to be near the chief, and followed by the officers of his suite, worthies of the Revolution, and hundreds of strangers without distinction of rank," Jackson walked to the Capitol, and at noon, on the East Portico, took the oath of office.

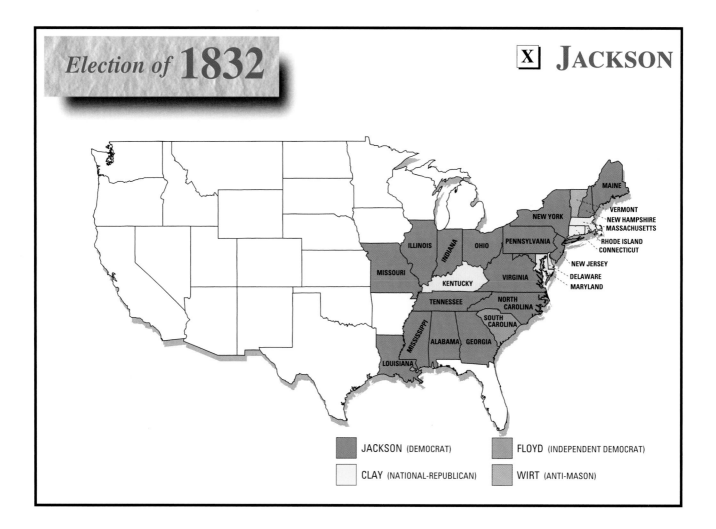

Election of 1832

☒ **JACKSON**

JACKSON (DEMOCRAT)   **FLOYD** (INDEPENDENT DEMOCRAT)

CLAY (NATIONAL-REPUBLICAN)   **WIRT** (ANTI-MASON)

States	Electoral Votes	Jackson	Clay	Floyd	Wirt
Alabama	(7)	7	-	-	-
Connecticut	(8)	-	8	-	-
Delaware	(3)	-	3	-	-
Georgia	(11)	11	-	-	-
Illinois	(5)	5	-	-	-
Indiana	(9)	9	-	-	-
Kentucky	(15)	-	15	-	-
Louisiana	(5)	5	-	-	-
Maine	(10)	10	-	-	-
Maryland	(10)	3	5	-	-
Massachusetts	(14)	-	14	-	-
Mississippi	(4)	4	-	-	-
Missouri	(4)	4	-	-	-
New Hampshire	(7)	7	-	-	-
New Jersey	(8)	8	-	-	-
New York	(42)	42	-	-	-
North Carolina	(15)	15	-	-	-
Ohio	(21)	21	-	-	-
Pennsylvania	(30)	30	-	-	-
Rhode Island	(4)	-	4	-	-
South Carolina	(11)	-	-	11	-
Tennessee	(15)	15	-	-	-
Vermont	(7)	-	-	-	7
Virginia	(23)	23	-	-	-
Totals	**(288)**	**219**	**49**	**11**	**7**

ELECTORAL VOTE

Election of 1832

STATE	TOTAL VOTE	ANDREW JACKSON (Democrat)		HENRY CLAY (National-Republican)		WILLIAM WIRT (Anti-Mason)		OTHER		PLURALITY	
		Votes	%	Votes	%	Votes	%	Votes	%		
Alabama	14,291	14,286	100.0	5		—		—		14,281	D
Connecticut	32,833	11,269	34.3	18,155	55.3	3,409	10.4	—		6,886	NR
Delaware	8,386	4,110	49.0	4,276	51.0	—		—		166	NR
Georgia	20,750	20,750	100.0	—		—		—		20,750	D
Illinois	21,481	14,609	68.0	6,745	31.4	97	0.5	30	0.1	7,864	D
Indiana	57,152	31,652	55.4	25,473	44.6	27		—		6,179	D
Kentucky	79,741	36,292	45.5	43,449	54.5	—		—		7,157	NR
Louisiana	6,337	3,908	61.7	2,429	38.3	—		—		1,479	D
Maine	62,153	33,978	54.7	27,331	44.0	844	1.4	—		6,647	D
Maryland	38,316	19,156	50.0	19,160	50.0	—		—		4	NR
Massachusetts	67,619	13,933	20.6	31,963	47.3	14,692	21.7	7,031	10.4	17,271	NR
Mississippi	5,750	5,750	100.0	—		—		—		5,750	D
Missouri	5,192	5,192	100.0	—		—		—		5,192	D
New Hampshire	43,793	24,855	56.8	18,938	43.2	—				5,917	D
New Jersey	47,760	23,826	49.9	23,466	49.1	468	1.0	—		360	D
New York	323,393	168,497	52.1	154,896	47.9	—		—		13,601	D
North Carolina	29,799	25,261	84.8	4,538	15.2	—		—		20,723	D
Ohio	158,350	81,246	51.3	76,566	48.4	538	0.3	—		4,680	D
Pennsylvania	157,679	90,973	57.7	—		66,706	42.3	—		24,267	D
Rhode Island	5,747	2,051	35.7	2,871	50.0	819	14.3	6	0.1	820	NR
Tennessee	29,425	28,078	95.4	1,347	4.6	—		—		26,731	D
Vermont	32,344	7,865	24.3	11,161	34.5	13,112	40.5	206	0.6	1,951	AM
Virginia	45,682	34,243	75.0	11,436	25.0	3		—		22,807	D
Totals	1,293,973	701,780	54.2	484,205	37.4	100,715	7.8	7,273	0.6	217,575	D

POPULAR VOTE

In 1832, Andrew Jackson was 65 years old. The reelection of this immensely popular president seemed inevitable. Jackson's supporters sent delegates to the Democratic Convention at Baltimore and the convention unanimously renominated him. It chose Martin Van Buren as Jackson's running mate, replacing John C. Calhoun. The opposition, the National Republican Party, nominated Henry Clay; the name Whig Party was formally adopted in 1834.

The Anti-Mason Party was involved in the campaign of 1832. It was a strange group: the first national third party in U.S. history; the first to hold a national nominating convention (September 1831); and the first to issue a party platform. It was a single issue party that was opposed to all kinds of secret societies. Freemasonry or Masonry is a secret fraternal order to which George Washington, Harry S. Truman, and other presidents belonged. The Anti-Masons opposed Jackson, who was a Freemason, and they would not endorse Clay because he had been a member. Their candidates, William Wirt and Amos Ellmaker, received 7.8 percent of the popular vote and carried Vermont in the election. In a few years, the party faded, gradually absorbed by the Whigs.

Jackson won another decisive victory. He received over 54.2 percent of the popular vote and 219 electoral votes to Clay's 49 electoral votes. Jackson carried 16 of the 24 states while Clay carried 6 states, including his home state of Kentucky. Clay received 37.4 percent of the popular vote.

The excitement that Andrew Jackson generated in his own time is reflected in the many studies of him, his supporters, and the meaning of Jacksonian democracy. Historians differ over Jackson's virtues and excesses—and those of the men who attached themselves to him. Some of his defenders were pro-labor and anti-business while others were anti-labor and pro-business. Almost all Jacksonians spoke of equality, but they meant it only for White men.

The Age of Jackson witnessed enormous economic changes in the United States. The factory system where the worker spent six days a week from dawn to dusk tending machines came into being during this period. Obscure places were transformed into industrial towns and cities. The U.S. Census Bureau's definition of an urban center was a concentration of 2,500 or more people. Using that definition, 5 percent of the United States was urban in 1790. By 1860, this figure rose to 25 percent. The population of the United States was 4 million in 1790. During Jackson's first term (1830),

it had tripled to 13 million. On the eve of the Civil War (1860), the population reached 32 million, making the United States as populous as Great Britain. This explosion fueled economic growth, creating demands for food, housing, transportation, consumer goods, communications, banking, and other financial services. The traffic at New Orleans reflected the rapid growth of new regions. In 1816, 37,000 bales of cotton were shipped from this port. By 1822, the figure was 161,000 bales; by 1830, it had jumped to 428,000. Most of the cotton went to British textile factories, although some fed the mills of New England. All these factors contributed to the mass politics which emerged during this era.

Andrew Jackson boldly used his party as a governing instrument. His success taught the lesson that a strong chief executive with a loyal, organized following can carry out a program even against powerful opposing forces. Jackson did not seek the presidency with the avowed purpose of promoting popular rule through the party system. He had hoped to rally a majority of the people behind his policies. The alliance of Jackson supporters throughout the nation came together as the new Democratic Party, which made Jackson the symbol for an Age. In addition to idolizing Jackson, this political movement seemed to have an underlying philosophy. It was national in that it opposed disunion but it also was anti-national in that it rejected Henry Clay's "American System." That is, the Democratic Party wanted roads, canals, and railroads to be supported by the states without any federal involvement.

The 1832 election decided the fate of the Bank of the United States. The story of the Bank is worth telling because, along with Jackson's personality, it became the most controversial issue in the election. Jackson had few ideas about economics. However, like most westerners, he had a distrust of banks and paper money. The Second Bank of the United States had been granted a federal charter for 20 years in 1816. The Bank, originally part of Alexander Hamilton's financial program, was a private corporation with immense financial power. It served as the depository for federal funds and did not pay interest for using these funds. In return, the Bank and its several branches cashed government drafts and transferred public money without charge. Through sound programs, the Bank established a reliable uniform currency. However, many farmers and merchants felt that the "monster bank" resembled an octopus "sucking the blood from the arteries of the toilers on the farm and in the shop." The "back country" people regarded banks as privileged institutions and they looked upon the losses which they themselves sustained because of a fluctuating currency as amounting to sheer robbery. In general, they supported liberal borrowing policies and inflationary programs in order to force the prices of their goods upward. Jackson's position appeared to them as another manifestation of democracy and they enthusiastically supported it. As the Bank grew, its branches competed with local banks for business. When several states taxed the branch offices, the Supreme Court stepped in. In *McCulloch v. Maryland* (1819), the Court ruled that a state could not tax a corporation chartered by the United States. "The power to tax" wrote Chief Justice John Marshall, "involves the power to destroy." Thus, the Bank and its branches had still another advantage in their competition with local financial institutions. This was another reason why animosity increased against the "monster."

In his first Annual Message to Congress in 1829, Jackson had attacked the Bank as being monopolistic and unconstitutional. The President served notice that he would not recommend renewal of the charter. Attorney General Roger B. Taney summarized the Jacksonian feeling when he described the "power concentrated in the hands of a few individuals—exercised in secret and unseen although felt—irresponsible and above the control of the people or the Government for the twenty years of its charter."

Backed by Henry Clay, Daniel Webster, and other opponents of Jackson, Nicholas Biddle, the president of the Bank of the United States, applied for a recharter in 1832, although the old charter had four years to run. Clay believed that Jackson's chances for reelection would be damaged, especially in the key state of Pennsylvania, if he vetoed renewal of the bank. Jackson, bedridden for the moment, grimly observed to his heir apparent, "The Bank, Mr. Van Buren, is trying to kill me, but I will kill it." He vetoed the bill on 10 July 1832. In a stinging message, the President criticized Marshall and Hamilton and lashed out at the rich men who

"have besought us to make them richer by act of Congress. By attempting to gratify their desires we have in the results of our legislation arrayed section against section, interest against interest, and man against man, in a fearful commotion which threatens to shake the foundations of our Union." The veto delighted Clay and the National Republicans. Nicholas Biddle described the message as "a manifesto of anarchy" and suggested that it was the kind of action one would expect of a leader of the French Revolution. The Bank now became a major issue in the 1832 campaign.

The National Republicans accused Jackson of being a tyrant. Their party newspaper said that the President would destroy every institution he could not control. The Bank aggravated matters by making a substantial contribution to Clay's campaign. Biddle had 30,000 copies of Jackson's veto message distributed because he was convinced it would serve his cause. However, the Bank issue hurt Clay and helped the President. Jackson emerged as the champion of the people, proving too popular for the Bank and the business interests which fought under its banner.

Each party distributed colorful ribbons and banners, and held party held parades, rallies, and festive barbecues, attended by thousands. This was another example of the increasing democratization of presidential elections. But it is the political cartoons of this campaign which have proved most memorable. The one which has obtained historical notoriety is entitled: "King Andrew the First." It depicted Jackson as a monarch, dressed in full royal attire, wearing a crown. In one hand he holds a rolled document labeled "veto," in the other a scepter, and he is shown standing on a torn copy of the Constitution. The words, "Born to Command" appear on one side, "King Andrew the First" on the other.

The real issue in the campaign was Andrew Jackson himself. Voters trusted him and rallied to his cause which they believed to be democratic. It was "Old Hickory's" great popularity which carried the election.

Election of 1836

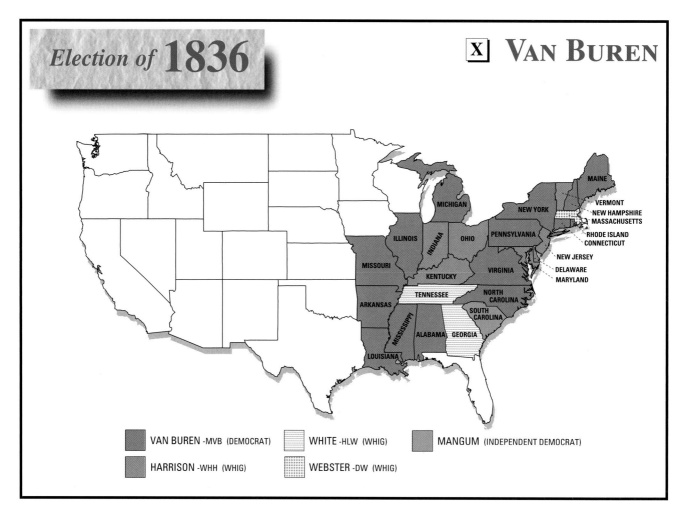

VAN BUREN -MVB (DEMOCRAT) **WHITE** -HLW (WHIG) **MANGUM** (INDEPENDENT DEMOCRAT)

HARRISON -WHH (WHIG) **WEBSTER** -DW (WHIG)

States	Electoral Votes	Van Buren	Harrison	White	Webster	Mangum
Alabama	(7)	7	-	-	-	-
Arkansas	(3)	3	-	-	-	-
Connecticut	(8)	8	-	-	-	-
Delaware	(3)	-	3	-	-	-
Georgia	(11)	-	-	11	-	-
Illinois	(5)	5	-	-	-	-
Indiana	(9)	-	9	-	-	-
Kentucky	(15)	-	15	-	-	-
Louisiana	(5)	5	-	-	-	-
Maine	(10)	10	-	-	-	-
Maryland	(10)	-	10	-	-	-
Massachusetts	(14)	-	-	-	14	-
Michigan	(3)	3	-	-	-	-
Mississippi	(4)	4	-	-	-	-
Missouri	(4)	4	-	-	-	-
New Hampshire	(7)	7	-	-	-	-
New Jersey	(8)	-	8	-	-	-
New York	(42)	42	-	-	-	-
North Carolina	(15)	15	-	-	-	-
Ohio	(21)	-	21	-	-	-
Pennsylvania	(30)	30	-	-	-	-
Rhode Island	(4)	4	-	-	-	-
South Carolina	(11)	-	-	-	-	11
Tennessee	(15)	-	-	15	-	-
Vermont	(7)	-	7	-	-	-
Virginia	(23)	23	-	-	-	-
Totals	**(294)**	**170**	**73**	**26**	**14**	**11**

ELECTORAL VOTE

Election of 1836

STATE	TOTAL VOTE	MARTIN VAN BUREN (Democrat)		WILLIAM H. HARRISON (Whig)		HUGH L. WHITE (Whig)		DANIEL WEBSTER (Whig)		OTHER		PLURALITY	
		Votes	%	Votes	%	Votes	%	Votes	%	Votes	%		
Alabama	37,296	20,638	55.3	—		16,658	44.7	—		—		3,980	MVB
Arkansas	3,714	2,380	64.1	—		1,334	35.9	—		—		1,046	MVB
Connecticut	38,093	19,294	50.6	18,799	49.4	—		—		—		495	MVB
Delaware	8,895	4,154	46.7	4,736	53.2	—		—		5	0.1	582	WHH
Georgia	47,259	22,778	48.2	—		24,481	51.8	—		—		1,703	HLW
Illinois	33,589	18,369	54.7	15,220	45.3	—		—		—		3,149	MVB
Indiana	74,423	33,084	44.5	41,339	55.5	—		—		—		8,255	WHH
Kentucky	70,090	33,229	47.4	36,861	52.6	—		—		—		3,632	WHH
Louisiana	7,425	3,842	51.7	—		3,583	48.3	—		—		259	MVB
Maine	38,740	22,825	58.9	14,803	38.2	—		—		1,112	2.9	8,022	MVB
Maryland	48,119	22,267	46.3	25,852	53.7	—		—		—		3,585	WHH
Massachusetts	74,732	33,486	44.8	—		—		41,201	55.1	45	0.1	33,486	DW
Michigan	12,052	6,507	54.0	5,545	46.0	—		—		—		962	MVB
Mississippi	20,079	10,297	51.3	—		9,782	48.7	—		—		515	MVB
Missouri	18,332	10,995	60.0	—		7,337	40.0	—		—		3,658	MVB
New Hampshire	24,925	18,697	75.0	6,228	25.0	—		—		—		12,469	MVB
New Jersey	51,729	25,592	49.5	26,137	50.5	—		—		—		545	WHH
New York	305,343	166,795	54.6	138,548	45.4	—		—		—		28,247	MVB
North Carolina	50,153	26,631	53.1	—		23,521	46.9	—		1		3,110	MVB
Ohio	202,931	97,122	47.9	105,809	52.1	—		—		—		8,687	WHH
Pennsylvania	178,701	91,466	51.2	87,235	48.8	—		—		—		4,231	MVB
Rhode Island	5,673	2,962	52.2	2,710	47.8	—		—		1		252	MVB
Tennessee	62,197	26,170	42.1	—		36,027	57.9	—		—		9,857	HLW
Vermont	35,099	14,040	4	20,994	59.8	—		—		65	0.2	6,954	WHH
Virginia	53,945	30,556	56.6	—		23,384	43.3	—		5		7,172	MVB
Totals	1,503,534	764,176	50.8	550,816	36.6	146,107	9.7	41,201	2.7	1,234	0.1	213,360	MVB

P O P U L A R   V O T E

[33]

Slavery dominated U.S. political history for the three decades following the election of 1836. Slaveholding states invariably supported states' rights over national sovereignty in order to prevent federal intervention and possibly the abolition of slavery. South Carolina's nullification of a federal law dominated Jackson's second term. Political groups which had opposed Jackson and his policies joined with the National Republicans to form the Whig Party, which would be one of the two major parties for the next 20 years.

Andrew Jackson chose Vice President Martin Van Buren as his successor, and the Democratic Convention promptly and unanimously nominated him. The Whig Party could not come close to reaching an agreement on a candidate. Party leaders decided not to hold a nominating convention but rather to adopt the strategy of running several candidates with strong local appeal. The Whigs wanted to have the election decided by the U.S. House of Representatives because they controlled the House. Van Buren, however, won with 170 electoral votes out of 294. He undoubtedly did well because of the Democratic Party's strong political organization and because of Jackson's powerful endorsement.

The Whig Party, which took form in the early 1830s to challenge Jacksonian Democracy, emerged as a major force in this election. Charging executive tyranny and calling Jackson "King Andrew," opponents of Jackson rallied together because they found themselves either opposed to him, the Democratic Party, or both. The three Whig candidates nominated to oppose Van Buren—William Henry Harrison, Daniel Webster, and Hugh L. White—were colorful figures. They differed on specific issues, but they were united in their opposition to Jackson. General William Henry Harrison, a military man like Jackson, supported national aid to build roads and canals, a position opposed by the Democrats. Harrison denounced Jackson for the growth of executive power and for the President's record use of the veto. The popular hero of the Battle of Tippecanoe emerged from this election as the leading Whig candidate. He received more than twice as many popular votes and almost twice as many electoral votes as Webster and White combined.

Senator Daniel Webster of Massachusetts received less than 3 percent of the popular vote and he carried only one state: his own. Americans used to love classic Senate debate—speeches hours long delivered from brief notes held in the palm of the hand and almost every word reported in newspapers. Webster concluded one such speech (in 1830) with the ringing declaration: "Liberty and Union, now and forever, one and inseparable!" These words were memorized by northern and western schoolchildren for a generation, including one young man, Abraham Lincoln, then living on the Indiana frontier.

Hugh L. White was elected to complete Jackson's unexpired term in the U.S. Senate (1825) and he held the seat for 15 years. Jackson threatened to ruin White if he publicly opposed Van Buren's nomination. White accepted the challenge and received the electoral votes of Georgia and his home state of Tennessee and less than 10 percent of the popular vote.

Willie P. Mangum, a U.S. senator from North Carolina, was chosen by the South Carolina legislature, the only state not to hold a popular vote for presidential electors. Mangum's opposition to the Force Bill (1833) made him very popular with South Carolinians. President Jackson had proclaimed that a state did not have the power to nullify a federal law, and he asked Congress for the Force Bill, giving him authorization to use the military to put down any rebellion.

John C. Calhoun was a Whig leader although not a presidential nominee. He had been Jackson's vice president, but he broke with him and resigned over the principles of states' rights and nullification. Now a United States senator from South Carolina, he denounced his former political ally as a power mad politician who was using his "imperious will" to perpetuate a dynasty by forcing the Democratic Party to accept Van Buren.

Vice President Martin Van Buren of New York was a professional politician who had held numerous state and national offices. Van Buren rarely became angry at even his worst enemies, and he saw no reason why political appointees could not be personal friends. Elected as Jackson's vice president in 1832, he became the General's protégé. His positions on various issues were clarified through a series of letters he wrote during the 1836 campaign. Van Buren opposed federal funds for internal improvements and, following Jackson's policy, he said that he would not recharter the Bank of the United States under any circumstances. In 1820, during the Missouri Compromise, he had opposed the extension of slavery into the territories. In this campaign, he declared himself a strong advocate of the right of slave states to control slavery within their boundaries. As vice president, he cast the deciding vote in the U.S. Senate (1836) in favor of the bill barring abolitionist material from the mails. Most importantly, he had the complete confidence of Andrew Jackson.

Each party staged public meetings with partisan speeches praising their candidates. Resolutions of support from an endless variety of organizations appeared in friendly newspapers including foreign language ones. Broadsides, handbills, pamphlets, pewter medals, engravings, and campaign biographies were distributed. Democratic state and local committees coordinated Van Buren's campaign. In Tennessee, for example, Congressman James K. Polk toured his district promoting Van Buren's election as well as his own. In contrast, the Whig campaign was weak because the party, with three presidential candidates, was fragmented and not able to generate much national excitement. Harrison appeared on the ballot of 15 of the 26 states then in the Union and Webster's name was on the ballot only in New England. Hugh White was on the ballot in only 10 states, mainly slaveholding states.

Voting began in Ohio and Pennsylvania on 4 November 1836 and concluded in Rhode Island three weeks later. In most states, the polls remained open for several days. The campaign continued up to the last minute. The Washington *Globe,* a Jacksonian newspaper, wrote that Van Buren "is the most powerful enemy of the abolitionists; and the safest president for the South." However, the Richmond *Whig* concluded its electioneering with a final attack on Van Buren calling him an anti-slavery Northerner.

Voter turnout was low for this period—Van Buren received 764,176 votes to 738,124 for the combined Whig candidates, a winning victory of 50.8 percent. In the electoral vote, he received 170 votes to a total of 124 for his four opponents.

When elected president at age 55, he became the first president born after the Declaration of Independence, the first of Dutch ancestry, the first from New York, and the first of several to go from the governor's mansion in Albany to the White House. Van Buren had been a unique figure in New York government and the first president to have headed a state political machine.

A minor, but unsettling event, took place in the vice presidential election—Richard M. Johnson failed to receive a majority of electoral votes because Virginia electors refused to vote for him. For the first and only time in U.S. history, the vice presidential election went to the U.S. Senate, which chose Johnson by a vote along party lines of 33 votes for Johnson and 16 votes for Whig candidate Representative Francis Granger of Massachusetts.

Richard M. Johnson, reared on the frontier, distinguished himself at the Battle of the Thames (1813) by devising a battlefield strategy for a regiment of riflemen. He was one of the few "war hawks" who actually fought in the War of 1812. As a member of the Kentucky legislature and then the U.S. Senate, he is given credit for the passage of the Kentucky law abolishing imprisonment for debt. He later helped promote similar legislation at the national level. Johnson took a considerable interest in public education and also was one of the founders of Columbian College (now George Washington University). In addition, he supported and supervised programs for educating Native Americans. Enormously popular among frontiersmen and urban workers, Andrew Jackson saw him as an eventual presidential candidate. Jackson chose him to be the Democratic vice presidential nominee, and the party convention obediently obliged. Johnson never married, but he had two daughters by a mulatto woman whom he inherited from his father's estate. This is the reason why the Virginia electors refused to vote for him, forcing the Senate to elect the vice president.

On 4 March 1837, Andrew Jackson, now nearing his seventieth birthday, witnessed the inauguration of his heir. Seated behind Van Buren, Jackson rode to the Capitol as the thousands who lined Pennsylvania Avenue cheered wildly for him. "For once," wrote Senator Thomas Hart Benton, "the rising was eclipsed by the setting sun. It was gratitude and admiration . . . the acclaim of posterity breaking from the bosoms of contemporaries." It remained to be seen if the great democratic society of which Jefferson had spoken and which continued under Jackson could be entrusted to Van Buren and Jackson's disciples.

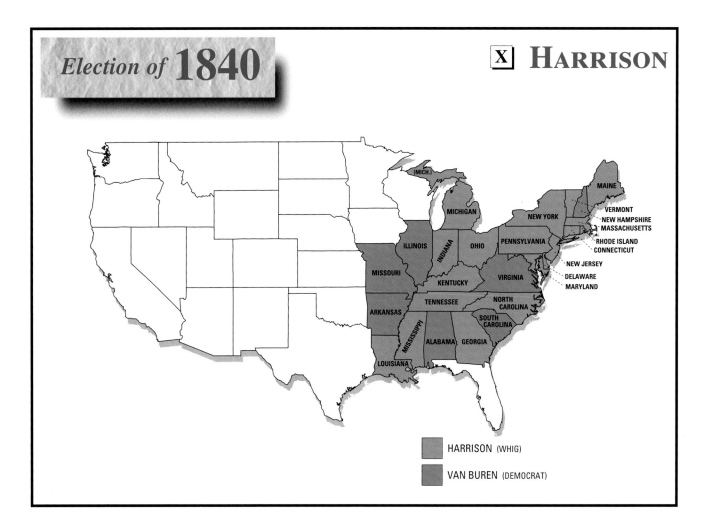

Election of 1840

☒ **HARRISON**

HARRISON (WHIG)

VAN BUREN (DEMOCRAT)

States	Electoral Votes	Harrison	Van Buren
Alabama	(7)	-	7
Arkansas	(3)	-	3
Connecticut	(8)	8	-
Delaware	(3)	3	-
Georgia	(11)	11	-
Illinois	(5)	-	5
Indiana	(9)	9	-
Kentucky	(15)	15	-
Louisiana	(5)	5	-
Maine	(10)	10	-
Maryland	(10)	10	-
Massachusetts	(14)	14	-
Michigan	(3)	3	-
Mississippi	(4)	4	-
Missouri	(4)	-	4
New Hampshire	(7)	-	7
New Jersey	(8)	8	-
New York	(42)	42	-
North Carolina	(15)	15	-
Ohio	(21)	21	-
Pennsylvania	(30)	30	-
Rhode Island	(4)	4	-
South Carolina	(11)	-	11
Tennessee	(15)	15	-
Vermont	(7)	7	-
Virginia	(23)	-	23
Totals	**(294)**	**234**	**60**

ELECTORAL VOTE

Election of 1840

STATE	TOTAL VOTE	WILLIAM H. HARRISON (Whig)		MARTIN VAN BUREN (Democrat)		JAMES G. BIRNEY (Liberty)		OTHER		PLURALITY	
		Votes	%	Votes	%	Votes	%	Votes	%		
Alabama	62,511	28,515	45.6	33,996	54.4	—		—		5,481	D
Arkansas	11,839	5,160	43.6	6,679	56.4	—		—		1,519	D
Connecticut	56,879	31,598	55.6	25,281	44.4	—		—		6,317	W
Delaware	10,852	5,967	55.0	4,872	44.9	—		13	0.1	1,095	W
Georgia	72,322	40,339	55.8	31,983	44.2	—		—		8,356	W
Illinois	93,175	45,574	48.9	47,441	50.9	160	0.2	—		1,867	D
Indiana	117,605	65,280	55.5	51,696	44.0	30		599	0.5	13,584	W
Kentucky	91,104	58,488	64.2	32,616	35.8	—		—		25,872	W
Louisiana	18,912	11,296	59.7	7,616	40.3	—		—		3,680	W
Maine	92,802	46,612	50.2	46,190	49.8	—		—		422	W
Maryland	62,280	33,528	53.8	28,752	46.2	—		—		4,776	W
Massachusetts	126,825	72,852	57.4	52,355	41.3	1,618	1.3	—		20,497	W
Michigan	44,029	22,933	52.1	21,096	47.9	—		—		1,837	W
Mississippi	36,525	19,515	53.4	17,010	46.6	—		—		2,505	W
Missouri	52,923	22,954	43.4	29,969	56.6	—		—		7,015	D
New Hampshire	59,956	26,310	43.9	32,774	54.7	872	1.5	—		6,464	D
New Jersey	64,454	33,351	51.7	31,034	48.1	69	0.1	—		2,317	W
New York	441,543	226,001	51.2	212,733	48.2	2,809	0.6	—		13,268	W
North Carolina	80,735	46,567	57.7	34,168	42.3	—		—		12,399	W
Ohio	272,890	148,043	54.3	123,944	45.4	903	0.3	—		24,099	W
Pennsylvania	287,695	144,023	50.1	143,672	49.9	—		—		351	W
Rhode Island	8,631	5,213	60.4	3,263	37.8	19	0.2	136	1.6	1,950	W
Tennessee	108,145	60,194	55.7	47,951	44.3	—		—		12,243	W
Vermont	50,782	32,440	63.9	18,006	35.5	317	0.6	19		14,434	W
Virginia	86,394	42,637	49.4	43,757	50.6	—		—		1,120	D
Totals	2,411,808	1,275,390	52.9	1,128,854	46.8	6,797	0.3	767		146,536	W

POPULAR VOTE

The election of 1840 is best remembered for its famous Log Cabin campaign. The Whig Party elected their first president and they also carried both Houses of Congress. The 1840 campaign was unique for its popular and emotional appeal, organized on an unprecedented scale. The credit of introducing every political device calculated to sway the "common man" belongs to the Whigs.

A major economic depression, caused by overspeculative investments in land and industry, swept the United States soon after President Martin Van Buren's inauguration in 1837. Stock prices tumbled and exports stopped almost completely. The price of cotton fell by almost one-half on the New Orleans market. In New York, unemployed workers demonstrated against evictions and the high price of food. Mobs broke into the city's flour warehouses and stole supplies. Farms and plantations were lost by people who had borrowed to purchase them and could not repay the loans. Many state governments defaulted on their bonds. Banks stopped paying interest and ships stood idle. Men, women, and children roamed about looking for jobs. City streets became crowded with a new class not seen before in the United States—hungry, frightened people who wanted work but could not find it.

Everyone blamed everyone else for the depression. Americans blamed British bankers and British bankers blamed American investors. Van Buren blamed the Second Bank of the United States, now operating with a state charter—and Nicholas Biddle, the Bank's president, blamed Van Buren. Some thought the cause of the depression came from too much beer and liquor drinking. The depression, which lasted until 1843, turned many Van Buren supporters against him.

Whig leaders were determined to win the 1840 presidential election. They decided to end party factionalism by nominating William Henry Harrison, the popular hero of the Battle of Tippecanoe. No attempt was made to frame a platform; indeed the only bond uniting the various groups under the Whig banner was a determination to defeat the Democrats. Rising through army ranks, Harrison had fought against the Native Americans in what was known as the Northwest Territory. Thomas Jefferson, then the territorial governor, granted him authority in 1802 to make treaties with the Native Americans to get them to give up as much land as possible. Through all kinds of deals, Harrison obtained millions of acres in what are now the states of Illinois and Indiana. While the British ceded this land to the United States under the treaty ending the American Revolution, the Native Americans did not accept the treaty as valid. They gradually united to resist the intrusion of settlers. The Shawnee warrior Tecumseh decreed that no chief of any tribe could cede land which belonged, he claimed, to all tribes in common. Harrison defeated Chief Tecumseh and the Shawnees at the Battle of Tippecanoe (1811) in northern Indiana. This event was immortalized in endless material objects, songs, and speeches during the 1840 campaign.

During the War of 1812, Harrison captured Fort Detroit from the British. He finally forced the British from the Northwest Territory at the Battle of the Thames (1813). Tecumseh, now an ally of the British, was killed and Harrison became a national military hero. Ironically, it was probably Van Buren's running mate, Richard M. Johnson, who actually killed Tecumseh.

Harrison faded from the public eye in the decades that followed. He became dependent on the income from his farm in North Bend, Ohio, and a small salary from being a county recorder. He had to support his extended family which included many children and grandchildren. Whig politicians discovered Harrison in obscurity and entered him as a sectional candidate in the 1836 campaign. He did surprisingly well. At age 67, Harrison, because of his military exploits a quarter of a century earlier, was able to unite the Whig Party. He led them to a decisive victory over Van Buren and the Democrats. For sectional balance, John Tyler, a former U.S. senator from Virginia and a supporter of states' rights, was chosen as his running mate.

What followed ranks as among the most colorful campaigns in U.S. political history. Biddle advised "Not one single word about [Harrison's] principles or his creed. . . . Let him say nothing—promise nothing." Issues blurred as the Whigs turned Harrison into a folk hero. Thurlow Weed, the powerful New York political leader, masterminded a brilliant campaign.

Late in 1839, a Democratic newspaper writer joked that if Harrison were given a pension of $200 a year and a barrel of hardcider, he would "sit the remainder of his days in his log cabin" and "study moral philosophy." The Whigs locked on to this and made it into their central campaign theme.

Harrison became the plain man of the people and Van Buren became the aristocrat. The symbolism caught on: the log cabin and hardcider image succeeded.

Harrison had studied medicine in college and he was descended from a distinguished Virginia family. His great-grandfather had signed the Declaration of Independence. However, Harrison's new image became a hardcider-drinking general who was born in a log cabin and had overcome social obstacles to become an Indian fighter and war hero. Van Buren and the Democrats were portrayed as the party of expensive wine and fancy mansions. As a matter of fact, Van Buren was the son of a tavernkeeper in Kinderhook, New York.

Items of every description imaginable bore the slogan "Tippecanoe and Tyler, Too." "Tippecanoe" song sheets saturated the market at the very moment when mass-produced pianos were finding their way into middle-class homes. Minstrel shows, glee clubs, and traveling performers all praised the now famous General from North Bend. Enameled glass broaches carried the log cabin and cider image; cotton bandannas depicted scenes form the General's early life; campaign flags, ceramic water pitchers, pewter coffee pots, Staffordshire china, teapots, glass plates, ribbons plus dozens of other items conveyed the charismatic image which Harrison's handlers had created for him. Deliberately avoiding issues, Harrison's supporters wore coonskin caps, built campaign log cabins in every town of consequence, and freely dispensed hardcider to the voters, who were persuaded that the General had saved the country from untold Indian atrocities. It turned out to be a brilliant strategy.

A great newspaper revolution had developed in the United States between 1830 and 1840. Technology made the "penny press" possible. Newspapers now became entertaining and sensational to build circulation. In 1830, about 900 newspapers existed, of which less than 100 were dailies; figures for 1840 reveal almost 1,600 newspapers of which more than 200 were dailies. The Whigs seized upon this opportunity by filling columns with lively copy about Harrison and his exploits. In addition, they created special campaign sheets which were inserted into newspapers that supported him. The most famous of the inserts was the *Log Cabin,* edited by Horace Greeley. Filled with jokes about the

Democrats, cartoons, campaign songs, and news of Tippecanoe clubs, the *Log Cabin* reached a printing of more than 80,000 copies a week. Other inserts reprinted Greeley's spirited material.

Breaking with tradition, Harrison became the first presidential candidate to give campaign speeches. He gave more than 23 speeches—each from one to three hours long. Newspapers and pamphlets carried his words to the nation, although they were mostly generalized, vague ambiguities. Whig speakers, including Abraham Lincoln and Daniel Webster, told huge crowds tales of a poor, hardworking, cabin-dwelling frontiersman who rose to be a general and commanded armies which achieved battlefield feats beyond description. "Here is a revolution in the habits and manners of the people," wrote John Quincy Adams in his diary, "When will it end?"

The Democratic campaign seemed dull. Their rallies fell short of the massive Whig outpourings. Newspapers friendly to the Democrats attacked Harrison for being on both sides of major issues. He was for the Bank of the United States as well as against it; for a protective tariff as well as being a freetrader. Andrew Jackson, now 73, was brought out of retirement to speak for "Little Van" as he never had done for himself. Van Buren's campaign failed to stir enthusiasm or to generate excitement. He followed tradition and made no speeches.

More than 80 percent of those eligible to vote did so, compared with 56 percent four years earlier. This record was not equaled or surpassed except in 1860 and 1876. Every state reached new levels of voter participation. Harrison received 52.9 percent of the popular vote to Van Buren's 46.8 percent. But the electoral vote was overwhelming. Harrison carried 19 states with 234 votes to Van Buren's 7 states and 60 votes.

Harrison's inauguration took place on a brisk day. Mounted on a white charger, the President-elect led the procession to the Capitol. Escorted to the East Portico, Harrison delivered a rambling and dull speech of 8,466 words—the longest inaugural address in U.S. history. He did not wear a coat, gloves, or a hat. He was later soaked in a rainstorm and caught a cold. One month later, on 4 April 1841, the President died of pneumonia.

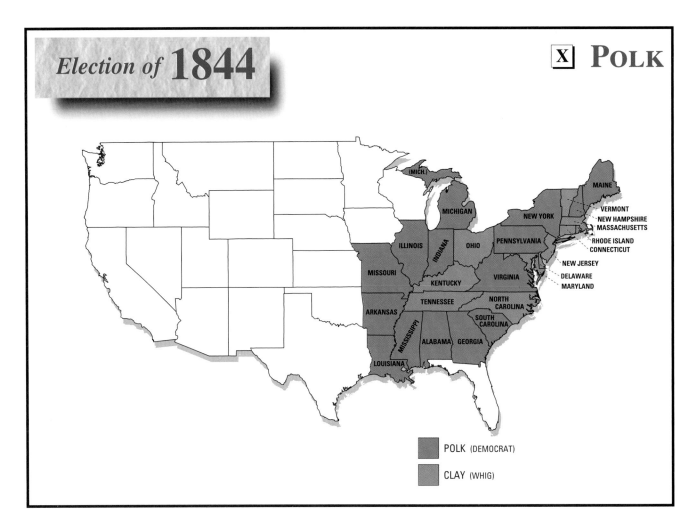

Election of 1844

☒ POLK

POLK (DEMOCRAT)

CLAY (WHIG)

States	Electoral Votes	Polk	Clay
Alabama	(9)	9	-
Arkansas	(3)	3	-
Connecticut	(6)	-	6
Delaware	(3)	-	3
Georgia	(10)	10	-
Illinois	(9)	9	-
Indiana	(12)	12	-
Kentucky	(12)	-	12
Louisiana	(6)	6	-
Maine	(9)	9	-
Maryland	(8)	-	8
Massachusetts	(12)	-	12
Michigan	(5)	5	-
Mississippi	(6)	6	-
Missouri	(7)	7	-
New Hampshire	(6)	6	-
New Jersey	(7)	-	7
New York	(36)	36	-
North Carolina	(11)	-	11
Ohio	(23)	-	23
Pennsylvania	(26)	26	-
Rhode Island	(4)	-	4
South Carolina	(9)	9	-
Tennessee	(13)	-	13
Vermont	(6)	-	6
Virginia	(17)	17	-
Totals	**(275)**	**170**	**105**

ELECTORAL VOTE

Election of 1844

STATE	TOTAL VOTE	JAMES K. POLK (Democrat)		HENRY CLAY (Whig)		JAMES G. BIRNEY (Liberty)		OTHER		PLURALITY	
		Votes	%	Votes	%	Votes	%	Votes	%		
Alabama	63,403	37,401	59.0	26,002	41.0	—		—		11,399	D
Arkansas	15,150	9,546	63.0	5,604	37.0	—		—		3,942	D
Connecticut	64,616	29,841	46.2	32,832	50.8	1,943	3.0	—		2,991	W
Delaware	12,247	5,970	48.7	6,271	51.2	—		6		301	W
Georgia	86,247	44,147	51.2	42,100	48.8	—		—		2,047	D
Illinois	109,057	58,795	53.9	45,854	42.0	3,469	3.2	939	0.9	12,941	D
Indiana	140,157	70,183	50.1	67,866	48.4	2,108	1.5	—		2,317	D
Kentucky	113,237	51,988	45.9	61,249	54.1	—		—		9,261	W
Louisiana	26,865	13,782	51.3	13,083	48.7	—		—		699	D
Maine	84,933	45,719	53.8	34,378	40.5	4,836	5.7	—		11,341	D
Maryland	68,690	32,706	47.6	35,984	52.4	—		—		3,278	W
Massachusetts	132,037	53,039	40.2	67,062	50.8	10,830	8.2	1,106	0.8	14,023	W
Michigan	55,560	27,737	49.9	24,185	43.5	3,638	6.5	—		3,552	D
Mississippi	45,004	25,846	57.4	19,158	42.6	—		—		6,688	D
Missouri	72,522	41,322	57.0	31,200	43.0	—		—		10,122	D
New Hampshire	49,187	27,160	55.2	17,866	36.3	4,161	8.5	—		9,294	D
New Jersey	75,944	37,495	49.4	38,318	50.5	131	0.2	—		823	W
New York	485,882	237,588	48.9	232,482	47.8	15,812	3.3	—		5,106	D
North Carolina	82,521	39,287	47.6	43,232	52.4	—		2		3,945	W
Ohio	312,300	149,127	47.8	155,091	49.7	8,082	2.6	—		5,964	W
Pennsylvania	331,645	167,311	50.4	161,195	48.6	3,139	0.9	—		6,116	D
Rhode Island	12,194	4,867	39.9	7,322	60.0	—		5		2,455	W
Tennessee	119,957	59,917	49.9	60,040	50.1	—		—		123	W
Vermont	48,765	18,041	37.0	26,770	54.9	3,954	8.1	—		8,729	W
Virginia	95,539	50,679	53.0	44,860	47.0	—		—		5,819	D
Totals	2,703,659	1,339,494	49.5	1,300,004	48.1	62,103	2.3	2,058	0.1	39,490	D

POPULAR VOTE

The issues raised in the 1844 presidential election led directly to the war with Mexico (1846–1848). This conflict reopened the question of slavery in the territories and was an ominous prelude to the Civil War (1861–1865).

The westward advancement from the Appalachian Mountains to the Mississippi River and then across the Great Plains to the Rocky Mountains, had a major impact on politics, economics, and thought. When Thomas Jefferson became president in 1801, the population stood at 5.3 million. Forty years later it had risen to about 17 million. There were 17 states comprising 460,537 square miles during Jefferson's administration. By 1845, there were 28 states and a land area of 1,239,060 square miles. Some 250,000 immigrants came to the United States between 1783 and 1820. In 1847 alone, more than that number arrived. Without pause, the frontier moved ever westward. "What the Mediterranean Sea was to the Greeks," wrote historian Frederick Jackson Turner, "breaking the bond of custom, offering new experience, calling out new institutions and activities, that, and more, the ever retreating frontier had been to the United States." By the end of President James K. Polk's administration in 1849, the United States had annexed Texas, the Oregon Territory, and the Mexican Cession (the future states of Nevada, Utah, Colorado, New Mexico, Arizona, and California). But, as the nation expanded, the problems that resulted tested the very foundation of the Republic.

Mexico had declared independence from Spain in 1821, with assistance from American frontiersmen and adventurers. The new Mexican Government invited Americans to settle in the area of Texas in order to strengthen the territory's economy and increase tax revenues. Connecticut-born Moses Austin, who had obtained a land grant from Mexico in 1820, pioneered American colonization there. He died before developing his Texas tract but Mexico validated the grant for his son, Stephen, who carried through the first colonization program. By 1830, about 20,000 Americans had settled in Texas. There were colonists from almost every state in the Union and from England, Ireland, and Germany; but most came from the southern slave states. Between 1820 and 1830, some 20,000 slaves had been brought across the Sabine and Red rivers into east Texas—ignoring the Mexican warning against non-Catholics and slaves.

In 1830, the Mexican Government sent troops to occupy Texas and to halt U.S. immigration, but it was too late to stop American settlers. In 1835, Mexico's leader, General Antonio Lopez Santa Anna, led an army across the Rio Grande River to oust the Americans. In February 1836, with over 2,000 troops, Santa Anna besieged some 200 Texans in the Alamo, a mission church at San Antonio. After two weeks of resistance, the Alamo fell. The Mexicans killed all the defenders but spared the noncombatants. "Remember the Alamo" became the cry of Texans in later battles with the Mexicans. The following month, on 2 March 1836, Americans in Texas declared their independence. They established a government under a constitution that allowed slavery. Sam Houston, commander of the Texas army, defeated Santa Anna's army on 21 April 1836 at San Jacinto and took the General captive. To obtain his release, Santa Anna signed a treaty giving Texas its independence, fixing a vague boundary between Texas and Mexico. The Mexican Congress disallowed the treaty but they were powerless to reverse it.

Texas had sought admission to the Union since gaining independence in 1836, but many Northerners feared that several additional slave states would be carved from this huge area equal in size to France. The South coveted Texas, said poet James Russell Lowell, to have "bigger pens to cram slaves in." Both Presidents Andrew Jackson and Martin Van Buren deferred action. Rebuffed, Sam Houston, then president of the Republic of Texas, spoke about diplomatic and economic ties with Great Britain. By 1841, these overtures had aroused many Americans. Would such an alliance abolish slavery and make the territory a haven for runaways? Would New England mills be denied cheap Texas cotton? Was American security endangered?

In 1844, the Democrats nominated James K. Polk, who became the first "dark horse," or unexpected candidate in U.S. history. Polk, a former congressmen and senator from Tennessee, had never wavered in his support of Andrew Jackson. Earlier in 1844, when former President Van Buren declared his opposition to the annexation of Texas on moral grounds, Andrew Jackson, now 77, took prompt political action. He summoned Democratic leaders to the Hermitage and declared that Van Buren had committed political suicide and could not be renominated. The party must have a candidate from the southwest who stood for annexation—and Jackson pointed to Polk. Van Buren had the support of a majority of the Democratic delegates, but he lacked the necessary two-thirds needed for nomination. Polk was nominated on the ninth ballot, as Jackson had predicted. The official proceedings of the Democratic Convention note at this point that, "the enthusiasm which now filled the convention was indescribable, and continued to increase up to the hour of adjournment."

Henry Clay, now 67 years old, the founder and leader of the Whig Party, became their nominee by acclamation. This was Clay's third try for the White House. He had an excellent reputation as a statesman and he was one of the most popular politicians in the country. His driving desire for higher office, however, and his lack of consistency on issues—he was nicknamed "The Great Compromiser"—set many voters against him. The annexation of Texas became the most important issue in the 1844 campaign. Clay originally opposed annexation believing it would lead to war with Mexico. "I consider the annexation of Texas at this time," explained Clay, "as a measure compromising the national character, involving us certainly in a war with Mexico, probably with other foreign nations . . . and not called for by any general expression of public opinion." However, Clay began to change his position on the Texas issue during the campaign. He thought that he had mis-judged American sentiment. On 1 July, he made public a letter explaining that personally he had no objection to annexation but he feared it might lead to the break-up of the Union because of strong northern opposition. This statement cost him his abolitionist supporters in the key state of New York which had 36 electoral votes. Polk won a narrow popular vote victory in the election, 49.5 percent to 48.1, percent, and 170 electoral votes to Clay's 105. As Van Buren had lost his party's renomination by being too specific on Texas, Clay lost the election to Polk by being too honest on the subject.

Banners and ribbons for Clay promoted him as a friend of agriculture and a strong supporter of the protective tariff. But the Democratic use of the American flag with one star (representing Texas) outside the standard summed up their campaign: they favored the immediate annexation of Texas. Democrats cleverly demanded the annexation of the entire Oregon Territory as well—all of Oregon, up to Russian Alaska's southern boundary at 54°40'—where slavery could never exist. "Fifty-four forty or fight!" became the Democratic campaign slogan. To counter this challenge, the Whig's scornfully asked, "Who is James K. Polk?" Polk, unlike Clay, remained silent and allowed his supporters to wage his campaign.

The outgoing Congress regarded the election results as a statement of the will of the people so they passed a joint resolution asking Texas to join the Union. President John Tyler signed it three days before the end of his term. Tyler, who had been denied renomination by the Whigs, had the satisfaction of sending a courier to inform Sam Houston that only the consent of the Lone Star Republic was neces-sary to make Texas the twenty-eighth state. On 4 July 1845, the Republic of Texas voted to give up its independence and become part of the United States. The border between Mexico and Texas, however, was still undetermined. Mexico immediately recalled its minister from Washington.

A Vermont congressman looked out a window in Washington on the morning after Polk's election and noticed a Democratic victory banner flying over the slave market. "That flag means *Texas*," he exclaimed, " and *Texas* means *civil war*, before we have done with it."

James G. Birney, the candidate of the abolitionist Liberty Party, received 2.3 percent of the popular vote. Third parties in U.S. politics appear and then disappear with a degree of rapidity. The Liberty Party, founded in 1839, however, was the first anti-slavery party in the United States. It became the focal point of the political opposition to slavery until the Free Soil Party replaced it in 1848. Because the Liberty Party had a single issue, it failed to attract those who opposed slavery but who were also were concerned about other issues. In spite of receiving a small percentage of the popular vote, Birney probably received enough votes in New York State to deprive Clay of winning the state's 36 electoral votes. Had Clay won New York, he would have won the election.

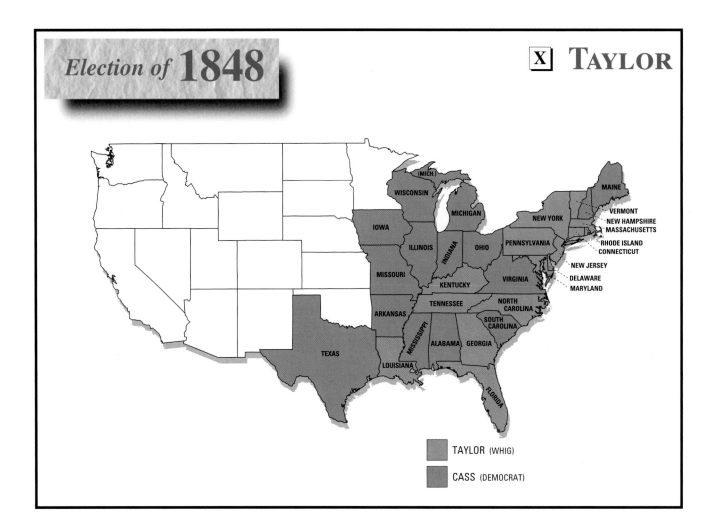

Election of **1848**

$\boxed{\text{X}}$ **TAYLOR**

TAYLOR (WHIG)

CASS (DEMOCRAT)

States	Electoral Votes	Taylor	Cass	States	Electoral Votes	Taylor	Cass
Alabama	(9)	-	9	Mississippi	(6)	-	6
Arkansas	(3)	-	3	Missouri	(7)	-	7
Connecticut	(6)	6	-	New Hampshire	(6)	-	6
Delaware	(3)	3	-	New Jersey	(7)	7	-
Florida	(3)	3	-	New York	(36)	36	-
Georgia	(10)	10	-	North Carolina	(11)	11	-
Illinois	(9)	-	9	Ohio	(23)	-	23
Indiana	(12)	-	12	Pennsylvania	(26)	26	-
Iowa	(4)	-	4	Rhode Island	(4)	4	-
Kentucky	(12)	12	-	South Carolina	(9)	-	9
Louisiana	(6)	6	-	Tennessee	(13)	13	-
Maine	(9)	-	9	Texas	(4)	-	4
Maryland	(8)	8	-	Vermont	(6)	6	-
Massachusetts	(12)	12	-	Virginia	(17)	-	17
Michigan	(5)	-	5	Wisconsin	(4)	-	4
				Totals	**(290)**	**163**	**127**

ELECTORAL VOTE

Election of 1848

STATE	TOTAL VOTE	ZACHARY TAYLOR (Whig)		LEWIS CASS (Democrat)		MARTIN VAN BUREN (Free Soil)		OTHER		PLURALITY	
		Votes	%	Votes	%	Votes	%	Votes	%		
Alabama	61,659	30,482	49.4	31,173	50.6	—		4		691	D
Arkansas	16,888	7,587	44.9	9,301	55.1	—		—		1,714	D
Connecticut	62,398	30,318	48.6	27,051	43.4	5,005	8.0	24		3,267	W
Delaware	12,432	6,440	51.8	5,910	47.5	82	0.7	—		530	W
Florida	7,203	4,120	57.2	3,083	42.8	—		—		1,037	W
Georgia	92,317	47,532	51.5	44,785	48.5	—		—		2,747	W
Illinois	124,596	52,853	42.4	55,952	44.9	15,702	12.6	89	0.1	3,099	D
Indiana	152,394	69,668	45.7	74,695	49.0	8,031	5.3	—		5,027	D
Iowa	22,271	9,930	44.6	11,238	50.5	1,103	5.0	—		1,308	D
Kentucky	116,865	67,145	57.5	49,720	42.5	—		—		17,425	W
Louisiana	33,866	18,487	54.6	15,379	45.4	—		—		3,108	W
Maine	87,625	35,273	40.3	40,195	45.9	12,157	13.9	—		4,922	D
Maryland	72,359	37,702	52.1	34,528	47.7	129	0.2	—		3,174	W
Massachusetts	134,748	61,072	45.3	35,281	26.2	38,333	28.4	62		22,739	W
Michigan	65,082	23,947	36.8	30,742	47.2	10,393	16.0	—		6,795	D
Mississippi	52,456	25,911	49.4	26,545	50.6	—		—		634	D
Missouri	72,748	32,671	44.9	40,077	55.1	—		—		7,406	D
New Hampshire	50,104	14,781	29.5	27,763	55.4	7,560	15.1	—		12,982	D
New Jersey	77,745	40,015	51.5	36,901	47.5	829	1.1	—		3,114	W
New York	455,944	218,583	47.9	114,319	25.1	120,497	26.4	2,545	0.6	98,086	W
North Carolina	79,826	44,054	55.2	35,772	44.8	—		—		8,282	W
Ohio	328,987	138,656	42.1	154,782	47.0	35,523	10.8	26		16,126	D
Pennsylvania	369,092	185,730	50.3	172,186	46.7	11,176	3.0	—		13,544	W
Rhode Island	11,049	6,705	60.7	3,613	32.7	726	6.6	5		3,092	W
Tennessee	122,463	64,321	52.5	58,142	47.5	—		—		6,179	W
Texas	17,000	5,281	31.1	11,644	68.5	—		75	0.4	6,363	D
Vermont	47,897	23,117	48.3	10,943	22.8	13,837	28.9	—		9,280	W
Virginia	92,004	45,265	49.2	46,739	50.8	—		—		1,474	D
Wisconsin	39,166	13,747	35.1	15,001	38.3	10,418	26.6	—		1,254	D
Totals	2,879,184	1,361,393	47.3	1,223,460	42.5	291,501	10.1	2,830	0.1	137,933	W

P O P U L A R   V O T E

In accepting the 1844 Democratic nomination, James K. Polk wrote that, if elected, he would not seek a second term. Polk achieved all of his objectives during one term. He added a significant corollary to the 1823 Monroe Doctrine—the people of "this continent alone" had the right to decide their own destiny. The question of the Oregon Territory was settled without a war with Great Britain by a compromise extending the existing continental line along the 49th parallel; and he obtained tariff reductions. The war with Mexico (1846–1848) showed Polk to be an expansionist rather than an imperialist, since he opposed retaining Mexico by force. This brief but decisive conflict settled the Texas boundary. Mexico ceded the enormous California and New Mexico territories, adding more than 1 million square miles to the national domain. Thus, the nation's borders stretched from the Atlantic Ocean to the Pacific Ocean, encompassing an area about five times larger than the combined lands of Germany, France, and Italy. Unfortunately, this broad expansion caused further sectional and party divisions.

Although a party man, Polk had supreme contempt for the spoils system. This unscrupulous method employed by congressmen to get offices for their supporters led him to "distrust the disinterestedness and honesty of all mankind." Convinced that the spoils system could crush any president who desired to do his duty, he resolved: "If God grants me length of days and health, I will, after the expiration of my term, give a history of the selfish and corrupt considerations which influence the course of public men, as a legacy to posterity." Polk died less than four months after leaving office, at age 54. He had little personal magnetism and only a few intimate friends to praise his record, but, seldom in U.S. history has such an ambitious agenda been completed in four years.

The Whig Party had been successful when it chose William Henry Harrison as their candidate in the 1840 presidential election. They attempted to duplicate their success when they nominated another general in the 1848 election, 64-year-old Zachary Taylor of Louisiana. He had joined the army in 1807 and had risen through the ranks. The Mexican War had made "Old Rough and Ready" a national hero.

Taylor confessed that he had never voted because he was always on duty on the frontier. However, he said that he supported Henry Clay. This was enough to convince Whig politicians that he belonged to their party. When several Whig leaders urged his nomination, Taylor wrote more than 50 letters to soldiers, public officials, and newspaper editors. He stated that he was not a candidate, and he doubted his qualification for the office. The mere idea of him as a presidential contender, he wrote, was "too visionary to require a serious answer. [It] never entered my head, nor is it likely to enter the head of any sane person."

The Whigs nominated Taylor on the fourth ballot over Henry Clay, Daniel Webster, and Winfield Scott. Millard Fillmore, a former New York congressman, was chosen as vice president to balance Taylor, who was a slaveholder. Zachary Taylor was one of the strangest presidential candidates in U.S. history. He was the first White House candidate without the slightest experience in any form of civil government. He wrote ungrammatical letters and could not spell. He stuttered and squinted. Lacking a formal education, he could not deliver a coherent speech. His legs were not only bowed but disproportionately short for his 5' 8" frame. The General hated military uniforms, preferring old clothes and tattered straw hats.

Since the Whigs could not agree on a party platform, the voters had to rely on Taylor's hazy statements. He repeated that if elected, his administration would be nonpartisan. "I am a Whig, but not an ultra Whig," he wrote. "If elected, I would not be the mere President of a Party. I would endeavor to act independent of party domination. I should feel bound to administer the government untrammeled by party schemes." Polk confided in his diary that the General impressed him as a well-meaning old man but "exceedingly ignorant of public affairs, and, I should judge, of very ordinary capacity."

The fact that the 1848 presidential election could be won by such an unlikely person demonstrated that the major issue of the day—slavery—was eating away at the two party system. The two national parties held themselves together by dealing with slavery as indirectly and vaguely as possible. By 1856, eight years later, the Whig Party virtually ceased to exist because of slavery. In 1860, the Democrats split into a northern and southern wing. The winning party in 1860—the Republicans—had its roots in the Liberty Party of 1844, but above all, in the Free Soil Party of 1848.

The Democrats nominated Lewis Cass on the fourth ballot, defeating James Buchanan of Pennsylvania and Levi Woodbury of New Hampshire. Cass was a distinguished soldier, diplomat, and statesman. In this election, he supported popular sovereignty. He felt that the question of slavery should be left up to the free people in the territories to be formed from the Mexican cessions. On the other hand, southern Democrats, led by South Carolina's John C. Calhoun, insisted that slaveowners be guaranteed the right to take their property into the territories. Free Soil Democrats and Conscience Whigs rejected such alternatives. To them, free soil meant free men. They felt that the western territories must be closed to slavery.

General William O. Butler of Kentucky was Cass's running mate. They tried their best to present their reasoned arguments to the voters. A new Democratic National Committee coordinated state activities. For the first time, a "Democratic Textbook" was issued; it was a collection of articles and resolutions praising the nominee and the party.

The Whigs turned out an endless variety of colorful prints depicting Taylor's military career, and they distributed them widely. The General was portrayed riding his charger, in full Napoleonic military dress. Every campaign tactic was used. Newspapers published catchy songs and an endless number of cartoons. Whig leaflets charged that Cass had illegally speculated in land while secretary of war and that he was a radical for supporting the 1848 Hungarian Revolution. Democrats poked fun at Taylor, claiming he could not read and would not understand the complexities of the presidency. Short campaign biographies glorified each candidate. The most widely circulated were a biography of Taylor by Washington newsman Ben Perley Poore and James Fenimore Cooper's lively biography of Cass. Both of these books were also published in German. Each party hired speakers to deliver orations in foreign languages. Every device imaginable was used to depict Cass and Taylor as the champion of this or that minority group. As the campaign drew to an end, torchlight processions and parades multiplied. Newspapers reported that election betting was common and that wagers "as high as $5,000 and $10,000 have been made in Cincinnati." The front page of one paper listed fantastic

odds—100 to 1—that Taylor would not carry 6 states and 500 to 1 that he would not be elected. Bribery went along with the gambling. In New Orleans, 500 laborers were hired to work on the new customshouse only after promising to vote for Cass. Democrats countered that Whigs had brought 13,000 men into Pennsylvania to do "pipe-laying" through Election Day. Desperate politicians pulled no punches. They were vicious at times; at other times, they were just silly.

Following a new federal law, this was the first presidential election to be held on a uniform day—the Tuesday following the first Monday in November. Nearly 3 million eligible men voted. Taylor won with 163 electoral votes, carrying 8 slave and 7 free states. Cass had 127 electoral votes, also carrying 8 free and 7 slave states. Taylor received 47.3 percent of the popular vote to Cass's 42.5 percent. Martin Van Buren and the Free Soil Party received slightly more than 10 percent of the popular vote, depriving Taylor of a majority.

The vote obtained by the Free Soil candidates—Martin Van Buren and his running mate Charles Francis Adams—is the most important event of the 1848 election. Their banner was "Free Soil, Free Speech, Free Labor, and Free Men." The new party opposed slavery in the territories, and supported federally funded internal improvements, free grants of public land to settlers, and a protective tariff to help the United States's growing industries against foreign competition. Although Van Buren and Adams won only 10 percent of the popular vote and no electoral votes, they may have affected the electoral outcome in at least 2states. Free Soil Party candidates were elected to state and local offices throughout the Northeast and the Midwest. They also elected nine congressmen to a closely divided U.S. House of Representatives, where they could influence the balance of power. They had demonstrated the potential strength and disruptive political power of a purely sectional party. In 1856, the Republican Party absorbed the Free Soilers, and their leaders and supporters helped elect Abraham Lincoln in 1860.

Election of 1852

X PIERCE

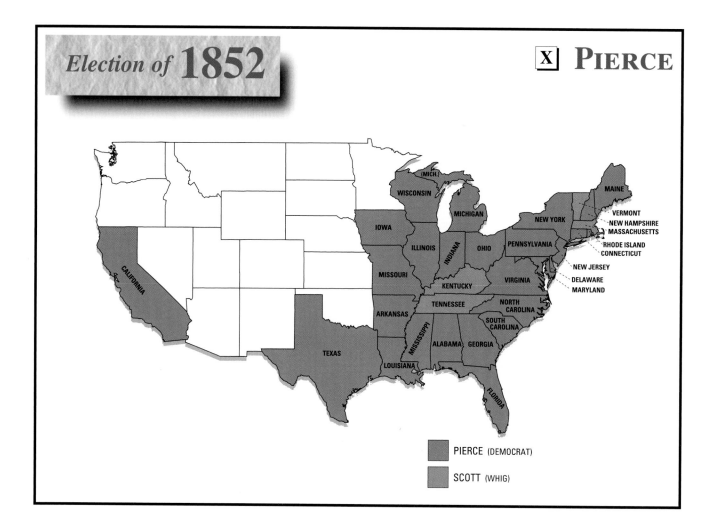

PIERCE (DEMOCRAT)

SCOTT (WHIG)

States	Electoral Votes	Pierce	Scott	States	Electoral Votes	Pierce	Scott
Alabama	(9)	9	-	Mississippi	(7)	7	-
Arkansas	(4)	4	-	Missouri	(9)	9	-
California	(4)	4	-	New Hampshire	(5)	5	-
Connecticut	(6)	6	-	New Jersey	(7)	7	-
Delaware	(3)	3	-	New York	(35)	35	-
Florida	(3)	3	-	North Carolina	(10)	10	-
Georgia	(10)	10	-	Ohio	(23)	23	-
Illinois	(11)	11	-	Pennsylvania	(27)	27	-
Indiana	(13)	13	-	Rhode Island	(4)	4	-
Iowa	(4)	4	-	South Carolina	(8)	8	-
Kentucky	(12)	-	12	Tennessee	(12)	-	12
Louisiana	(6)	6	-	Texas	(4)	4	-
Maine	(8)	8	-	Vermont	(5)	-	5
Maryland	(8)	8	-	Virginia	(15)	15	-
Massachusetts	(13)	-	13	Wisconsin	(5)	5	-
Michigan	(6)	6	-	**Totals**	**(296)**	**254**	**42**

ELECTORAL VOTE

Election of 1852

STATE	TOTAL VOTE	FRANKLIN PIERCE (Democrat)		WINFIELD SCOTT (Whig)		JOHN P. HALE (Free Soil)		OTHER		PLURALITY	
		Votes	%	Votes	%	Votes	%	Votes	%		
Alabama	44,147	26,881	60.9	15,061	34.1	—		2,205	5.0	11,820	D
Arkansas	19,577	12,173	62.2	7,404	37.8	—		—		4,769	D
California	76,810	40,721	53.0	35,972	46.8	61	0.1	56	0.1	4,749	D
Connecticut	66,781	33,249	49.8	30,359	45.5	3,161	4.7	12		2,890	D
Delaware	12,673	6,318	49.9	6,293	49.7	62	0.5	—		25	D
Florida	7,193	4,318	60.0	2,875	40.0	—		—		1,443	D
Georgia	62,626	40,516	64.7	16,660	26.6	—		5,450	8.7	23,856	D
Illinois	154,974	80,378	51.9	64,733	41.8	9,863	6.4	—		15,645	D
Indiana	183,176	95,340	52.0	80,907	44.2	6,929	3.8	—		14,433	D
Iowa	35,364	17,763	50.2	15,856	44.8	1,606	4.5	139	0.4	1,907	D
Kentucky	111,643	53,949	48.3	57,428	51.4	266	0.2	—		3,479	W
Louisiana	35,902	18,647	51.9	17,255	48.1	—		—		1,392	D
Maine	82,182	41,609	50.6	32,543	39.6	8,030	9.8	—		9,066	D
Maryland	75,120	40,022	53.3	35,077	46.7	21		—		4,945	D
Massachusetts	127,103	44,569	35.1	52,683	41.4	28,023	22.0	1,828	1.4	8,114	W
Michigan	82,939	41,842	50.4	33,860	40.8	7,237	8.7	—		7,982	D
Mississippi	44,454	26,896	60.5	17,558	39.5	—		—		9,338	D
Missouri	68,801	38,817	56.4	29,984	43.6	—		—		8,833	D
New Hampshire	50,535	28,503	56.4	15,486	30.6	6,546	13.0	—		13,017	D
New Jersey	83,926	44,301	52.8	38,551	45.9	336	0.4	738	0.9	5,750	D
New York	522,294	262,083	50.2	234,882	45.0	25,329	4.8	—		27,201	D
North Carolina	78,891	39,788	50.4	39,043	49.5	—		60	0.1	745	D
Ohio	352,903	169,193	47.9	152,577	43.2	31,133	8.8	—		16,616	D
Pennsylvania	387,920	198,568	51.2	179,182	46.2	8,500	2.2	1,670	0.4	19,386	D
Rhode Island	17,005	8,735	51.4	7,626	44.8	644	3.8	—		1,109	D
Tennessee	115,486	56,900	49.3	58,586	50.7	—		—		1,686	W
Texas	20,223	14,857	73.5	5,356	26.5	—		10		9,501	D
Vermont	43,838	13,044	29.8	22,173	50.6	8,621	19.7	—		9,129	W
Virginia	132,604	73,872	55.7	58,732	44.3	—		—		15,140	D
Wisconsin	64,740	33,658	52.0	22,240	34.4	8,842	13.7	—		11,418	D
Totals	**3,161,830**	**1,607,510**	**50.8**	**1,386,942**	**43.9**	**155,210**	**4.9**	**12,168**	**0.4**	**220,568**	**D**

POPULAR VOTE

Both the Whig and Democratic parties struggled with how to deal with the issues of sectionalism and factionalism in the election of 1852. In many ways, the United States had broken into several distinct sections, each facing different economic, political, and social problems. National parties—and the presidency—held these different sections together. Every problem could be compromised but slavery defied such a solution. The slavery issue dominated the election of 1852, the last contest between the Democratic Party and the Whig Party. The Compromise of 1850 revealed serious differences between and within both political parties.

The nation stood equally divided into 15 slave and 15 free states in 1850. When California petitioned for admission as a free state, sectional disagreements threatened to disrupt the Union. Congress met in 1850 to debate the spread of slavery. The Great Triumvirate—Henry Clay, John C. Calhoun, and Daniel Webster— met again, for the last time. Clay, a three-time candidate for the presidency, wanted to retire quietly, but he returned to the U.S. Senate in 1849. He wrote to a friend that he wished "to be a calm and quiet looker-on, rarely speaking, and, when I do, endeavoring to throw oil upon the troubled waters." He soon found himself leading one of the most important debates in U.S. history.

Henry Clay, now 73, forged the Compromise of 1850— a series of resolutions to save the nation. These resolutions proposed the admission of California as a free state; the organization of New Mexico and Utah as territories without mention of slavery; the establishment of a more efficient procedure for returning fugitive slaves to their masters as the Constitution had approved; the ending of the slave trade in the District of Columbia but the continuation of slavery there unless Maryland consented otherwise; and federal compensation to Texas for some land ceded to New Mexico. All sides of the slavery problem would give up something but the Union would be preserved.

On 4 March 1850, John C. Calhoun, too ill and feeble to speak himself, had his speech read by Senator James Murray Mason of Virginia. It predicted that the South could no longer remain in the Union. Calhoun pessimistically discussed sectional divisions. He maintained that the South had to defend slavery in order to stay alive. The Union, so near its end, could not be saved by cries of "Union, Union,

glorious Union," but by an unbreakable guarantee to preserve slavery while giving the South her equal rights in the territories. Would the North agree to this, he asked? The old champion of slavery died four weeks later. Calhoun's last words were: "The South, the poor South."

On 7 March, Daniel Webster rose to speak "not as a Massachusetts man, nor as a Northern man, but as an American. . . . I speak to-day for the preservation of the Union." The greatest Senate orator embraced compromise, equally denouncing those who thought peaceable secession possible as well as the abolitionists who despised all fugitive slave laws. Senator William Seward of New York spoke four days later and opposed the Compromise from the opposite perspective. While admitting that Congress had the power to permit slavery in the territories, he was against it. He said that, "there is a higher law than the Constitution which regulates our authority over the domain"—the law of God, from which alone the laws of man derive their sanction. Seward said that the Fugitive Slave Act would endanger the Union far more than any other anti-slavery measure. Historian William E. Gienapp wrote that it revealed "the growing moral chasm separating North and South in this decade."

The Fugitive Slave Act was intended to appease Southerners who felt that existing obligations to return runaway slaves to their owners were not strong enough. Anti-slavery people hated this law. For this very reason, Southerners insisted that it be enforced. As historian Carl Schurz noted, "the compromise of 1850, instead of securing peace and harmony, contained in the most important of its provisions the seeds of new and greater conflicts."

As this dramatic debate raged in Congress, President Zachary Taylor, who firmly opposed the Compromise, died. Taylor was a slaveholder and he had told his son-in-law, Jefferson Davis, that he would not permit any weakening of the rights of the slaveholding states. Millard Fillmore, who succeeded him, was now decisive in persuading Congress to pass the legislation. Fillmore favored "the safe middle course."

The Compromise of 1850 was separated into five bills, and one by one these bills passed both the House and the Senate. They received their most consistent support from northern Democrats and southern Whigs. The issues of manifest destiny and slavery were now linked for the next decade. Southerners felt that passage of the Fugitive Slave

Law was essential and Fillmore signed this legislation. Northerners found this law most offensive. The abolitionists unleashed a torrent of abuse against the President, but he enforced the unpopular law.

The Democratic National Convention met in Baltimore on 1 June. Because of the two-thirds requirement for nomination, the Democrats again deadlocked, passing over Stephen A. Douglas, James Buchanan, William Marcy, and Lewis Cass, the presidential candidate in 1848. On the forty-ninth ballot, an exhausted convention chose a compromise candidate: Franklin Pierce of New Hampshire. Pierce's great claim seemed to be that he was a Northerner who opposed slavery but supported the Compromise of 1850. He himself was not enthusiastic about his candidacy. He lacked both the temperament and the experience to deal with the complex problem facing the nation. Senator William Rufus DeVane King of Alabama, was chosen to run for vice president.

On the fifty-third ballot, the Whigs turned to 66-year-old General Winfield Scott. Scott had been a hero in the War of 1812, and he became general in chief of the army in 1841. His handlers urged him to practice "masterly silence" but the General immediately endorsed strict enforcement of the Fugitive Slave Law. The many factions within the Whig Party—which was formed originally to oppose Andrew Jackson and to support Clay's "American System"—just dissolved. Webster, utterly crushed by his failure to be nominated, tearfully asked: "How will this look in history?" He sank into a deep depression and died five days before the election—but not before repudiating Scott's nomination. At the same time, Clay was growing weaker. He had told friends that he wanted to die in service to his country. He did so on 29 June 1852, just days after the Whigs ended their last convention.

Pierce did not make any speeches during the campaign. His supporters called him "Young Hickory of the Granite Hills" to remind voters of Andrew Jackson. His personality—and that of Scott—became the chief subject of party orators and newspaper articles. Pierce was, in the Whig press,

"a fourth-rate lawyer," a drunk, and a coward during service in the Mexican War. Democrats called Scott silly and inept. They actually published a pamphlet titled "Dangers of Electing an Incompetent Man President." Pierce answered the sneering Whig inquiry "Who is Franklin Pierce?" by asking Nathaniel Hawthorne, his notable Bowdoin College classmate, to write a campaign biography.

Both parties also sought the immigrant, Catholic vote, crucial in such states as Ohio and Indiana. Foreign language pamphlets of each party accused the other of "nativist" prejudices. As Democrats continued to attack Scott's hostility to immigrants as well as his military record, his supporters became alarmed. They sent the General, still on active service, to pick sites for military hospitals. He took a long tour of the Ohio Valley and found time to address Irish and German voters, who had been angered by his earlier statements about immigrants. Scott awkwardly told them of his love for the "sweet German accent" and the "rich Irish brogue."

Scott's campaigning did not help him. Pierce won the most lopsided victory since Andrew Jackson's reelection in 1832. He carried all but four states: Kentucky, Massachusetts, Tennessee, and Vermont. He received 254 electoral votes to Scott's 42, and 50.8 percent of the popular vote to Scott's 43.9 percent. The Whig Party was not only defeated; it was wiped out. Some suggested that its epitaph should read: "Here lies the Whig Party, which died of an effort to swallow the Fugitive Law." John P. Hale, the Free Soil Party candidate, received about 5 percent of the popular vote, chiefly from Massachusetts, New York, and Ohio. Voter participation was the lowest of any election between 1840 and 1860. Perhaps the most significant event of this election was the disintegration of the Whig Party because of factional and sectional differences. A compromise president in the White House was the result. Pierce was a good man but a poor leader, and his administration moved the country closer to civil war.

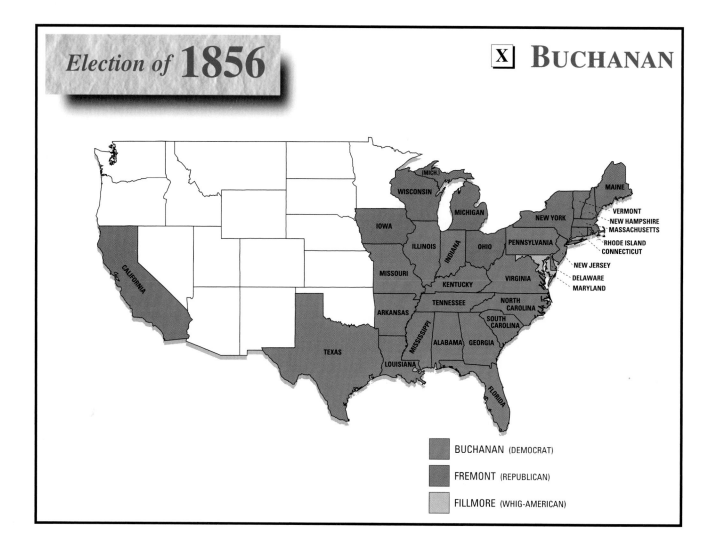

Election of 1856

☒ BUCHANAN

BUCHANAN (DEMOCRAT)

FREMONT (REPUBLICAN)

FILLMORE (WHIG-AMERICAN)

States	Electoral Votes	Buchanan	Fremont	Fillmore	States	Electoral Votes	Buchanan	Fremont	Fillmore
Alabama	(9)	9	-	-	Mississippi	(7)	7	-	-
Arkansas	(4)	4	-	-	Missouri	(9)	9	-	-
California	(4)	4	-	-	New Hampshire	(5)	-	5	-
Connecticut	(6)	-	6	-	New Jersey	(7)	7	-	-
Delaware	(3)	3	-	-	New York	(35)	-	35	-
Florida	(3)	3	-	-	North Carolina	(10)	10	-	-
Georgia	(10)	10	-	-	Ohio	(23)	-	23	-
Illinois	(11)	11	-	-	Pennsylvania	(27)	27	-	-
Indiana	(13)	13	-	-	Rhode Island	(4)	-	4	-
Iowa	(4)	-	4	-	South Carolina	(8)	8	-	-
Kentucky	(12)	12	-	-	Tennessee	(12)	12	-	-
Louisiana	(6)	6	-	-	Texas	(4)	4	-	-
Maine	(8)	-	8	-	Vermont	(5)	-	5	-
Maryland	(8)	-	-	8	Virginia	(15)	15	-	-
Massachusetts	(13)	-	13	-	Wisconsin	(5)	-	5	-
Michigan	(6)	-	6	-	**Totals**	**(296)**	**174**	**114**	**8**

ELECTORAL VOTE

Election of 1856

STATE	TOTAL VOTE	JAMES BUCHANAN (Democrat)		JOHN C. FREMONT (Republican)		MILLARD FILLMORE (Whig-American)		OTHER		PLURALITY	
		Votes	%	Votes	%	Votes	%	Votes	%		
Alabama	75,291	46,739	62.1	—		28,552	37.9	—		18,187	D
Arkansas	32,642	21,910	67.1	—		10,732	32.9	—		11,178	D
California	110,255	53,342	48.4	20,704	18.8	36,195	32.8	14		17,147	D
Connecticut	80,360	35,028	43.6	42,717	53.2	2,615	3.3	—		7,689	R
Delaware	14,598	8,004	54.8	310	2.1	6,275	43.0	9	0.1	1,729	D
Florida	11,191	6,358	56.8	—		4,833	43.2	—		1,525	D
Georgia	99,020	56,581	57.1	—		42,439	42.9	—		14,142	D
Illinois	239,334	105,528	44.1	96,275	40.2	37,531	15.7	—		9,253	D
Indiana	235,401	118,670	50.4	94,375	40.1	22,356	9.5	—		24,295	D
Iowa	92,310	37,568	40.7	45,073	48.8	9,669	10.5	—		7,505	R
Kentucky	142,058	74,642	52.5	—		67,416	47.5	—		7,226	D
Louisiana	42,873	22,164	51.7	—		20,709	48.3	—		1,455	D
Maine	109,689	39,140	35.7	67,279	61.3	3,270	3.0	—		28,139	R
Maryland	86,860	39,123	45.0	285	0.3	47,452	54.6	—		8,329	WA
Massachusetts	170,048	39,244	23.1	108,172	63.6	19,626	11.5	3,006	1.8	68,928	R
Michigan	125,558	52,136	41.5	71,762	57.2	1,660	1.3	—		19,626	R
Mississippi	59,647	35,456	59.4	—		24,191	40.6	—		11,265	D
Missouri	106,486	57,964	54.4	—		48,522	45.6	—		9,442	D
New Hampshire	69,774	31,891	45.7	37,473	53.7	410	0.6	—		5,582	R
New Jersey	99,396	46,943	47.2	28,338	28.5	24,115	24.3	—		18,605	D
New York	596,486	195,878	32.8	276,004	46.3	124,604	20.9	—		80,126	R
North Carolina	84,963	48,243	56.8	—		36,720	43.2	—		11,523	D
Ohio	386,640	170,874	44.2	187,497	48.5	28,121	7.3	148		16,623	R
Pennsylvania	460,937	230,772	50.1	147,963	32.1	82,202	17.8	—		82,809	D
Rhode Island	19,822	6,680	33.7	11,467	57.8	1,675	8.5	—		4,787	R
Tennessee	133,582	69,704	52.2	—		63,878	47.8	—		5,826	D
Texas	48,005	31,995	66.6	—		16,010	33.4	—		15,985	D
Vermont	50,675	10,569	20.9	39,561	78.1	545	1.1	—		28,992	R
Virginia	150,233	90,083	60.0	—		60,150	40.0	—		29,933	D
Wisconsin	120,513	52,843	43.8	67,090	55.7	580	0.5	—		14,247	R
Totals	4,054,647	1,836,072	45.3	1,342,345	33.1	873,053	21.5	3,177	0.1	493,727	D

POPULAR VOTE

Many hoped that the Compromise of 1850 had settled the slavery problem. Within four years, however, the question of slavery in the territories resurfaced and became the major issue in the election of 1856. Another significant issue was the powerful sentiment throughout the nation against immigrants and Catholics.

The 1856 election revolved around the assignment of blame—or guilt—for the Kansas-Nebraska Act and the bloodshed which followed its passage. When Franklin Pierce became president in 1853, the Democrats gained control of Congress. Stephen A. Douglas of Illinois became chairman of the Senate Committee on Territories. Douglas decided to deal with the pressing problem of the northern section of the Louisiana Purchase stretching west from Missouri, Iowa, and the Minnesota Territory to the Rocky Mountains. Douglas did not intend to provoke sectional controversy. Rather, he wanted to promote rapid settlement of the region west of Missouri, and to encourage the building of a transcontinental railroad westward from Chicago. Douglas's bill quickly passed the Senate, and the House approved it after a bitter debate. President Pierce signed the bill into law on 30 May 1854.

The Kansas-Nebraska Act divided the area into two territories: Kansas and Nebraska. It repealed the Missouri Compromise of 1820 which had prohibited slavery above the 36° 30′ line—the southern border of Missouri. Both Kansas and Nebraska were north of this line and had been closed to slavery. Now slavery could exist in this area, since the Act declared that all questions regarding slavery would be decided by the people living there. Congressional approval of popular sovereignty ended the idea that the federal government could exclude slavery from a territory.

Settlers started to move into Kansas at once, and it became a race to see whether more people would come from the slave states or the free states. The struggle between pro-slavery and anti-slavery groups became an armed conflict, a civil war. More than 200 settlers were killed between November 1855 and December 1856 and $2 million in property was destroyed. Some pro-slavery thugs pillaged and looted Lawrence, Kansas, and John Brown, a fanatical abolitionist, retaliated. Brown, his four sons, and two friends carried out the Osawatomie Massacre (24–25 May 1856). They dragged five pro-slavery men from their beds, split open their skulls and cut off their hands while chanting hymns. Violence and terrorism now increased. Temporary peace came to Kansas in late 1856 with the aid of federal troops.

The Missouri Compromise had become a sacred guarantee to many. Consequently, the fury unleashed against Douglas because of the Kansas-Nebraska Act was unmatched—he was burned in effigy and cursed throughout the North as a traitor. When Douglas tried to explain his actions in Chicago, his native city, he was stoned from the speaker's platform. Northerners flocked to another party which firmly opposed the expansion of slavery in the territories—the Republican Party.

The new Republican Party, which came into existence because of the Act, accused President Pierce and the Democrats of being criminals. In language rarely used in a party platform, the Republicans declared: "We arraign . . . the President, his advisers, agents, supporters, apologists, and accessories . . . before the country and before the world; and it is our fixed purpose to bring the actual perpetrators of these atrocious outrages and their accomplices to a sure [and swift] . . . punishment."

By the end of 1854, the new Republican Party began to spread throughout the North. Composed of anti-slavery men, Free Soilers, and former Whigs, the party demanded the immediate repeal of the Kansas-Nebraska Act and the 1850 Fugitive Slave Law. The Republicans were also in favor of the abolition of slavery in the District of Columbia. They were uncertain about how to handle nativism and, therefore, they avoided direct discussion of it. At their first national convention held in Philadelphia in June 1856, the Republicans unanimously chose 43-year-old John C. Frémont as their presidential nominee. Frémont was a popular, but reckless, explorer and former army officer who had served briefly in the U.S. Senate from California. Chanting their slogan: "Free Speech, Free Soil and Frémont," the Republicans prepared to go before the nation in a great moral crusade against slavery. William L. Dayton, a former Whig and U.S. senator from New Jersey, was chosen as his running mate.

The Democrats held their convention in Cincinnati during the first week of June. While divided along sectional lines, the party was, nevertheless, the heir of Jacksonian democracy. They counted many nationally known public figures within their ranks, and the party machine controlled federal patronage. It had the backing of a nearly solid South and a loyal following in the North and West. The vicious acts of John Brown preceded their convention by two weeks, causing an unaccustomed quietness among the delegates. James Buchanan of Pennsylvania received the nomination on the seventeenth ballot. Franklin Pierce and Stephen A. Douglas had been rejected because of their close association with the Kansas-Nebraska Act. Buchanan had served in the U.S. Congress for 20 years and he had been secretary of state under President James K. Polk. Buchanan offered security, experience, and, hopefully, peaceful solutions to an agitated nation. The Democrats did not want a nominee who had been involved in the bitter debate over the Kansas-Nebraska Act. Buchanan had been U.S. minister to Great Britain during that period. Former Representative John C. Breckinridge of Kentucky was chosen as the Democratic vice presidential candidate. Breckinridge later was indicted for treason for supporting the Confederate States of America.

The American Party emerged as a political force in the 1856 election. It was dedicated to halting immigration to the United States. It started as a secret society, the Order of the Star Spangled Banner. Members would reply: "I know nothing about it" when asked for information. Hence, they became known as Know-Nothings. Their slogan was: "Americans must rule America." They adopted a platform which, among other things, stated that only native-born men should be allowed to vote. Native Americanism as a political influence had existed in the United States for decades, but it grew rapidly in response to the arrival of almost 4.5 million immigrants, mainly German and Irish Catholics between 1840 and 1860. Many were attracted to the party, but its anti-immigrant/Catholic stance antagonized many others. One of them was Abraham Lincoln who wrote in 1855: "I am not a know-nothing. That is certain. How could I be? . . . As a nation, we began by declaring that 'all men are created equal.' We now practically read it 'all men are created equal except Negroes.' When the Know-Nothings get control, it will read 'all men are created equal except Negroes and foreigners and Catholics.' When it comes to this I should prefer emigrating to some country where they make no pretense of loving liberty." Despite

such objections, the new party won astounding victories in the state elections of 1854.

Former President Millard Fillmore became the nominee of the American (Know-Nothing) Party. He won 21.5 percent of the total popular vote and Maryland's 8 electoral votes. Fillmore, who opposed the sole nativist appeal of the party, nevertheless endorsed it. He tried to attract former Whigs as well as those who thought that immigration could divert attention from the explosive slavery issue. Fillmore tried to appeal to both anti-slavery and anti-immigrant voters but most of the latter chose Frémont and the Republican Party, especially when the American Party's national convention voted to support the Kansas-Nebraska Act. Most of Fillmore's support came from the South. After the 1856 elections, the party collapsed.

Each party focused on particular states and regions in order to win a majority of the electoral vote in this three-way race. The Democrats used their excellent state organizations. Republicans relied on the enthusiasm of their supporters. They held rallies and torchlight parades with floats and drum corps. Noted authors such as Edward Everett Hale, Ralph Waldo Emerson, and William Cullen Bryant gave speeches for Frémont as did Abraham Lincoln and Carl Schurz, the popular German American orator. John Greenleaf Whittier composed an ode for the Republican cause.

The election results had been predicted—Buchanan won. With about 4 million votes cast, he defeated Frémont by a half million, and Fillmore by 1 million. Buchanan received 174 electoral votes; Frémont 114; and Fillmore 8. Frémont had carried 11 of the 16 northern states and came within 35 electoral votes of winning the election. If the Republicans had carried Pennsylvania and 9 additional electoral votes, they would have elected Frémont eventhough he did not receive a single vote in 11 slave states and a total of only 595 votes in 2 other states, Delaware and Maryland. This possibility raised the fear that the anti-slavery party could come to power in the future without a southern vote, and could cause the breakup of the Union.

Election of 1860

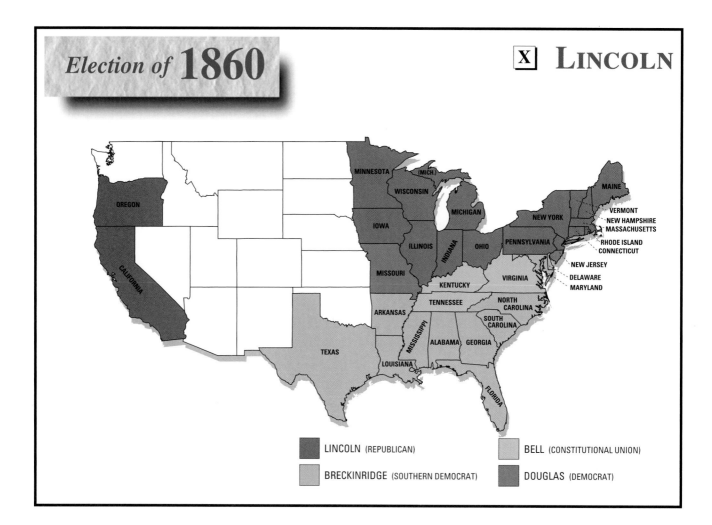

LINCOLN (REPUBLICAN)

BELL (CONSTITUTIONAL UNION)

BRECKINRIDGE (SOUTHERN DEMOCRAT)

DOUGLAS (DEMOCRAT)

States	Electoral Votes	Lincoln	Breckinridge	Bell	Douglas	States	Electoral Votes	Lincoln	Breckinridge	Bell	Douglas
Alabama	(9)	-	9	-	-	Mississippi	(7)	-	7	-	-
Arkansas	(4)	-	4	-	-	Missouri	(9)	-	-	-	9
California	(4)	4	-	-	-	New Hampshire	(5)	5	-	-	-
Connecticut	(6)	6	-	-	-	New Jersey	(7)	4	-	-	3
Delaware	(3)	-	3	-	-	New York	(35)	35	-	-	-
Florida	(3)	-	3	-	-	North Carolina	(10)	-	10	-	-
Georgia	(10)	-	10	-	-	Ohio	(23)	23	-	-	-
Illinois	(11)	11	-	-	-	Oregon	(3)	3	-	-	-
Indiana	(13)	13	-	-	-	Pennsylvania	(27)	27	-	-	-
Iowa	(4)	4	-	-	-	Rhode Island	(4)	4	-	-	-
Kentucky	(12)	-	-	12	-	South Carolina	(8)	-	8	-	-
Louisiana	(6)	-	6	-	-	Tennessee	(12)	-	-	12	-
Maine	(8)	8	-	-	-	Texas	(4)	-	4	-	-
Maryland	(8)	-	8	-	-	Vermont	(5)	5	-	-	-
Massachusetts	(13)	13	-	-	-	Virginia	(15)	-	-	15	-
Michigan	(6)	6	-	-	-	Wisconsin	(5)	5	-	-	-
Minnesota	(4)	4	-	-	-	**Totals**	**(303)**	**180**	**72**	**39**	**12**

ELECTORAL VOTE

Election of **1860**

STATE	TOTAL VOTE	ABRAHAM LINCOLN (Republican)		STEPHEN A. DOUGLAS (Democrat)		JOHN C. BRECKINRIDGE (Southern Democrat)		JOHN BELL (Constitutional Union)		OTHER		PLURALITY	
		Votes	%	Votes	%	Votes	%	Votes	%	Votes	%		
Alabama	90,122	—		13,618	15.1	48,669	54.0	27,835	30.9	—		20,834	SD
Arkansas	54,152	—		5,357	9.9	28,732	53.1	20,063	37.0	—		8,669	SD
California	119,827	38,733	32.3	37,999	31.7	33,969	28.3	9,111	7.6	15		734	R
Connecticut	74,819	43,488	58.1	15,431	20.6	14,372	19.2	1,528	2.0	—		28,057	R
Delaware	16,115	3,822	23.7	1,066	6.6	7,339	45.5	3,888	24.1	—		3,451	SD
Florida	13,301	—		223	1.7	8,277	62.2	4,801	36.1	—		3,476	SD
Georgia	106,717	—		11,581	10.9	52,176	48.9	42,960	40.3	—		9,216	SD
Illinois	339,666	172,171	50.7	160,215	47.2	2,331	0.7	4,914	1.4	35		11,956	R
Indiana	272,143	139,033	51.1	115,509	42.4	12,295	4.5	5,306	1.9	—		23,524	R
Iowa	128,739	70,302	54.6	55,639	43.2	1,035	0.8	1,763	1.4	—		14,663	R
Kentucky	146,216	1,364	0.9	25,651	17.5	53,143	36.3	66,058	45.2	—		12,915	CU
Louisiana	50,510	—		7,625	15.1	22,681	44.9	20,204	40.0	—		2,477	SD
Maine	100,918	62,811	62.2	29,693	29.4	6,368	6.3	2,046	2.0	—		33,118	R
Maryland	92,502	2,294	2.5	5,966	6.4	42,482	45.9	41,760	45.1	—		722	SD
Massachusetts	169,876	106,684	62.8	34,370	20.2	6,163	3.6	22,331	13.1	328	0.2	72,314	R
Michigan	154,758	88,481	57.2	65,057	42.0	805	0.5	415	0.3	—		23,424	R
Minnesota	34,804	22,069	63.4	11,920	34.2	748	2.1	50	0.1	17		10,149	R
Mississippi	69,095	—		3,282	4.7	40,768	59.0	25,045	36.2	—		15,723	SD
Missouri	165,563	17,028	10.3	58,801	35.5	31,362	18.9	58,372	35.3	—		429	D
New Hampshire	65,943	37,519	56.9	25,887	39.3	2,125	3.2	412	0.6	—		11,632	R
New Jersey	121,215	58,346	48.1	62,869	51.9	—		—		—		4,523	D
New York	675,156	362,646	53.7	312,510	46.3	—		—		—		50,136	R
North Carolina	96,712	—		2,737	2.8	48,846	50.5	45,129	46.7	—		3,717	SD
Ohio	442,866	231,709	52.3	187,421	42.3	11,406	2.6	12,194	2.8	136		44,288	R
Oregon	14,758	5,329	36.1	4,136	28.0	5,075	34.4	218	1.5	—		254	R
Pennsylvania	476,442	268,030	56.3	16,765	3.5	178,871	37.5	12,776	2.7	—		89,159	R
Rhode Island	19,951	12,244	61.4	7,707	38.6	—		—		—		4,537	R
Tennessee	146,106	—		11,281	7.7	65,097	44.6	69,728	47.7	—		4,631	CU
Texas	62,855	—		18		47,454	75.5	15,383	24.5	—		32,071	SD
Vermont	44,644	33,808	75.7	8,649	19.4	218	0.5	1,969	4.4	—		25,159	R
Virginia	166,891	1,887	1.1	16,198	9.7	74,325	44.5	74,481	44.6	—		156	CU
Wisconsin	152,179	86,110	56.6	65,021	42.7	887	0.6	161	0.1	—		21,089	R
Totals	4,685,561	1,865,908	39.9	1,380,202	29.5	848,019	18.1	590,901	12.6	531		485,706	R

POPULAR VOTE

The presidential election of 1860 is the most momentous in U.S. history because the losing states refused to accept the results peacefully. The election was like the eye of a hurricane, a moment of dreadful calm with the foreboding sense of a greater storm to come.

During President James Buchanan's administration sectional disputes between the North and the South had become more bitter and passionate. The Dred Scot decision (1857) and John Brown's attempt to incite a slave revolt in a raid at Harper's Ferry, Virginia (1859) further intensified the burning slavery issue. With the fatalism of a Greek tragedy, the nation appeared to be rushing toward destruction.

There were four candidates in the 1860 election: John Bell (Constitutional Union Party); Stephen A. Douglas (Democratic Party); John C. Breckinridge (Southern Democratic Party); and Abraham Lincoln (Republican Party). The dominant issue was the extension of slavery. All other economic, political, and social issues clustered around slavery. Bell had no solution; Douglas favored popular sovereignty and worked for compromise; Breckinridge was pro-slavery and thought the issue irreconcilable. Lincoln argued that the Union must be preserved.

The Republican Party met in Chicago in the middle of May and nominated 53-year-old Abraham Lincoln on the third ballot. He was the inoffensive second choice of most delegates. Lincoln had served as a Whig representative in the U.S. Congress for one term (1847–1849) and then returned to his law practice in Springfield, Illinois. "Honest Abe" embodied the American success story. Born in a log cabin, self-educated, he rose to become a noted lawyer and shrewd politician. He was not an abolitionist but was rock-solid on the fundamental Republican principle: slavery must be banned from the territories. Both the Republican platform and Lincoln stated that the Constitution protected slavery in those states where it existed. Lincoln had avoided association with the Know-Nothings and could count on support from naturalized citizens. Moderate and humane, his speeches struck a note of humility and hope.

The Republican Party platform also supported a high protective tariff to aid U.S. industries; the construction of a transcontinental railroad built with federal assistance; a liberal immigration policy; and a homestead act which would grant free land to settlers. The platform condemned attempts to reopen the African slave trade and denied the authority of Congress or a territorial legislature to give legal status to slavery in the territories. The Republican Party attracted eastern capitalists, western farmers, industrial laborers, and voters of New England descent wherever they lived. It also aimed its appeal at the key states of Illinois, Indiana, Pennsylvania, and New Jersey, which had supported Buchanan in 1856 and now were vitally important for an 1860 Republican victory. In short, Lincoln and the Republicans carefully avoided offending any of the several factions which comprised the Republican Party and yet crafted a message to the South that they were not a party of anti-slavery fanatics.

Stephen A. Douglas remained the most commanding figure within the Democratic Party. During the 1858 Illinois Senate campaign, he held seven debates with Abraham Lincoln, his opponent. During what is known as the "Lincoln-Douglas" debates, he formulated the "Freeport Doctrine" which helped him to a narrow win in the senatorial election. The people of a territory, reasoned Douglas, could, by lawful means, exclude slavery prior to the formation of a state constitution. The Senator tried to reconcile his "popular sovereignty" belief with the Dred Scott decision. However, this caused him to lose his southern support for the 1860 Democratic nomination. The issue was slavery in the territories: Lincoln opposed it and Douglas hedged his position.

Douglas insisted on a platform supporting popular sovereignty, that is, local control of the slave question. The Democratic Party had met in Charleston, South Carolina, but many southern delegates walked out after the platform was adopted. The Democrats convened again in Baltimore, Maryland two months later. After the nomination of Douglas and Herschel V. Johnson of Georgia, more Southerners walked out. The next day, they nominated John C. Breckinridge of Kentucky, for president, and Joseph Lane of Oregon, for vice president. They called themselves the Southern Democratic Party and they adopted a strong pro-slavery platform. After more than 30 years as a national party which had been founded by Andrew Jackson, the Democrats split over an irreconcilable issue—the power of the national government to regulate slavery in the western territories.

The Constitutional Union Party, a remnant of the old-line Whig and American parties, chose John Bell of Tennessee, as their presidential candidate and Edward Everett of Massachusetts, as his running mate. Their platform, which condemned subordination of the states to the federal government, was a simple one: "The Constitution of the country, the Union of the States and the enforcement of the laws." Essentially, they avoided the question of slavery.

The campaign followed the same pattern as the Tippecanoe campaign of William Henry Harrison in 1840, and it was the most exciting since then. The Republican Party had superb organization and adequate money to wage an aggressive assault into virtually every county in the northern and midwestern states. They held torchlight parades, published biographies, and issued pamphlets, silk ribbons, medals, and all sorts of trinkets. To illustrate Lincoln's humble origins, the Republicans used symbols such as axes and rail fences. Lincoln's portrait appeared on more than a dozen different silk ribbons. More than 120 different mass-produced photographs of Lincoln were sold. Horace Greeley, editor of the influential New York *Tribune,* compiled Republican documents in a *Political Textbook for 1860.* It went through 14 editions. The journalist and novelist William Dean Howells wrote a campaign biography praising Lincoln, who later rewarded him with an appointment as counsel in Venice, Italy. Carl Schurz, a noted German American newspaper publisher, led a Republican group which appealed to naturalized voters. Campaign literature circulated in at least five languages.

Many myths now surround Lincoln—the tall, frugal, plain spoken man. Lincoln himself carefully cultivated stories about his humble origins. He was an excellent politician, although he was the least active of the four candidates. He greeted visitors in Springfield, Illinois, but said little of substance. He did not deliver a single speech, but his positions were readily known as the book version of his famed debates with Stephen A. Douglas had gone through many printings. Instead, the major Republican innovation—marching clubs, called "Wide Awakes"—excelled in parades attracting attention with their colorful uniforms and unusual marching routines.

More than 400,000 "Wide Awakes" participated in the campaign. One gigantic parade with horse-drawn floats was held in New York City two weeks before the election. It took almost five hours for the parade to pass. The other candidates tried to imitate the Republicans. Processions supporting Bell featured the ringing of a giant bell symbolizing alarm

for the Union. Douglas supporters circulated sheet music, pamphlets, and cartoons attempting to identify Lincoln with the radical abolitionists. Republican spokesmen denied he had any intention of interfering with slavery. It was expansion into the territories that he opposed. In the end, this message worked. Republicans convinced enough Midwesterners in critical states that a Lincoln defeat would mean that the Great Plains would be carved into slave plantations rather than free homesteads.

Douglas believed that he would carry most of the southern states and enough free states to insure his election. By mid summer, however, he admitted that Lincoln would be elected. When the returns were counted, Lincoln received 180 of the 303 electoral votes, a clear majority. All of the 180 votes were from free states. Breckinridge carried 11 slave states and 72 electoral votes; Bell ran third with 39, winning 3 border slave states: Kentucky, Tennessee, and Virginia. Douglas carried only Missouri and won 3 New Jersey votes for a total of 12 electoral votes. In the popular vote columns, Lincoln had received only 39.9 percent of the total; 60.1 percent did not vote for him. Voter turnout exceeded 80 percent but Lincoln did not receive a single vote in any future Confederate state except in Virginia where he polled less than 2,000 votes. The popular vote was a personal but hollow triumph for Douglas because he was the only candidate to draw votes from every region of the nation. The election, however, shows a distinct sectional voting pattern. It was almost as if two elections had been held: Lincoln vs. Douglas in the North and West; Bell vs. Breckinridge in the South.

Lincoln's victory caused secession. It is unclear if he thought this would be the consequence. Lincoln had said southern leaders, "had too much commonsense and good temper to break-up" the nation. An analysis of the final voting figures support his contention. In almost every southern state Douglas and Bell together carried a majority of the counties. This suggests that the people of the South were not so solidly in favor of secession. A middle ground had a strong hold upon them as well as most Americans, but southern extremists concluded that the southern way of life could not survive under Lincoln. Lincoln's objective was to preserve the Union—this mystical source of the political process which he placed beyond all other considerations. However, the slave states began to secede in December 1860.

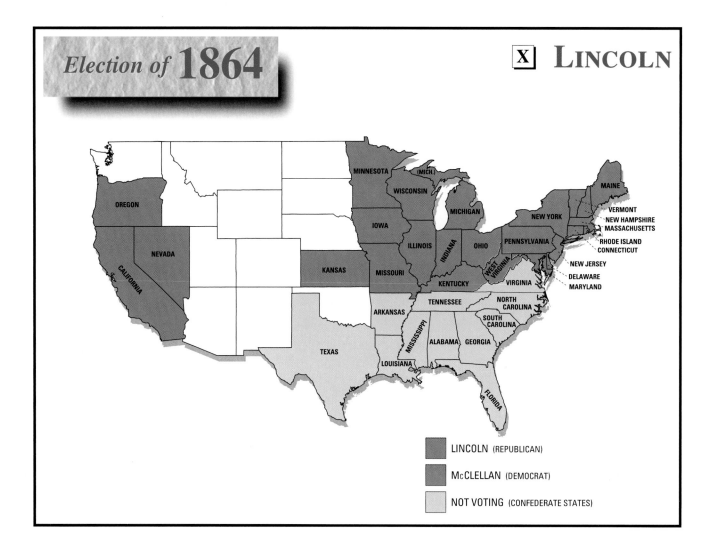

Election of 1864

☒ LINCOLN

LINCOLN (REPUBLICAN)

McCLELLAN (DEMOCRAT)

NOT VOTING (CONFEDERATE STATES)

States	Electoral Votes	Lincoln	McClellan	States	Electoral Votes	Lincoln	McClellan
California	(5)	5	-	Missouri	(11)	11	-
Connecticut	(6)	6	-	Nevada	(3)	2	-
Delaware	(3)	-	3	New Hampshire	(5)	5	-
Illinois	(16)	16	-	New Jersey	(7)	-	7
Indiana	(13)	13	-	New York	(33)	33	-
Iowa	(8)	8	-	Ohio	(21)	21	-
Kansas	(3)	3	-	Oregon	(3)	3	-
Kentucky	(11)	-	11	Pennsylvania	(26)	26	-
Maine	(7)	7	-	Rhode Island	(4)	4	-
Maryland	(7)	7	-	Vermont	(5)	5	-
Massachusetts	(12)	12	-	West Virginia	(5)	5	-
Michigan	(8)	8	-	Wisconsin	(8)	8	-
Minnesota	(4)	4	-	**Totals**	**(234)**	**212**	**21**

ELECTORAL VOTE

Election of 1864

STATE	TOTAL VOTE	ABRAHAM LINCOLN (Republican)		GEORGE B. McCLELLAN (Democrat)		OTHER		PLURALITY	
		Votes	%	Votes	%	Votes	%		
California	105,890	62,053	58.6	43,837	41.4	—		18,216	R
Connecticut	86,958	44,673	51.4	42,285	48.6	—		2,388	R
Delaware	16,922	8,155	48.2	8,767	51.8	—		612	D
Illinois	348,236	189,512	54.4	158,724	45.6	—		30,788	R
Indiana	280,117	149,887	53.5	130,230	46.5	—		19,657	R
Iowa	132,947	83,858	63.1	49,089	36.9	—		34,769	R
Kansas	21,580	17,089	79.2	3,836	17.8	655	3.0	13,253	R
Kentucky	92,088	27,787	30.2	64,301	69.8	—		36,514	D
Maine	114,797	67,805	59.1	46,992	40.9	—		20,813	R
Maryland	72,892	40,153	55.1	32,739	44.9	—		7,414	R
Massachusetts	175,493	126,742	72.2	48,745	27.8	6		77,997	R
Michigan	165,279	91,133	55.1	74,146	44.9	—		16,987	R
Minnesota	42,433	25,031	59.0	17,376	40.9	26	0.1	7,655	R
Missouri	104,346	72,750	69.7	31,596	30.3	—		41,154	R
Nevada	16,420	9,826	59.8	6,594	40.2	—		3,232	R
New Hampshire	69,630	36,596	52.6	33,034	47.4	—		3,562	R
New Jersey	128,744	60,724	47.2	68,020	52.8	—		7,296	D
New York	730,721	368,735	50.5	361,986	49.5	—		6,749	R
Ohio	471,283	265,674	56.4	205,609	43.6	—		60,065	R
Oregon	18,350	9,888	53.9	8,457	46.1	5		1,431	R
Pennsylvania	573,735	296,292	51.6	277,443	48.4	—		18,849	R
Rhode Island	23,067	14,349	62.2	8,718	37.8	—		5,631	R
Vermont	55,740	42,419	76.1	13,321	23.9	—		29,098	R
West Virginia	34,877	23,799	68.2	11,078	31.8	—		12,721	R
Wisconsin	149,342	83,458	55.9	65,884	44.1	—		17,574	R
Totals	4,031,887	2,218,388	55.0	1,812,807	45.0	692		405,581	R

The Constitution does not provide for suspending elections. For, as Abraham Lincoln said: "We cannot have free government without elections; and if the rebellion could force us to forego or postpone a national election, it might fairly claim to have already conquered and ruined us." The 1864 presidential election took place even though it was the third year of the Civil War.

The National Union Convention representing both Republicans and War Democrats renominated Lincoln by acclamation on 7 June. Republican leaders desired to appeal to Union sentiment and do away with partisan influence as much as possible. The use of the Republican name was carefully avoided. News of General Ulysses S. Grant's loss of more than 12,000 men at Cold Harbor on 3 June dampened the enthusiasm of the delegates. The Baltimore convention chose Andrew Johnson as the vice presidential candidate. Johnson was a life-long Democrat and a former senator from the slave state of Tennessee. As a War Democrat, Johnson, who had been Lincoln's military governor of Tennessee (1862–1864), symbolized the coalition character of the National Union Party. This decision to nominate Johnson had major ramifications for the nation.

The Republican Party was not united in support of Lincoln. Those who called themselves Radicals, for example, had become increasingly distrustful of the President's commitment to ending slavery totally. The preservation of the Union still remained the most essential war goal for them, but they now insisted on emancipation without any compensation to the slaveholder. They were shocked when, in 1862, Lincoln suggested that District of Columbia owners be paid an average of $300 per slave to achieve emancipation in the nation's capital. The Radicals also found Lincoln inconsistent as well as contradictory on the question of Reconstruction: how the South should be treated after a military victory had been achieved.

One week prior to the National Union Convention (Republican Party), a group of Radical Republicans nominated John C. Frémont for president. Their short platform spoke about equality for all and it demanded the confiscation of Confederate owned lands for redistribution among the freedmen. Frémont's candidacy disturbed Lincoln. The erratic general retained a fiercely loyal following especially in Missouri, where, through an 1861 military proclamation, Frémont freed the slaves. Although northern Radicals rejoiced at Frémont's action, Lincoln thought it premature and unconstitutional, and relieved him of his command. Now, the President feared Frémont could take away enough votes to cost the Republicans Indiana, Illinois, and Missouri—and the election. Lincoln's friends placed pressure on friendly abolitionists who urged Frémont to withdraw. Dissonant voices told Frémont to stick with his principles, but he ungracefully withdrew six weeks before the election. In a public letter, he announced he had not changed his negative opinion of Lincoln whose "administration had been politically, militarily, and financially a failure, but [withdrew] because a Democratic Party victory would restore the Union with slavery." The next day, Lincoln dismissed Montgomery Blair from his cabinet. Blair had bluntly denounced the ending of slavery as a crackpot idea, and he fiercely opposed Radical plans for Reconstruction of the South.

Lincoln's skillful political maneuver held his party together. By accepting Andrew Johnson as his running mate, moderate Republicans seemed satisfied. The Radicals also seemed satisfied by Lincoln's agreeing to the platform plank calling for "unconditional surrender" and by his dismissing Blair. In short, the Republican Party now accepted the preservation of the Union at all costs, and emancipation as well.

Within a few weeks of Lincoln's renomination, however, this shaky Republican coalition came apart. Secretary of the Treasury Salmon P. Chase, whom Lincoln had forced to resign, joined with Horace Greeley in concluding that the President could not win the election. They insisted that another convention must convene. "Mr. Lincoln is already beaten," wrote Greeley, perhaps the Republican Party's most important journalist. "He cannot be elected. We must have another ticket to save us from overthrow." He suggested Generals Ulysses S. Grant, William T. Sherman, or Benjamin Butler for president, and Admiral David Farragut for vice president.

Senator Charles Sumner of Massachusetts agreed. Lincoln's renomination, he wrote, had been "ill-considered," but there could be no other candidate "unless he withdraws patriotically and kindly so as to leave no breach in the Party." It was an alarming situation. Lincoln received letters from some of his most loyal supporters declaring the election already lost. On 23 August, the President confided his thoughts to paper: "This morning, as for some days past, it seems exceedingly probable that this administration will not be re-elected. Then it will be my duty to co-operate with the President-elect, as to save the Union between the election and the inauguration; as he will have secured his election on such ground that he cannot possibly save it afterward."

"You think I don't know I am going to be beaten," he said to a friend, "*but I do* and unless some great change takes place *badly beaten."* Then Union victories came in rapid succession: Admiral Farragut's victory in Mobile Bay, the last major Gulf port in Confederate hands; General Sherman's capture of Atlanta, Georgia; and General Philip Sheridan's victory at Winchester, Virginia. The Republican opposition to Lincoln collapsed. They now joined together against the party which stood for ending the war—the Democrats.

The Democrats assembled in Chicago at the end of August. While also pledged to preserve the Union, their platform condemned the war and called for an end to the fighting. They key plank declared: "After four years of failure to restore the Union by the experiment of war . . . [we] demand that immediate efforts be made for a cessation of hostilities, with a view to an ultimate convention of the states, or other peaceable means, to the end that, at the earliest practical moment, peace may be restored on the basis of the Federal Union." Like the Republicans, the Democrats had their internal divisions. The Peace Democrats favored an armistice followed by negotiations, and the War Democrats favored continuing the fighting. With the peace platform plank in place, the party proceeded to nominate General George McClellan, whom Lincoln had removed from command of the Army of the Potomac in November 1862. McClellan had political aspirations. He had declared his opposition to Lincoln and discreetly made known his availability for the presidency. The General opposed emancipation but favored restoration of the Union by military force.

Democratic leaders thought they could win with their peace plank and they believed that McClellan was a victim of an unjust, unfair, despotic administration. He accepted the nomination and tried to harmonize the party's inconsis-

tencies but without success. During the campaign, the Peace Democrats stressed the platform while the War Democrats played up McClellan's determination for a military victory.

The 1864 presidential election was a referendum on the Lincoln administration's conduct of the war. No one could be quite sure, however, what a Democratic victory would mean. A halt in the fighting? Could the war then ever resume? A restoration of the Union with slavery? A Republican triumph meant a continuation of the war until the South surrendered and the end of slavery. To achieve these goals, the Republicans closed ranks and campaigned for Lincoln.

On 8 November, voters in 25 states reelected Lincoln by a sweeping electoral majority of 212 to 21. McClellan carried only Delaware, Kentucky, and New Jersey. Lincoln received 55 percent of the popular vote, more than 15 percent greater than in 1860. "The outcome," said Lincoln, proved that "a people's government can sustain a national election in the midst of a great Civil War."

A remarkable event took place during this election—more than 150,000 soldiers voted. The warriors participated in an election in which they were being asked if they should continue the fighting. Some states made it possible for their troops to vote in the field while others accepted absentee ballots. Since the Republicans considered the soldier vote essential, thousands received furloughs in early November so they could go home and vote in those states which made no provision for an absentee ballot. By an overwhelming majority, 77.6 percent, the soldiers cast their ballot for Lincoln, as few wished to support the Democratic Party which had declared the war a failure. In the midst of the Civil War, the nation peacefully held an election and those fighting to defend it also participated.

Lincoln wrote: "Our circumstances are novel and exceptional." Exceptional indeed! In the midst of the western world's largest and most destructive war since Napoleon's defeat, the United States voted to determine basic civil and military policies—as well as the future of millions of African Americans.

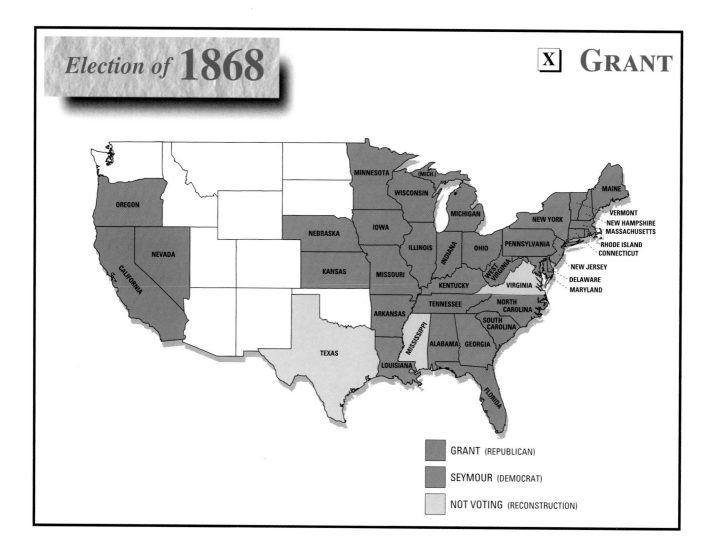

Election of 1868

X GRANT

GRANT (REPUBLICAN)

SEYMOUR (DEMOCRAT)

NOT VOTING (RECONSTRUCTION)

States	Electoral Votes	Grant	Seymour	States	Electoral Votes	Grant	Seymour
Alabama	(8)	8	-	Missouri	(11)	11	-
Arkansas	(5)	5	-	Nebraska	(3)	3	-
California	(5)	5	-	Nevada	(3)	3	-
Connecticut	(6)	6	-	New Hampshire	(5)	5	-
Delaware	(3)	-	3	New Jersey	(7)	-	7
Florida	(3)	3	-	New York	(33)	-	33
Georgia	(9)	-	9	North Carolina	(9)	9	-
Illinois	(16)	16	-	Ohio	(21)	21	-
Indiana	(13)	13	-	Oregon	(3)	-	3
Iowa	(8)	8	-	Pennsylvania	(26)	26	-
Kansas	(3)	3	-	Rhode Island	(4)	4	-
Kentucky	(11)	-	11	South Carolina	(6)	6	-
Louisiana	(7)	-	7	Tennessee	(10)	10	-
Maine	(7)	7	-	Vermont	(5)	5	-
Maryland	(7)	-	7	West Virginia	(5)	5	-
Massachusetts	(12)	12	-	Wisconsin	(8)	8	-
Michigan	(8)	8	-				
Minnesota	(4)	4	-	**Totals**	**(294)**	**214**	**80**

E L E C T O R A L   V O T E

Election of 1868

STATE	TOTAL VOTE	ULYSSES S. GRANT (Republican)		HORATIO SEYMOUR (Democrat)		OTHER		PLURALITY	
		Votes	%	Votes	%	Votes	%		
Alabama	149,594	76,667	51.3	72,921	48.7	6		3,746	R
Arkansas	41,190	22,112	53.7	19,078	46.3	—		3,034	R
California	108,656	54,588	50.2	54,068	49.8	—		520	R
Connecticut	98,570	50,789	51.5	47,781	48.5	—		3,008	R
Delaware	18,571	7,614	41.0	10,957	59.0	—		3,343	D
Georgia	159,816	57,109	35.7	102,707	64.3	—		45,598	D
Illinois	449,420	250,304	55.7	199,116	44.3	—		51,188	R
Indiana	343,528	176,548	51.4	166,980	48.6	—		9,568	R
Iowa	194,439	120,399	61.9	74,040	38.1	—		46,359	R
Kansas	43,630	30,027	68.8	13,600	31.2	3		16,427	R
Kentucky	155,455	39,566	25.5	115,889	74.5	—		76,323	D
Louisiana	113,488	33,263	29.3	80,225	70.7	—		46,962	D
Maine	112,962	70,502	62.4	42,460	37.6	—		28,042	R
Maryland	92,795	30,438	32.8	62,357	67.2	—		31,919	D
Massachusetts	195,508	136,379	69.8	59,103	30.2	26		77,276	R
Michigan	225,632	128,563	57.0	97,069	43.0	—		31,494	R
Minnesota	71,620	43,545	60.8	28,075	39.2	—		15,470	R
Missouri	152,488	86,860	57.0	65,628	43.0	—		21,232	R
Nebraska	15,291	9,772	63.9	5,519	36.1	—		4,253	R
Nevada	11,689	6,474	55.4	5,215	44.6	—		1,259	R
New Hampshire	68,304	37,718	55.2	30,575	44.8	11		7,143	R
New Jersey	163,133	80,132	49.1	83,001	50.9	—		2,869	D
New York	849,771	419,888	49.4	429,883	50.6	—		9,995	D
North Carolina	181,498	96,939	53.4	84,559	46.6	—		12,380	R
Ohio	518,665	280,159	54.0	238,506	46.0	—		41,653	R
Oregon	22,086	10,961	49.6	11,125	50.4	—		164	D
Pennsylvania	655,662	342,280	52.2	313,382	47.8	—		28,898	R
Rhode Island	19,511	13,017	66.7	6,494	33.3	—		6,523	R
South Carolina	107,538	62,301	57.9	45,237	42.1	—		17,064	R
Tennessee	82,757	56,628	68.4	26,129	31.6	—		30,499	R
Vermont	56,224	44,173	78.6	12,051	21.4	—		32,122	R
West Virginia	49,321	29,015	58.8	20,306	41.2	—		8,709	R
Wisconsin	193,628	108,920	56.3	84,708	43.7	—		24,212	R
Totals	5,722,440	3,013,650	52.7	2,708,744	47.3	46		304,906	R

P O P U L A R   V O T E

The 1868 presidential election was the most emotional in U.S. history. At issue was the future of some 4 million newly freed people, nearly 14 percent of the nation's total population.

The Democratic Party promised a dramatic slowdown in the process of racial equality. They pledged that Reconstruction of the former Confederate states would be left to each state and amnesty would be granted to all who had supported the Confederacy.

The Republican Party, dominated by Radicals, believed unconditional surrender by the South meant not only emancipation but also enforcement of the Fourteenth Amendment, which defined citizenship to include African Americans and guaranteed basic civil rights to all, including the right to vote for males. The penalty clause of the Amendment effectively disqualified most Confederates from holding state or federal office. Political power now passed, therefore, to the freedmen, the "carpetbaggers" (northern Whites who had moved to the South after the war) and to the "scalawags"(the small percentage of southern Whites who had opposed secession).

Lincoln had been assassinated in 1865. His successor, Andrew Johnson, had been impeached by the U.S. House of Representatives and tried before the U.S. Senate for defying Republican Reconstruction policies. Further exhilarated by victories in the 1866 congressional elections, the Republicans thought they had a mandate to proceed with their goal of racial equality. While halted, if not reversed, eight years later, these programs would become the blueprint for a civil rights movement a century later.

The Democratic Convention met in July. Party leadership had shifted. Stephen A. Douglas, James Buchanan, and Lewis Cass were dead. Power passed to Senator Thomas Hendricks of Indiana, George H. Pendleton of Ohio, Missouri's Francis Preston Blair, and General Winfield Hancock. Andrew Johnson returned to the party. On the twenty-second ballot, to break a deadlock, the Democrats unanimously nominated former New York Governor Horatio Seymour.

In his acceptance letter, Seymour wrote he had neither sought nor expected the nomination. He then attacked the "menacing attitude" of the Radicals and their attempt to destroy the rights of southern Whites by imposing Black suffrage on them. Blair, the vice presidential nominee, wrote in a similar vein. He claimed Radical programs had subjugated the rights of southern Whites through a policy of illegal military force. Ulysses S. Grant, the leading Republican candidate, had exclaimed, "Let us have peace," while Blair told a Kansas City audience, "The white race is the only race in the world that has shown itself capable of maintaining free institutions of a free government." A Richmond newspaper reported that throughout the South "the Democratic nominations are received with the most emphatic applause." After the election, Seymour said that accepting the nomination was the greatest mistake of his life.

Seymour and Blair's allusions to race are prudent and cautious when compared to the virulent, offensive language used by Democratic Party newspapers. Racism has rarely been as overt, so vicious, as what newspapers published during the 1868 campaign. "Universal Nigger Suffrage is the Great Issue of the Campaign," screamed a *New York Herald* editorial. "There is no other issue . . . the whole campaign burns purely and simply upon this point of the political status of the nigger in the Southern States and . . . universal nigger suffrage and the correlated oppression of the white man. . . [These] divide the parties and the people." Democratic pamphlets echoed this theme and printed graphic reports of alleged atrocities committed by Blacks on the "good white folk of the South." Grant became a Democratic target as well. They asked, "Was he not a ruthless drunk whose troops were butchered? Had he not expelled Jews from the Department of Tennessee in December 1862 only to have President Abraham Lincoln reverse him?"

The Republican Convention met in May. More than a dozen African Americans attended as delegates from former Confederate states. Carpetbaggers dominated every southern delegation. The platform reaffirmed the vote for freedmen but left the matter of "equal suffrage in the loyal states" up to the states themselves. Abolitionists denounced this plank as contradictory and mean-spirited. (The Fifteenth Amendment, adopted in 1870, however, extended the right to vote to all men in every state.) The platform, as would every Republican Party platform for the next generation, praised the sacrifice of Union veterans, widows, and orphans and promised them well-paying pensions.

The Republican Convention nominated Ulysses S. Grant by acclamation on the first ballot. Former Speaker of the House Schuyler Colfax of Indiana was the vice presidential candidate. Grant had no party affiliation. He had voted for president only once and that was for James Buchanan because, he said, "I knew Frémont." During 1868, he became the rallying figure for the Radicals. He disliked politics, but he had no intention of allowing the defeated Southerners to influence Reconstruction. Grant took no active part in the campaign. Ironically, the great wartime military commander made a poor transition to the tumultuous world of politics. Historians continually rank him as one of the worst presidents in U.S. history.

Race dominated the campaign. The Republicans obviously appealed to the newly enfranchised Black voter. Black leaders themselves well understood the importance of a Republican victory. Republicans repeatedly waved the "bloody shirt"—a campaign technique of linking Democrats with violence and secession in the South. Pamphlets accused the Democratic Party of being the party of traitors to the Union, and said that a Democratic victory would end veteran pensions.

Francis Blair, the Democratic vice presidential nominee, became an early Republican target. Blair had said many times that Republican Reconstruction laws were null and void. This contributed to violence throughout the South as other Democrats took their cue from him. Inflammatory Democratic speeches predicted domination by "an inferior and barbarous race." Groups led by the Ku Klux Klan used force, intimidation, and violence to prevent Blacks from voting. One prominent South Carolinian wrote: "Negroes are daily shot dead or wounded. Nobody is convicted because no adequate testimony is found or the magistrates don't prosecute."

Violence against Blacks accelerated during September and October. In Louisiana, some 3,000 Whites clashed with Blacks in a race riot, and more than 100 persons were killed. Two hundred political murders were reported in Arkansas, including the ambush killing of a Republican congressman. Terror reigned in parts of Texas and Mississippi. Most of the violence against Blacks was perpetrated by a new group, the Ku Klux Klan.

Founded in 1866 as a secret order, the Klan recruited members from all classes of southern White society. Many former Confederate soldiers joined the Klan, giving it the characteristics of a military guerrilla force. What united the Klansmen was a fear and hatred of Blacks. During the 1868 campaign, Nathan Bedford Forrest, the Klan founder, warned Republican leaders that they would be killed if they used state militias against the Klan: "I have no powder to burn killing negroes. I intend to kill radicals . . . There is not a radical leader in this town [Memphis] but is a marked man, and if trouble should break out, none of them would be left alive." The Klan effectively kept Blacks from voting in many areas of the South. In 22 Georgia counties, for example, with a total Black registration of more than 9,300, Grant received only 87 votes. Republicans received no votes in 11 Georgia counties.

Alarmed Democrats feared a violent racial revolution if they lost the election. Seymour's refusal to campaign and Blair's continued racially charged speeches caused some Democratic leaders to urge another convention. Seymour even said he would withdraw. But August Belmont, publisher of the New York *World*, and Samuel J. Tilden, a distinguished lawyer, among others, concluded the party must pull itself together. Seymour, they insisted, had to use his oratorical skills to explain that a Democratic victory would bring neither a race war nor a resumption of fighting.

Three weeks before the election, Seymour reluctantly began an extensive tour that took him from Syracuse to Chicago and back through Pennsylvania to New York City. He tried to focus on issues such as those affecting banking and currency. Although these speeches sounded good, the race issue could not be ignored. Nevertheless, he steadfastly maintained a rigorous schedule down to election day.

Grant beat Seymour badly in the electoral vote, receiving 214 votes to the Governor's 80 votes. Seymour carried Oregon, New Jersey, and New York, the last by one percentage point. He also won three border states: Delaware, Kentucky, and Maryland. Seymour received a majority of the popular vote in the South but won the electoral vote in only two of these states, Georgia and Louisiana. Grant received 52.7 percent of the total popular vote to Seymour's 47.3 percent. Surprisingly though, Grant's popular majority was only a little more than 300,000 votes out of 5,722,440. Grant received virtually the same proportion of the northern popular vote (55 percent) as did Lincoln in 1864. In defiance of Klan threats, approximately 700,000 Blacks voted in six southern states then under Radical domination, and Grant received most of their votes. His majority, therefore, depended on Black support. Republicans now urged universal male suffrage—and they submitted the Fifteenth Amendment to the states for ratification.

Election of 1872

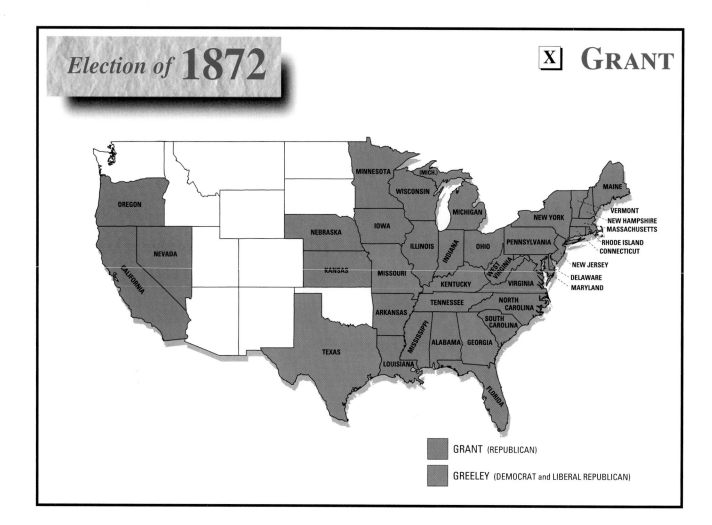

GRANT (REPUBLICAN)

GREELEY (DEMOCRAT and LIBERAL REPUBLICAN)

States	Electoral Votes	Grant	Hendricks	Brown	Jenkins	Davis
Alabama	(10)	10	-	-	-	-
Arkansas	(6)	-	-	-	-	-
California	(6)	6	-	-	-	-
Connecticut	(6)	6	-	-	-	-
Delaware	(3)	3	-	-	-	-
Florida	(4)	4	-	-	-	-
Georgia	(11)	-	-	6	2	-
Illinois	(21)	21	-	-	-	-
Indiana	(15)	15	-	-	-	-
Iowa	(11)	11	-	-	-	-
Kansas	(5)	5	-	-	-	-
Kentucky	(12)	-	8	4	-	-
Louisiana	(8)	-	-	-	-	-
Maine	(7)	7	-	-	-	-
Maryland	(8)	-	8	-	-	-
Massachusetts	(13)	13	-	-	-	-
Michigan	(11)	11	-	-	-	-
Minnesota	(5)	5	-	-	-	-
Mississippi	(8)	8	-	-	-	-
Missouri	(15)	-	6	8	-	1
Nebraska	(3)	3	-	-	-	-
Nevada	(3)	3	-	-	-	-
New Hampshire	(5)	5	-	-	-	-
New Jersey	(9)	9	-	-	-	-
New York	(35)	35	-	-	-	-
North Carolina	(10)	10	-	-	-	-
Ohio	(22)	22	-	-	-	-
Oregon	(3)	3	-	-	-	-
Pennsylvania	(29)	29	-	-	-	-
Rhode Island	(4)	4	-	-	-	-
South Carolina	(7)	7	-	-	-	-
Tennessee	(12)	-	12	-	-	-
Texas	(8)	-	8	-	-	-
Vermont	(5)	5	-	-	-	-
Virginia	(11)	11	-	-	-	-
West Virginia	(5)	5	-	-	-	-
Wisconsin	(10)	10	-	-	-	-
Totals	**(366)**	**286**	**42**	**18**	**2**	**1**

ELECTORAL VOTE

Election of 1872

STATE	TOTAL VOTE	ULYSSES S. GRANT (Republican)		HORACE GREELEY (Democrat, Liberal Republican)		CHARLES O'CONOR (Straight Out Democrat)		OTHER		PLURALITY	
		Votes	%	Votes	%	Votes	%	Votes	%		
Alabama	169,716	90,272	53.2	79,444	46.8	—		—		10,828	R
Arkansas	79,300	41,373	52.2	37,927	47.8	—		—		3,446	R
California	95,785	54,007	56.4	40,717	42.5	1,061	1.1	—		13,290	R
Connecticut	95,992	50,307	52.4	45,685	47.6	—		—		4,622	R
Delaware	21,822	11,129	51.0	10,205	46.8	488	2.2	—		924	R
Florida	33,190	17,763	53.5	15,427	46.5	—		—		2,336	R
Georgia	138,906	62,550	45.0	76,356	55.0	—		—		13,806	D
Illinois	429,971	241,936	56.3	184,884	43.0	3,151	0.7	—		57,052	R
Indiana	349,779	186,147	53.2	163,632	46.8	—		—		22,515	R
Iowa	216,365	131,566	60.8	71,189	32.9	2,221	1.0	11,389	5.3	60,377	R
Kansas	100,512	66,805	66.5	32,970	32.8	156	0.2	581	0.6	33,835	R
Kentucky	191,135	88,766	46.4	99,995	52.3	2,374	1.2	—		11,229	D
Louisiana	128,692	71,663	55.7	57,029	44.3	—		—		14,634	R
Maine	90,523	61,426	67.9	29,097	32.1	—		—		32,329	R
Maryland	134,447	66,760	49.7	67,687	50.3	—		—		927	D
Massachusetts	192,650	133,455	69.3	59,195	30.7	—		—		74,260	R
Michigan	221,569	138,768	62.6	78,651	35.5	2,879	1.3	1,271	0.6	60,117	R
Minnesota	91,339	56,040	61.4	35,131	38.5	—		168	0.2	20,909	R
Mississippi	129,457	82,175	63.5	47,282	36.5	—		—		34,893	R
Missouri	273,059	119,196	43.7	151,434	55.5	2,429	0.9	—		32,238	D
Nebraska	25,932	18,329	70.7	7,603	29.3	—		—		10,726	R
Nevada	14,649	8,413	57.4	6,236	42.6	—		—		2,177	R
New Hampshire	68,906	37,168	53.9	31,425	45.6	—		313	0.5	5,743	R
New Jersey	168,112	91,656	54.5	76,456	45.5	—		—		15,200	R
New York	828,020	440,738	53.2	387,282	46.8	—		—		53,456	R
North Carolina	165,163	94,772	57.4	70,130	42.5	261	0.2	—		24,642	R
Ohio	529,435	281,852	53.2	244,320	46.1	1,163	0.2	2,100	0.4	37,532	R
Oregon	20,107	11,818	58.8	7,742	38.5	547	2.7	—		4,076	R
Pennsylvania	561,629	349,589	62.2	212,040	37.8	—		—		137,549	R
Rhode Island	18,994	13,665	71.9	5,329	28.1	—		—		8,336	R
South Carolina	95,452	72,290	75.7	22,699	23.8	204	0.2	259	0.3	49,591	R
Tennessee	179,046	85,655	47.8	93,391	52.2	—		—		7,736	D
Texas	115,700	47,910	41.4	67,675	58.5	115	0.1	—		19,765	D
Vermont	52,408	41,481	79.2	10,927	20.8	—		—		30,554	R
Virginia	185,195	93,463	50.5	91,647	49.5	85		—		1,816	R
West Virginia	62,467	32,320	51.7	29,532	47.3	615	1.0	—		2,788	R
Wisconsin	192,255	105,012	54.6	86,390	44.9	853	0.4	—		18,622	R
Totals	6,467,679	3,598,235	55.6	2,834,761	43.8	18,602	0.3	16,081	0.3	763,474	R

P O P U L A R   V O T E

Ulysses S. Grant angered many prominent Republicans during his first term as president. Some party leaders opposed his renomination for many reasons: his plan to annex the Dominican Republic; the use of military troops in the South to enforce Radical Reconstruction, and his opposition to civil service reform. Above all, the suspicion of corruption at the highest levels of government had become an issue. Many of Grant's appointees were involved with graft and scandal. These issues added up to what his critics called "Grantism." Grant the politician, unlike Grant the general, had proved to be indecisive and weak.

Dissatisfied Missouri Reform Republicans took the lead in opposing Grant, hoping to deny him a second term. These reformers tried to make "Grantism" the main campaign issue in 1872. They met at the state capital in Jefferson City and formally launched the Liberal Republican Party on 24 January 1872. Their leaders called for a national convention to meet in Cincinnati, Ohio on 1 May 1872.

The most influential Liberal Republicans were the intellectual elite and editors and writers of leading eastern newspapers and journals, including Edwin L. Godkin, editor of *The Nation,* George William Curtis of *Harper's Weekly*, and William Cullen Bryant of the New York *Evening Post.* Senator Charles Sumner of Massachusetts and the distinguished writer Henry Adams also joined the new party. "It looks as though we might carry the country . . . by a whirlwind," boasted the noted economist David A. Wells.

More than 700 enthusiastic delegates gathered in Cincinnati to attend the first and only Liberal Republican Convention. They believed that Liberal Republicans would begin a new era of national improvements which would include sectional reconciliation, tariff reductions, and strong civil service laws to end political patronage. Speakers confidently predicted that their new movement would end "Grantism." The question was who could beat him.

The brief Liberal Republican platform contained contradictory statements except for the specific demand for immediate civil service reform to end "arbitrary favoritism and patronage." The platform continued, "To this end, it is imperatively required that no President shall be a candidate for re-election." Two planks pledged fidelity to "the equality of all men before the law . . . equal and exact justice to all of whatever nativity, race, color or persuasion." But other planks demanded amnesty for all former Confederates, advocated

"the supremacy of the civil over the military authority," called for "local self-government" (already a code phrase for white rule in the South), and condemned Grant's use of "arbitrary measures." Since "military authority" and "arbitrary measures" had proven to be the only way to protect the freedmen in the South, these platform phrases were recognized as an appeal for an alliance with the Democrats.

On the fifth ballot, the delegates nominated Horace Greeley for president and Missouri's Governor B. Gratz Brown as his running mate. Almost immediately, dissension divided the reformers. On 6 May, Samuel Bowles, editor of the *Springfield* (Massachusetts) *Republican* and a Liberal Republican founder, questioned the wisdom of choosing Greeley. On 9 May, Godkin of *The Nation* wrote that the convention must "be pronounced a failure . . . [Greeley] has long been associated intimately with the worst political trash to be found anywhere, who would in all probability be followed by them to Washington, and who, if left in their hands there, would set up the most corrupt administration ever seen." On 18 May, *Harper's Weekly* joined in criticizing Greeley's selection "with amusement and astonishment. It was probably the only nomination for president ever made which was received with a good-humored laugh." Henry Adams remarked: "If the Gods insist on making Mr. Greeley our President, I give up."

Horace Greeley had gained fame as the founder and editor of the New York *Tribune* (1841), one of the finest newspapers in the country. The paper also served as a forum for Greeley's social and economic views, which included abolitionism, temperance, vegetarianism, women's rights, and utopianism. Through the years, Greeley had lent his support to a wide range of unpopular and curious organizations. By often taking stands on different sides of the same issue, Greeley presented an image of a confused person to his critics.

Greeley had been an early supporter of the Republican Party (1854) and had backed Lincoln's nomination (1860). During the Civil War, however, he aligned himself with the anti-slavery faction which demanded immediate emancipation. In 1864, his attempt to initiate a peace conference between Lincoln and Jefferson Davis, president of the Confederacy, ended in a fiasco. Greeley kept changing his mind. In one year (1864 to 1865), he first advocated total war to defeat the southern traitors. He then proposed a negotiated peace as well as a harsh reconstruction policy combined with amnesty for the Confederates. Greeley's appearance was also a problem. An awkward man with a large round face and bald head, he had long white whiskers and he wore drooping eyeglasses and wrinkled clothing.

The Republican Convention assembled in Philadelphia on 5 June. Grant's renomination was a formality. At the President's request, the delegates replaced Vice President Schuyler Colfax, whom Grant detested, with Senator Henry Wilson of Massachusetts. Speakers denounced the Liberal Republican defectors but Grant was glad to get rid of them. He called them "soreheads" who made trouble when they could not have their own way. The platform called for the vigorous enforcement of the Fourteenth and Fifteenth Amendments. Surprisingly, the platform also pledged the party to end "the evils of patronage" and "opposed further grants of public lands to corporations." African Americans were urged to stay with the party which had obtained their freedom and guaranteed their right to vote. As Frederick Douglass explained: "If the Republican Party goes down, freedom goes down with it."

The Democratic Convention met in Baltimore on 9 July. It was an unusual meeting, lasting less than six hours. No Democrat sought the presidential nomination, and party leaders had already decided that Greeley would be their choice. The delegates adopted the Liberal Republican platform word for word. Dissenters protesting Greeley's nomination obtained less than 10 percent on a roll call vote. Many Democrats, however, broke with their leaders. Greeley had a long record of partisan attacks on them, and his nomination by the Democratic Party seemed ludicrous. Across the nation, state chairmen urged support for local candidates but ignored mentioning the national ticket. Of 50 Pennsylvania Democratic newspapers, only 2 endorsed Greeley.

Greeley set off on an exhaustive speaking tour although he was a sick man. A chronic insomniac, he also suffered from a degenerative neurological disease. He made nearly 200 speeches during one 11-day period. Curious but enthusiastic crowds were emotionally moved by his simple eloquent pleas for reconciliation between the North and the South. Groups of veterans sometimes jeered him when he spoke of a

full amnesty for all Confederates, including Jefferson Davis. Greeley was confident that he would defeat Grant.

Thomas Nast, the famous cartoonist for *Harper's Weekly*, viciously attacked Greeley as a fool and an eccentric. Although *Harper's Weekly* reached a minority of voters, these brilliant cartoons often were torn-out and tacked on walls for public display. Greeley took Nast's insults to heart, remarking dejectedly that he scarcely knew whether he was "running for the presidency or the penitentiary."

Grant spent the campaign months on the porch of his sea-side cottage in New Jersey. He refused to make any speeches. George William Childs, the editor of the Philadelphia *Public Ledger*, told of a visit he and other Republicans made to Grant's summer retreat. After relaying their anxieties about the campaign without his active participation, Grant "said nothing but sent for a map of the United States. He laid the map on the table, went over it with a pencil, and said, 'We will carry this State, that State' . . . When the election came, the result was that Grant carried every State that he said he would."

Grant received a greater percentage of the popular vote (55.6 percent) than did Lincoln in 1864, carrying 31 of the 37 states. During the counting of the electoral vote, objections were raised about the Arkansas and Louisiana votes. As a result, the returns of both states were not included. Greeley's total of 66 electoral votes was the lowest received by any major candidate between 1864 and 1932. Greeley received almost 130,000 more popular votes than did the Democratic candidate in 1868 because 4 states—Mississippi, Texas, Virginia, and Florida—voted in 1872 but had not in 1868. But this increase paled beside the rise of almost 600,000 in the Republican vote. When Godkin was asked to summarize the meaning of the election, he replied: "Contempt for Greeley." Fusion with the Liberal Republicans meant political disaster for the Democratic Party, which reached a historic low-point. The Liberal Republican Party disappeared. Greeley died 24 days after the election, on 29 November 1872. Since his death occurred before the Electoral College met, his votes were redistributed among several men.

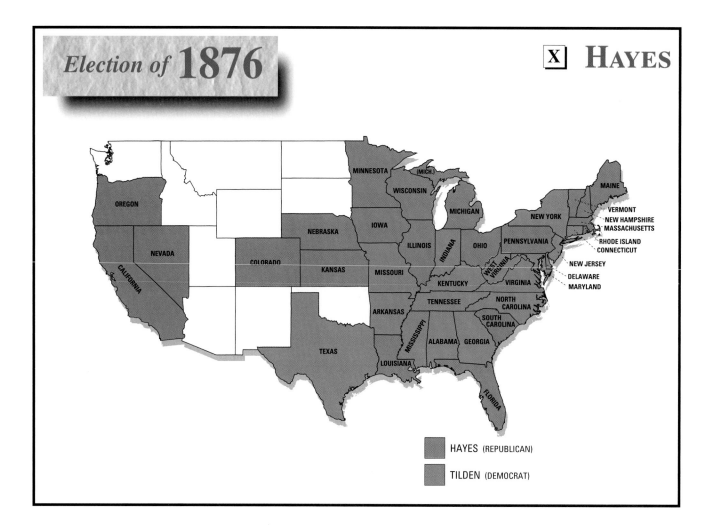

Election of **1876**

X **HAYES**

HAYES (REPUBLICAN)

TILDEN (DEMOCRAT)

States	Electoral Votes	Hayes	Tilden	States	Electoral Votes	Hayes	Tilden
Alabama	(10)	-	10	Missouri	(15)	-	15
Arkansas	(6)	-	6	Nebraska	(3)	3	-
California	(6)	6	-	Nevada	(3)	3	-
Colorado	(3)	3	-	New Hampshire	(5)	5	-
Connecticut	(6)	-	6	New Jersey	(9)	-	9
Delaware	(3)	-	3	New York	(35)	-	35
Florida	(4)	4	-	North Carolina	(10)	-	10
Georgia	(11)	-	11	Ohio	(22)	22	-
Illinois	(21)	21	-	Oregon	(3)	3	-
Indiana	(15)	-	15	Pennsylvania	(29)	29	-
Iowa	(11)	11	-	Rhode Island	(4)	4	-
Kansas	(5)	5	-	South Carolina	(7)	7	-
Kentucky	(12)	-	12	Tennessee	(12)	-	12
Louisiana	(8)	8	-	Texas	(8)	-	8
Maine	(7)	7	-	Vermont	(5)	5	-
Maryland	(8)	-	8	Virginia	(11)	-	11
Massachusetts	(13)	13	-	West Virginia	(5)	-	5
Michigan	(11)	11	-	Wisconsin	(10)	10	-
Minnesota	(5)	5	-	**Totals**	**(369)**	**185**	**184**
Mississippi	(8)	-	8				

E L E C T O R A L V O T E

Election of 1876

STATE	TOTAL VOTE	RUTHERFORD B. HAYES (Republican)		SAMUEL J. TILDEN (Democrat)		PETER COOPER (Greenback)		OTHER		PLURALITY	
		Votes	%	Votes	%	Votes	%	Votes	%		
Alabama	171,699	68,708	40.0	102,989	60.0	—		2		34,281	D
Arkansas	96,946	38,649	39.9	58,086	59.9	211	0.2	—		19,437	D
California	155,784	79,258	50.9	76,460	49.1	47		19		2,798	R
Connecticut	122,134	59,033	48.3	61,927	50.7	774	0.6	400	0.3	2,894	D
Delaware	24,133	10,752	44.6	13,381	55.4	—		—		2,629	D
Florida	46,776	23,849	51.0	22,927	49.0	—		—		922	R
Georgia	180,690	50,533	28.0	130,157	72.0	—		—		79,624	D
Illinois	554,368	278,232	50.2	258,611	46.6	17,207	3.1	318	0.1	19,621	R
Indiana	431,073	208,011	48.3	213,529	49.5	9,533	2.2	—		5,518	D
Iowa	293,398	171,326	58.4	112,121	38.2	9,431	3.2	520	0.2	59,205	R
Kansas	124,134	78,324	63.1	37,902	30.5	7,770	6.3	138	0.1	40,422	R
Kentucky	260,626	97,568	37.4	160,060	61.4	—		2,998	1.2	62,492	D
Louisiana	145,823	75,315	51.6	70,508	48.4	—		—		4,807	R
Maine	117,045	66,300	56.6	49,917	42.6	—		828	0.7	16,383	R
Maryland	163,759	71,980	44.0	91,779	56.0	—		—		19,799	D
Massachusetts	259,619	150,063	57.8	108,777	41.9	—		779	0.3	41,286	R
Michigan	318,426	166,901	52.4	141,665	44.5	9,023	2.8	837	0.3	25,236	R
Minnesota	124,160	72,962	58.8	48,799	39.3	2,399	1.9	—		24,163	R
Mississippi	164,776	52,603	31.9	112,173	68.1	—		—		59,570	D
Missouri	350,610	145,027	41.4	202,086	57.6	3,497	1.0	—		57,059	D
Nebraska	49,258	31,915	64.8	17,343	35.2	—		—		14,572	R
Nevada	19,691	10,383	52.7	9,308	47.3	—		—		1,075	R
New Hampshire	80,143	41,540	51.8	38,510	48.1	—		93	0.1	3,030	R
New Jersey	220,193	103,517	47.0	115,962	52.7	714	0.3	—		12,445	D
New York	1,015,503	489,207	48.2	521,949	51.4	1,978	0.2	2,369	0.2	32,742	D
North Carolina	233,911	108,484	46.4	125,427	53.6	—		—		16,943	D
Ohio	658,650	330,698	50.2	323,182	49.1	3,058	0.5	1,712	0.3	7,516	R
Oregon	29,873	15,207	50.9	14,157	47.4	509	1.7	—		1,050	R
Pennsylvania	758,973	384,157	50.6	366,204	48.2	7,209	0.9	1,403	0.2	17,953	R
Rhode Island	26,499	15,787	59.6	10,712	40.4	—		—		5,075	R
South Carolina	182,683	91,786	50.2	90,897	49.8	—		—		889	R
Tennessee	222,743	89,566	40.2	133,177	59.8	—		—		43,611	D
Texas	151,431	45,013	29.7	106,372	70.2	—		46		61,359	D
Vermont	64,460	44,092	68.4	20,254	31.4	—		114	0.2	23,838	R
Virginia	236,288	95,518	40.4	140,770	59.6	—		—		45,252	D
West Virginia	99,647	41,997	42.1	56,546	56.7	1,104	1.1	—		14,549	D
Wisconsin	257,176	130,050	50.6	123,922	48.2	1,509	0.6	1,695	0.7	6,128	R
Totals	**8,413,101**	**4,034,311**	**48.0**	**4,288,546**	**51.0**	**75,973**	**0.9**	**14,271**	**0.2**	**254,235**	**D**

P O P U L A R   V O T E

The 1876 presidential election marked the political end of the era of the Civil War and Reconstruction. A majority of Americans, preoccupied with unprecedented economic growth, conveniently forgot about the enforcement of the Fourteenth and Fifteenth Amendments and racial equality for African Americans. The 1876 campaign is memorable because it resulted in the famous disputed presidential election.

On 8 November 1876, the Republican New York *Tribune* announced the election of Democrat Samuel J. Tilden as the president of the United States. Four months later, on 2 March 1877, the Democratic New York *World* ran a headline account of how Republican Rutherford B. Hayes had been finally "elevated" to the presidency. The events surrounding this startling reversal make up one of the most dramatic episodes in U.S. political history.

Day after day, month after month, public officials resigned or were dismissed from their positions as scandal after scandal shattered the Republican Party during the second term of Grant's administration. By the beginning of 1876, his administration approached complete breakdown as new exposés rocked the very foundation of the government. The scandals had not touched Grant personally, and he was eager to run for a third term in 1876.

A majority of Republican leaders ruled out Grant as a candidate. In 1874, the Democrats had won control of the U.S. House of Representatives for the first time in 18 years. They gained 77 seats in the House and 10 in the U.S. Senate, with gains occurring in every region. Impressed by the revived Democratic Party, some Republican leaders felt that a Grant candidacy would raise the issue about a president serving more than two terms. They searched for a candidate who was not associated with the scandals of the past 8 years and one who could bring the Liberal Republicans back to the party. They were determined to hold the executive branch with all of its patronage.

The Republican Convention met in Cincinnati on 14 June 1876. The delegates divided into Stalwarts and Half-Breeds. Stalwarts were the hard-core party professionals who supported political patronage. They also felt that, if business interests wanted favors from government, they should pay for them. Half-Breeds were Republican civil service reformers who had not deserted to the Liberal Republicans in 1872. They favored removing federal troops from the southern states while the Stalwarts wanted to maintain the troops there to enforce the Fourteenth and Fifteenth Amendments. Stalwarts, closest to Grant, still favored him to run for a third term. Half-Breeds supported Congressman James G. Blaine of Maine. When the attempt to renominate Grant failed and Blaine's candidacy lost momentum, the party united behind Ohio's three-term governor, Rutherford B. Hayes. William A. Wheeler, a congressman from New York, was nominated for vice president. Hayes, who had achieved an admirable record as an efficient state administrator, proved to be the perfect answer for the divided party. He portrayed himself as the new image of honest and moderate Republicanism.

The Democratic Party met in St. Louis on 27 June. They nominated Samuel J. Tilden, the governor of New York; Indiana Governor Thomas Hendricks was chosen for vice president. Tilden's name had become synonymous with governmental reform. As chairman of the New York State Democratic Party, he had led the fight against New York City's "Tweed Ring," led by the unscrupulous William M. Tweed. It controlled the city's political appointments and had stolen millions from the city's treasury through fraudulent contracts. The brief Democratic platform used the word "reform" 12 times. It also called for a final end to Radical Reconstruction by removing federal troops from South Carolina, Florida, and Louisiana.

As tradition dictated, neither candidate campaigned. Tilden had suffered a stroke in 1875, and he remained at his New York City home. Both candidates, however, gave advice to party leaders. Hayes, opposed to the use of public funds for religious schools, thought a proposed Sixteenth Amendment forbidding such practices could be a winning issue. He cautioned William Dean Howells, his campaign biographer, to portray him "as a public servant of sense and sensibility" and not to comment "on religion, temperance, or free trade." Each party saturated key states with prominent speakers. Mark Twain spoke for Hayes and economist Henry George campaigned for Tilden. Thomas Nast, the cartoonist for *Harper's Weekly*, irresponsibly linked Tilden to the Tweed Ring. John A. Dix, whom Tilden had defeated in the 1876 New York gubernatorial race, denounced him as "a sham reformer." But the Democratic Party seemed to have the better issues. The Grant scandals, the severity of the mid-1870s depression and the demand for civil service reform all appeared to work to their advantage. Little separated

Tilden from Hayes on economic issues, aside from technical differences on the tariff. Both were conservatives who favored "sound money" and limited government.

Both Tilden and Hayes gave only token support to the rights of African Americans guaranteed by the Fourteenth and Fifteenth Amendments. They each were practical politicians who cared more about industrial growth in both the North and the South than in racial equality. Tilden supported "home rule" in the South. He thought Black males should be excluded from the political process wherever possible. Hayes, in accepting the Republican nomination, gave his support to "honorable and capable local government." In other words, he agreed to White rule in the South and the nullification of the Fourteenth Amendment as it applied to Blacks. Racist decisions of the Supreme Court also encouraged ignoring both amendments.

On Election Day, a record 82.6 percent of those eligible voted. Tilden won 51 percent of the popular vote to 48 percent for Hayes. Early returns claimed Tilden had been elected but within a day, it appeared that the electoral result was in doubt. As the situation developed, the electoral vote stood at 184 for Tilden, 1 vote short of the needed majority, and 165 for Hayes, with 20 votes in dispute: Florida's 4; Louisiana's 8; and South Carolina's 7. One Oregon electoral vote also was disputed for technical reasons. Tilden needed 1 vote for an electoral victory; Hayes needed all 20. Written records and the spoken word later recorded in diaries and memoirs have resulted in an amazingly thorough documentation of the complex maneuvering which followed. In 1879, the Joint Congressional Committee on Alleged Frauds in the Late Presidential Election compiled detailed testimony, authenticated evidence, and deciphered coded telegrams. The report of that committee fully detailed the most complex event in U.S. political history.

If all the disputed electoral votes went to Hayes, he would be elected with 185 votes to Tilden's 184. The well-organized Republican machine, supported by federal troops, sought to hold Florida, Louisiana, and South Carolina for their candidates while the Democrats claimed election boards dominated by Radical Republicans had fraudulently voided Tilden ballots. As a result, two sets of returns went to Congress from these three states.

Congress met in December amidst great excitement and confusion. The Constitution states that "the President of the Senate shall, in the presence of the Senate and the House of Representatives, open all certificates, and the vote shall then be counted." But, counted by whom? If the Republican Senate had the power, Hayes would be chosen. Conversely, the Democrats had a majority in the House and they would sustain Tilden electors.

Congress created a special Electoral Commission to deal with this unprecedented situation. This bipartisan group was to consist of five members each from the House, the Senate, and the Supreme Court. It was expected that there would be seven Republicans, seven Democrats, and one Independent on the Commission. Four of the justices were designated by name in the bill (two Democrats and two Republicans) with power to choose the fifth justice. Justice David Davis, an independent, was elected to the U.S. Senate by the Illinois legislature, removing him from consideration. Justice Joseph P. Bradley, a Republican, became the fifteenth person on the Electoral Commission. The Commission met on 31 January 1877 and adjourned on 2 March. Voting strictly along party lines, it awarded all of the disputed electoral votes to Hayes.

The famous Compromise of 1877 was reached two days before the scheduled inauguration. Southern Democrats agreed to allow the Commission's recommendation to be accepted. In return, Republicans agreed to withdraw federal troops from the South, effectively ending Reconstruction and the rights of African American males to vote. In addition, Hayes promised to appoint at least one Southern Democrat to his cabinet and to support federal aid for railroad construction in the South as well as grants to rebuild bridges and harbors. On 2 March 1877, a joint session of Congress witnessed Thomas Ferry, president pro tem of the U.S. Senate, read the ballots and declare Hayes and Wheeler elected. An aide rapped on the door of Hayes's sleeping compartment on a train bound for Washington to inform him of his election.

All historians who have studied the electoral crisis of 1876–1877 applaud the extraordinary calm with which the mass of the people accepted the Commission's decision. In many countries, a similar situation might have caused civil war.

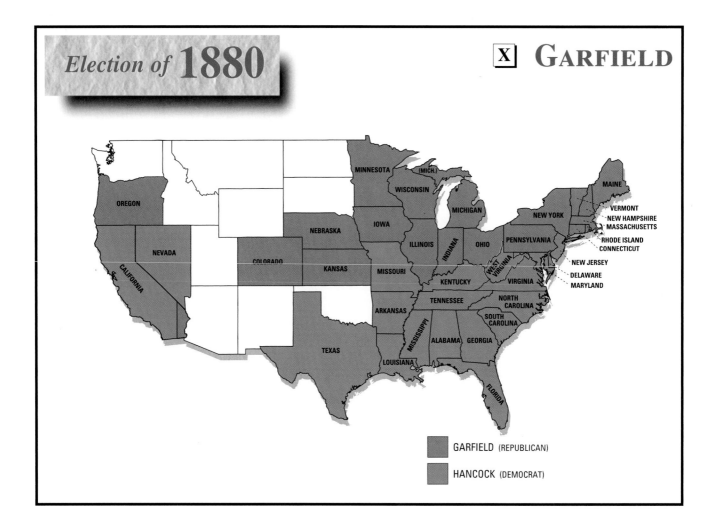

Election of 1880

GARFIELD (REPUBLICAN)

HANCOCK (DEMOCRAT)

States	Electoral Votes	Garfield	Hancock	States	Electoral Votes	Garfield	Hancock
Alabama	(10)	-	10	Mississippi	(8)	-	8
Arkansas	(6)	-	6	Missouri	(15)	-	15
California	(6)	1	5	Nebraska	(3)	3	-
Colorado	(3)	3	-	Nevada	(3)	-	3
Connecticut	(6)	6	-	New Hampshire	(5)	5	-
Delaware	(3)	-	3	New Jersey	(9)	-	9
Florida	(4)	-	4	New York	(35)	35	-
Georgia	(11)	-	11	North Carolina	(10)	-	10
Illinois	(21)	21	-	Ohio	(22)	22	-
Indiana	(15)	15	-	Oregon	(3)	3	-
Iowa	(11)	11	-	Pennsylvania	(29)	29	-
Kansas	(5)	5	-	Rhode Island	(4)	4	-
Kentucky	(12)	-	12	South Carolina	(7)	-	7
Louisiana	(8)	-	8	Tennessee	(12)	-	12
Maine	(7)	7	-	Texas	(8)	-	8
Maryland	(8)	-	8	Vermont	(5)	5	-
Massachusetts	(13)	13	-	Virginia	(11)	-	11
Michigan	(11)	11	-	West Virginia	(5)	-	5
Minnesota	(5)	5	-	Wisconsin	(10)	10	-
				Totals	**(369)**	**214**	**155**

ELECTORAL VOTE

Election of 1880

STATE	TOTAL VOTE	JAMES A. GARFIELD (Republican)		WINFIELD S. HANCOCK (Democrat)		JAMES B. WEAVER (Greenback)		OTHER		PLURALITY	
		Votes	%	Votes	%	Votes	%	Votes	%		
Alabama	151,902	56,350	37.1	91,130	60.0	4,422	2.9	—		34,780	D
Arkansas	107,772	41,661	38.7	60,489	56.1	4,079	3.8	1,543	1.4	18,828	D
California	164,218	80,282	48.9	80,426	49.0	3,381	2.1	129	0.1	144	D
Colorado	53,546	27,450	51.3	24,647	46.0	1,435	2.7	14		2,803	R
Connecticut	132,798	67,071	50.5	64,411	48.5	868	0.7	448	0.3	2,660	R
Delaware	29,458	14,148	48.0	15,181	51.5	129	0.4	—		1,033	D
Florida	51,618	23,654	45.8	27,964	54.2	—		—		4,310	D
Georgia	157,451	54,470	34.6	102,981	65.4	—		—		48,511	D
Illinois	622,305	318,036	51.1	277,321	44.6	26,358	4.2	590	0.1	40,715	R
Indiana	470,758	232,169	49.3	225,523	47.9	13,066	2.8	—		6,646	R
Iowa	323,140	183,904	56.9	105,845	32.8	32,327	10.0	1,064	0.3	78,059	R
Kansas	201,054	121,520	60.4	59,789	29.7	19,710	9.8	35		61,731	R
Kentucky	267,104	106,490	39.9	148,875	55.7	11,506	4.3	233	0.1	42,385	D
Louisiana	104,462	38,978	37.3	65,047	62.3	437	0.4	—		26,069	D
Maine	143,903	74,052	51.5	65,211	45.3	4,409	3.1	231	0.2	8,841	R
Maryland	172,221	78,515	45.6	93,706	54.4	—		—		15,191	D
Massachusetts	282,505	165,198	58.5	111,960	39.6	4,548	1.6	799	0.3	53,238	R
Michigan	353,076	185,335	52.5	131,596	37.3	34,895	9.9	1,250	0.4	53,739	R
Minnesota	150,806	93,939	62.3	53,314	35.4	3,267	2.2	286	0.2	40,625	R
Mississippi	117,068	34,844	29.8	75,750	64.7	5,797	5.0	677	0.6	40,906	D
Missouri	397,289	153,647	38.7	208,600	52.5	35,042	8.8	—		54,953	D
Nebraska	87,355	54,979	62.9	28,523	32.7	3,853	4.4	—		26,456	R
Nevada	18,343	8,732	47.6	9,611	52.4	—		—		879	D
New Hampshire	86,361	44,856	51.9	40,797	47.2	528	0.6	180	0.2	4,059	R
New Jersey	245,928	120,555	49.0	122,565	49.8	2,617	1.1	191	0.1	2,010	D
New York	1,103,945	555,544	50.3	534,511	48.4	12,373	1.1	1,517	0.1	21,033	R
North Carolina	240,946	115,616	48.0	124,204	51.5	1,126	0.5	—		8,588	D
Ohio	724,984	375,048	51.7	340,867	47.0	6,456	0.9	2,613	0.4	34,181	R
Oregon	40,841	20,619	50.5	19,955	48.9	267	0.7	—		664	R
Pennsylvania	874,783	444,704	50.8	407,428	46.6	20,667	2.4	1,984	0.2	37,276	R
Rhode Island	29,235	18,195	62.2	10,779	36.9	236	0.8	25	0.1	7,416	R
South Carolina	169,793	57,954	34.1	111,236	65.5	567	0.3	36		53,282	D
Tennessee	243,263	107,677	44.3	129,569	53.3	6,017	2.5	—		21,892	D
Texas	233,632	50,217	21.5	156,010	66.8	27,405	11.7	—		105,793	D
Vermont	65,098	45,567	70.0	18,316	28.1	1,215	1.9	—		27,251	R
Virginia	211,616	83,533	39.5	128,083	60.5	—		—		44,550	D
West Virginia	112,641	46,243	41.1	57,390	50.9	9,008	8.0	—		11,147	D
Wisconsin	267,202	144,406	54.0	114,650	42.9	7,986	3.0	160	0.1	29,756	R
Totals	9,210,420	4,446,158	48.3	4,444,260	48.3	305,997	3.3	14,005	0.2	1,898	R

POPULAR VOTE

The 1880 presidential election is regarded by many as the most forgotten in U. S. history. The Democratic and the Republican parties offered little choice to the voters. Statesmanship was never so uninspiring and statesmen so inadequate. The drab procession of political nonentities can be compared to a puppet show: control of the strings remained in the hands of political bosses and big business. The 1880 campaign, filled with pompous oratory, did not focus on the major concerns confronting the nation.

One of these major concerns was the technological revolution which had begun to sweep across the country after the Civil War. The war had created a greater demand for iron, lumber, brick, glass, and petroleum products. The market grew for agricultural implements and transportation equipment. New and more powerful locomotives and the change from single-track to double-track roadbeds made the railroads more important than ever before. Rapid changes took place in almost every industry, and the invention of the telephone, the phonograph, and the incandescent light bulb altered basic life patterns drastically. Giant companies built large meat-packing houses in Chicago. Power-driven sewing machines, cloth cutters, and ready-made clothes changed the clothing business from small tailor shops to big businesses. Between 1870 and 1880, total capital invested in U.S. manufacturing almost doubled.

Another major concern was immigration. The 10 million immigrants who poured into the United States between 1870 and 1890 added to the rapidly growing labor force. Wages averaged $1 per day and factory work weeks ranged from 60 to more than 80 hours. The seven-day work week remained the rule in steel and paper mills. Long hours and worker fatigue increased accidents and deaths. The number of women wage workers in manufacturing increased from 226,000 in 1850 to 850,000 in 1880 by which time nearly 1 of every 6 workers was female. Attempts to organize laborers into unions failed. "The period was poor in purpose and barren in results," noted historian Henry Adams. Promises of investigation and reform deceived the voter into believing that political abuses would be corrected. "All being corrupt together," wrote Edwin L. Godkin, editor of *The Nation,* "what is the use of investigating each other?"

Ulysses S. Grant was the leading candidate for the 1880 Republican nomination. The General had embarked on a 28-month tour around the world with his wife and family soon after he left the White House in 1876. Grant had become more popular than ever before. His tour took him through Europe to Egypt, India, China, and Japan. Statesmen praised and honored him and monarchs competed for the pleasure of his company. The Khedive of Egypt gave them a palace to stay in and a boat for exploring the Nile River. In China, they were guests at a seventy course dinner. In a tradition-breaking ceremony, Grant accompanied the Emperor of Japan on a review of the army. Reporters accompanying the Grants dispatched glowing stories of elaborate receptions, mile-long processions, and gala balls which dazzled the imagination.

Republican leaders wrote to Grant discussing a third term. They advised him to stay abroad as long as he could, returning just before the 1880 convention. But Grant grew tired of the trip. His ship docked in San Francisco in September 1879 where a huge, enthusiastic crowd cheered him. As his train crossed the country, towns and cities entertained him at lavish banquets. Grant and his advisers were convinced that the Republican Party would select him as their presidential nominee again.

The Republican Convention assembled in Chicago on 2 June 1880. When Grant's name was placed in nomination, it was greeted by a deafening ovation that lasted more than half an hour. In the first ballot, 756 votes were cast, and Grant fell 75 votes short of a majority. Senator James G. Blaine of Maine was his closest rival. Republican reformers were horrified at the thought of Grant in the White House for another term. Blaine's campaign manager reported hearing people say that war, famine, and pestilence could not be worse than another four years of the General. Grant's vote stayed virtually the same through 35 ballots. On the thirty-sixth ballot, a remarkable "stop Grant" shift occurred. The former congressman and newly elected senator from Ohio, James A. Garfield, received 20 more votes than a majority. Senator Roscoe Conkling of New York, Grant's floor manager, moved that the nomination be made unanimous and the delegates shouted their approval. Garfield personally asked Chester A. Arthur of New York, a Grant supporter, to accept the vice presidential nomination. Arthur agreed.

The Democratic Convention opened in Cincinnati on 22 June. General Winfield Scott Hancock of Pennsylvania received the nomination on the second ballot. Hancock had graduated from the United States Military Academy,

West Point, in a class of 25 that included George McClellan, Thomas "Stonewall" Jackson and Grant. Hancock emerged as a hero after the Battle of Gettysburg (1863). He was popular in the South because he administered Radical Reconstruction policies leniently as military governor in Louisiana and Texas. The convention chose former Indiana Congressman William English for vice president. The Democratic strategy was to win the election by holding on to the solid Democratic South, and carrying New York and Indiana.

Both parties campaigned similarly and avoided the issues. There were parades, bandannas, brass badges, song books, sheet music, and satirical booklets poking fun at both candidates. One Republican pamphlet attacked Hancock's lack of experience. "A Record of the Statesmanship of General Winfield Scott Hancock . . . compiled from the Records," summarized his "achievements." Upon opening it, one found seven blank pages and one word at the bottom of the eighth page: "finis." The Democrats also produced biting pamphlets. One compared the "Bright Record of the Patriot Hancock" with the "Black Record of the Politician Garfield." The Republicans continually reminded voters that they had fought to save the Union and the Democrats recalled how the election of 1876 had been stolen from Samuel J. Tilden. One biting cartoon by Thomas Nast received wide distribution. A puzzled Hancock is asking a New Jersey Senator: "Who is Tariff and why is he for revenue only?" This suggested that Hancock was ignorant of a key issue in the campaign.

Republicans and Democrats spent enormous sums in the key states of New York, with 35 electoral votes, and Indiana, with 15 electoral votes. Both parties ignored the problems caused by the industrial transformation of the United States. Each party accused the other of the most outrageous acts. In Indiana, the Democrats claimed that southern African Americans had been brought into the state to increase the Republican vote. Republicans countered with stinging rebukes of the Democratic Party's treatment of Blacks. The buying of votes was rampant. Chester A. Arthur explained after the election, "Indiana was really, I suppose, a Democratic State. It had been put down on the books as a State that might

be carried by close and perfect organization and a great deal of [laughter and cries of "soap" from the audience]. I see the reporters are present, therefore I will simply say that everybody showed a great deal of interest in the occasion and distributed tracts and political documents throughout the State." In New York, both parties suffered from major internal divisions, but Garfield personally managed to bring together the various Republican factions within the state. He promised them patronage if he carried New York and won the election. Hancock, however, could not resolve the Democratic feuds which involved state aid to parochial schools and a divisive New York City mayoralty election.

Garfield carried both New York and Indiana, winning the election with 214 electoral votes to Hancock's 155. Hancock lost New York by only 21,033 out of more than 1 million votes cast. Had the state given its electoral votes to Hancock, the Democrats would have elected their first president since 1856. In the national popular vote, Garfield's margin was slightly more than 2,000 out of more than 9 million votes cast.

In The Politicos, historian Matthew Josephson wrote that the interlude between the election and the inauguration was one of "fabulous intrigue, fabulous even in the quarrelsome annals of the American republic. Behind the scenes, while the public heard only confusing or distorted reports [rival factions] fought without quarter for control of the new government." Garfield's own diary reveals his bewilderment by the maddening demands for political appointments. "I have been dealing all these years with ideas," the distraught Garfield told Blaine. "I have been heretofore treating of the fundamental principles of government and here I am considering all day whether A or B shall be appointed to this or that office . . . My God! What is there in this place that a man should ever want to get into it?" In July 1881, President Garfield was shot by one of those office seekers.

The 1880 election began a decade of marginal victories. Between 1880 and 1892, neither the Democrats nor the Republicans would command a substantial majority of the popular vote. In 1880, the Democrats failed to win a popular plurality but they did so in the next three presidential elections—1884, 1888, and 1892.

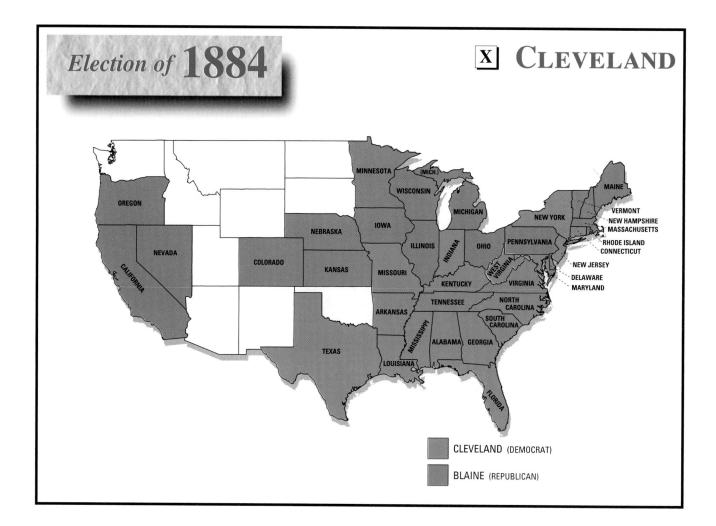

Election of 1884

☒ CLEVELAND

CLEVELAND (DEMOCRAT)

BLAINE (REPUBLICAN)

States	Electoral Votes	Cleveland	Blaine	States	Electoral Votes	Cleveland	Blaine
Alabama	(10)	10	-	Mississippi	(9)	9	-
Arkansas	(7)	7	-	Missouri	(16)	16	-
California	(8)	-	8	Nebraska	(5)	-	5
Colorado	(3)	-	3	Nevada	(3)	-	3
Connecticut	(6)	6	-	New Hampshire	(4)	-	4
Delaware	(3)	3	-	New Jersey	(9)	9	-
Florida	(4)	4	-	New York	(36)	36	-
Georgia	(12)	12	-	North Carolina	(11)	11	-
Illinois	(22)	-	22	Ohio	(23)	-	23
Indiana	(15)	15	-	Oregon	(3)	-	3
Iowa	(13)	-	13	Pennsylvania	(30)	-	30
Kansas	(9)	-	9	Rhode Island	(4)	-	4
Kentucky	(13)	13	-	South Carolina	(9)	9	-
Louisiana	(8)	8	-	Tennessee	(12)	12	-
Maine	(6)	-	6	Texas	(13)	13	-
Maryland	(8)	8	-	Vermont	(4)	-	4
Massachusetts	(14)	-	14	Virginia	(12)	12	-
Michigan	(13)	-	13	West Virginia	(6)	6	-
Minnesota	(7)	-	7	Wisconsin	(11)	-	11
				Totals	**(401)**	**219**	**182**

ELECTORAL VOTE

Election of 1884

STATE	TOTAL VOTE	GROVER CLEVELAND (Democrat)		JAMES G. BLAINE (Republican)		BENJAMIN F. BUTLER (Greenback)		JOHN P. ST. JOHN (Prohibition)		OTHER		PLURALITY	
		Votes	%	Votes	%	Votes	%	Votes	%	Votes	%		
Alabama	153,624	92,736	60.4	59,444	38.7	762	0.5	610	0.4	72		33,292	D
Arkansas	125,779	72,734	57.8	51,198	40.7	1,847	1.5	—		—		21,536	D
California	196,988	89,288	45.3	102,369	52.0	2,037	1.0	2,965	1.5	329	0.2	13,081	R
Colorado	66,519	27,723	41.7	36,084	54.2	1,956	2.9	756	1.1	—		8,361	R
Connecticut	137,221	67,167	48.9	65,879	48.0	1,682	1.2	2,493	1.8	—		1,288	D
Delaware	29,984	16,957	56.6	12,953	43.2	10		64	0.2	—		4,004	D
Florida	59,990	31,769	53.0	28,031	46.7	—		72	0.1	118	0.2	3,738	D
Georgia	143,610	94,667	65.9	48,603	33.8	145	0.1	195	0.1	—		46,064	D
Illinois	672,670	312,351	46.4	337,469	50.2	10,776	1.6	12,074	1.8	—		25,118	R
Indiana	491,649	244,989	49.8	238,466	48.5	8,194	1.7	—		—		6,523	D
Iowa	393,542	177,316	45.1	197,089	50.1	16,341	4.2	1,499	0.4	1,297	0.3	19,773	R
Kansas	250,991	90,111	35.9	154,410	61.5	1,691	0.7	4,311	1.7	468	0.2	64,299	R
Kentucky	274,910	152,961	55.6	118,690	43.2	120		3,139	1.1	—		34,271	D
Louisiana	113,234	62,594	55.3	46,347	40.9	3,955	3.5	338	0.3	—		16,247	D
Maine	127,114	52,153	41.0	72,217	56.8	578	0.5	2,160	1.7	6		20,064	R
Maryland	209,823	96,866	46.2	85,748	40.9	24,382	11.6	2,827	1.3	—		11,118	D
Massachusetts	321,253	122,352	38.1	146,724	45.7	42,252	13.2	9,923	3.1	2		24,372	R
Michigan	364,490	149,835	41.1	192,669	52.9	3,583	1.0	18,403	5.0	—		42,834	R
Minnesota	186,434	70,065	37.6	111,685	59.9	—		4,684	2.5	—		41,620	R
Mississippi	120,688	77,653	64.3	43,035	35.7	—		—		—		34,618	D
Missouri	441,268	236,023	53.5	203,081	46.0	—		2,164	0.5	—		32,942	D
Nebraska	134,202	54,391	40.5	76,912	57.3	—		2,899	2.2	—		22,521	R
Nevada	12,779	5,577	43.6	7,176	56.2	26	0.2	—		—		1,599	R
New Hampshire	84,586	39,198	46.3	43,254	51.1	554	0.7	1,580	1.9	—		4,056	R
New Jersey	260,853	127,747	49.0	123,436	47.3	3,486	1.3	6,156	2.4	28		4,311	D
New York	1,167,003	563,048	48.2	562,001	48.2	16,955	1.5	24,999	2.1	—		1,047	D
North Carolina	268,356	142,905	53.3	125,021	46.6	—		430	0.2	—		17,884	D
Ohio	784,620	368,280	46.9	400,092	51.0	5,179	0.7	11,069	1.4	—		31,812	R
Oregon	52,683	24,598	46.7	26,845	51.0	726	1.4	479	0.9	35	0.1	2,247	R
Pennsylvania	899,710	394,772	43.9	472,792	52.5	16,992	1.9	15,154	1.7	—		78,020	R
Rhode Island	32,771	12,391	37.8	19,030	58.1	422	1.3	928	2.8	—		6,639	R
South Carolina	92,812	69,845	75.3	21,730	23.4	—		—		1,237	1.3	48,115	D
Tennessee	259,978	133,770	51.5	124,101	47.7	957	0.4	1,150	0.4	—		9,669	D
Texas	321,242	223,209	69.5	91,234	28.4	3,310	1.0	3,489	1.1	—		131,975	D
Vermont	59,409	17,331	29.2	39,514	66.5	785	1.3	1,752	2.9	27		22,183	R
Virginia	284,977	145,491	51.1	139,356	48.9	—		130		—		6,135	D
West Virginia	132,145	67,311	50.9	63,096	47.7	799	0.6	939	0.7	—		4,215	D
Wisconsin	319,847	146,447	45.8	161,155	50.4	4,594	1.4	7,651	2.4	—		14,708	R
Totals	**10,049,754**	**4,874,621**	**48.5**	**4,848,936**	**48.2**	**175,096**	**1.7**	**147,482**	**1.5**	**3,619**		**25,685**	**D**

The 1884 presidential campaign was the most abusive and insulting in U.S. history. The Republican and Democratic parties ignored the major issues confronting the nation. Personal character attacks on each candidate dominated the campaign.

On 2 July 1881, President James A. Garfield had been shot by an insane office seeker. He clung to life until 19 September. Public reaction to Garfield's assassination led to the passage of the Pendleton Act of 1883, which established the nonpartisan Civil Service Commission. Although the number of jobs placed under the merit system was relatively small—approximately 10 percent—a promising start had been made to end the spoils system. Arthur's otherwise placid administration ended with the rowdy 1884 presidential campaign where control of the national government remained the chief issue.

The Republican Convention met in Chicago on 3 June 1884. James G. Blaine, who had so narrowly missed the nomination in 1880, had emerged as the party's most commanding figure. He had served in Congress for many years and as secretary of state in both the Garfield and Arthur administrations. Blaine resigned from the cabinet in December 1881 to write *Twenty Years of Congress,* a thousand-page history of his career. The convention bypassed Arthur and chose Blaine on the fourth ballot.

Blaine may have been a "Plumed Knight" to the rank and file of the party, but he was a simple grafter to other Republicans. The principal charge against him was the use of the House speakership for personal monetary gain. Liberal Republicans also opposed Blaine for his stand against further civil service reform. This reform wing, now called "Mugwumps," bolted from the convention and promised to support any decent Democratic nominee. Younger and shrewder politicians, like Henry Cabot Lodge and Theodore Roosevelt, supported Blaine while admitting the worst about him. Even Roscoe Conkling, the New York Stalwart leader, refused to campaign for Blaine. Later in the campaign, when a group of Blaine supporters pleaded with Conkling to reconsider and to endorse Blaine, he told the delegates: "Gentlemen, you have been misinformed. I have given up criminal law."

The Democrats met in Chicago on 8 July. The delegates nominated Grover Cleveland, the governor of New York, on the second ballot and chose Thomas Hendricks of Indiana for vice president. The states of New York and Indiana were critical to the Democratic strategy for winning the election. In 1881, Grover Cleveland had been elected mayor of Buffalo as a reform candidate. Two years later, the "unknown candidate," as his supporters called him, was elected governor of New York. He alienated New York's powerful Tammany Hall bosses by refusing to award the usual patronage jobs to the state party leaders. In 1884, the Democratic National Convention seized upon Cleveland as the man who could initiate a new and cleaner era in U.S. politics. "We love him for the enemies he has made," said General Edward S. Bragg of Wisconsin in seconding Cleveland's nomination.

The 1884 campaign is the first in which the public morality of one candidate, Blaine, and the sexual morality of the other, Cleveland, received such attention. In the early weeks of the campaign, before mudslinging began, Blaine spoke of "constructive action" by the federal government. He talked about improving the nation's internal waterways, encouraging foreign trade and of the benefits of a productive tariff to all sections of the nation. "Emphasize *wages,* especially *wages,"* he told Republican editors when they wrote tariff editorials. But Cleveland would not engage him in a debate on the tariff. Rather, the Democratic Party described Blaine as a man of shabby political morals whose party had been in power too long.

The Democrats publicized the so-called Mulligan Letters as an example of Blaine using his political position for personal financial gain. In 1869, when he was Speaker of the House, he sold railroad bonds to fellow congressmen on a highly generous commission basis. Blaine promised them a $3 return for every $1 invested within two years. A series of embarrassing letters that he wrote to a railroad executive came into the possession of one James Mulligan. One letter ended with the request: "Burn this letter when you have read it." *The New York Times* reprinted the letters on its front page with an editorial conclusion that Blaine had exposed himself as "a prostitute of public trusts, a scheming jobber, and a reckless falsifier."

The New York Times was one of six New York newspapers that had supported Garfield in 1880 but had now switched to the Democratic nominee. Their editorials attacked Blaine without mercy throughout the summer of 1884. Likewise, *The Nation* reprinted, in parallel columns, a series of contradictory statements made by Blaine.

Cartoonists Thomas Nast in *Harper's Weekly* and Bernhard Gillam in *Puck* continually attacked him. Nast showed Blaine fawning before bloated railroad tycoons. Gillam drew Blaine as the Tattooed Man, with phrases from the Mulligan letters all over his body.

The Democrats had their own campaign scandal. On 21 July, the Buffalo *Evening Telegraph* published the story of a relationship between Cleveland and a Buffalo widow. He acknowledged that a boy, born on 14 September 1874, was his son. Cleveland had assumed full responsibility and supported the child. When the mother became an uncontrollable alcoholic, Cleveland arranged for her to receive treatment. He then supervised the adoption of the boy by a childless couple living in the Buffalo area. He never saw his son or the mother again. Republican newspapers referred to Cleveland's bachelor apartment in Buffalo as a "harem;" that he had "lusted his victims in the city and surrounding villages." The difference between Cleveland and Blaine, they said, was "between the brothel and the family, between lust and law." Republican editors teased their readers with allusions to "perverse enjoyments" and "bestial conduct." Blaine supporters pushed carriages, complete with dolls, and chanted in falsetto tones: "Ma! Ma!/Where's my Pa!"

When the story broke, Cleveland wired his Buffalo supporters a three-word telegram: "Tell the Truth!" Democrats rallied to his defense. Edwin L. Godkin, editor of *The Nation*, wrote that although chastity was a fine thing, "every man knows in his heart that it is not the greatest of virtues." Reverend Henry Ward Beecher informed a reporter that if all New Yorkers who had committed adultery voted for Cleveland, he would carry the state by a landslide. Actually, Cleveland emerged a stronger candidate from this scandal.

Cleveland did not campaign. Blaine, however, made an extensive six-week tour. He delivered more than 400 speeches. Exhausted, his last major stop was New York City on 29 October. He met several hundred Protestant ministers in the lobby of the Fifth Avenue Hotel before a scheduled dinner. The ministers, all Republican, had passed resolutions supporting Blaine and condemning the Democrats. On their behalf, Samuel D. Burchard, a Presbyterian minister, greeted Blaine: "We are Republicans, and don't propose to leave our party and identify with the party whose antecedents have been Rum, Romanism and Rebellion. We are loyal to our flag, we are loyal to you."

Within hours the major newspapers were being bombarded with news of the anti-Catholic remark. When Blaine passed through New Haven the following day, handbills advertising the three R's had preceded him. "Rum, Romanism and Rebellion" now became the Democratic taunt. Blaine probably lost thousands of Catholic votes because he had allowed such an insulting remark to pass unchallenged. The following week, John Kelly, the political boss of New York City, told him: "All is over."

If 29 October had started out discouragingly for Blaine, it wound up disastrously. He had dinner that evening at Delmonico's with about 200 Republicans, mostly millionaires. Blaine spoke of the glorious role the Republican Party had in furthering wealth. The next day, Joseph Pulitzer's newspaper, the New York *World*, reported in banner headlines: "THE ROYAL FEAST OF BELSHAZZAR . . . BLAINE AND MONEY KINGS . . . AN OCCASION FOR THE COLLECTION OF A REPUBLICAN CORRUPTION FUND."

More than 10 million Americans went to the polls on 4 November 1884. Cleveland received 48.5 percent of the popular vote to Blaine's 48.2 percent. Cleveland had captured the South, the border states of Delaware, Kentucky, Maryland, Missouri, and West Virginia, as well as New Jersey, Indiana, and Connecticut, for a total of 20 states with 219 electoral votes. Blaine had won 18 states and 182 electoral votes. The popular vote in New York was almost a tie. A careful recounting of the New York votes witnessed by a distinguished group of lawyers concluded that Cleveland won the state with a plurality of 1,047 votes. Blaine said that he would have carried New York and won the election if it had not been for the intolerant and utterly improper remark of Dr. Burchard.

Blaine lost the election because of his shortcomings, mistakes, and mishaps. But Cleveland was the right man at the right time. "Everyone takes part," wrote historian Henry Adams of the 1884 election, "We are all doing our best, and swearing at each other like demons. But the amusing thing is that no one talks about real interests. By common consent they agree to let these alone."

Election of 1888

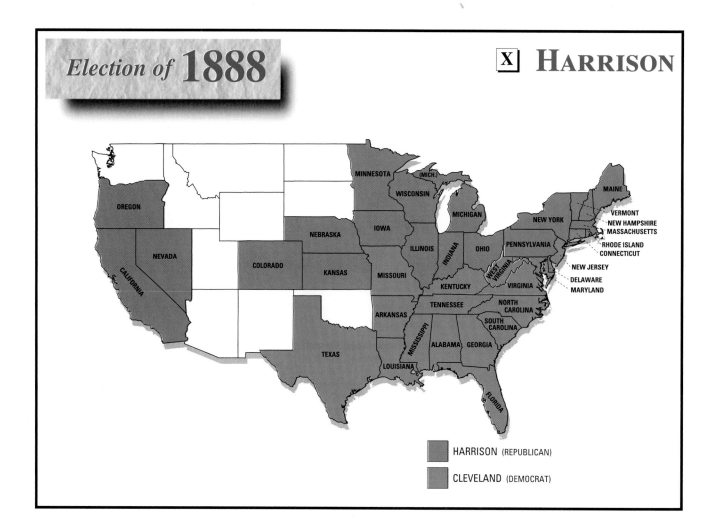

HARRISON (REPUBLICAN)

CLEVELAND (DEMOCRAT)

States	Electoral Votes	Harrison	Cleveland	States	Electoral Votes	Harrison	Cleveland
Alabama	(10)	-	10	Mississippi	(9)	-	9
Arkansas	(7)	-	7	Missouri	(16)	-	16
California	(8)	8	-	Nebraska	(5)	5	-
Colorado	(3)	3	-	Nevada	(3)	3	-
Connecticut	(6)	-	6	New Hampshire	(4)	4	-
Delaware	(3)	-	3	New Jersey	(9)	-	9
Florida	(4)	-	4	New York	(36)	36	-
Georgia	(12)	-	12	North Carolina	(11)	-	11
Illinois	(22)	22	-	Ohio	(23)	23	-
Indiana	(15)	15	-	Oregon	(3)	3	-
Iowa	(13)	13	-	Pennsylvania	(30)	30	-
Kansas	(9)	9	-	Rhode Island	(4)	4	-
Kentucky	(13)	-	13	South Carolina	(9)	-	9
Louisiana	(8)	-	8	Tennessee	(12)	-	12
Maine	(6)	6	-	Texas	(13)	-	13
Maryland	(8)	-	8	Vermont	(4)	4	-
Massachusetts	(14)	14	-	Virginia	(12)	-	12
Michigan	(13)	13	-	West Virginia	(6)	-	6
Minnesota	(7)	7	-	Wisconsin	(11)	11	-
				Totals	**(401)**	**233**	**168**

ELECTORAL VOTE

Election of 1888

STATE	TOTAL VOTE	BENJAMIN HARRISON (Republican)		GROVER CLEVELAND (Democrat)		CLINTON B. FISK (Prohibition)		ALSON J. STREETER (Union Labor)		OTHER		PLURALITY	
		Votes	%	Votes	%	Votes	%	Votes	%	Votes	%		
Alabama	175,085	57,177	32.7	117,314	67.0	594	0.3	—		—		60,137	D
Arkansas	157,058	59,752	38.0	86,062	54.8	614	0.4	10,630	6.8	—		26,310	D
California	251,339	124,816	49.7	117,729	46.8	5,761	2.3	—		3,033	1.2	7,087	R
Colorado	91,946	50,772	55.2	37,549	40.8	2,182	2.4	1,266	1.4	177	0.2	13,223	R
Connecticut	153,978	74,584	48.4	74,920	48.7	4,234	2.7	240	0.2	—		336	D
Delaware	29,764	12,950	43.5	16,414	55.1	399	1.3	—		1		3,464	D
Florida	66,500	26,529	39.9	39,557	59.5	414	0.6	—		—		13,028	D
Georgia	142,936	40,499	28.3	100,493	70.3	1,808	1.3	136	0.1	—		59,994	D
Illinois	747,813	370,475	49.5	348,351	46.6	21,703	2.9	7,134	1.0	150		22,124	R
Indiana	536,988	263,366	49.0	260,990	48.6	9,939	1.9	2,693	0.5	—		2,376	R
Iowa	404,694	211,607	52.3	179,876	44.4	3,550	0.9	9,105	2.2	556	0.1	31,731	R
Kansas	331,133	182,845	55.2	102,739	31.0	6,774	2.0	37,838	11.4	937	0.3	80,106	R
Kentucky	344,868	155,138	45.0	183,830	53.3	5,223	1.5	677	0.2	—		28,692	D
Louisiana	115,891	30,660	26.5	85,032	73.4	160	0.1	39		—		54,372	D
Maine	128,253	73,730	57.5	50,472	39.4	2,691	2.1	1,344	1.0	16		23,258	R
Maryland	210,941	99,986	47.4	106,188	50.3	4,767	2.3	—		—		6,202	D
Massachusetts	344,243	183,892	53.4	151,590	44.0	8,701	2.5	—		60		32,302	R
Michigan	475,356	236,387	49.7	213,469	44.9	20,945	4.4	4,555	1.0	—		22,918	R
Minnesota	263,162	142,492	54.1	104,372	39.7	15,201	5.8	1,097	0.4	—		38,120	R
Mississippi	115,786	30,095	26.0	85,451	73.8	240	0.2	—		—		55,356	D
Missouri	521,359	236,252	45.3	261,943	50.2	4,539	0.9	18,625	3.6	—		25,691	D
Nebraska	202,630	108,417	53.5	80,552	39.8	9,435	4.7	4,226	2.1	—		27,865	R
Nevada	12,573	7,229	57.5	5,303	42.2	41	0.3	—		—		1,926	R
New Hampshire	90,770	45,734	50.4	43,382	47.8	1,596	1.8	—		58	0.1	2,352	R
New Jersey	303,634	144,347	47.5	151,493	49.9	7,794	2.6	—		—		7,146	D
New York	1,319,748	650,338	49.3	635,965	48.2	30,231	2.3	627		2,587	0.2	14,373	R
North Carolina	285,563	134,784	47.2	147,902	51.8	2,840	1.0	—		37		13,118	D
Ohio	839,357	416,054	49.6	395,456	47.1	24,356	2.9	3,491	0.4	—		20,598	R
Oregon	61,889	33,291	53.8	26,518	42.8	1,676	2.7	—		404	0.7	6,773	R
Pennsylvania	997,568	526,091	52.7	446,633	44.8	20,947	2.1	3,873	0.4	24		79,458	R
Rhode Island	40,775	21,969	53.9	17,530	43.0	1,251	3.1	18		7		4,439	R
South Carolina	79,997	13,736	17.2	65,824	82.3	—		—		437	0.5	52,088	D
Tennessee	303,694	138,978	45.8	158,699	52.3	5,969	2.0	48		—		19,721	D
Texas	354,412	88,604	25.0	232,189	65.5	4,739	1.3	28,880	8.1	—		143,585	D
Vermont	63,476	45,193	71.2	16,788	26.4	1,460	2.3	—		35	0.1	28,405	R
Virginia	304,087	150,399	49.5	152,004	50.0	1,684	0.6	—		—		1,605	D
West Virginia	159,440	78,171	49.0	78,677	49.3	1,084	0.7	1,508	0.9	—		506	D
Wisconsin	354,614	176,553	49.8	155,232	43.8	14,277	4.0	8,552	2.4	—		21,321	R
Totals	11,383,320	5,443,892	47.8	5,534,488	48.6	249,819	2.2	146,602	1.3	8,519	0.1	90,596	D

P O P U L A R   V O T E

The 1888 presidential election was the first since the Civil War in which the parties had a major economic difference—the tariff issue. The campaign ranks as one of the most corrupt in U.S. political history. Both parties resorted to the usual fraudulent methods of the day. The Republicans, however, had a campaign fund contributed to by apprehensive business interests and were the worst offenders.

The principal achievements of Cleveland's first administration were the extension of civil service, the veto of undeserved pensions for Civil War veterans, and tariff revision. In the 1880s the United States faced the unusual problem of having a surplus in the treasury, indicating that taxes were too high. Extravagant pension bills and "pork barrel" legislation for rivers and harbors would have readily disposed of the surplus, but Cleveland boldly decided to attack the cause of the problem: the tariff. His advisers warned about the political repercussions of a tariff battle with the Republicans. "What is the use of being elected or re-elected, unless you stand for something?" he asked them.

On 6 December 1887, the President focused the attention of the nation on the need for tariff reform by devoting his third annual State of the Union message exclusively to this subject. "Our present tariff laws," he declared, "the vicious, inequitable, and illogical source of unnecessary taxation, ought to be at once revised and amended." He explained that the existing law protected U.S. industries from foreign competition, but the tariff also had correspondingly increased consumer prices. It had provided an additional "burden upon those with moderate means and the poor, the employed and unemployed, the sick and well, and the young and old." Cleveland vividly described the tariff as "a tax which with relentless grasp is fastened upon the clothing of every man, woman, and child in the land." The tariff debate raged in and out of Congress from the conclusion of his message through Election Day, 1888.

The Democratic controlled House Ways and Means Committee, chaired by Roger Mills of Texas, prepared a tariff bill with an estimated total revenue reduction of $80 million per year. For several months, the House debated, amended, criticized, and praised the administration's bill. Congressmen representing special interest groups as well as their sectional interests delivered both partisan and moral appeals for and against enactment. During the course of the extensive debates, the Republican Party became committed to a protective tariff

sufficiently high to maintain a domestic monopoly for U.S. industrialists—in other words, protection for the sake of protection. On 21 July 1888, the Mills bill passed the House by a vote cast along strict party lines and was sent to the U.S. Senate. However, the Republican controlled Senate rewrote it and passed legislation which maintained a high level of duties. Cleveland's State of the Union message and the tariff bill became the chief campaign issue of 1888.

The Democratic Party met in St. Louis on 5 June and unanimously renominated Grover Cleveland on the first ballot. Vice President Thomas Hendricks had died in November 1885. Former Ohio Senator Allen G. Thurman was chosen as Cleveland's running mate years earlier. Cleveland received the convention's decision as a mixed blessing. On 2 June 1886, at age 49, the bachelor President had married 21-year-old Frances Folsom, daughter of one of his former Buffalo law partners. He wrote during the 1888 campaign: "I absolutely long to be able to live with her as other people do with their wives. Well! Perhaps I can after the 4th of next March."

The Republican Convention met in Chicago on 19 June. Almost every leader fought for the chance to run against Cleveland. James G. Blaine, vacationing at the Scottish castle of his friend Andrew Carnegie, asked not to be considered. The anti-Blaine forces knew, nevertheless, that his supporters controlled the delegates. The dozen or so favorite-son candidates stayed in the race through seven ballots. The delegates were waiting to hear from Blaine. Then word came from Scotland that Blaine preferred former Indiana Senator Benjamin Harrison. The convention nominated Harrison for president on the next ballot. Levi P. Morton, a New York financier, had Blaine's support for vice president, and the delegates dutifully chose him.

Harrison came from a distinguished political family. His great-grandfather, also named Benjamin Harrison, had signed the Declaration of Independence; his grandfather, William Henry Harrison, had been a military hero and president of the United States; his father, John A. Harrison, had been a two-term member of the U.S. House of Representatives. The Harrison family's participation in government is equaled by few in the United States. Benjamin Harrison spoke about his Civil War experiences in a Chicago speech during the Republican Convention. He received a citation signed by Abraham Lincoln describing his "ability . . . manifest energy and gallantry." Harrison spoke of how the Republican Party had taken "the ship of state when there was a treachery at the helm, when there was mutiny on the deck, when the ship was among the rocks, and we put loyalty at the helm." From this point on, he was General Harrison to the nation, the war hero grandson of Old Tippecanoe.

The Republican Party launched a most ambitious campaign. Their strategy again centered on winning the key states of Indiana and New York. All during the summer and fall, manufacturers were told how to explain to their workers the connection between jobs and the protective tariff. The Iron and Steel Association made a massive effort to promote the tariff through pamphlets and newspaper stories. Harrison conducted an effective "front porch" campaign making a large number of short speeches to visiting delegations.

Cleveland refused to become involved in his own re-election campaign. He cited a busy White House schedule, the dignity of his office, and vacation plans with his wife. Without a doubt, the Democratic Party's best campaigner was Allen G. Thurman, their 75-year-old vice presidential nominee. Thurman had served in both the House of Representatives and the Senate for many years. In August, Thurman criss-crossed Ohio and went on to Michigan; in September, he made an extensive tour of New York and New Jersey; in October, he concentrated on Indiana, West Virginia, and back to Ohio. The serious side of Thurman's speeches about lowering the tariff, however, often gave way to the ludicrous. He complained about the charge that he "was a weak and decrepit old man." He complained of dizziness at a huge New York rally in Madison Square Garden on 6 September. Two days later, he spoke for 25 minutes in Newark berating the Republican tariff program. Then his voice broke; he tottered on the platform and was saved from falling into the audience by the outstretched arms of his son. His family refused to allow him to return to New York for a final rally in early November because of his health.

Ironically, the infirm vice presidential nominee became a symbol of virility. He had pulled from his pocket, on hundreds of occasions, a bright red silk bandanna to wipe his brow or absorb his sneezes, which were caused by snuff. Suddenly, audiences also wore red bandannas, and they cheered affectionately for "Old Snuff." At a Port Huron, Michigan rally, to wild applause, he held up his bandanna and shouted: "Well gentlemen, this is a good honest hand-kerchief, and I could have bought it a good deal cheaper if it had not been for the tariff tax." Red bandannas poured from textile mills. About 22 inches square, they carried pictures of Cleveland and Thurman and slogans such as "Tariff Reform." Many varieties of campaign bandannas appeared for each party during the 1888 election. The red bandanna, however, was the one associated with Allen G. Thurman.

The campaign was mainly waged on the tariff issue until the introduction of the "Murchison" letter in late September. The British Minister to Washington, Sir Lionel Sackville-West, fell into a carefully planned Republican trap. He advised a California Republican who claimed to be Charles A. Murchison, a naturalized citizen of English birth, to vote for Cleveland. This intervention into U.S. politics by the British Minister undoubtedly cost Cleveland the support of many Irish Americans, and consequently the loss of New York and perhaps the election.

Cleveland obtained about 100,000 popular votes more than Harrison. Harrison, however, carried the key states of New York and Indiana, receiving an electoral count of 233 to Cleveland's 168. Harrison piously attributed his victory to God. But Republican National Chairman Matthew Quay, who had purchased untold votes in Indiana, said: "Providence hadn't a damn thing to do with it." He added that he supposed Harrison would "never know how close a number of men were compelled to approach the gates of the penitentiary to make him President."

The Republican Party returned to power in the election of 1888. They won control of the presidency and both Houses of Congress. The election results show no major shift in political allegiances. In fact, the voting patterns in 1888 were very similar to those in the three preceding presidential elections.

Election of 1892

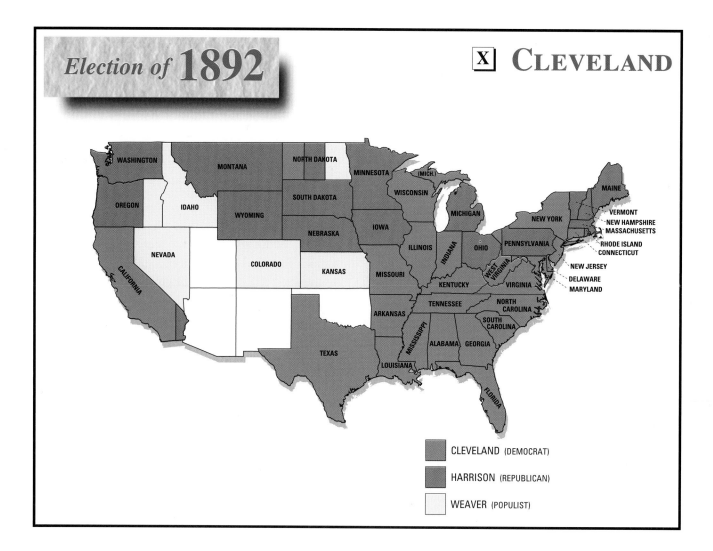

X CLEVELAND

CLEVELAND (DEMOCRAT)

HARRISON (REPUBLICAN)

WEAVER (POPULIST)

States	Electoral Votes	Cleveland	Harrison	Weaver
Alabama	(11)	11	-	-
Arkansas	(8)	8	-	-
California	(9)	8	1	-
Colorado	(4)	-	-	4
Connecticut	(6)	6	-	-
Delaware	(3)	3	-	-
Florida	(4)	4	-	-
Georgia	(13)	13	-	-
Idaho	(3)	-	-	3
Illinois	(24)	24	-	-
Indiana	(15)	15	-	-
Iowa	(13)	-	13	-
Kansas	(10)	-	-	10
Kentucky	(13)	13	-	-
Louisiana	(8)	8	-	-
Maine	(6)	-	6	-
Maryland	(8)	8	-	-
Massachusetts	(15)	-	15	-
Michigan	(14)	5	9	-
Minnesota	(9)	-	9	-
Mississippi	(9)	9	-	-
Missouri	(17)	17	-	-
Montana	(3)	-	3	-
Nebraska	(8)	-	8	-
Nevada	(3)	-	-	3
New Hampshire	(4)	-	4	-
New Jersey	(10)	10	-	-
New York	(36)	36	-	-
North Carolina	(11)	11	-	-
North Dakota	(3)	1	1	1
Ohio	(23)	1	22	-
Oregon	(4)	-	3	1
Pennsylvania	(32)	-	32	-
Rhode Island	(4)	-	4	-
South Carolina	(9)	9	-	-
South Dakota	(4)	-	4	-
Tennessee	(12)	12	-	-
Texas	(15)	15	-	-
Vermont	(4)	-	4	-
Virginia	(12)	12	-	-
Washington	(4)	-	4	-
West Virginia	(6)	6	-	-
Wisconsin	(12)	12	-	-
Wyoming	(3)	-	3	-
Totals	**(444)**	**277**	**145**	**22**

ELECTORAL VOTE

Election of 1892

STATE	TOTAL VOTE	GROVER CLEVELAND (Democrat)		BENJAMIN HARRISON (Republican)		JAMES B. WEAVER (Populist)		JOHN BIDWELL (Prohibition)		OTHER		PLURALITY	
		Votes	%	Votes	%	Votes	%	Votes	%	Votes	%		
Alabama	232,543	138,135	59.4	9,184	3.9	84,984	36.5	240	0.1	—		53,151	D
Arkansas	148,117	87,834	59.3	47,072	31.8	11,831	8.0	113	0.1	1,267	0.9	40,762	D
California	269,585	118,151	43.8	118,027	43.8	25,311	9.4	8,096	3.0	—		124	D
Colorado	93,881	—		38,620	41.1	53,584	57.1	1,677	1.8	—		14,964	POP
Connecticut	164,593	82,395	50.1	77,030	46.8	809	0.5	4,026	2.4	333	0.2	5,365	D
Delaware	37,235	18,581	49.9	18,077	48.5	—		564	1.5	13		504	D
Florida	35,471	30,153	85.0	—		4,843	13.7	475	1.3	—		25,310	D
Georgia	223,126	129,446	58.0	48,408	21.7	41,939	18.8	988	0.4	2,345	1.1	81,038	D
Idaho	19,407	—		8,599	44.3	10,520	54.2	288	1.5	—		1,921	POP
Illinois	873,667	426,281	48.8	399,308	45.7	22,207	2.5	25,871	3.0	—		26,973	D
Indiana	553,613	262,740	47.5	255,615	46.2	22,208	4.0	13,050	2.4	—		7,125	D
Iowa	443,159	196,367	44.3	219,795	49.6	20,595	4.6	6,402	1.4	—		23,428	R
Kansas	323,591	—		156,134	48.3	162,888	50.3	4,569	1.4	—		6,754	POP
Kentucky	340,864	175,461	51.5	135,462	39.7	23,500	6.9	6,441	1.9	—		39,999	D
Louisiana	114,889	87,926	76.5	26,963	23.5	—		—		—		60,963	D
Maine	116,451	48,049	41.3	62,936	54.0	2,396	2.1	3,066	2.6	4		14,887	R
Maryland	213,275	113,866	53.4	92,736	43.5	796	0.4	5,877	2.8	—		21,130	D
Massachusetts	391,028	176,813	45.2	202,814	51.9	3,210	0.8	7,539	1.9	652	0.2	26,001	R
Michigan	466,917	202,396	43.3	222,708	47.7	20,031	4.3	20,857	4.5	925	0.2	20,312	R
Minnesota	267,841	100,589	37.6	122,736	45.8	30,399	11.3	14,117	5.3	—		22,147	R
Mississippi	52,519	40,030	76.2	1,398	2.7	10,118	19.3	973	1.9	—		29,912	D
Missouri	541,583	268,400	49.6	227,646	42.0	41,204	7.6	4,333	0.8	—		40,754	D
Montana	44,461	17,690	39.8	18,871	42.4	7,338	16.5	562	1.3	—		1,181	R
Nebraska	200,205	24,956	12.5	87,213	43.6	83,134	41.5	4,902	2.4	—		4,079	R
Nevada	10,826	703	6.5	2,811	26.0	7,226	66.7	86	0.8	—		4,415	POP
New Hampshire	89,328	42,081	47.1	45,658	51.1	292	0.3	1,297	1.5	—		3,577	R
New Jersey	337,485	170,987	50.7	156,059	46.2	969	0.3	8,133	2.4	1,337	0.4	14,928	D
New York	1,336,793	654,868	49.0	609,350	45.6	16,429	1.2	38,190	2.9	17,956	1.3	45,518	D
North Carolina	280,270	132,951	47.4	100,346	35.8	44,336	15.8	2,637	0.9	—		32,605	D
North Dakota	36,118	—		17,519	48.5	17,700	49.0	899	2.5	—		181	POP
Ohio	850,164	404,115	47.5	405,187	47.7	14,850	1.7	26,012	3.1	—		1,072	R
Oregon	78,378	14,243	18.2	35,002	44.7	26,875	34.3	2,258	2.9	—		8,127	R
Pennsylvania	1,003,000	452,264	45.1	516,011	51.4	8,714	0.9	25,123	2.5	888	0.1	63,747	R
Rhode Island	53,196	24,336	45.7	26,975	50.7	228	0.4	1,654	3.1	3		2,639	R
South Carolina	70,504	54,680	77.6	13,345	18.9	2,407	3.4	—		72	0.1	41,335	D
South Dakota	70,160	8,894	12.7	34,714	49.5	26,552	37.8	—		—		8,162	R
Tennessee	265,732	136,468	51.4	100,537	37.8	23,918	9.0	4,809	1.8	—		35,931	D
Texas	410,860	236,979	57.7	70,982	17.3	96,649	23.5	2,164	0.5	4,086	1.0	140,330	D
Vermont	55,793	16,325	29.3	37,992	68.1	42	0.1	1,424	2.6	10		21,667	R
Virginia	292,238	164,136	56.2	113,098	38.7	12,275	4.2	2,729	0.9	—		51,038	D
Washington	87,968	29,802	33.9	36,459	41.4	19,165	21.8	2,542	2.9	—		6,657	R
West Virginia	171,079	84,467	49.4	80,292	46.9	4,167	2.4	2,153	1.3	—		4,175	D
Wisconsin	371,481	177,325	47.7	171,101	46.1	9,919	2.7	13,136	3.5	—		6,224	D
Wyoming	16,703	—		8,454	50.6	7,722	46.2	498	3.0	29	0.2	732	R
Totals	12,056,097	5,551,883	46.1	5,179,244	43.0	1,024,280	8.5	270,770	2.2	29,920	0.2	372,639	D

POPULAR VOTE

On 7 June 1892, the Republican Convention met at Minneapolis and renominated President Benjamin Harrison. Later that month, the Democrats convened in Chicago and again chose Grover Cleveland as their presidential candidate. Harrison lost his spirit for campaigning after his wife died and Cleveland spent the summer at his beach home in Massachusetts. The dull campaign which followed was enlivened by a third candidate, James Weaver of Iowa, who ran on the Populist ticket.

During the first two years of Benjamin Harrison's administration, the Republicans had enjoyed a majority in both Houses of Congress. It was here, under the relentless leadership of the party bosses, that the power resided. The conservative, fiercely partisan Harrison, referred to by his contemporaries as a human icicle, seemed almost unaware of the growing unrest of the farmer and the predicament of the urban laborer.

Determined Republican legislators honored their 1888 campaign pledge by passing the McKinley Tariff Act (1890), which raised duties to a new high. But the growing western agrarian bloc extracted a major concession in return for their congressional support of the tariff. They demanded a more liberal silver purchase act. Also, to quiet the growing public sentiment against business monopolies, Republican leaders agreed to the Sherman Anti-Trust Act (1890). The key clauses were made so vague that almost all knew it would be ineffective. Veterans of the Union army supported Republican policies because the party leaders had given them pensions that were much too generous. The debt-ridden farmers probably understood the tariff better by the 1890 congressional elections, and, as a result, the Republicans lost control of the House. Nine representatives of a new party, the People's Party or, more commonly, the Populists, were elected.

In the 1890s, most farmers believed that neither political party was doing anything to solve their problems. Much of the economic, cultural, and political turmoil of the decade focused on agriculture. Farmers protested declining prices for their crops and higher fees charged by the middlemen: mortgage lenders, bankers, grain elevator operators, and railroad owners. The political movement which resulted raised serious doubts about the survival of capitalism. The jurist Oliver Wendell Holmes, Jr. recalled 1892 as the year "a vague terror went over the earth and the word socialism began to be heard."

The manufacturing and transportation industries had made great progress after the Civil War. However, industrial development still largely depended on agriculture. Agriculture was also undergoing a revolution due to the rapid expansion of farming across the Great Plains and the use of new machinery. The construction of an extensive railroad network carried farm goods to markets all over the United States. Some goods were shipped abroad.

The post–Civil War industrial revolution forced farmers to become part of an interconnected system which exposed them to complex economic forces. These forces adversely affected their income. Farmers were the last economic group in the United States to realize that they needed federal regulations in order to survive. Industrialists spoke about *laissez-faire* capitalism but they supported protective tariffs for their industries as well as monopolistic business practices. The farmers slowly realized that the protective tariff discriminated against them. They purchased their farm machinery and other manufactured goods, such as harnesses and sewing machines, in a protected market but sold their goods in competitive markets of supply and demand.

Between 1860 and 1890 more land was brought under cultivation than in all the previous history of the nation. Dramatic increases occurred in the production of wheat, corn, cotton, and other staples. In 1830, for example, it required something over half-an-hour to prepare the ground and sow one bushel of wheat; in 1900, this operation took only 2 minutes. In 1830, a man could harvest 20 bushels of grain in 61 hours using a hand-cradle; by 1900, he could perform this same task in less than 3 hours. It took 21 hours to harvest a ton of hay in 1850; it took only 4 hours half a century later. However, by 1900, the farmers' share of the national wealth was less than half that of 1860. While the agricultural market for goods had expanded, the economic and political position of the farmers had contracted. They especially blamed the bankers and the railroad barons for the high rates that they charged. They would not accept the idea that they were part of a highly sophisticated capitalist system. Rather, they fought it. They refused to admit that they produced more than could be consumed. A large amount of the Populist rhetoric was phrased in conspiratorial terms. They campaigned by saying that the good farmers, rather than being rewarded for feeding the nation, were being punished by falling prices, foreclosures, and bankruptcies.

Wheat brought $1.20 a bushel in 1881 and 50 cents in 1895. Farmers sold cotton for 10.5 cents a pound in 1881 and 4.5 cents in 1894. The fall in farm prices hit the farmers especially hard as they were debtors with fixed monetary obligations. They had purchased new land and machinery when prices were high and money was cheap. Now, with declining prices, they faced a sharp deflation. They blamed the cold-blooded Wall Street cabal, led by tycoons, for crushing the nation's hardest workers. This theme was expressed repeatedly through letters, speeches, pamphlets, and songs. "The Farmer Is the Man" was among the best known of the Populist ballads. Two of the verses are:

The farmer is the man,
The farmer is the man,
Lives on credit till the fall;
Then they take him by the hand,
And they lead him from the land,
And the merchant is the one who gets it all.

When the banker says he's broke
And the merchant's up in smoke,
They forget that it's the farmer feeds them all.
It would put them to the test
If the farmer took a rest;
Then they'd know that it's the farmer feeds them all.

Leonidas Polk and other farm leaders first urged the formation of cooperatives to free the farmers from bankers and mortgage lenders. In 1889, when Polk became president of the National Farmers' Alliance, it had more than 1 million members. Polk, like most other southern alliance members, feared that a third political party would split southern Democrats and bring back African American domination in Republican state governments. Both Republican and Democratic leaders, however, ignored his ideas of agrarian reform. It was difficult for them to believe that anything was wrong. The older parties felt that foreign agitators and anarchists were to blame for discontented workers or poverty-stricken farmers.

In the 1890 elections in the southern states, the Farmers' Alliance sought to gain control of the Democratic Party machinery. The reformers won majorities in 5 state legislatures and elected 3 governors, 1 U.S. senator and 44 Representatives. In the West, farmers formed third parties with various names to challenge the dominant Republicans. They made a most impressive showing, especially in Kansas, where the People's Party won control of the lower House of the state legislature, and elected 1 U.S. senator and 5 representatives.

In February 1892, Polk presided over the great Industrial Conference of 22 reform groups which met in St. Louis. Success in the 1890 elections convinced the delegates to launch a new national political party. The Populist Convention that convened in Omaha on that Independence Day resembled a huge old-fashioned camp meeting. The platform described a melancholy America, "brought to the verge of moral, political, and material ruin." It said that government injustice bred "two great classes—tramps and millionaires." Specifically, the platform demanded an inflation through the free and unlimited coinage of silver; a graduated income tax; public ownership of the railroads, telegraph, and telephones; prohibition of land ownership by aliens; immigration restriction; an eight-hour work day for laborers; the prohibition of the use of labor spies; and the direct election of senators. To many, especially the leaders of the Republican and Democratic parties in 1892, the platform was the first step toward communism. The issues raised by the Populists outlasted their political party. Solutions to the problems they spoke about finally occurred some 40 years later, under Franklin D. Roosevelt's "New Deal" of the 1930s.

Cleveland received 5,551,883 popular votes to Harrison's 5,179,244. Weaver polled 1,024,280 (8.5 percent of the total). Cleveland won 227 electoral votes to Harrison's 145 and Weaver's 22. For the first time since before the Civil War, the President and both Houses of Congress were Democratic. The Populists carried four states—Colorado, Idaho, Kansas, and Nevada. In large sections of the Midwest and especially in the South, reluctance to vote for a third party caused the election of many Democrats sympathetic to the Populist cause.

In defeat, the Populists scored a major triumph. They did extremely well in the West. In the South, farmers stayed within the Democratic Party, regardless of grievances, because the party meant White supremacy. The Populist goal now became to win control of the Democratic Party and to be victorious in the 1896 presidential election.

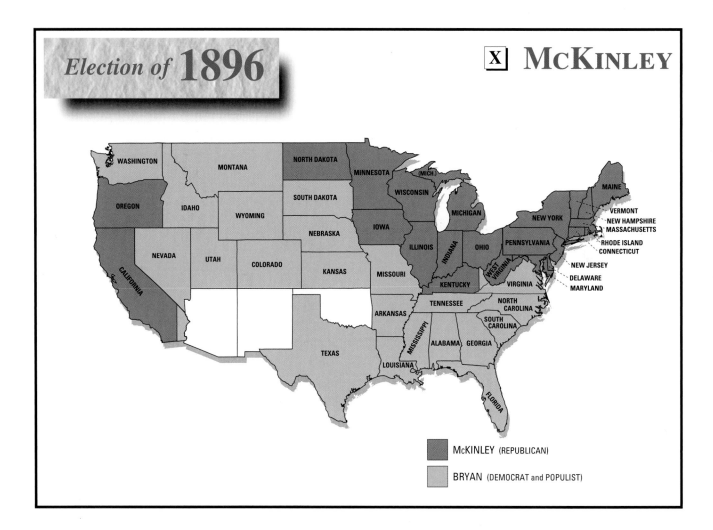

Election of 1896

☒ **McKinley**

McKINLEY (REPUBLICAN)

BRYAN (DEMOCRAT and POPULIST)

States	Electoral Votes	McKinley	Bryan	States	Electoral Votes	McKinley	Bryan
Alabama	(11)	-	11	Nebraska	(8)	-	8
Arkansas	(8)	-	8	Nevada	(3)	-	3
California	(9)	8	1	New Hampshire	(4)	4	-
Colorado	(4)	-	4	New Jersey	(10)	10	-
Connecticut	(6)	6	-	New York	(36)	36	-
Delaware	(3)	3	-	North Carolina	(11)	-	11
Florida	(4)	-	4	North Dakota	(3)	3	-
Georgia	(13)	-	13	Ohio	(23)	23	-
Idaho	(3)	-	3	Oregon	(4)	4	-
Illinois	(24)	24	-	Pennsylvania	(32)	32	-
Indiana	(15)	15	-	Rhode Island	(4)	4	-
Iowa	(13)	13	-	South Carolina	(9)	-	9
Kansas	(10)	-	10	South Dakota	(4)	-	4
Kentucky	(13)	12	1	Tennessee	(12)	-	12
Louisiana	(8)	-	8	Texas	(15)	-	15
Maine	(6)	6	-	Utah	(3)	-	3
Maryland	(8)	8	-	Vermont	(4)	4	-
Massachusetts	(15)	15	-	Virginia	(12)	-	12
Michigan	(14)	14	-	Washington	(4)	-	4
Minnesota	(9)	9	-	West Virginia	(6)	6	-
Mississippi	(9)	-	9	Wisconsin	(12)	12	-
Missouri	(17)	-	17	Wyoming	(3)	-	3
Montana	(3)	-	3	**Totals**	**(447)**	**271**	**176**

ELECTORAL VOTE

Election of 1896

STATE	TOTAL VOTE	WILLIAM McKINLEY (Republican)		WILLIAM J. BRYAN (Democrat, Populist)		JOHN M. PALMER (National Democrat)		JOSHUA LEVERING (Prohibition)		OTHER		PLURALITY	
		Votes	%	Votes	%	Votes	%	Votes	%	Votes	%		
Alabama	194,580	55,673	28.6	130,298	67.0	6,375	3.3	2,234	1.1	—		74,625	D
Arkansas	149,396	37,512	25.1	110,103	73.7	—		889	0.6	892	0.6	72,591	D
California	298,598	146,756	49.1	144,877	48.5	1,730	0.6	2,573	0.9	2,662	0.9	1,879	R
Colorado	189,539	26,271	13.9	161,005	84.9	1		1,717	0.9	545	0.3	134,734	D
Connecticut	174,394	110,285	63.2	56,740	32.5	4,336	2.5	1,806	1.0	1,227	0.7	53,545	R
Delaware	38,456	20,450	53.2	16,574	43.1	966	2.5	466	1.2	—		3,876	R
Florida	46,488	11,298	24.3	32,756	70.5	1,778	3.8	656	1.4	—		21,458	D
Georgia	162,480	59,395	36.6	93,885	57.8	3,670	2.3	5,483	3.4	47		34,490	D
Idaho	29,631	6,324	21.3	23,135	78.1	—		172	0.6	—		16,811	D
Illinois	1,090,766	607,130	55.7	465,593	42.7	6,307	0.6	9,796	0.9	1,940	0.2	141,537	R
Indiana	637,089	323,754	50.8	305,538	48.0	2,145	0.3	3,061	0.5	2,591	0.4	18,216	R
Iowa	521,550	289,293	55.5	223,744	42.9	4,516	0.9	3,192	0.6	805	0.2	65,549	R
Kansas	336,085	159,484	47.5	173,049	51.5	1,209	0.4	1,723	0.5	620	0.2	13,565	D
Kentucky	445,928	218,171	48.9	217,894	48.9	5,084	1.1	4,779	1.1	—		277	R
Louisiana	101,046	22,037	21.8	77,175	76.4	1,834	1.8	—		—		55,138	D
Maine	118,419	80,403	67.9	34,587	29.2	1,867	1.6	1,562	1.3	—		45,816	R
Maryland	250,249	136,959	54.7	104,150	41.6	2,499	1.0	5,918	2.4	723	0.3	32,809	R
Massachusetts	401,269	278,976	69.5	105,414	26.3	11,749	2.9	2,998	0.7	2,132	0.5	173,562	R
Michigan	545,583	293,336	53.8	237,164	43.5	6,923	1.3	4,978	0.9	3,182	0.6	56,172	R
Minnesota	341,762	193,503	56.6	139,735	40.9	3,222	0.9	4,348	1.3	954	0.3	53,768	R
Mississippi	69,591	4,819	6.9	63,355	91.0	1,021	1.5	396	0.6	—		58,536	D
Missouri	674,032	304,940	45.2	363,667	54.0	2,365	0.4	2,169	0.3	891	0.1	58,727	D
Montana	53,330	10,509	19.7	42,628	79.9	—		193	0.4	—		32,119	D
Nebraska	223,181	103,064	46.2	115,007	51.5	2,885	1.3	1,242	0.6	983	0.4	11,943	D
Nevada	10,286	1,938	18.8	8,348	81.2	—		—		—		6,410	D
New Hampshire	83,670	57,444	68.7	21,650	25.9	3,520	4.2	779	0.9	277	0.3	35,794	R
New Jersey	371,014	221,367	59.7	133,675	36.0	6,373	1.7	—		9,599	2.6	87,692	R
New York	1,423,876	819,838	57.6	551,369	38.7	18,950	1.3	16,052	1.1	17,667	1.2	268,469	R
North Carolina	331,337	155,122	46.8	174,408	52.6	578	0.2	635	0.2	594	0.2	19,286	D
North Dakota	47,391	26,335	55.6	20,686	43.6	—		358	0.8	12		5,649	R
Ohio	1,014,295	525,991	51.9	477,497	47.1	1,858	0.2	5,068	0.5	3,881	0.4	48,494	R
Oregon	97,335	48,700	50.0	46,739	48.0	977	1.0	919	0.9	—		1,961	R
Pennsylvania	1,194,355	728,300	61.0	433,228	36.3	11,000	0.9	19,274	1.6	2,553	0.2	295,072	R
Rhode Island	54,785	37,437	68.3	14,459	26.4	1,166	2.1	1,160	2.1	563	1.0	22,978	R
South Carolina	68,938	9,313	13.5	58,801	85.3	824	1.2	—		—		49,488	D
South Dakota	82,937	41,040	49.5	41,225	49.7	—		672	0.8	—		185	D
Tennessee	320,903	148,683	46.3	167,168	52.1	1,953	0.6	3,099	1.0	—		18,485	D
Texas	541,018	163,894	30.3	370,308	68.4	5,022	0.9	1,794	0.3	—		206,414	D
Utah	78,098	13,491	17.3	64,607	82.7	—		—		—		51,116	D
Vermont	63,568	51,127	80.4	10,367	16.3	1,341	2.1	733	1.2	—		40,760	R
Virginia	294,674	135,379	45.9	154,708	52.5	2,129	0.7	2,350	0.8	108		19,329	D
Washington	93,583	39,153	41.8	53,314	57.0	—		968	1.0	148	0.2	14,161	D
West Virginia	201,757	105,379	52.2	94,480	46.8	678	0.3	1,220	0.6	—		10,899	R
Wisconsin	447,409	268,135	59.9	165,523	37.0	4,584	1.0	7,507	1.7	1,660	0.4	102,612	R
Wyoming	21,067	10,072	47.8	10,862	51.6	—		133	0.6	—		790	D
Totals	13,935,738	7,108,480	51.0	6,511,495	46.7	133,435	1.0	125,072	0.9	57,256	0.4	596,985	R

P O P U L A R   V O T E

The 1896 presidential election took place in an atmosphere of national crisis. The economic system seemed to operate mainly to benefit the rich and it was now under attack. During 1893 and 1894, scattered jobless men formed into "armies" because of mass unemployment. The best known is Coxey's Army. Jacob S. Coxey, a wealthy Ohio quarry owner, paid for several hundred unemployed men to march to Washington and to present Congress with their demands. Soon, "armies" from all over the nation were said to be heading for Washington. President Grover Cleveland did not understand the seriousness of the root causes leading to this event. The Capitol police dispersed the "army" and arrested Coxey for trespassing.

In 1892, violence at the Carnegie steelworks near Homestead, Pennsylvania and in the mining community of Coeur d'Alene, Idaho were preludes to the bloody Pullman Strike of June–July 1894. George S. Pullman had refused to allow labor leader Eugene V. Debs to organize his workers. Their wages had been cut but the rent and the prices in stores in Pullman's company town, located near Chicago, were not. By late June, more than 120,000 railroad workers joined in a sympathy strike, paralyzing the nation. President Cleveland, against the advice of Illinois Governor John Peter Altgeld, ordered 14,000 soldiers to Chicago to break the strike. The union movement disintegrated. Debs was sentenced to jail. "Shall law and order prevail" asked one congressman," or shall mobacracy triumph?"

The so-called panic of 1893 lasted at least four years. By mid-1894, some 56 railroads with 30,000 miles of track had passed into receivership. Thousands of industrial plants had closed. At least 20 percent of the work force was unemployed. An estimated 2.5 million homeless men and women drifted the streets looking for nonexistent jobs. Terence V. Powderly, former head of the Knights of Labor, observed that "charity has been strained as it was never strained before, but still the cry for bread from starving throats is heard all over the land."

By 1896, farmers had become completely frustrated as government, both national and state, remained indifferent to their worsening predicament. The farmers had many problems including droughts, high interest rates, falling farm prices, insect plagues, and discriminatory railroad rates. The farmers became more bitter as Washington continued to ignore agricultural problems. Prices continued to decline and

debt continued to increase. "Send me to Washington," South Carolina's Benjamin Tillman yelled at frantic mobs, "and I'll stick my pitchfork into his [Cleveland's] old ribs!"

Although western agricultural protest movements date back to the 1860s, the aggressive Populists demanded immediate relief through direct political action in the 1890s. They carried their message to farm picnics, rural crossroads, and county fairs. Newspaper editor William Allen White recalled the Populist fervor during the 1894 congressional elections: "Far into the night the voices rose—women's voices, children's voices, the voices of old men, of youth and maidens, rose on the ebbing prairie breezes as the crusaders of the revolution rode home, praising the people's will as though it were God's will and cursing wealth for its iniquity."

In the 1894 congressional elections, Populist candidates had polled 1,471,590 votes, an increase of about 400,000 or 42 percent, over 1892. This outcome represented a dissatisfaction with both major parties. Populist spokesmen had preached an agrarian radicalism that shocked and appalled "respectable" groups in the East. In a speech typical of Populist campaign oratory, Mary Lease, a populist leader in Kansas, attacked Wall Street and said: "The people are at bay, let the bloodhounds of money who have dogged us thus far beware."

The 1896 presidential election revived political life in the United States. Not since the Civil War had people's emotions been so aroused either for or against an issue. Free silver became the great rallying cry—the free and unlimited coinage of silver at the ratio to gold of 16:1. Farmers believed that this would cause an inflation, creating higher farm prices and ending every agricultural inequality. In 1895, William Jennings Bryan, an Omaha editor and former congressman from Nebraska, predicted: "There is no question now that the campaign of 1896 will be fought on the money question between the capitalists of the Northeast and the rest of the people of the country."

The Democratic Convention met in Chicago on 7 July 1896. The party was bitterly divided. The platform repudiated the Cleveland administration. Cleveland firmly opposed free silver as "dangerous and reckless" even though one state convention after another had chosen delegates pledged to the silver crusade. It was silver—and silver alone—that brought the delegates to the point of hysteria. The uncompromising silver platform plank, adopted 628 to 301, indicated that the bimetallists controlled a majority of the delegates.

On the evening of 9 July, Bryan rose to defend the platform. Before he finished speaking, the assembled convention knew that they had found their new leader. The words of the 36-year-old Bryan thrilled the delegates: "You come to us and tell us that the great cities are in favor of the gold standard. We reply that the great cities rest upon our broad and fertile prairies. Burn down your cities and leave our farms, and your cities will spring up again as if by magic; but destroy our farms, and the grass will grow in the streets of every city in the country."

He delivered his memorable conclusion to a half-hysterical audience: "Having behind us the producing masses of this nation and the world, the laboring interests, and the toilers everywhere, we will answer their demand for a gold standard by saying to them: You shall not press down upon the brow of labor this crown of thorns—you shall not crucify mankind upon a cross of gold!"

Bryan was nominated for president on the fifth ballot. The forces of agrarian discontent had found a spokesman at long last. The Populist Party, assembled the following month, also nominated Bryan. Fusion with the Democrats virtually finished the Populists as a separate political party.

The Republican Convention chose William McKinley, governor of Ohio and a former congressman who had been chairman of the Ways and Means Committee that had drafted the high protective Tariff Act of 1890. Republicans embraced the gold standard and opposed the free coinage of silver. "We are unalterably opposed to every measure calculated to debase our currency," declared their platform. Although McKinley had supported pro-silver bills when he was in Congress, he now assured eastern Republicans of his complete acceptance of the gold plank. Thirty-four western convention delegates bolted from the convention and urged their followers to support Bryan. The issue between the parties was clearly drawn.

The 1896 presidential campaign became the most memorable and exciting since that of 1860. Bryan traveled more than 18,000 miles, making over 600 speeches in 29 states. The Democratic strategy attempted to unite the eastern worker with the agrarian masses. On some days, Bryan spoke to as many as 100,000 people. The "Great Commoner," as his followers affectionately called him, assaulted the "money power" and conveyed a message of hope. "Mr. Bryan stands for the people—as Lincoln did," commented the Topeka (Kansas) *Advocate*. Bryan, however, remained an outsider and a sectional candidate east of the Ohio River. He once referred to the East, and to New York City in particular, as "the enemy's country" that he intended to invade. Cleveland, the Democratic standard-bearer in the three preceding presidential elections, called the silverites "madmen and criminals."

McKinley remained at his home in Canton, Ohio, delivering talks to visiting delegations. Well-paid Republican speakers predicted that a Bryan victory would be followed by a reign of terror. Writers accused Bryan of being a demagogue, a traitor, an anarchist, and a communist. John P. Newman, the Methodist bishop of Omaha, criticized Bryan's "Cross of Gold" speech: "The crown of thorns was for the Savior's brow, and not for those who would overthrow the best government on earth."

McKinley received 271 electoral votes to Bryan's 176. In the popular vote column, the election was considerably closer. McKinley polled some 7 million votes to 6.5 million for Bryan. The Democrats carried no state north of the former Confederacy or east of the Mississippi River. A majority of the traditionally Republican farmers in the Midwest, especially in Iowa and Ohio, stayed with McKinley. Outside of the South, where maintaining White supremacy was the issue, Bryan's greatest success was among the prairie and Great Plains farmers. Most members of the non-agrarian middle class considered Bryan a threat to their property and savings. Industrial workers had difficulty in identifying with the silver issue. Also, factory owners had told them that "the whistle will not blow Wednesday morning" if Bryan was elected. "The issue [was] the single gold standard," observed historian Henry Adams, "and the majority at last declared itself, once and for all, in favor of a capitalistic system with all its necessary machinery. All one's friends, all one's best citizens, reformers, churches, colleges, educated classes, had joined the banks to force submission to capitalism; a submission long foreseen by the mere law of mass."

Election of 1900

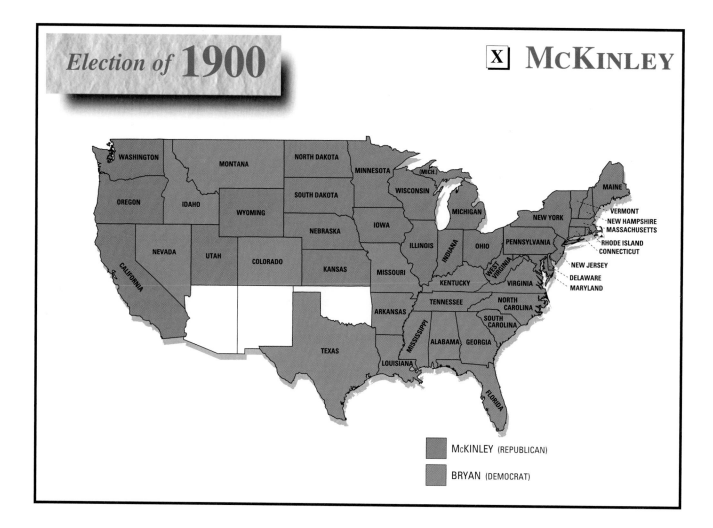

McKINLEY (REPUBLICAN)

BRYAN (DEMOCRAT)

States	Electoral Votes	McKinley	Bryan	States	Electoral Votes	McKinley	Bryan
Alabama	(11)	-	11	Nebraska	(8)	8	-
Arkansas	(8)	-	8	Nevada	(3)	-	3
California	(9)	9	-	New Hampshire	(4)	4	-
Colorado	(4)	-	4	New Jersey	(10)	10	-
Connecticut	(6)	6	-	New York	(36)	36	-
Delaware	(3)	3	-	North Carolina	(11)	-	11
Florida	(4)	-	4	North Dakota	(3)	3	-
Georgia	(13)	-	13	Ohio	(23)	23	-
Idaho	(3)	-	3	Oregon	(4)	4	-
Illinois	(24)	24	-	Pennsylvania	(32)	32	-
Indiana	(15)	15	-	Rhode Island	(4)	4	-
Iowa	(13)	13	-	South Carolina	(9)	-	9
Kansas	(10)	10	-	South Dakota	(4)	4	-
Kentucky	(13)	-	13	Tennessee	(12)	-	12
Louisiana	(8)	-	8	Texas	(15)	-	15
Maine	(6)	6	-	Utah	(3)	3	-
Maryland	(8)	8	-	Vermont	(4)	4	-
Massachusetts	(15)	15	-	Virginia	(12)	-	12
Michigan	(14)	14	-	Washington	(4)	4	-
Minnesota	(9)	9	-	West Virginia	(6)	6	-
Mississippi	(9)	-	9	Wisconsin	(12)	12	-
Missouri	(17)	-	17	Wyoming	(3)	3	-
Montana	(3)	-	3	**Totals**	**(447)**	**292**	**155**

E L E C T O R A L   V O T E

Election of 1900

STATE	TOTAL VOTE	WILLIAM McKINLEY (Republican)		WILLIAM J. BRYAN (Democrat)		JOHN G. WOOLEY (Prohibition)		EUGENE V. DEBS (Socialist)		OTHER		PLURALITY	
		Votes	%	Votes	%	Votes	%	Votes	%	Votes	%		
Alabama	159,692	55,612	34.8	97,129	60.8	2,763	1.7	—		4,188	2.6	41,517	D
Arkansas	127,966	44,800	35.0	81,242	63.5	584	0.5	—		1,340	1.0	36,442	D
California	302,318	164,755	54.5	124,985	41.3	5,024	1.7	—		7,554	2.5	39,770	R
Colorado	220,895	92,701	42.0	122,705	55.5	3,790	1.7	686	0.3	1,013	0.5	30,004	D
Connecticut	180,195	102,572	56.9	74,014	41.1	1,617	0.9	1,029	0.6	963	0.5	28,558	R
Delaware	41,989	22,535	53.7	18,852	44.9	546	1.3	56	0.1	—		3,683	R
Florida	39,649	7,355	18.6	28,273	71.3	2,244	5.7	634	1.6	1,143	2.9	20,918	D
Georgia	121,410	34,260	28.2	81,180	66.9	1,402	1.2	—		4,568	3.8	46,920	D
Idaho	57,984	27,198	46.9	29,484	50.8	857	1.5	—		445	0.8	2,286	R
Illinois	1,131,898	597,985	52.8	503,061	44.4	17,626	1.6	9,687	0.9	3,539	0.3	94,924	R
Indiana	664,094	336,063	50.6	309,584	46.6	13,718	2.1	2,374	0.4	2,355	0.4	26,479	R
Iowa	530,345	307,799	58.0	209,261	39.5	9,502	1.8	2,743	0.5	1,040	0.2	98,538	R
Kansas	353,766	185,955	52.6	162,601	46.0	3,605	1.0	1,605	0.5	—		23,354	R
Kentucky	468,265	227,132	48.5	235,126	50.2	2,890	0.6	766	0.2	2,351	0.5	7,994	D
Louisiana	67,906	14,234	21.0	53,668	79.0	—		—		4		39,434	D
Maine	105,693	65,412	61.9	36,822	34.8	2,581	2.4	878	0.8	—		28,590	R
Maryland	264,386	136,151	51.5	122,237	46.2	4,574	1.7	900	0.3	524	0.2	13,914	R
Massachusetts	414,804	238,866	57.6	156,997	37.8	6,202	1.5	9,607	2.3	3,132	0.8	81,869	R
Michigan	543,789	316,014	58.1	211,432	38.9	11,804	2.2	2,820	0.5	1,719	0.3	104,582	R
Minnesota	316,311	190,461	60.2	112,901	35.7	8,555	2.7	3,065	1.0	1,329	0.4	77,560	R
Mississippi	59,055	5,707	9.7	51,706	87.6	—		—		1,642	2.8	45,999	D
Missouri	683,658	314,092	45.9	351,922	51.5	5,965	0.9	6,139	0.9	5,540	0.8	37,830	D
Montana	63,856	25,409	39.8	37,311	58.4	306	0.5	711	1.1	119	0.2	11,902	D
Nebraska	241,430	121,835	50.5	114,013	47.2	3,655	1.5	823	0.3	1,104	0.5	7,822	R
Nevada	10,196	3,849	37.8	6,347	62.2	—		—		—		2,498	D
New Hampshire	92,364	54,799	59.3	35,489	38.4	1,270	1.4	790	0.9	16		19,310	R
New Jersey	401,050	221,707	55.3	164,808	41.1	7,183	1.8	4,609	1.1	2,743	0.7	56,899	R
New York	1,548,043	822,013	53.1	678,462	43.8	22,077	1.4	12,869	0.8	12,622	0.8	143,551	R
North Carolina	292,518	132,997	45.5	157,733	53.9	990	0.3	—		798	0.3	24,736	D
North Dakota	57,783	35,898	62.1	20,524	35.5	735	1.3	517	0.9	109	0.2	15,374	R
Ohio	1,040,073	543,918	52.3	474,882	45.7	10,203	1.0	4,847	0.5	6,223	0.6	69,036	R
Oregon	83,251	46,172	55.5	32,810	39.4	2,536	3.0	1,464	1.8	269	0.3	13,362	R
Pennsylvania	1,173,210	712,665	60.7	424,232	36.2	27,908	2.4	4,831	0.4	3,574	0.3	288,433	R
Rhode Island	56,548	33,784	59.7	19,812	35.0	1,529	2.7	—		1,423	2.5	13,972	R
South Carolina	50,698	3,525	7.0	47,173	93.0	—		—		—		43,648	D
South Dakota	96,169	54,574	56.7	39,538	41.1	1,541	1.6	176	0.2	340	0.4	15,036	R
Tennessee	273,860	123,108	45.0	145,240	53.0	3,844	1.4	346	0.1	1,322	0.5	22,132	D
Texas	424,334	131,174	30.9	267,945	63.1	2,642	0.6	1,846	0.4	20,727	4.9	136,771	D
Utah	93,071	47,089	50.6	44,949	48.3	205	0.2	717	0.8	111	0.1	2,140	R
Vermont	56,212	42,569	75.7	12,849	22.9	383	0.7	39	0.1	372	0.7	29,720	R
Virginia	264,208	115,769	43.8	146,079	55.3	2,130	0.8	—		230	0.1	30,310	D
Washington	107,523	57,455	53.4	44,833	41.7	2,363	2.2	2,006	1.9	866	0.8	12,622	R
West Virginia	220,796	119,829	54.3	98,807	44.8	1,628	0.7	286	0.1	246	0.1	21,022	R
Wisconsin	442,501	265,760	60.1	159,163	36.0	10,027	2.3	7,048	1.6	503	0.1	106,597	R
Wyoming	24,708	14,482	58.6	10,164	41.1	—		21	0.1	41	0.2	4,318	R
Totals	13,970,470	7,218,039	51.7	6,358,345	45.5	209,004	1.5	86,935	0.6	98,147	0.7	859,694	R

P O P U L A R   V O T E

The principal issue in the 1900 presidential election was a moral one. The issue that most divided the parties was imperialism. The last two years of the nineteenth century were a major turning point in U.S. history. Within a short time, the United States had acquired Hawaii and received part of Samoa through legislation, and obtained Cuba, Puerto Rico, Guam, and the Philippine Islands by cession from Spain as a result of the Spanish-American War. Until this time, the new lands acquired, except for Alaska (1867), shared common boundaries. They were places for settlement as Americans moved westward across the continent. However, the new possessions were to be held as territories or colonies with little chance they would ever be used for settlement or become states.

By 1899, the United States was suppressing an independence movement in the Philippines with armed force. Ironically, the Filipino nationalist leader had been inspired by the Declaration of Independence. Anti-imperialists argued against acquiring colonies without the consent of the governed. They maintained that the Constitution did not provide for the acquisition of extraterritorial possessions and rule over peoples without their consent.

The new expansion represented commercial imperialism. The United States was producing more than the domestic market could absorb at profitable prices, and new markets were essential. American industries also needed foreign raw materials and cheap labor. Investments overseas began to soar in 1900. Military bases in these new acquisitions protected the international trade routes of the United States and suppressed local nationalistic uprisings. The 1897 catalogue of Sears Roebuck listed more than 10,000 items for sale. With one exception, Cuban cigars, every item was made in American factories. By 1910, the Sears Company boasted: "Our trade reaches around the world." The United States, the world's leading democratic nation, had become one of the world's leading imperialist powers.

Thomas Jefferson's dream of a nation composed of independent self-sufficient farmers had been replaced by an extremely different economic system. Between 1860 and 1890, the non-agrarian work force grew by 300 percent. By 1890, more than 4.6 million Americans were working in factories; another 3 million were divided equally between the transportation and construction industries. A ten-hour work day and a six-day work week were almost standard.

The 10 million immigrants who arrived between 1870 and 1890 added to the rapidly growing labor force. Skilled craftsmen slowly faded away. Commercial capitalism rapidly had created a new class of people—the industrial worker.

The movement of population between 1860 and 1900 was from the farm to the cities. In 1860, one out of six Americans lived in a city; by 1900, it had changed to one out of three. The population of New York City was 1.2 million; by 1900, it had grown to more than 3 million. By 1910, it approached 5 million. During the same period, the population of Philadelphia grew from 560,000 to over 1.5 million. In 1831, Chicago was a muddy trading post with 12 families. At the time of the Civil War, 100,000 people lived there. By 1900 the population had leaped to nearly 2 million, making it the second largest city in the United States.

William McKinley had taken office on 4 March 1897. Within four months, the Republican controlled Congress, and the President signed the Dingley Tariff. It raised rates to a new high, averaging 57 percent, effectively insulating U.S. industry against foreign competition. The Republican motto became "Protection for American Industries." Good harvests and rising prices brought relief to farmers. Republicans credited their policies for the return of prosperity. Their 1900 campaign was: "The Full Dinner Pail."

McKinley defended the overseas empire by saying it was God's will. There was nothing else for the nation to do but "to take them all, and to educate the Filipinos, and to uplift and civilize and Christianize them, and by God's grace do the very best we can by them as our fellowmen for whom Christ also died." The Republicans, meeting in Philadelphia, on 19 June 1900, renominated William McKinley. At his suggestion, the party chose 41-year-old Theodore Roosevelt as his vice presidential running mate to replace Garret Hobart who had died in 1899. In 1898, Roosevelt had resigned as assistant secretary of the navy to raise his own regiment (the Rough Riders) in the Spanish-American War. He had led his forces up San Juan Hill (Cuba) in a well-publicized victory. Roosevelt, elected governor of New York in 1898, seemed the perfect spokesman to defend McKinley's decision to annex the Philippine Islands and to campaign for American overseas expansion.

The Democrats met in Kansas City 10 days after the Republicans adjourned. William Jennings Bryan was renominated and former Vice President Adlai E. Stevenson of

Illinois was chosen as his running mate. The 1900 Democratic platform differed with McKinley regarding imperialism. It stated: "All governments instituted among men derive their just power from the consent of the governed; that any government not based upon the consent of the governed is a tyranny; to impose upon any people a government of force is to substitute the methods of imperialism for those of a republic."

Roosevelt called this Democratic platform plank "a policy of infamy," a stand "for lawlessness and disorder; for dishonesty and dishonor, for license and disaster at home, and cowardly shrinking from duty abroad." However, this plank attracted many supporters who spoke against imperialism during the 1900 campaign. Edwin L. Godkin, editor of *The Nation,* and Samuel Bowles of the *Springfield Republican* wrote scathing editorials against McKinley's policies. Samuel Gompers, president of the American Federation of Labor, lectured against annexation of foreign lands. Andrew Carnegie financed the Anti-Imperialist League. Mark Twain charged McKinley with "playing the European game of imperialism." He suggested that the flag of the United States be changed with "the white stripes painted black and the stars replaced by the skull and cross bones." Overseas expansion was the most important issue between the two parties.

However, the issue was more philosophical than it was the key reason for supporting one party over another. In the words of the *Literary Digest:* "Democrats of the East and South disagree with the Democrats of the West, and the Republicans of the West disagree with the Republicans of the East." Mary Lease, the populist orator from Kansas in 1896, supported McKinley in 1900 because "this anti-expansion . . . policy of the Democratic Party presents the most unpatriotic, un-American, unwise issue from a purely material point of view that has ever come before the people of this country." Bryan asked Carnegie not to support him publicly: "You and I agree in opposing militarism and imperialism, but when these questions are settled we may find ourselves upon opposite sides as heretofore."

Another issue dividing the parties was silver. Until 1873, the United States issued paper currency based upon the treasury's holdings of gold and silver at the ratio of 16 parts

of silver to one part of gold: the "16:1 ratio." In 1873 , the United States went on a gold standard whereby paper currency was backed only by gold. Subsequently, large silver deposits were discovered in Nevada. Bryan and his supporters wanted the government to resume the free, that is the unlimited, coinage of silver at the old ratio of 16:1. Since the ratio had been disrupted by new mineral discoveries, an inflation would be created, resulting in higher crop prices.

Joseph Pulitzer, editor of the New York *World,* urged Bryan "to keep silent on Silver east of the Blue Ridge mountains." Newspaper publisher William Randolph Hearst, then a Democrat, advised him: "My people everywhere from the Atlantic to the Pacific tell me there is no free silver sentiment." The Democratic platform framing committee adopted the free silver plank by one vote. The issue still remained a passionate one for Bryan, the "Great Commoner," and for so many of his loyal followers. He sincerely believed that anti-imperialism was the perfect companion for free silver and that supporters of each issue, linked together, would elect him.

Bryan's determination to "stand where I stood" on the silver issue seemed puzzling. By 1898, world gold production had doubled that of 1890. The discovery of gold in the Klondike region of Alaska helped the money supply, virtually eliminating the free silver issue. The free and unlimited coinage of silver at the 16:1 ratio with gold could not be supported by precious metal production tables. However, Bryan refused to drop silver as a political issue. Republican House Speaker Thomas B. Reed, who resigned from Congress in protest against McKinley's annexation policies, remarked: "Bryan had rather be wrong than president."

Bryan's defeat was a crushing one. McKinley won 21 more electoral votes than he had in 1896, for a total of 292 electoral votes to Bryan's 155. McKinley received 51.7 percent of the popular vote to Bryan's 45.5 percent. Voter turnout slipped to 71.6 percent compared with 78.3 percent four years earlier. Bryan won the border and southern states plus Montana, Idaho, Nevada, and Colorado. McKinley carried the rest of the Great Plains states including Nebraska, Bryan's home state. Voters had sent a message that they agreed with the Republican policies that had brought prosperity. They chose "The Full Dinner Pail."

Election of 1904

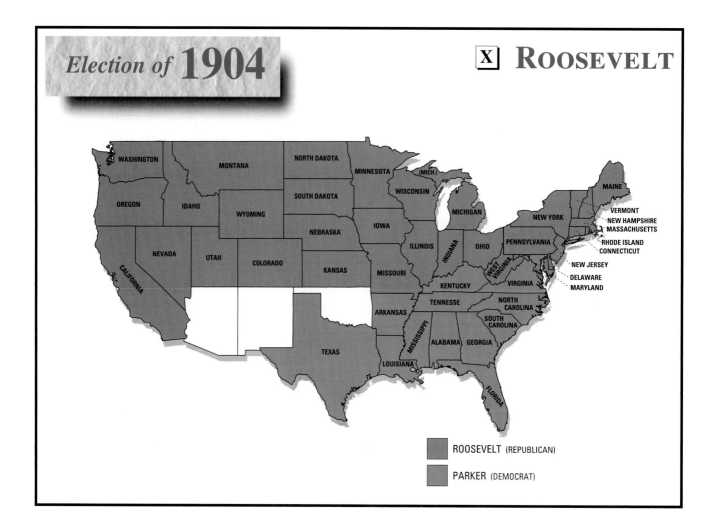

ROOSEVELT (REPUBLICAN)

PARKER (DEMOCRAT)

States	Electoral Votes	Roosevelt	Parker	States	Electoral Votes	Roosevelt	Parker
Alabama	(11)	-	11	Nebraska	(8)	8	-
Arkansas	(9)	-	9	Nevada	(3)	3	-
California	(10)	10	-	New Hampshire	(4)	4	-
Colorado	(5)	5	-	New Jersey	(12)	12	-
Connecticut	(7)	7	-	New York	(39)	39	-
Delaware	(3)	3	-	North Carolina	(12)	-	12
Florida	(5)	-	5	North Dakota	(4)	4	-
Georgia	(13)	-	13	Ohio	(23)	23	-
Idaho	(3)	3	-	Oregon	(4)	4	-
Illinois	(27)	27	-	Pennsylvania	(34)	34	-
Indiana	(15)	15	-	Rhode Island	(4)	4	-
Iowa	(13)	13	-	South Carolina	(9)	-	9
Kansas	(10)	10	-	South Dakota	(4)	4	-
Kentucky	(13)	-	13	Tennessee	(12)	-	12
Louisiana	(9)	-	9	Texas	(18)	-	18
Maine	(6)	6	-	Utah	(3)	3	-
Maryland	(8)	1	7	Vermont	(4)	4	-
Massachusetts	(16)	16	-	Virginia	(12)	-	12
Michigan	(14)	14	-	Washington	(5)	5	-
Minnesota	(11)	11	-	West Virginia	(7)	7	-
Mississippi	(10)	-	10	Wisconsin	(13)	13	-
Missouri	(18)	18	-	Wyoming	(3)	3	-
Montana	(3)	3	-	**Totals**	**(476)**	**336**	**140**

ELECTORAL VOTE

Election of 1904

STATE	TOTAL VOTE	THEODORE ROOSEVELT (Republican)		ALTON B. PARKER (Democrat)		EUGENE V. DEBS (Socialist)		SILAS C. SWALLOW (Prohibition)		OTHER		PLURALITY	
		Votes	%	Votes	%	Votes	%	Votes	%	Votes	%		
Alabama	108,785	22,472	20.7	79,797	73.4	853	0.8	612	0.6	5,051	4.6	57,325	D
Arkansas	116,328	46,760	40.2	64,434	55.4	1,816	1.6	992	0.9	2,326	2.0	17,674	D
California	331,768	205,226	61.9	89,294	26.9	29,535	8.9	7,380	2.2	333	0.1	115,932	R
Colorado	243,667	134,661	55.3	100,105	41.1	4,304	1.8	3,438	1.4	1,159	0.5	34,556	R
Connecticut	191,136	111,089	58.1	72,909	38.1	4,543	2.4	1,506	0.8	1,089	0.6	38,180	R
Delaware	43,856	23,705	54.1	19,347	44.1	146	0.3	607	1.4	51	0.1	4,358	R
Florida	38,705	8,314	21.5	26,449	68.3	2,337	6.0	—		1,605	4.1	18,135	D
Georgia	130,986	24,004	18.3	83,466	63.7	196	0.1	685	0.5	22,635	17.3	59,462	D
Idaho	72,577	47,783	65.8	18,480	25.5	4,949	6.8	1,013	1.4	352	0.5	29,303	R
Illinois	1,076,495	632,645	58.8	327,606	30.4	69,225	6.4	34,770	3.2	12,249	1.1	305,039	R
Indiana	682,206	368,289	54.0	274,356	40.2	12,023	1.8	23,496	3.4	4,042	0.6	93,933	R
Iowa	485,703	307,907	63.4	149,141	30.7	14,847	3.1	11,601	2.4	2,207	0.5	158,766	R
Kansas	329,047	213,455	64.9	86,164	26.2	15,869	4.8	7,306	2.2	6,253	1.9	127,291	R
Kentucky	435,946	205,457	47.1	217,170	49.8	3,599	0.8	6,603	1.5	3,117	0.7	11,713	D
Louisiana	53,908	5,205	9.7	47,708	88.5	995	1.8	—		—		42,503	D
Maine	97,023	65,432	67.4	27,642	28.5	2,102	2.2	1,510	1.6	337	0.3	37,790	R
Maryland	224,229	109,497	48.8	109,446	48.8	2,247	1.0	3,034	1.4	5		51	R
Massachusetts	445,100	257,813	57.9	165,746	37.2	13,604	3.1	4,279	1.0	3,658	0.8	92,067	R
Michigan	520,443	361,863	69.5	134,163	25.8	8,942	1.7	13,312	2.6	2,163	0.4	227,700	R
Minnesota	292,860	216,651	74.0	55,187	18.8	11,692	4.0	6,253	2.1	3,077	1.1	161,464	R
Mississippi	58,721	3,280	5.6	53,480	91.1	462	0.8	—		1,499	2.6	50,200	D
Missouri	643,861	321,449	49.9	296,312	46.0	13,009	2.0	7,191	1.1	5,900	0.9	25,137	R
Montana	63,568	33,994	53.5	21,816	34.3	5,675	8.9	339	0.5	1,744	2.7	12,178	R
Nebraska	225,732	138,558	61.4	52,921	23.4	7,412	3.3	6,323	2.8	20,518	9.1	85,637	R
Nevada	12,115	6,864	56.7	3,982	32.9	925	7.6	—		344	2.8	2,882	R
New Hampshire	90,151	54,157	60.1	34,071	37.8	1,090	1.2	750	0.8	83	0.1	20,086	R
New Jersey	432,247	245,164	56.7	164,566	38.1	9,587	2.2	6,845	1.6	6,085	1.4	80,598	R
New York	1,617,765	859,533	53.1	683,981	42.3	36,883	2.3	20,787	1.3	16,581	1.0	175,552	R
North Carolina	207,818	82,442	39.7	124,091	59.7	124	0.1	342	0.2	819	0.4	41,649	D
North Dakota	70,014	52,595	75.1	14,273	20.4	2,009	2.9	1,137	1.6	—		38,322	R
Ohio	1,004,395	600,095	59.7	344,674	34.3	36,260	3.6	19,339	1.9	4,027	0.4	255,421	R
Oregon	89,656	60,309	67.3	17,327	19.3	7,479	8.3	3,795	4.2	746	0.8	42,982	R
Pennsylvania	1,236,738	840,949	68.0	337,998	27.3	21,863	1.8	33,717	2.7	2,211	0.2	502,951	R
Rhode Island	68,656	41,605	60.6	24,839	36.2	956	1.4	768	1.1	488	0.7	16,766	R
South Carolina	55,890	2,570	4.6	53,320	95.4	—		—		—		50,750	D
South Dakota	101,395	72,083	71.1	21,969	21.7	3,138	3.1	2,965	2.9	1,240	1.2	50,114	R
Tennessee	242,750	105,363	43.4	131,653	54.2	1,354	0.6	1,889	0.8	2,491	1.0	26,290	D
Texas	233,609	51,307	22.0	167,088	71.5	2,788	1.2	3,933	1.7	8,493	3.6	115,781	D
Utah	101,626	62,446	61.4	33,413	32.9	5,767	5.7	—		—		29,033	R
Vermont	51,888	40,459	78.0	9,777	18.8	859	1.7	792	1.5	1		30,682	R
Virginia	130,410	48,180	36.9	80,649	61.8	202	0.2	1,379	1.1	—		32,469	D
Washington	145,151	101,540	70.0	28,098	19.4	10,023	6.9	3,229	2.2	2,261	1.6	73,442	R
West Virginia	239,986	132,620	55.3	100,855	42.0	1,573	0.7	4,599	1.9	339	0.1	31,765	R
Wisconsin	443,440	280,314	63.2	124,205	28.0	28,240	6.4	9,872	2.2	809	0.2	156,109	R
Wyoming	30,614	20,489	66.9	8,930	29.2	987	3.2	208	0.7	—		11,559	R
Totals	**13,518,964**	**7,626,593**	**56.4**	**5,082,898**	**37.6**	**402,489**	**3.0**	**258,596**	**1.9**	**148,388**	**1.1**	**2,543,695**	**R**

POPULAR VOTE

The presidential election of 1904 can be summarized in two words: Theodore Roosevelt. No other election in U.S. history has revolved so completely around the personality of one man. Theodore Roosevelt, not quite 43, became the youngest president of the United States after the assassination of President William McKinley in September 1901. Rancher, soldier, naturalist, musician, scholar, plus a dozen other things, Roosevelt had served as a member of the New York State Assembly and then as a civil service commissioner under Presidents Benjamin Harrison and Grover Cleveland. In both capacities, he had identified himself with the reform faction of the Republican Party. He had also written the four-volume *Winning of the West* (1894–1896).

Theodore Roosevelt was born in 1858 in New York City. His mother and father had inherited wealth and were part of "fashionable society." Roosevelt, a sickly boy, had led a sheltered childhood. He later taught himself to ride a horse, to shoot a rifle, and to box, although handicapped by chronic asthma and poor eyesight. He graduated Phi Beta Kappa from Harvard College and then wrote *The Naval War of 1812* (1882), still considered a definitive study. He dreaded that he might become one of "these small men who do most of the history teaching in the colleges." Fortunately for him, a local Republican boss needed a "respectable" candidate for a New York City assembly district. In the Assembly, his seniors found him irritating, but Roosevelt became wonderful copy for reporters.

In 1897, President McKinley appointed Roosevelt assistant secretary of the navy. When the Spanish-American War began, he organized the famous Rough Riders and fought his way to national fame at San Juan Hill in Cuba. He came home a war hero, and now was known as "Teddy" to everybody, in spite of his intense dislike of the nickname.

Roosevelt was elected governor of New York in 1898. Although his administration was a popular one, Roosevelt's independence of patronage caused Republican bosses to want him out of state politics. They decided to "kick Roosevelt upstairs" into the vice presidency. Mark Hanna, chairman of the Republican National Committee, warned them that Roosevelt's 1900 election would mean that there was "only one life between this madman and the White House." Roosevelt reluctantly accepted the nomination, saying, "I would greatly rather be anything else."

His first statement as president gave comfort, at least temporarily, to Republican conservatives: "I wish to say that it shall be my aim to continue, absolutely unbroken, the policy of President McKinley for the peace, the prosperity, and the honor of our beloved country." A bitter Mark Hanna remarked: "I told William McKinley it was a mistake to nominate that wild man at Philadelphia. I asked him if he realized what would happen if he should die. Now look, that damned cowboy is President of the United States."

The days of the post–Civil War docile president had ended. Roosevelt, with his inexhaustible energy and tremendous personal magnetism, brought a new energy to the White House from the moment he, his wife, and six children moved in. University men regarded him as one of them because of his many superior works of history. Westerners identified with his ranching experience and his cowboy adventures. Southerners recalled that his mother's family had fought for the Confederacy. People everywhere considered him as a democratic American whose every action showed good sportsmanship.

The public soon became intrigued with their new president. Cartoonists were never at a loss for ideas, and journalists predicted his collapse unless he slowed his pace. Roosevelt was always at the center of action. "When Theodore attends a wedding," a relative sighed, "he wants to be the bride, and when he attends a funeral he wants to be the corpse." Beneath his charm, however, was a strong national leader who dramatized the immense powers connected with his office.

The President demanded a "square deal" for all Americans and pledged enforcement of existing anti-trust laws and stricter supervision of big business. Hailed as "the trust-buster," Roosevelt lashed out at the "malefactors of great wealth." He stated: "We do not wish to destroy corporations but we do wish to make them subserve the public good." Roosevelt's most enduring contribution to future generations may have been his support of many conservation initiatives. He withdrew millions of acres of government forest lands from public sale. He also captured the popular fancy by calling for, among other things, the construction of a canal across Central America, a larger navy and a better army, increased pensions for Civil War veterans through liberalized eligibility requirements, extension of civil service, an assertive foreign policy, and stricter regulation regarding corporate mergers.

Roosevelt became a symbol of the progressive spirit to millions of Americans. Using what he called a "bully pulpit," he dramatized popular issues, such as anti-trust legislation, pure food and drug laws, and labor reform. The President made reform movements seem respectable. Reformer Frances Perkins wrote, "We were all . . . under his spell. . . . He had recommended to the people Jacob Riis's book *How the Other Half Lives*. I had read it, and . . . straightaway felt that the pursuit of social justice would be my vocation."

Roosevelt's popularity soared. He made an unprecedented campaign tour of New England and the Midwest to help congressional candidates in the 1902 elections. His railroad journey the following year to a reunion of the Rough Riders at the Grand Canyon became a triumphal trip across the country. However, the President's use of his executive power and patronage infuriated business leaders who traditionally supported the Republican Party. They never seemed to know which industry he would attack next. "It really seems hard," complained railroad baron James J. Hill, "that we should be compelled to fight for our lives against . . . political adventurers."

Roosevelt controlled the Republican Convention which met in Chicago on 21 June 1904. He chose the temporary and permanent chairmen, named the nominating and secondary speakers—and then told them what to say. Senator Charles W. Fairbanks of Indiana was selected for vice president. The convention was a formality. Leaders had to sustain interest by creating a debate over the eligibility of the Hawaiian delegation. Roosevelt felt insecure about being elected in his own right. "The criminal rich and the foul rich," he exclaimed more than once, "will do all they can to beat me." His progressive reforms, he thought, might very well cost him the election. Roosevelt explained to his friend Cecil Spring-Rice that the presidency "tends to put a premium on a man's keeping out of trouble rather than upon his accomplishing results."

The Democrats remained divided between the supporters of William Jennings Bryan and the rest of the party. The "Great Commoner" unsuccessfully demanded that the 1904 platform reaffirm the free silver and anti-imperialist planks of 1896 and 1900. "The folks down South like you," protested one delegate to the St. Louis convention "but they are tired of having their mail handed them by a Republican." Bryan blocked the nomination of newspaper publisher William Randolph Hearst, now a congressman. Hearst advocated an eight-hour work day, a graduated income tax, and government ownership of the railroads. He would have been the presidential nominee but Bryan refused his endorsement because of Hearst's support of imperialism.

The disheartened convention finally settled on Alton B. Parker, chief judge of the New York State Court of Appeals, whose dream was to be appointed to the United States Supreme Court. The platform was a cautious compromise that omitted the silver plank because Parker refused to run if it were included. Former President Grover Cleveland felt that Parker, a "clean, decent man," would not be a strong candidate because he lacked charisma. The Democrats nominated 81-year-old Henry G. Davis, a former senator from West Virginia, for vice president; they hoped Davis would make a generous contribution to the party from his personal fortune, and he did.

The campaign was not exciting. Roosevelt remained at his home in Sagamore Hill, New York. Parker attempted a front porch type campaign from his home on the Hudson River but very few Democrats came to see him. In October, Bryan began to campaign for Parker, shrugging off his earlier remark about the judge's "absolute unfitness" to be president. He attacked Roosevelt's "militarism" and "imperialism," but the election outcome was a foregone conclusion. There is an impression, observed Joseph Pulitzer's New York *World*, "that we are to elect a President next November. It is a mistake . . . We are to elect a czar."

Roosevelt won a decisive victory, 336 electoral votes to Parker's 140. He carried every state outside of the South except the border states of Kentucky and Maryland. (A later recount in Maryland gave the state to Roosevelt with a 51-vote plurality, and he lost in Kentucky by 11,713 votes out of 435,946 cast.) Roosevelt received 56.4 percent of the popular vote to Parker's 37.6 percent. The New York *Sun*, which had supported Parker, admitted Roosevelt's election was "one of the most illustrious personal triumphs in all political history." As the results were coming in, Roosevelt exclaimed to his wife that he was "no longer a political accident."

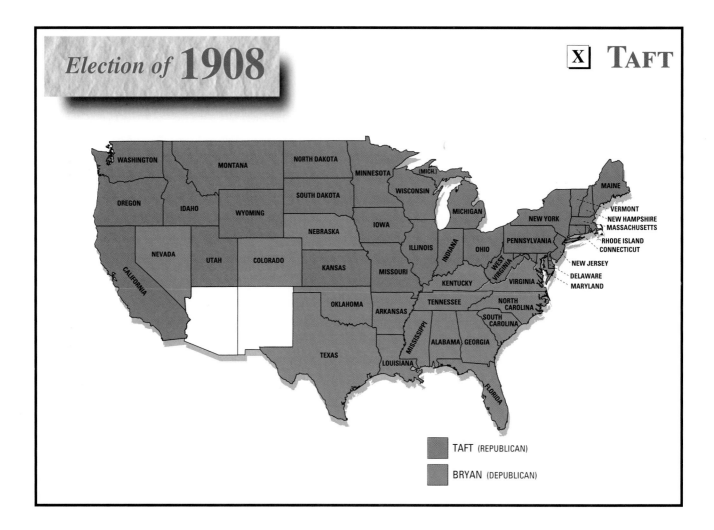

TAFT (REPUBLICAN)

BRYAN (DEPUBLICAN)

States	Electoral Votes	Taft	Bryan	States	Electoral Votes	Taft	Bryan
Alabama	(11)	-	11	Nebraska	(8)	-	8
Arkansas	(9)	-	9	Nevada	(3)	-	3
California	(10)	10	-	New Hampshire	(4)	4	-
Colorado	(5)	-	5	New Jersey	(12)	12	-
Connecticut	(7)	7	-	New York	(39)	39	-
Delaware	(3)	3	-	North Carolina	(12)	-	12
Florida	(5)	-	5	North Dakota	(4)	4	-
Georgia	(13)	-	13	Ohio	(23)	23	-
Idaho	(3)	3	-	Oklahoma	(7)	-	7
Illinois	(27)	27	-	Oregon	(4)	4	-
Indiana	(15)	15	-	Pennsylvania	(34)	34	-
Iowa	(13)	13	-	Rhode Island	(4)	4	-
Kansas	(10)	10	-	South Carolina	(9)	-	9
Kentucky	(13)	-	13	South Dakota	(4)	4	-
Louisiana	(9)	-	9	Tennessee	(12)	-	12
Maine	(6)	6	-	Texas	(18)	-	18
Maryland	(8)	2	6	Utah	(3)	3	-
Massachusetts	(16)	16	-	Vermont	(4)	4	-
Michigan	(14)	14	-	Virginia	(12)	-	12
Minnesota	(11)	11	-	Washington	(5)	5	-
Mississippi	(10)	-	10	West Virginia	(7)	7	-
Missouri	(18)	18	-	Wisconsin	(13)	13	-
Montana	(3)	3	-	Wyoming	(3)	3	-
				Totals	**(483)**	**321**	**162**

ELECTORAL VOTE

Election of 1908

STATE	TOTAL VOTE	WILLIAM H. TAFT (Republican)		WILLIAM J. BRYAN (Democrat)		EUGENE V. DEBS (Socialist)		EUGENE W. CHAFIN (Prohibition)		OTHER		PLURALITY	
		Votes	%	Votes	%	Votes	%	Votes	%	Votes	%		
Alabama	105,152	25,561	24.3	74,391	70.7	1,450	1.4	690	0.7	3,060	2.9	48,830	D
Arkansas	151,845	56,684	37.3	87,020	57.3	5,842	3.8	1,026	0.7	1,273	0.8	30,336	D
California	386,625	214,398	55.5	127,492	33.0	28,659	7.4	11,770	3.0	4,306	1.1	86,906	R
Colorado	263,858	123,693	46.9	126,644	48.0	7,960	3.0	5,559	2.1	2		2,951	D
Connecticut	189,903	112,815	59.4	68,255	35.9	5,113	2.7	2,380	1.3	1,340	0.7	44,560	R
Delaware	48,007	25,014	52.1	22,055	45.9	239	0.5	670	1.4	29	0.1	2,959	R
Florida	49,360	10,654	21.6	31,104	63.0	3,747	7.6	1,356	2.7	2,499	5.1	20,450	D
Georgia	132,504	41,355	31.2	72,350	54.6	584	0.4	1,452	1.1	16,763	12.7	30,995	D
Idaho	97,293	52,621	54.1	36,162	37.2	6,400	6.6	1,986	2.0	124	0.1	16,459	R
Illinois	1,155,254	629,932	54.5	450,810	39.0	34,711	3.0	29,364	2.5	10,437	0.9	179,122	R
Indiana	721,117	348,993	48.4	338,262	46.9	13,476	1.9	18,036	2.5	2,350	0.3	10,731	R
Iowa	494,770	275,210	55.6	200,771	40.6	8,287	1.7	9,837	2.0	665	0.1	74,439	R
Kansas	376,043	197,316	52.5	161,209	42.9	12,420	3.3	5,030	1.3	68		36,107	R
Kentucky	490,719	235,711	48.0	244,092	49.7	4,093	0.8	5,885	1.2	938	0.2	8,381	D
Louisiana	75,117	8,958	11.9	63,568	84.6	2,514	3.3	—		77	0.1	54,610	D
Maine	106,335	66,987	63.0	35,403	33.3	1,758	1.7	1,487	1.4	700	0.7	31,584	R
Maryland	238,531	116,513	48.8	115,908	48.6	2,323	1.0	3,302	1.4	485	0.2	605	R
Massachusetts	456,905	265,966	58.2	155,533	34.0	10,778	2.4	4,373	1.0	20,255	4.4	110,433	R
Michigan	538,124	333,313	61.9	174,619	32.4	11,527	2.1	16,785	3.1	1,880	0.3	158,694	R
Minnesota	330,254	195,843	59.3	109,401	33.1	14,472	4.4	10,114	3.1	424	0.1	86,442	R
Mississippi	66,904	4,363	6.5	60,287	90.1	978	1.5	—		1,276	1.9	55,924	D
Missouri	715,841	347,203	48.5	346,574	48.4	15,431	2.2	4,209	0.6	2,424	0.3	629	R
Montana	69,233	32,471	46.9	29,511	42.6	5,920	8.6	838	1.2	493	0.7	2,960	R
Nebraska	266,799	126,997	47.6	131,099	49.1	3,524	1.3	5,179	1.9	—		4,102	D
Nevada	24,526	10,775	43.9	11,212	45.7	2,103	8.6	—		436	1.8	437	D
New Hampshire	89,595	53,144	59.3	33,655	37.6	1,299	1.4	905	1.0	592	0.7	19,489	R
New Jersey	467,111	265,298	56.8	182,522	39.1	10,249	2.2	4,930	1.1	4,112	0.9	82,776	R
New York	1,638,350	870,070	53.1	667,468	40.7	38,451	2.3	22,667	1.4	39,694	2.4	202,602	R
North Carolina	252,554	114,887	45.5	136,928	54.2	372	0.1	354	0.1	13		22,041	D
North Dakota	94,524	57,680	61.0	32,884	34.8	2,421	2.6	1,496	1.6	43		24,796	R
Ohio	1,121,552	572,312	51.0	502,721	44.8	33,795	3.0	11,402	1.0	1,322	0.1	69,591	R
Oklahoma	254,260	110,473	43.4	122,362	48.1	21,425	8.4	—				11,889	D
Oregon	110,539	62,454	56.5	37,792	34.2	7,322	6.6	2,682	2.4	289	0.3	24,662	R
Pennvylvania	1,267,450	745,779	58.8	448,782	35.4	33,914	2.7	36,694	2.9	2,281	0.2	296,997	R
Rhode Island	72,317	43,942	60.8	24,706	34.2	1,365	1.9	1,016	1.4	1,288	1.8	19,236	R
South Carolina	66,379	3,945	5.9	62,288	93.8	100	0.2	—		46	0.1	58,343	D
South Dakota	114,775	67,536	58.8	40,266	35.1	2,846	2.5	4,039	3.5	88	0.1	27,270	R
Tennessee	257,180	117,977	45.9	135,608	52.7	1,870	0.7	301	0.1	1,424	0.6	17,631	D
Texas	292,913	65,605	22.4	216,662	74.0	7,779	2.7	1,626	0.6	1,241	0.4	151,057	D
Utah	108,757	61,165	56.2	42,610	39.2	4,890	4.5	—		92	0.1	18,555	R
Vermont	52,680	39,552	75.1	11,496	21.8	—		799	1.5	833	1.6	28,056	R
Virginia	137,065	52,572	38.4	82,946	60.5	255	0.2	1,111	0.8	181	0.1	30,374	D
Washington	183,570	106,062	57.8	58,383	31.8	14,177	7.7	4,700	2.6	248	0.1	47,679	R
West Virginia	258,098	137,869	53.4	111,410	43.2	3,679	1.4	5,140	2.0	—		26,459	R
Wisconsin	454,438	247,744	54.5	166,662	36.7	28,147	6.2	11,565	2.5	320	0.1	81,082	R
Wyoming	37,608	20,846	55.4	14,918	39.7	1,715	4.6	66	0.2	63	0.2	5,928	R
Totals	14,882,734	7,676,258	51.6	6,406,801	43.0	420,380	2.8	252,821	1.7	126,474	0.8	1,269,457	R

The presidential election of 1908 was an endorsement of Theodore Roosevelt's eight years in the White House. Although Roosevelt easily could have been renominated, he had declared in 1904 that "under no circumstances" would he be a candidate to succeed himself. Theodore Roosevelt's presidency ranks as one of the most outstanding of the twentieth century. He had vigorously asserted executive leadership. "Never sit still," Roosevelt said, "get action, do things . . . take a place wherever you are and be somebody."

Roosevelt's years in the White House corresponded with the transformation of the United States from an agrarian to an industrial nation. By 1900, the United States had surpassed Great Britain to become the world's leading manufacturing power. Between 1900 and 1909 automobile output had increased some 3,500 percent. There was a corresponding increase in the demand for steel, rubber, and petroleum products. These increases in material production were accompanied by an array of social problems inherent in an industrial society. The progressive leaders believed that the nation's great democratic heritage could be adjusted to the hard facts of the new age.

Roosevelt's administrations helped shape the idea of a positive state where the national government assumes a responsibility to correct the economic and social problems created by the industrial revolution. "Under this interpretation of executive power," wrote Roosevelt, "I did and caused to be done many things not previously done by the President and the heads of departments. I did not usurp power, but I did greatly broaden the use of executive power. In other words, I acted for the public welfare, I acted for the common well-being of all our people." It remained to be seen whether his successor could continue in this direction.

Roosevelt chose Secretary of War William Howard Taft to be the 1908 Republican nominee. They had known and trusted each other for many years. Roosevelt and Taft made an excellent team. Taft's easy-going conservatism counteracted Roosevelt's impulsive qualities. Taft became a close adviser, in effect, the "trouble shooter" of the administration. He took on the task of starting the actual construction of the Panama Canal and hurried to the Canal Zone for that purpose. When Roosevelt left Washington for a vacation, he placed Taft in charge. Everything was all right, Roosevelt often said, with Taft "sitting on the lid."

The story is told that one night in the White House

library, Roosevelt spoke about his successor with Taft and his wife, Nellie. Roosevelt said, "I am the seventh son of a seventh daughter and I have clairvoyant powers. I see a man weighing three hundred and fifty pounds. There is something hanging over his head. . . . at one time it looks like the presidency, then again it looks life the chief justiceship." Mrs. Taft said, "Make it the presidency." Taft said, "Make it the chief justiceship." Taft had, on various occasions, told friends: "I am not a politician and I dislike parties. I do want to go on the bench, and my ambition is to be Chief Justice of the United States. I would be of more service there to the United States than I could be as President."

Taft's protests grew weaker by mid-1905. During the 1906 congressional elections, Roosevelt sent Taft on a speaking tour. Taft did well, although he complained that "politics, when I am in it, makes me sick." He was convinced that William Jennings Bryan would again be the Democratic nominee in 1908. He wrote Roosevelt late in October 1906: "It is always a doubtful question whether [Bryan] does not do more good for the major party than the minority for if he puts excitement into the campaign at all he is likely to bring out the Republicans." In March 1907, Taft received definite word that he was the President's chosen candidate. And, on 18 June 1908, the Republican Convention dutifully nominated Taft on the first ballot.

On 30 August 1906, Bryan returned from a one-year trip around the world. Every well-known Democrat had contributed toward the costs of a great reception for him in New York City, and most were there to personally welcome him home. The following day, Bryan outlined the mission of the 1908 campaign to a cheering audience of 12,000 in Madison Square Garden. "He did it," Roosevelt wrote his friend Henry Cabot Lodge, "I think he has helped us immensely. Down at bottom Bryan is a cheap soul. He felt that he had to take an attitude that would show that he was really a great deal more radical than I was." Taft, however, remarked to newspaper publisher Whitelaw Reid: "His party is dreadfully hard up for Presidential timber."

In 1908, the Democrats nominated William Jennings Bryan for the third time. Bryan had quickly regained control of the party organization after Alton B. Parker's stunning 1904 defeat. He believed that Parker's defeat proved that the Democrats would not win with a conservative at the head of the ticket. Bryan had put the free silver issue behind him and claimed that he was Theodore Roosevelt's heir: the true reformer and the candidate of the people.

Bryan's many supporters were devoted to him with all their hearts and souls. Bryan was the last great spokesmen for idealistic agrarian democracy, and he demanded that the Democratic Party be progressive. The election of 1904 was a complete failure, he said, because Democrats had shunned the "fixed principle—equal rights to all and special privileges to none." He believed that every great political issue was economic; every great economic issue was moral; and moral questions must be settled by an appeal to "the moral sense" of the nation. Immoral trusts had to be abolished; labor disputes had to be settled by arbitration; and the Philippines had to be granted independence. Bryan commanded his followers to help Roosevelt carry out "whatever is good." He had written the President in September 1905: "Stand by your guns. You have developed a reform element in the Republican Party; you must lead it or suffer the humiliation of seeing the leadership pass to someone else."

By 1906, Roosevelt had come to agree with so many of Bryan's demands that the newspapers wrote of a "Roosevelt-Bryan merger." The President now referred to himself as "a progressive conservative" who was "trying to keep the left center together." In 1900, he had called Bryan a "demagogue and agitator;" now he called him a "kindly well-meaning, emotional man." Roosevelt had adopted Bryan's key proposals: federal ownership of railroads; a ban on corporate contributions to political campaigns; pure food and drug legislation; and the federal licensing of all interstate businesses. Few of these programs, if any, appealed to Taft.

Bryan spent 60 days campaigning, delivering from 16 to 30 speeches a day. As the campaign progressed, his liberalism broadened. He reached out to the American Federation of Labor (AFL), becoming the first major candidate to oppose injunctions against workers' strikes. Samuel Gompers, president of the AFL, campaigned for him in many states. Bryan endorsed major rule changes to democratize the U.S. House of Representatives; the initiative and the referendum; and direct primaries. Bryan repeatedly asserted that he, not

Taft, was the heir to Roosevelt's policies.

Taft preferred a front porch style campaign. It took a great deal of prodding from Roosevelt to change his mind. As he began to enjoy himself, he put aside prepared texts and spoke extemporaneously. He made continuity his major theme and his delivery grew stronger. "You are making a great campaign," said Roosevelt. Wall Street agreed with Roosevelt and gave odds of 3 to 1 that Taft would win.

Election Day brought a solid victory for Taft and the Republican Party. He received 321 electoral votes to Bryan's 162. Taft had a popular majority of 51.6 percent to 43 percent for Bryan. The Republicans retained control of both houses of Congress. Bryan carried the Solid South plus Kentucky, Colorado, Oklahoma, Nebraska, and Nevada. Bryan polled 1.3 million votes more than Parker had received in 1904. This showed that those Democrats who had supported the "radical" Roosevelt over the "conservative" Parker had returned to the fold. The election of 1908, however, was a sweeping endorsement of Theodore Roosevelt and his policies.

Taft could barely believe that he had won, and Bryan could not understand why he had lost. He publicly asked for guidance to help him comprehend "the mystery of 1908." Bryan always seemed too radical, especially in the East. For many years, he had felt a burning dislike for the northeastern states and for large cities in particular. He knew that Yankees made fun of him and regarded him with amused contempt. He firmly believed that he spoke for the great underclass in American society.

After the election, Roosevelt interpreted its significance. He said: "Taft will carry on the work substantially as I have. . . . I have the profound satisfaction of knowing that he will do all in his power to further . . . the great causes for which I have fought." The election was also a victory for progressivism and Bryan. The Democrats increased their strength in almost every state legislature and won 11 governorships, including those in 5 states Taft had carried. Those Democrats who had supported Theodore Roosevelt over Parker in 1904 had returned to the party of Bryan.

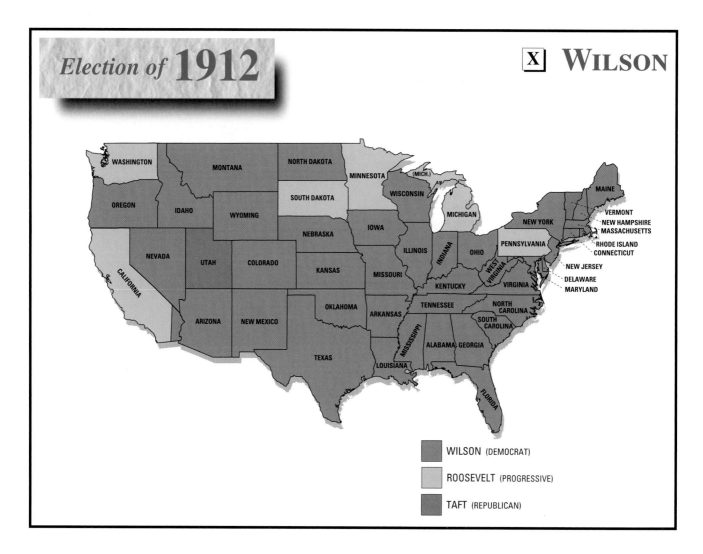

Election of 1912

WILSON (DEMOCRAT)

ROOSEVELT (PROGRESSIVE)

TAFT (REPUBLICAN)

States	Electoral Votes	Wilson	Roosevelt	Taft	States	Electoral Votes	Wilson	Roosevelt	Taft
Alabama	(12)	12	-	-	Nebraska	(8)	8	-	-
Arizona	(3)	3	-	-	Nevada	(3)	3	-	-
Arkansas	(9)	9	-	-	New Hampshire	(4)	4	-	-
California	(13)	2	11	-	New Jersey	(14)	14	-	-
Colorado	(6)	6	-	-	New Mexico	(3)	3	-	-
Connecticut	(7)	7	-	-	New York	(45)	45	-	-
Delaware	(3)	3	-	-	North Carolina	(12)	12	-	-
Florida	(6)	6	-	-	North Dakota	(5)	5	-	-
Georgia	(14)	14	-	-	Ohio	(24)	24	-	-
Idaho	(4)	4	-	-	Oklahoma	(10)	10	-	-
Illinois	(29)	29	-	-	Oregon	(5)	5	-	-
Indiana	(15)	15	-	-	Pennsylvania	(38)	-	38	-
Iowa	(13)	13	-	-	Rhode Island	(5)	5	-	-
Kansas	(10)	10	-	-	South Carolina	(9)	9	-	-
Kentucky	(13)	13	-	-	South Dakota	(5)	-	5	-
Louisiana	(10)	10	-	-	Tennessee	(12)	12	-	-
Maine	(6)	6	-	-	Texas	(20)	20	-	-
Maryland	(8)	8	-	-	Utah	(4)	-	-	4
Massachusetts	(18)	18	-	-	Vermont	(4)	-	-	4
Michigan	(15)	-	15	-	Virginia	(12)	12	-	-
Minnesota	(12)	-	12	-	Washington	(7)	-	7	-
Mississippi	(10)	10	-	-	West Virginia	(8)	8	-	-
Missouri	(18)	18	-	-	Wisconsin	(13)	13	-	-
Montana	(4)	4	-	-	Wyoming	(3)	3	-	-
					Totals	**(531)**	**435**	**88**	**8**

ELECTORAL VOTE

Election of 1912

STATE	TOTAL VOTE	WOODROW WILSON (Democrat)		THEODORE ROOSEVELT (Progressive)		WILLIAM H. TAFT (Republican)		EUGENE V. DEBS (Socialist)		OTHER		PLURALITY	
		Votes	%	Votes	%	Votes	%	Votes	%	Votes	%		
Alabama	117,959	82,438	69.9	22,680	19.2	9,807	8.3	3,029	2.6	5		59,758	D
Arizona	23,687	10,324	43.6	6,949	29.3	2,986	12.6	3,163	13.4	265	1.1	3,375	D
Arkansas	125,104	68,814	55.0	21,644	17.3	25,585	20.5	8,153	6.5	908	0.7	43,229	D
California	677,877	283,436	41.8	283,610	41.8	3,847	0.6	79,201	11.7	27,783	4.1	174	P
Colorado	265,954	113,912	42.8	71,752	27.0	58,386	22.0	16,366	6.2	5,538	2.1	42,160	D
Connecticut	190,404	74,561	39.2	34,129	17.9	68,324	35.9	10,056	5.3	3,334	1.8	6,237	D
Delaware	48,690	22,631	46.5	8,886	18.3	15,997	32.9	556	1.1	620	1.3	6,634	D
Florida	50,837	35,343	69.5	4,555	9.0	4,279	8.4	4,806	9.5	1,854	3.6	30,788	D
Georgia	121,470	93,087	76.6	21,985	18.1	5,191	4.3	1,058	0.9	149	0.1	71,102	D
Idaho	105,754	33,921	32.1	25,527	24.1	32,810	31.0	11,960	11.3	1,536	1.5	1,111	D
Illinois	1,146,173	405,048	35.3	386,478	33.7	253,593	22.1	81,278	7.1	19,776	1.7	18,570	D
Indiana	654,474	281,890	43.1	162,007	24.8	151,267	23.1	36,931	5.6	22,379	3.4	119,883	D
Iowa	492,353	185,322	37.6	161,819	32.9	119,805	24.3	16,967	3.4	8,440	1.7	23,503	D
Kansas	365,560	143,663	39.3	120,210	32.9	74,845	20.5	26,779	7.3	63		23,453	D
Kentucky	452,714	219,484	48.5	101,766	22.5	115,510	25.5	11,646	2.6	4,308	1.0	103,974	D
Louisiana	79,248	60,871	76.8	9,283	11.7	3,833	4.8	5,261	6.6	—		51,588	D
Maine	129,641	51,113	39.4	48,495	37.4	26,545	20.5	2,541	2.0	947	0.7	2,618	D
Maryland	231,981	112,674	48.6	57,789	24.9	54,956	23.7	3,996	1.7	2,566	1.1	54,885	D
Massachusetts	488,056	173,408	35.5	142,228	29.1	155,948	32.0	12,616	2.6	3,856	0.8	17,460	D
Michigan	547,971	150,201	27.4	213,243	38.9	151,434	27.6	23,060	4.2	10,033	1.8	61,809	P
Minnesota	334,219	106,426	31.8	125,856	37.7	64,334	19.2	27,505	8.2	10,098	3.0	19,430	P
Mississippi	64,483	57,324	88.9	3,549	5.5	1,560	2.4	2,050	3.2	—		53,775	D
Missouri	698,566	330,746	47.3	124,375	17.8	207,821	29.7	28,466	4.1	7,158	1.0	122,925	D
Montana	80,256	28,129	35.0	22,709	28.3	18,575	23.1	10,811	13.5	32		5,420	D
Nebraska	249,483	109,008	43.7	72,681	29.1	54,226	21.7	10,185	4.1	3,383	1.4	36,327	D
Nevada	20,115	7,986	39.7	5,620	27.9	3,196	15.9	3,313	16.5	—		2,366	D
New Hampshire	87,961	34,724	39.5	17,794	20.2	32,927	37.4	1,981	2.3	535	0.6	1,797	D
New Jersey	433,663	178,638	41.2	145,679	33.6	89,066	20.5	15,948	3.7	4,332	1.0	32,959	D
New Mexico	48,807	20,437	41.9	8,347	17.1	17,164	35.2	2,859	5.9	—		3,273	D
New York	1,588,315	655,573	41.3	390,093	24.6	455,487	28.7	63,434	4.0	23,728	1.5	200,086	D
North Carolina	243,776	144,407	59.2	69,135	28.4	29,129	11.9	987	0.4	118		75,272	D
North Dakota	86,474	29,549	34.2	25,726	29.7	22,990	26.6	6,966	8.1	1,243	1.4	3,823	D
Ohio	1,037,114	424,834	41.0	229,807	22.2	278,168	26.8	90,164	8.7	14,141	1.4	146,666	D
Oklahoma	253,694	119,143	47.0	—		90,726	35.8	41,630	16.4	2,195	0.9	28,417	D
Oregon	137,040	47,064	34.3	37,600	27.4	34,673	25.3	13,343	9.7	4,360	3.2	9,464	D
Pennsylvania	1,217,736	395,637	32.5	444,894	36.5	273,360	22.4	83,614	6.9	20,231	1.7	49,257	P
Rhode Island	77,894	30,412	39.0	16,878	21.7	27,703	35.6	2,049	2.6	852	1.1	2,709	D
South Carolina	50,403	48,355	95.9	1,293	2.6	536	1.1	164	0.3	55	0.1	47,062	D
South Dakota	116,327	48,942	42.1	58,811	50.6	—		4,664	4.0	3,910	3.4	9,869	P
Tennessee	251,933	133,021	52.8	54,041	21.5	60,475	24.0	3,564	1.4	832	0.3	72,546	D
Texas	300,961	218,921	72.7	26,715	8.9	28,310	9.4	24,884	8.3	2,131	0.7	190,611	D
Utah	112,272	36,576	32.6	24,174	21.5	42,013	37.4	8,999	8.0	510	0.5	5,437	R
Vermont	62,804	15,350	24.4	22,129	35.2	23,303	37.1	928	1.5	1,094	1.7	1,174	R
Virginia	136,975	90,332	65.9	21,776	15.9	23,288	17.0	820	0.6	759	0.6	67,044	D
Washington	322,799	86,840	26.9	113,698	35.2	70,445	21.8	40,134	12.4	11,682	3.6	26,858	P
West Virginia	268,728	113,097	42.1	79,112	29.4	56,754	21.1	15,248	5.7	4,517	1.7	33,985	D
Wisconsin	399,975	164,230	41.1	62,448	15.6	130,596	32.7	33,476	8.4	9,225	2.3	33,634	D
Wyoming	42,283	15,310	36.2	9,232	21.8	14,560	34.4	2,760	6.5	421	1.0	750	D
Totals	15,040,963	6,293,152	41.8	4,119,207	27.4	3,486,333	23.2	900,369	6.0	241,902	1.6	2,173,945	D

POPULAR VOTE

The most significant result of the presidential election of 1912 was the emergence of Woodrow Wilson as a national leader. The election also demonstrated that the country was in favor of reform and had become overwhelmingly progressive in temperament.

William Howard Taft had entered the presidency in 1909 after a solid election triumph with the support of Theodore Roosevelt. Taft, a former judge, was acutely aware of the constitutional limitations imposed on his office. He held to the more traditional belief in a distinct separation of powers between the three branches of government. Roosevelt, on the other hand, often assumed an irreverent attitude toward the Constitution. Taft had difficulty speaking to crowds whereas Roosevelt had developed a wonderful bond with the American people. Roosevelt aroused enthusiasm with new ideas and new goals, but Taft was unprepared to go forward with a program of his own. Roosevelt was primarily a man of action; Taft, essentially, was a man of deliberation. Therefore, the progressive initiative stalled.

Taft seemed unwilling to antagonize the conservative Old Guard congressional leaders of his own party who thought reform had gone far enough. Republican Progressives were angered at the President's support of the protective Payne-Aldrich Tariff (1909) despite his campaign pledge to lower the tariff. Taft's dismissal of Gifford Pinchot, the Chief Forester in the Department of Agriculture, further angered conservationists. Pinchot was a good friend of Roosevelt's, but he had acted with deliberate insubordination in a policy debate over public land. His firing was interpreted as a dramatic reversal of Roosevelt's conservation programs. Western Republican Progressives almost unanimously supported Pinchot and were drawn closer to Roosevelt. Roosevelt was now convinced that Taft had allowed the Old Guard to maneuver him into a position which would split the party.

Taft championed many liberal reforms: the Mann-Elkins Act (1910), which strengthened the jurisdiction of the Interstate Commerce Commission, the Postal Savings Bank (1910), where workers could safely deposit their money, and an antitrust program. Nevertheless, Progressive Republicans, led by Senator Robert La Follette of Wisconsin, were convinced that Roosevelt's reform policies had been stalled.

Taft seemed to ignore major social conditions, especially the predicament of the farmer and laborer. He increasingly accepted recommendations from the business community.

Instead of attempting to appease dissidents within his party, he seemed to go out of his way to antagonize them. The surprising triumph of Republican Progressives, as well as heavy Democratic gains in the 1910 congressional elections clearly indicated that the President's prestige had been weakened. Encouraged by their success, and looking forward to capturing the Republican Party in 1912, Taft's critics formed the National Progressive Republican League (1911).

Theodore Roosevelt had been on a hunting trip in Africa and had taken a triumphal tour of Europe. He returned to New York in June 1910 and pursued some of his many non-political interests. However, he was soon speaking to huge audiences in the West. His one year absence abroad had not dulled his zeal for reform. Rather, his ideas had become distilled into a new creed—the New Nationalism. In addition to the old policies of trust regulation and conservation, Roosevelt now spoke about social justice—reconstructing society through political action. Conservative Republicans shuddered at the concept of the New Nationalism and feared a party split.

Roosevelt and Taft continued a friendly correspondence for several months. Taft wrote to his old friend, "I have been conscientiously trying to carry out your policies, but my method of doing so has not worked smoothly." After the Democrats regained the U.S. House of Representatives in a landslide in 1910, Roosevelt knew that Taft could not be reelected. The division between them now widened. Taft publicly denounced those who supported the New Nationalism as "political emotionalists" and "neurotics." Roosevelt's restless energy combined with Taft's conservatism convinced him to enter the 1912 Republican primaries. "My hat is in the ring," Roosevelt announced in February 1912.

The next four months witnessed a lively fight for Republican delegates. Roosevelt described it as "the most momentous struggle since the close of the Civil War." Taft said, "I do not want to fight Theodore Roosevelt, but I am going to fight." Abusive behavior and name-calling at state and local conventions obscured the major issues. A majority of states holding direct primaries overwhelmingly chose pro-Roosevelt delegates, but the Old Guard conservatives and political bosses controlled the convention machinery in Chicago. Taft was renominated on the first ballot.

Roosevelt was convinced that he had been cheated out of the nomination by corrupt politicians. He announced his willingness to run on a third-party ticket "even if only one State should support me." His followers took immediate steps to found a new party. On 6 August 1912, the new party—the Progressive Party—nominated their hero. Roosevelt declared to the hastily summoned convention, "We have put forth a platform which shall be a contract with the people." The statement of principles which he delivered was the most advanced social thought of the time. He spoke about a minimum wage, equal rights for women, prohibition of child labor, and the need for workmen's compensation. "I am feeling like a bull moose," commented the beloved leader. The bull moose became the symbol of the new party.

The Democrats, realizing that the White House was within their grasp, battled fiercely before selecting their presidential nominee. It had been 16 years since William Jennings Bryan and his followers had captured leadership of the party, but Bryan still commanded the loyal devotion of many rural Democrats. However, he knew that the party must have a new leader and announced that he would not seek a fourth nomination. Almost every Democratic newspaper in the country agreed that it was essential to reorganize the party.

The delegates at the 1912 Democratic Convention chose Governor Woodrow Wilson of New Jersey on the forty-sixth ballot. A former president of Princeton University, Wilson had an impressive record as a progressive governor. He had championed a workmen's compensation act, a direct primary law, labor reform, and a state corrupt practices act. Wilson had earned a Ph.D. in political science and history from Johns Hopkins University, and his thesis is still considered a brilliant analysis of the federal legislative system. He did not have a commanding presence and conducted his campaign rallies like a teacher in a classroom. His sentences were polished and each word was precise. He always seemed to be preaching about visions, purposes, and responsibilities.

The ensuing campaign was the first serious three-cornered presidential election since 1860. However, Taft had privately conceded defeat by mid-July. Except for his acceptance speech, Taft refused to deliver any campaign speeches. Wilson and Roosevelt carried the burden of the campaign. Roosevelt's New Nationalism called for the extension of federal powers while Wilson's New Freedom stressed his confidence in the states. Neither denied the need for major

political and social changes. Although both their programs were progressive, they differed greatly. As the campaign progressed, Roosevelt became more specific. He explained the need for social justice programs: a minimum wage for women workers, health care programs, the use of tariff proceeds to increase wages to industrial laborers, and federal intervention in labor disputes. Roosevelt waged a magnificent campaign. However, he failed to draw enough progressive Democrats away from Wilson. This caused his inevitable defeat.

Wilson's reform thinking was not as developed as Roosevelt's. Basically, he was a states' rights Democrat. That is, he believed that the federal government should be used only to end special privileges. Wilson objected to Roosevelt's labor programs as paternalistic. He thought that they would make workers too dependent on the government. Wilson saw Roosevelt's New Nationalism as a threat to the free enterprise system.

The Socialist Party nominated Eugene V. Debs for a fourth time. Debs praised Karl Marx and called for a class revolution. He attacked both Roosevelt and Wilson. Both, he said, were supported by capitalists who would never emancipate the working class. After a transcontinental speaking tour on a train called the "Red Special," he ended his campaign with a bitter denunciation of all progressives.

The results of the 1912 election were not surprising. Wilson won 435 electoral votes to Roosevelt's 88 and Taft's 8. Taft carried only two states: Utah and Vermont. However, the popular vote told another story: Wilson received 6,293,152 (41.8 percent); Roosevelt received 4,119,207 (27.4 percent); Taft received 3,486,333 (23.2 percent); and Debs received 900,369 (6 percent). Wilson clearly was not the choice of a majority of voters. In each of his three elections, Bryan had received more popular votes than Wilson. Thousands of voters, therefore, who had supported Bryan in 1896, 1900, and 1908, now voted for either Roosevelt or Debs. Roosevelt received a higher percentage of the popular vote than any other third party candidate in U.S. history. The vote, however, was a tribute to his personality, and the Progressive Party rapidly disappeared.

Theodore Roosevelt's New Nationalism became the basis of his distant cousin Franklin's New Deal in the 1930s. After several years of arguments among themselves and with a split in the Republican Party, Woodrow Wilson emerged as the new progressive leader.

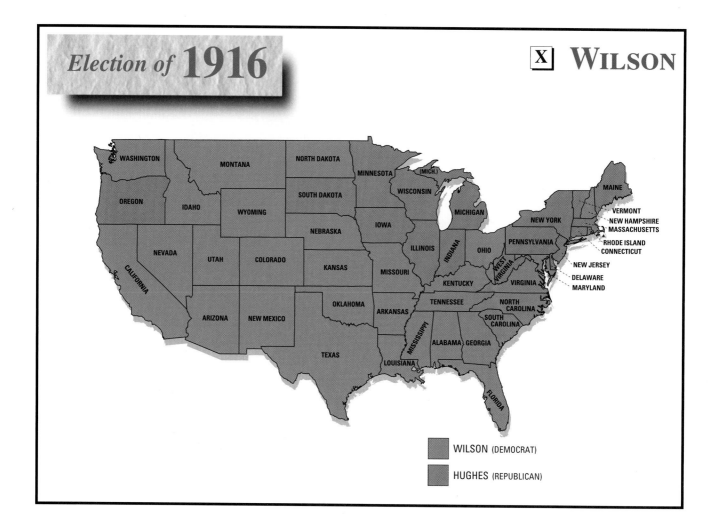

Election of 1916

WILSON (DEMOCRAT)

HUGHES (REPUBLICAN)

States	Electoral Votes	Wilson	Hughes	States	Electoral Votes	Wilson	Hughes
Alabama	(12)	12	-	Nebraska	(8)	8	-
Arizona	(3)	3	-	Nevada	(3)	3	-
Arkansas	(9)	9	-	New Hampshire	(4)	4	-
California	(13)	13	-	New Jersey	(14)	-	14
Colorado	(6)	6	-	New Mexico	(3)	3	-
Connecticut	(7)	-	7	New York	(45)	-	45
Delaware	(3)	-	3	North Carolina	(12)	12	-
Florida	(6)	6	-	North Dakota	(5)	5	-
Georgia	(14)	14	-	Ohio	(24)	24	-
Idaho	(4)	4	-	Oklahoma	(10)	10	-
Illinois	(29)	-	29	Oregon	(5)	-	5
Indiana	(15)	-	15	Pennsylvania	(38)	-	38
Iowa	(13)	-	13	Rhode Island	(5)	-	5
Kansas	(10)	10	-	South Carolina	(9)	9	-
Kentucky	(13)	13	-	South Dakota	(5)	-	5
Louisiana	(10)	10	-	Tennessee	(12)	12	-
Maine	(6)	-	6	Texas	(20)	20	-
Maryland	(8)	8	-	Utah	(4)	4	-
Massachusetts	(18)	-	18	Vermont	(4)	-	4
Michigan	(15)	-	15	Virginia	(12)	12	-
Minnesota	(12)	-	12	Washington	(7)	7	-
Mississippi	(10)	10	-	West Virginia	(8)	1	7
Missouri	(18)	18	-	Wisconsin	(13)	-	13
Montana	(4)	4	-	Wyoming	(3)	3	-
				Totals	**(531)**	**277**	**254**

ELECTORAL VOTE

Election of 1916

STATE	TOTAL VOTE	WOODROW WILSON (Democrat)		CHARLES E. HUGHES (Republican)		ALLAN L. BENSON (Socialist)		J. FRANK HANLY (Prohibition)		OTHER		PLURALITY	
		Votes	%	Votes	%	Votes	%	Votes	%	Votes	%		
Alabama	130,435	99,116	76.0	28,662	22.0	1,916	1.5	741	0.6	—		70,454	D
Arizona	58,019	33,170	57.2	20,522	35.4	3,174	5.5	1,153	2.0	—		12,648	D
Arkansas	170,104	112,211	66.0	48,879	28.7	6,999	4.1	2,015	1.2	—		63,332	D
California	999,250	465,936	46.6	462,516	46.3	42,898	4.3	27,713	2.8	187	0.1	3,420	D
Colorado	292,037	177,496	60.8	101,388	34.7	9,951	3.4	2,793	1.0	409	0.1	76,108	D
Connecticut	213,874	99,786	46.7	106,514	49.8	5,179	2.4	1,789	0.8	606	0.3	6,728	R
Delaware	51,810	24,753	47.8	26,011	50.2	480	0.9	566	1.1	—		1,258	R
Florida	80,734	55,984	69.3	14,611	18.1	5,353	6.6	4,786	5.9	—		41,373	D
Georgia	160,681	127,754	79.5	11,294	7.0	941	0.6	—		20,692	12.9	107,062	D
Idaho	134,615	70,054	52.0	55,368	41.1	8,066	6.0	1,127	0.8	—		14,686	D
Illinois	2,192,707	950,229	43.3	1,152,549	52.6	61,394	2.8	26,047	1.2	2,488	0.1	202,320	R
Indiana	718,853	334,063	46.5	341,005	47.4	21,860	3.0	16,368	2.3	5,557	0.8	6,942	R
Iowa	518,738	221,699	42.7	280,439	54.1	10,976	2.1	3,371	0.6	2,253	0.4	58,740	R
Kansas	629,813	314,588	49.9	277,658	44.1	24,685	3.9	12,882	2.0	—		36,930	D
Kentucky	520,078	269,990	51.9	241,854	46.5	4,734	0.9	3,039	0.6	461	0.1	28,136	D
Louisiana	92,974	79,875	85.9	6,466	7.0	284	0.3	—		6,349	6.8	73,409	D
Maine	136,314	64,033	47.0	69,508	51.0	2,177	1.6	596	0.4	—		5,475	R
Maryland	262,039	138,359	52.8	117,347	44.8	2,674	1.0	2,903	1.1	756	0.3	21,012	D
Massachusetts	531,822	247,885	46.6	268,784	50.5	11,058	2.1	2,993	0.6	1,102	0.2	20,899	R
Michigan	646,873	283,993	43.9	337,952	52.2	16,012	2.5	8,085	1.2	831	0.1	53,959	R
Minnesota	387,367	179,155	46.2	179,544	46.3	20,117	5.2	7,793	2.0	758	0.2	389	R
Mississippi	86,679	80,422	92.8	4,253	4.9	1,484	1.7	—		520	0.6	76,169	D
Missouri	786,773	398,032	50.6	369,339	46.9	14,612	1.9	3,887	0.5	903	0.1	28,693	D
Montana	178,009	101,104	56.8	66,933	37.6	9,634	5.4	—		338	0.2	34,171	D
Nebraska	287,315	158,827	55.3	117,771	41.0	7,141	2.5	2,952	1.0	624	0.2	41,056	D
Nevada	33,314	17,776	53.4	12,127	36.4	3,065	9.2	346	1.0	—		5,649	D
New Hampshire	89,127	43,781	49.1	43,725	49.1	1,318	1.5	303	0.3	—		56	D
New Jersey	494,442	211,018	42.7	268,982	54.4	10,405	2.1	3,182	0.6	855	0.2.	57,964	R
New Mexico	66,879	33,693	50.4	31,097	46.5	1,977	3.0	112	0.2	—		2,596	D
New York	1,706,305	759,426	44.5	879,238	51.5	45,944	2.7	19,031	1.1	2,666	0.2	119,812	R
North Carolina	289,837	168,383	58.1	120,890	41.7	509	0.2	55		—		47,493	D
North Dakota	115,390	55,206	47.8	53,471	46.3	5,716	5.0	997	0.9	—		1,735	D
Ohio	1,165,091	604,161	51.9	514,753	44.2	38,092	3.3	8,085	0.7	—		89,408	D
Oklahoma	292,327	148,123	50.7	97,233	33.3	45,091	15.4	1,646	0.6	234	0.1	50,890	D
Oregon	261,650	120,087	45.9	126,813	48.5	9,711	3.7	4,729	1.8	310	0.1	6,726	R
Pennsylvania	1,297,189	521,784	40.2	703,823	54.3	42,638	3.3	28,525	2.2	419		182,039	R
Rhode Island	87,816	40,394	46.0	44,858	51.1	1,914	2.2	470	0.5	180	0.2	4,464	R
South Carolina	63,950	61,845	96.7	1,550	2.4	135	0.2	—		420	0.7	60,295	D
South Dakota	128,942	59,191	45.9	64,217	49.8	3,760	2.9	1,774	1.4	—		5,026	R
Tennessee	272,190	153,280	56.3	116,223	42.7	2,542	0.9	145	0.1	—		37,057	D
Texas	373,310	287,415	77.0	64,999	17.4	18,960	5.1	1,936	0.5	—		222,416	D
Utah	143,145	84,145	58.8	54,137	37.8	4,460	3.1	149	0.1	254	0.2	30,008	D
Vermont	64,475	22,708	35.2	40,250	62.4	798	1.2	709	1.1	10		17,542	R
Virginia	152,025	101,840	67.0	48,384	31.8	1,056	0.7	678	0.4	67		53,456	D
Washington	380,994	183,388	48.1	167,208	43.9	22,800	6.0	6,868	1.8	730	0.2	16,180	D
West Virginia	289,671	140,403	48.5	143,124	49.4	6,144	2.1	—		—		2,721	R
Wisconsin	447,134	191,363	42.8	220,822	49.4	27,631	6.2	7,318	1.6	—		29,459	R
Wyoming	51,906	28,376	54.7	21,698	41.8	1,459	2.8	373	0.7	—		6,678	D
Totals	**18,535,022**	**9,126,300**	**49.2**	**8,546,789**	**46.1**	**589,924**	**3.2**	**221,030**	**1.2**	**50,979**	**0.3**	**579,511**	**D**

The 1916 presidential election was a referendum on Woodrow Wilson's commitments to progressivism and to peace. Wilson's reelection campaign emphasized that the Democratic Party had enacted almost every plank in the Progressive Party platform of 1912, and it also stressed Wilson's policy of neutrality. It was a dull and boring campaign that resulted in a very close election.

Wilson's talent for leadership, combined with the progressive temper of the times, resulted in an amazing amount of legislation during his first term. After four years in the White House, the President confidently stated that "no equal period in our history has been so fruitful of important reforms in our economic and industrial life or so full of significant changes in the spirit and purpose of our political action." Wilson had established his firm control over Congress and the Democratic Party.

Wilson wanted to return the nation to "economic freedom"—free of high tariffs, industrial and financial monopolies, and the almost unlimited power of the employer over his employees. Wilson said that the government had to intervene to remove the "unnatural" restraints on freedom of competition and on equality of opportunity in order to achieve this free economy. He called his policy the New Freedom.

Reduction of the high tariff was the first plank in the Democratic platform. Wilson was determined to smash the privileged tariff protection policy that the Republican Party had supported since 1861. High duties imposed on European imports had helped to protect America's growing industries from foreign competition. However, as the American economy thrived, high tariff duties kept out lower priced goods from abroad, raising the American cost of living to an unnatural level. Thus, Wilson looked at the protective tariff as a symbol of privilege as well as a subsidy to business paid for by the consumer.

On 8 April 1913, Wilson delivered a brief tariff message to a special session of Congress. This was the first time since John Adams in 1800 that a President had appeared personally before the legislative branch. After months of negotiations, Congress reversed protectionism on 3 October. The Underwood Tariff Act (1913) lowered the average duty rate to 30 percent, compared with 57 percent in the 1897 Dingley Tariff. Iron, steel, raw wool, and sugar were placed on the duty free list. To compensate for the loss of revenue, Congress passed the first income tax law. A flat 1 percent tax was imposed on all income, individual or corporate, over $4,000. (The average worker's annual income in 1913 was between $300 and $400.) "It is hard to speak of these things without seeming to go off into campaign eloquence," Wilson told those who witnessed the signing ceremony, "but that is not my feeling. It is . . . a feeling of profound gratitude."

Passage of the Federal Reserve Act (1913) was the second major plank of the New Freedom. Prior to 1913, the nation's banks (approximately 7,000) operated without federal control or coordination among themselves. There was no uniform currency but rather an assortment of gold and silver coins, local bank certificates, greenbacks, and National Bank notes. The new system provided the country with a sound currency and a method for mobilizing the banking reserves of the nation in a financial emergency. It preserved private enterprise in banking while, at the same time, imposing a degree of public regulation. It is a technical banking law which has succeeded remarkably well.

Wilson held to his broad principles but he was not inflexible. He believed that the Democratic Party must stay in power to assure progressive change. By the 1916 campaign, many laws had been passed which progressives had championed during the previous two decades: The Clayton Anti-Trust Act (1914) contained provisions for breaking up business trusts; the Smith-Lever Act (1914) provided funds to help educate farmers in the latest techniques of scientific agriculture; the Federal Trade Commission (1914) issued rulings outlawing unfair business practices; the Harrison Narcotic Act (1914) listed addictive drugs that were not to be sold without a doctor's prescription; the Warehouse Act (1916) made it possible for farmers to hold crops off the market until prices were favorable; the Federal Farm Loan Act (1916) provided low interest, long term loans to farmers; the Adamson Act (1916) established an eight-hour work day for railroad workers; the Keating-Owens Act (1916) outlawed child labor but was declared unconstitutional in 1918. In four years, Wilson tried to convince the American people that progressivism transcended party lines and government was their servant.

Shockingly though, Wilson believed in total segregation of the races. Shortly after his inauguration, federal agencies segregated workers in offices, shops, restrooms, and restaurants. Employees who objected were discharged. African American educational leader Booker T. Washington wrote,

"I have recently spent several days in Washington, and I have never seen the colored people so discouraged and bitter as they are at the present time." Many progressive leaders protested to Wilson but he stood firm. In fact, he was surprised at the opposition, contending that segregation was being instituted to help African Americans.

Although Europe had been on the brink of a conflict for more than a decade, most Americans were shocked when war broke out in August 1914. On 19 August, Wilson appealed to the nation to remain impartial in thought as well as in action. The President, a devoted admirer of the British parliamentary system, privately confided that "if Germany wins, it will change the course of our civilization, and make the United States a military nation." However, both the American people and the administration desired neutrality. Throughout 1915 and 1916, the President attempted to remain neutral despite provocative British and German incidents. A major crisis resulted from the sinking of the British ship *Lusitania* by a German U-boat on 7 May 1915. One hundred and twenty-eight Americans were killed. After strong diplomatic protests, Germany announced that it would not attack unarmed passenger liners. "He kept us out of war" became the Democratic Party's rallying cry during the 1916 campaign.

When the Republican Convention convened in Chicago on 7 June 1916, harmony prevailed. Everyone seemed to agree that the debacle of 1912, when Theodore Roosevelt left the party, would not be repeated. Roosevelt had returned to the party. He had campaigned for the nomination during the spring but had won little support. Likewise, former President William Howard Taft wrote that the chance of his own nomination was "resting in a tomb." On the third ballot, the delegates selected Charles Evans Hughes, a former reform governor of New York. Hughes had made no statements on public policy since he had been appointed to the Supreme Court by President Taft in 1910. No one knew where he stood on the issues and there was doubt that he would even accept the nomination. This is why Hughes appealed to the diverse factions within the Republican Party. When he received the official notice of his selection, Hughes immediately resigned from the Court. He sent a brief message to the convention that he could not turn down their call to duty.

The Democrats gathered in St. Louis on 14 June 1916 and renominated Wilson by acclamation. Wilson had written the draft for the platform which was adopted without opposition. The President then returned to affairs of state. Hughes criticized Wilson, and Wilson focused on his administration's accomplishments and his commitment to peace. A Democratic victory was far from certain because the country still had a Republican majority.

Early election returns indicated an easy win for Hughes, who carried most of the large eastern and midwestern states. *The New York Times* declared Hughes elected shortly after 10:00 P.M. The New York *World* soon followed. Reporters demanded a victory statement from Hughes who wisely decided to wait for Wilson's concession. The margin narrowed on the following day. Wilson won all the doubtful states and received a total of 277 electoral votes to 254 for Hughes. This was the closest electoral victory since 1876. Wilson had gained nearly 3 million popular votes over 1912 but still defeated Hughes by fewer than 600,000 popular votes out of 18.5 million votes cast. The Democrats again captured both houses of Congress.

Wilson had succeeded in putting together a coalition of progressive supporters. Journalist Walter Lippmann spoke for many of these progressives when he wrote: "I shall vote not for the Wilson who has uttered a few too many noble sentiments but for the Wilson who is evolving under experience and is remaking his philosophy in the light of it. . . . The Wilson who is temporarily at least creating out of the reactionary, parochial fragments of the Democracy the only party which at this moment is national in scope, liberal in purpose, and effective in action." Labor leaders and farm leaders endorsed him. Almost every independent newspaper and journal of opinion supported Wilson. Herbert Croly, editor of the *New Republic* wrote: "I shall vote for him because he has succeeded, at least for the time being, in transforming the Democracy into the more promising of the two major party organizations . . . For the first time in several generations the party has the chance of becoming the embodiment of a genuinely national democracy." The support of this great progressive coalition which backed Wilson in 1916 became the base of Franklin D. Roosevelt's support 16 years later.

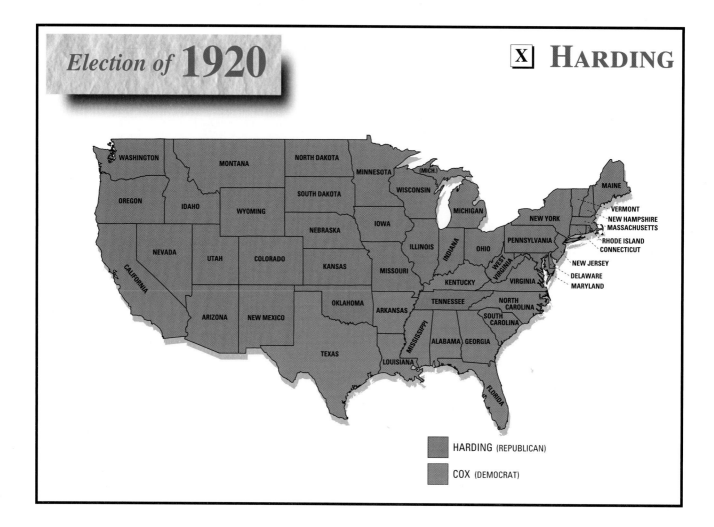

Election of 1920

HARDING (REPUBLICAN)

COX (DEMOCRAT)

States	Electoral Votes	Harding	Cox	States	Electoral Votes	Harding	Cox
Alabama	(12)	-	12	Nebraska	(8)	8	-
Arizona	(3)	3	-	Nevada	(3)	3	-
Arkansas	(9)	-	9	New Hampshire	(4)	4	-
California	(13)	13	-	New Jersey	(14)	14	-
Colorado	(6)	6	-	New Mexico	(3)	3	-
Connecticut	(7)	7	-	New York	(45)	45	-
Delaware	(3)	3	-	North Carolina	(12)	-	12
Florida	(6)	-	6	North Dakota	(5)	5	-
Georgia	(14)	-	14	Ohio	(24)	24	-
Idaho	(4)	4	-	Oklahoma	(10)	10	-
Illinois	(29)	29	-	Oregon	(5)	5	-
Indiana	(15)	15	-	Pennsylvania	(38)	38	-
Iowa	(13)	13	-	Rhode Island	(5)	5	-
Kansas	(10)	10	-	South Carolina	(9)	-	9
Kentucky	(13)	-	13	South Dakota	(5)	5	-
Louisiana	(10)	-	10	Tennessee	(12)	12	-
Maine	(6)	6	-	Texas	(20)	-	20
Maryland	(8)	8	-	Utah	(4)	4	-
Massachusetts	(18)	18	-	Vermont	(4)	4	-
Michigan	(15)	15	-	Virginia	(12)	-	12
Minnesota	(12)	12	-	Washington	(7)	7	-
Mississippi	(10)	-	10	West Virginia	(8)	8	-
Missouri	(18)	18	-	Wisconsin	(13)	13	-
Montana	(4)	4	-	Wyoming	(3)	3	-
				Totals	**(531)**	**404**	**127**

ELECTORAL VOTE

Election of 1920

STATE	TOTAL VOTE	WARREN G. HARDING (Republican)		JAMES M. COX (Democrat)		EUGENE V. DEBS (Socialist)		PARLEY P. CHRISTENSEN (Farmer-Labor)		OTHER		PLURALITY	
		Votes	%	Votes	%	Votes	%	Votes	%	Votes	%		
Alabama	233,951	74,719	31.9	156,064	66.7	2,402	1.0	—		766	0.3	81,345	D
Arizona	66,803	37,016	55.4	29,546	44.2	222	0.3	15		4		7,470	R
Arkansas	183,871	72,316	39.3	106,427	57.9	5,128	2.8	—		—		34,111	D
California	943,463	624,992	66.2	229,191	24.3	64,076	6.8	—		25,204	2.7	395,801	R
Colorado	292,053	173,248	59.3	104,936	35.9	8,046	2.8	3,016	1.0	2,807	1.0	68,312	R
Connecticut	365,518	229,238	62.7	120,721	33.0	10,350	2.8	1,947	0.5	3,262	0.9	108,517	R
Delaware	94,875	52,858	55.7	39,911	42.1	988	1.0	93	0.1	1,025	1.1	12,947	R
Florida	145,684	44,853	30.8	90,515	62.1	5,189	3.6	—		5,127	3.5	45,662	D
Georgia	149,558	42,981	28.7	106,112	71.0	465	0.3	—		—		63,131	D
Idaho	138,281	91,351	66.1	46,930	33.9							44,421	R
Illinois	2,094,714	1,420,480	67.8	534,395	25.5	74,747	3.6	49,630	2.4	15,462	0.7	886,085	R
Indiana	1,262,974	696,370	55.1	511,364	40.5	24,713	2.0	16,499	1.3	14,028	1.1	185,006	R
Iowa	894,959	634,674	70.9	227,804	25.5	16,981	1.9	10,321	1.2	5,179	0.6	406,870	R
Kansas	570,243	369,268	64.8	185,464	32.5	15,511	2.7	—		—		183,804	R
Kentucky	918,636	452,480	49.3	456,497	49.7	6,409	0.7	—		3,250	0.4	4,017	D
Louisiana	126,397	38,539	30.5	87,519	69.2	—		—		339	0.3	48,980	D
Maine	197,840	136,355	68.9	58,961	29.8	2,214	1.1	—		310	0.2	77,394	R
Maryland	428,443	236,117	55.1	180,626	42.2	8,876	2.1	1,645	0.4	1,179	0.3	55,491	R
Massachusetts	993,718	681,153	68.5	276,691	27.8	32,267	3.2	—		3,607	0.4	404,462	R
Michigan	1,048,411	762,865	72.8	233,450	22.3	28,947	2.8	10,480	1.0	12,669	1.2	529,415	R
Minnesota	735,838	519,421	70.6	142,994	19.4	56,106	7.6	—		17,317	2.4	376,427	R
Mississippi	82,351	11,576	14.1	69,136	84.0	1,639	2.0	—		—		57,560	D
Missouri	1,332,140	727,252	54.6	574,699	43.1	20,342	1.5	3,108	0.2	6,739	0.5	152,553	R
Montana	179,006	109,430	61.1	57,372	32.1	—		12,204	6.8	—		52,058	R
Nebraska	382,743	247,498	64.7	119,608	31.3	9,600	2.5	—		6,037	1.6	127,890	R
Nevada	27,194	15,479	56.9	9,851	36.2	1,864	6.9	—		—		5,628	R
New Hampshire	159,092	95,196	59.8	62,662	39.4	1,234	0.8	—		—		32,534	R
New Jersey	910,251	615,333	67.6	258,761	28.4	27,385	3.0	2,264	0.2	6,508	0.7	356,572	R
New Mexico	105,412	57,634	54.7	46,668	44.3	2		1,104	1.0	4		10,966	R
New York	2,898,513	1,871,167	64.6	781,238	27.0	203,201	7.0	18,413	0.6	24,494	0.8	1,089,929	R
North Carolina	538,649	232,819	43.2	305,367	56.7	446	0.1	—		17		72,548	D
North Dakota	205,786	160,082	77.8	37,422	18.2	8,282	4.0	—		—		122,660	R
Ohio	2,021,653	1,182,022	58.5	780,037	38.6	57,147	2.8	—		2,447	0.1	401,985	R
Oklahoma	485,678	243,840	50.2	216,122	44.5	25,716	5.3	—		—		27,718	R
Oregon	238,522	143,592	60.2	80,019	33.5	9,801	4.1	—		5,110	2.1	63,573	R
Pennsylvania	1,851,248	1,218,215	65.8	503,202	27.2	70,021	3.8	15,642	0.8	44,168	2.4	715,013	R
Rhode Island	167,981	107,463	64.0	55,062	32.8	4,351	2.6	—		1,105	0.7	52,401	R
South Carolina	66,808	2,610	3.9	64,170	96.1	28		—		—		61,560	D
South Dakota	182,237	110,692	60.7	35,938	19.7	—		34,707	19.0	900	0.5	74,754	R
Tennessee	428,036	219,229	51.2	206,558	48.3	2,249	0.5	—		—		12,671	R
Texas	486,109	114,658	23.6	287,920	59.2	8,124	1.7	—		75,407	15.5	173,262	D
Utah	145,828	81,555	55.9	56,639	38.8	3,159	2.2	4,475	3.1	—		24,916	R
Vermont	89,961	68,212	75.8	20,919	23.3	—		—		830	0.9	47,293	R
Virginia	231,000	87,456	37.9	141,670	61.3	808	0.3	240	0.1	826	0.4	54,214	D
Washington	398,715	223,137	56.0	84,298	21.1	8,913	2.2	77,246	19.4	5,121	1.3	138,839	R
West Virginia	509,936	282,007	55.3	220,785	43.3	5,618	1.1	—		1,526	0.3	61,222	R
Wisconsin	701,281	498,576	71.1	113,422	16.2	80,635	11.5	—		8,648	1.2	385,154	R
Wyoming	56,253	35,091	62.4	17,429	31.0	1,288	2.3	2,180	3.9	265	0.5	17,662	R
Totals	26,768,613	16,153,115	60.3	9,133,092	34.1	915,490	3.4	265,229	1.0	301,687	1.1	7,020,023	R

POPULAR VOTE

The 1920 presidential election was a repudiation of Wilsonian idealism. More specifically, it was a rejection of the League of Nations. The odds against the Democrats repeating their last two victories were 7 to 1 in mid-October and 10 to 1 on Election Day. If it were a prize fight, said Senator Hiram Johnson, "the police would interfere on the grounds of brutality."

Wilson's war message to Congress on 2 April 1917 had condemned German submarine warfare as "warfare against mankind." By going to war, the United States pledged "to make the world safe for democracy." On 8 January 1918, Wilson outlined Fourteen Points summarizing for the world his ideas for a just and fair peace. He spoke about justice, prosperity, freedom of the seas, removal of trade barriers, disarmament, national self-determination in central and eastern Europe, and a new era of collective security. Point 14 described an international association, a League of Nations, which would guarantee "political independence and territorial integrity to great and small states alike."

Even before the armistice of 11 November 1918, Wilson had decided to shatter precedent by taking personal charge of the peace negotiations. He pleaded with the nation to keep Democratic majorities in Congress as an approval of his wartime leadership and as a vote of confidence in his planned peace efforts. Republican leaders had generally supported Wilson's efforts to promote a lasting peace. Now, however, they saw an opportunity for political gain. They appealed to the Midwest's traditional isolationism and to the general war weariness of the American people. They attacked the President's foreign policy.

Wilson's appeal failed, and the voters chose a Republican majority in both the House and the Senate. Nevertheless, he ignored the humiliating defeat and sailed for Europe on 13 December for the peace negotiations. He angered both parties by not appointing a single member of Congress to the commission that accompanied him to the peace talks. Theodore Roosevelt warned "our allies, our enemies and Mr. Wilson himself" that Wilson "had no authority whatever to speak for the American people at this time. His leadership has just been emphatically repudiated by them."

The harsh realities of the peace treaty which Wilson signed at Versailles on 28 June 1919 angered many Americans. The President's hope for a better world through the League of Nations now was attacked as an "entangling alliance." Nevertheless, more than the needed two-thirds of the Senate seemed ready to vote for the treaty with some form of League membership for the United States. A majority of Americans would probably have backed them.

However, Wilson grew more stubborn about even minor changes in the agreements which he had signed. He undertook an exhausting speaking tour to rally public opinion for the League without any reservations or changes. He suffered a stroke on 25 September 1919 after a speech at Boulder, Colorado, and was rushed back to Washington. Wilson's crippling illness deprived the cause of the League of Nations of its leader. From his sickbed, the President appealed to "all true friends of the treaty" to reject any changes to the document. The Senate failed to ratify the treaty in two separate votes. Wilson decided to appeal to the people once again. He proclaimed that the presidential election of 1920 would be a referendum on the League of Nations.

By the beginning of 1920, most political observers predicted that any Republican candidate would be elected. After being involved in a horrible war, the nation had grown tired of crusades "to make the world safe for democracy." Combined Allied war losses were staggering. Of the 65 million men mobilized for combat, 10 million had been killed and some 20 million wounded. Almost 50,000 Americans were killed in battle between 1917 and 1918. Approximately 237,000 were wounded and nearly 3,000 were reported missing.

Strikes had flared up throughout the country, involving more than 4 million workers in 1919. Programs lagged for easing men back into peacetime activities. Millions of Americans had come to believe that the nation was faced by the menace of a communist revolution. During this period of the "red scare," traditional American freedoms were endangered by the extreme actions of Wilson's Attorney General A. Mitchell Palmer against alleged radicals.

The Republican Convention met in Chicago on 8 June 1920. The two leading candidates for the presidential nomination were General Leonard Wood and Governor Frank O. Lowden. Theodore Roosevelt had died in 1919, and many of his supporters backed Wood, who was Roosevelt's commander during the Spanish-American War and a close friend thereafter. Lowden, an efficient governor of Illinois, had access to large campaign funds from oil interests. Progressive Republicans claimed that both men were too indebted to big business interests. William Allen White, editor of the Emporia, Kansas *Gazette* wrote: "I have never seen a convention—and I have watched most of them since McKinley's first nomination—so completely dominated by sinister predatory economic forces as was this." The convention deadlocked. Late one night, in a smoke-filled room, a group of senators led by Henry Cabot Lodge of Massachusetts, agreed to back Senator Warren G. Harding of Ohio. The convention nominated Harding on the tenth ballot and chose Massachusetts Governor Calvin Coolidge as his running mate. These two were thoroughly conservative candidates running on a thoroughly conservative platform. The Republican platform remained intentionally vague on the important League of Nations issue. It pledged the party "to such agreements with other nations of the world as shall meet the full duty of America to civilization and humanity."

Harding, a handsome and outgoing party regular with a notably undistinguished senatorial record, represented a return to "normalcy." He made no pretense to intellectualism. Even his friends described him as a second-rater. In a Boston speech a month before the convention, Harding caught the spirit of the country in urging a return to "not heroism, but healing, not nostrums (false remedies) but normalcy." He was convinced that the Republican Party was the only one fit to rule. Above all, Harding "looked like a President" and he appeared willing to cooperate with the party bosses.

The Democratic Convention met in San Francisco in late June. No one knew who might receive the party's presidential nomination. Three-quarters of the delegates were uncommitted to any candidate. Others were pledged to vote for favorite sons. Secretary of the Treasury William McAdoo, Wilson's son-in-law, seemed to be a front-runner. Rumors spread that William Jennings Bryan controlled some 125 delegates and planned to stampede the convention again. Wilson, who could have easily designated a candidate, seemed to be waiting to be chosen for a third term. His supporters, however, decided not to encourage his renomination. In the end, the urban bosses stepped in and secured the nomination of an anti-prohibition candidate who might save their city tickets for them. The delegates nominated Governor James Cox of Ohio on the forty-fourth ballot. Cox had not been closely identified with Wilson's policies.

Cox later wrote that he personally selected 38-year-old Assistant Secretary of the Navy Franklin D. Roosevelt as his running mate. "He met the geographical requirement," said Cox, "[He] was recognized as an Independent," and had "a well-known name."

The Socialists nominated Eugene V. Debs for president for the fifth and last time. Debs had spoken against the involvement of the United States in World War I, and he was sentenced to a ten-year term for violation of the Espionage Act (1917). Debs conducted his campaign from behind the walls of the Atlanta Federal Penitentiary. The Department of Justice allowed him to give interviews to visitors, send out some letters, and issue press releases of 500 words a week.

Cox and Roosevelt campaigned hard to make the election a referendum on the League of Nations. Cox strongly favored the League but wavered on what amendments he might be willing to accept. Harding, following the advice of his manager, made few speeches and avoided taking positions on the issues of the day except to promise a return to the "good old days." The ambivalence he displayed was politically successful. At first he gave the impression he supported American membership in the League; then he gave the impression he was against it. "Keep Warren at home," advised Boies Penrose, the political boss of Pennsylvania. "Don't let him make any speeches. If he goes out on a tour somebody's sure to ask him questions, and Warren's just the sort of damned fool that will try to answer them."

The Election Day landslide exceeded the expectation of the Republicans. Harding received more than 16,153,000 votes, 60.3 percent of the total, and carried every state outside of the Solid South. Harding also lost in Kentucky by 4,000 votes. For the first time in history, Tennessee went Republican. Cox received some 9,133,000 votes, 34.1 percent. Eugene V. Debs obtained 915,000 votes, 3.4 percent. The sweep brought a Republican majority of 22 in the Senate and 167 in the House. Joseph Tumulty, Wilson's secretary exclaimed: "It wasn't a landslide; it was an earthquake."

The American people were tired of the debate over the League of Nations. They were concerned about the rising cost of living, the number of people out of work, high taxes, and labor violence. After eight years of Wilson's relentless idealism, a return to "normalcy" was a welcome change.

Election of 1924

X COOLIDGE

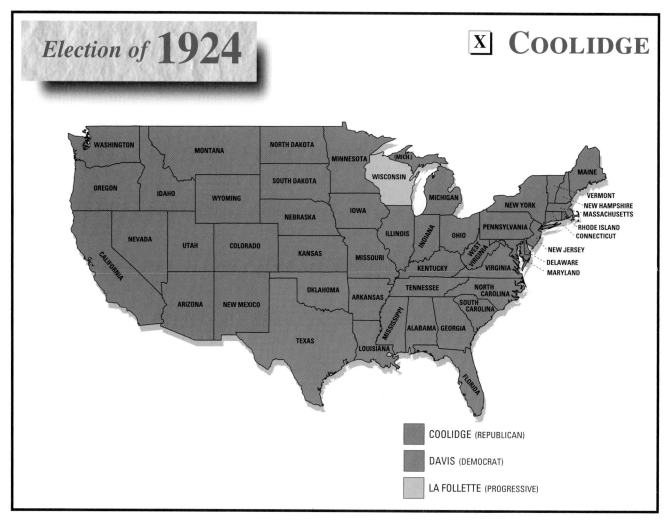

COOLIDGE (REPUBLICAN)

DAVIS (DEMOCRAT)

LA FOLLETTE (PROGRESSIVE)

States	Electoral Votes	Coolidge	Davis	La Follette	States	Electoral Votes	Coolidge	Davis	La Follette
Alabama	(12)	-	12	-	Nebraska	(8)	8	-	-
Arizona	(3)	3	-	-	Nevada	(3)	3	-	-
Arkansas	(9)	-	9	-	New Hampshire	(4)	4	-	-
California	(13)	13	-	-	New Jersey	(14)	14	-	-
Colorado	(6)	6	-	-	New Mexico	(3)	3	-	-
Connecticut	(7)	7	-	-	New York	(45)	45	-	-
Delaware	(3)	3	-	-	North Carolina	(12)	-	12	-
Florida	(6)	-	6	-	North Dakota	(5)	5	-	-
Georgia	(14)	-	14	-	Ohio	(24)	24	-	-
Idaho	(4)	4	-	-	Oklahoma	(10)	-	10	-
Illinois	(29)	29	-	-	Oregon	(5)	5	-	-
Indiana	(15)	15	-	-	Pennsylvania	(38)	38	-	-
Iowa	(13)	13	-	-	Rhode Island	(5)	5	-	-
Kansas	(10)	10	-	-	South Carolina	(9)	-	9	-
Kentucky	(13)	13	-	-	South Dakota	(5)	5	-	-
Louisiana	(10)	-	10	-	Tennessee	(12)	-	12	-
Maine	(6)	6	-	-	Texas	(20)	-	20	-
Maryland	(8)	8	-	-	Utah	(4)	4	-	-
Massachusetts	(18)	18	-	-	Vermont	(4)	4	-	-
Michigan	(15)	15	-	-	Virginia	(12)	-	12	-
Minnesota	(12)	12	-	-	Washington	(7)	7	-	-
Mississippi	(10)	-	10	-	West Virginia	(8)	8	-	-
Missouri	(18)	18	-	-	Wisconsin	(13)	-	-	13
Montana	(4)	4	-	-	Wyoming	(3)	3	-	-
					Totals	(531)	382	136	13

ELECTORAL VOTE

Election of 1924

STATE	TOTAL VOTE	CALVIN COOLIDGE (Republican)		JOHN W. DAVIS (Democrat)		ROBERT M. LA FOLLETTE (Progressive)		HERMAN P. FARIS (Prohibition)		OTHER		PLURALITY	
		Votes	%	Votes	%	Votes	%	Votes	%	Votes	%		
Alabama	164,563	42,823	26.0	113,138	68.8	8,040	4.9	562	0.3	—		70,315	D
Arizona	73,961	30,516	41.3	26,235	35.5	17,210	23.3	—		—		4,281	R
Arkansas	138,540	40,583	29.3	84,790	61.2	13,167	9.5	—		—		44,207	D
California	1,281,778	733,250	57.2	105,514	8.2	424,649	33.1	18,365	1.4	—		308,601	R
Colorado	342,261	195,171	57.0	75,238	22.0	69,946	20.4	966	0.3	940	0.3	119,933	R
Connecticut	400,396	246,322	61.5	110,184	27.5	42,416	10.6	—		1,474	0.4	136,138	R
Delaware	90,885	52,441	57.7	33,445	36.8	4,979	5.5	—		20		18,996	R
Florida	109,158	30,633	28.1	62,083	56.9	8,625	7.9	5,498	5.0	2,319	2.1	31,450	D
Georgia	166,635	30,300	18.2	123,262	74.0	12,687	7.6	231	0.1	155	0.1	92,962	D
Idaho	147,690	69,791	47.3	23,951	16.2	53,948	36.5	—		—		15,843	R
Illinois	2,470,067	1,453,321	58.8	576,975	23.4	432,027	17.5	2,367	0.1	5,377	0.2	876,346	R
Indiana	1,272,390	703,042	55.3	492,245	38.7	71,700	5.6	4,416	0.3	987	0.1	210,797	R
Iowa	976,770	537,458	55.0	160,382	16.4	274,448	28.1	—		4,482	0.5	263,010	R
Kansas	662,456	407,671	61.5	156,320	23.6	98,461	14.9	—		4		251,351	R
Kentucky	813,843	396,758	48.8	375,593	46.2	38,465	4.7	—		3,027	0.4	21,165	R
Louisiana	121,951	24,670	20.2	93,218	76.4			—		4,063	3.3	68,548	D
Maine	192,192	138,440	72.0	41,964	21.8	11,382	5.9	—		406	0.2	96,476	R
Maryland	358,630	162,414	45.3	148,072	41.3	47,157	13.1	—		987	0.3	14,342	R
Massachusetts	1,129,837	703,476	62.3	280,831	24.9	141,225	12.5	—		4,305	0.4	422,645	R
Michigan	1,160,419	874,631	75.4	152,359	13.1	122,014	10.5	6,085	0.5	5,330	0.5	722,272	R
Minnesota	822,146	420,759	51.2	55,913	6.8	339,192	41.3	—		6,282	0.8	81,567	R
Mississippi	112,442	8,494	7.6	100,474	89.4	3,474	3.1	—		—		91,980	D
Missouri	1,310,095	648,488	49.5	574,962	43.9	83,996	6.4	1,418	0.1	1,231	0.1	73,526	R
Montana	174,425	74,138	42.5	33,805	19.4	66,124	37.9	—		358	0.2	8,014	R
Nebraska	463,559	218,985	47.2	137,299	29.6	105,681	22.8	1,594	0.3	—		81,686	R
Nevada	26,921	11,243	41.8	5,909	21.9	9,769	36.3	—		—		1,474	R
New Hampshire	164,769	98,575	59.8	57,201	34.7	8,993	5.5	—		—		41,374	R
New Jersey	1,088,054	676,277	62.2	298,043	27.4	109,028	10.0	1,660	0.2	3,046	0.3	378,234	R
New Mexico	112,830	54,745	48.5	48,542	43.0	9,543	8.5	—		—		6,203	R
New York	3,263,939	1,820,058	55.8	950,796	29.1	474,913	14.6	—		18,172	0.6	869,262	R
North Carolina	481,608	190,754	39.6	284,190	59.0	6,651	1.4	13		—		93,436	D
North Dakota	199,081	94,931	47.7	13,858	7.0	89,922	45.2	—		370	0.2	5,009	R
Ohio	2,016,296	1,176,130	58.3	477,887	23.7	358,008	17.8	—		4,271	0.2	698,243	R
Oklahoma	527,828	225,756	42.8	255,798	48.5	46,274	8.8	—		—		30,042	D
Oregon	279,488	142,579	51.0	67,589	24.2	68,403	24.5	—		917	0.3	74,176	R
Pennsylvania	2,144,850	1,401,481	65.3	409,192	19.1	307,567	14.3	9,779	0.5	16,831	0.8	992,289	R
Rhode Island	210,115	125,286	59.6	76,606	36.5	7,628	3.6	—		595	0.3	48,680	R
South Carolina	50,755	1,123	2.2	49,008	96.6	623	1.2	—		1		47,885	D
South Dakota	203,868	101,299	49.7	27,214	13.3	75,355	37.0	—		—		25,944	R
Tennessee	301,030	130,831	43.5	159,339	52.9	10,666	3.5	94		100		28,508	D
Texas	657,054	130,794	19.9	483,381	73.6	42,879	6.5	—		—		352,587	D
Utah	156,990	77,327	49.3	47,001	29.9	32,662	20.8	—		—		30,326	R
Vermont	102,917	80,498	78.2	16,124	15.7	5,964	5.8	326	0.3	5		64,374	R
Virginia	223,603	73,328	32.8	139,717	62.5	10,369	4.6	—		189	0.1	66,389	D
Washington	421,549	220,224	52.2	42,842	10.2	150,727	35.8	—		7,756	1.8	69,497	R
West Virginia	583,662	288,635	49.5	257,232	44.1	36,723	6.3	—		1,072	0.2	31,403	R
Wisconsin	840,827	311,614	37.1	68,115	8.1	453,678	54.0	2,918	0.3	4,502	0.5	142,064	P
Wyoming	79,900	41,858	52.4	12,868	16.1	25,174	31.5	—		—		16,684	R
Totals	29,095,023	15,719,921	54.0	8,386,704	28.8	4,832,532	16.6	56,292	0.2	99,574	0.3	7,333,217	R

POPULAR VOTE

The Republicans entered the 1924 campaign with some fears and doubts. By the spring of 1923, Washington buzzed with continued revelations about the Teapot Dome scandal which involved the bribery of Albert Fall, Warren G. Harding's secretary of the interior. There were also rumors about other scandals within the highest levels of government. After Harding's death in August 1923, investigations confirmed the suspicions. The nation did not blame Calvin Coolidge, Harding's vice president, for Harding's weaknesses. Coolidge, a strong believer in thrift and hard work, offered a return to honesty briefly interrupted by the Harding years. "I want things as they used to be—before," said the new President. This stern, unimaginative man represented the essence of conservatism. His calm faith in the wisdom of the business class—plus governmental economies, a balanced budget, lower taxes, and a protective tariff—won him wide support. Prosperity became the issue in the 1924 campaign.

"The business of America is business," said the new President. Secretary of the Treasury Andrew Mellon, the millionaire industrialist, was dedicated to the reduction of taxes for the rich and the transfer of much of that burden to the middle and lower income groups. Mellon reasoned that the wealthy would create more jobs for more people and add to the nation's prosperity, if they were left alone.

Smaller businessmen had their champion in Secretary of Commerce Herbert Hoover. He tried to help small businessmen become more profitable. He obtained foreign orders for them and he also supported a high tariff to protect U.S. industries. It was "not the function of the government to manage business," Hoover wrote, but it was the function of government "to distribute economic information; to investigate economic . . . problems; to point out the remedy for economic failure or the road to progress."

What was of "real importance to wage-earners," Coolidge wrote, "was not how they might conduct a quarrel with their employers but how the business of the country might be so organized so as to insure steady employment at a fair rate of pay. If that were done there would be no occasion for a quarrel, and if it were not done a quarrel would do no good." But, what was a "fair rate of pay?" The average salary was less than $1,500 a year, less than what was needed to maintain a minimum decent living standard. Membership in unions declined from 5.1 million in 1920 to 3.6 million in 1929.

Federal courts rapidly issued injunctions to break strikes, boycotts, or to enforce anti-union ("yellow-dog") contracts. The Supreme Court struck down child-labor laws and a minimum wage law for women. Many progressives who had voted for Woodrow Wilson and Theodore Roosevelt now abandoned the cause of labor as too radical. Coolidge had broken the Boston police strike when he was governor of Massachusetts. At that time, he said, "There is no right to strike against the public safety by anybody, anywhere, at any time." He became the new hero of those who were frightened by the wide-spread strikes of 1919 and 1920.

Coolidge avoided most issues, especially the divisive ones. When his legislative proposals failed in Congress, he did not seem bothered. "I am for economy," he said in vetoing the Bonus Bill for World War I veterans. Congress easily overrode his veto. "Four-fifths of all our troubles in this life would disappear if we would only sit down and keep still," said the President. "I have not been hurt," he once remarked, "by what I have not said." The Republican Party's 1924 campaign slogan was most appropriate: "Keep cool with Coolidge."

The Republican Convention nominated Coolidge on the first ballot in 1924. After Governor Frank Lowden of Illinois refused the vice presidential nomination, it went to Charles G. Dawes, former director of the budget. The platform emphasized the party's "record unsurpassed" in economy and debt reduction. It praised the protective tariff as a major contribution to prosperity. The platform, like the candidate, was unexciting but safe.

No such unanimity marked the Democratic Convention that assembled in New York City on 24 June 1924. The delegates battled for 17 days before they agreed on a platform and a candidate. The Democratic Party had become divided by regional differences. The southern delegates, fearing racial and labor problems, opposed any program that seemed similar to Wilson's New Freedom. Many of the eastern delegates were Catholic and bitterly opposed the Ku Klux Klan. The South, with its growing industrialization, was losing interest in a tariff for revenue only. The delegates from urban centers opposed prohibition but those from small towns and rural areas supported it. A serious disagreement arose over a resolution asking for the denunciation of the Ku Klux Klan by name. The Klan had carried its programs of racial and religious discrimination into politics, scoring dramatic victories in the rural South and the West. The Klan hated Blacks, immigrants, Jews, Catholics, and anyone who favored "foreign ideas." After a bitter debate, the resolution was defeated by one vote. The convention divided in the same way on choosing a presidential nominee. The two leading contenders were William G. McAdoo, Wilson's former secretary of the treasury and a favorite son of the South and the West, and New York Governor Alfred E. Smith. After 95 ballots, Smith and McAdoo withdrew by agreement. Finally, on the 103rd ballot, the tired and unhappy delegates chose John W. Davis, a distinguished New York corporation lawyer. Davis had been solicitor general in Wilson's administration and later ambassador to Great Britain. The choice of Charles W. Bryan, brother of William Jennings Bryan, as Davis's running mate did little to heal the seriously divided party. Senator Hiram Johnson of California wrote, "How true was Grant's exclamation that the Democratic Party could be relied upon at the right time to do the wrong thing!"

Senator Robert La Follette of Wisconsin had hoped to win the 1924 Republican nomination and was disappointed in the political trend away from liberalism. When Coolidge was nominated, La Follette called for a second convention to meet on 4 July in Cleveland. His aim was to unite the various progressive forces from both parties and to revive the movement for social justice. The Progressive Party nominated La Follette for president and Senator Burton Wheeler of Montana for vice president. In contrast to the platforms of the Republicans and Democrats, they took an advanced progressive position, attacking monopoly and promising reforms for the farmers and workingmen. Their chief support came from farmers from the Great Plains.

La Follette wrote the brief 14-point platform which called for, among other things: the public control of all natural resources; the direct election of federal judges; congressional power to override federal judicial decisions; and the outlawing of war. However, La Follette had very little money for waging a campaign and did not have state, country, or municipal followers running with him. The Progressive Party of 1924 was not really a third party but rather a third presidential and vice presidential ticket.

Davis could not get his campaign organized. As he recalled in his memoirs: "They had to put a name on the ticket, and so they turned and put mine on . . . every time I'd reach out into the eastern group personalized by Al Smith, the McAdoo group would run away from me. Then when I'd reach out and try to get the McAdoo group somewhere back into the corral, the Smith group would run away from me." Davis had sided with management against hard-pressed unions in several law cases, a fact which made labor leader Samuel Gompers skeptical of him as a friend of the workingman. Woodrow Wilson had described Davis as "a fine man, but he is a formalist. If you want a stand-still, he is just the man to nominate." Thirty years later, Davis represented the segregationist Board of Education of Topeka, Kansas, before the Supreme Court in *Brown v. Board of Education.*

It was clear from the start of the campaign that Coolidge would sweep the country. Almost all progressive Republican officeholders supported him in order not to lose their seniority. The group that concerned Republicans the most, the agricultural West, was experiencing higher prices for their crops. Republicans warned that Coolidge was the alternative to La Follette's "red radicalism," and Republican farmers stayed within the party. Likewise, the voters ignored the Harding scandals as a thing of the distant past. The future promised only prosperity with "Honest Cal."

The election of 1924 was a relatively dull campaign, characterized by public indifference to politics. Only 51.1 percent of the eligible voters went to the polls. Coolidge was decisively elected. His popular vote exceeded the total of his two opponents by more than 2 million. Coolidge won 382 electoral votes, leaving Davis with 136 in 12 states and La Follette with Wisconsin's 13. Coolidge won the eastern states and all of the Midwest and West except Wisconsin. The Democratic Party held onto its stable base in the Solid South. The *New Republic* magazine commented: "The election of 1920 was a great Democratic defeat. This election is a great Republican victory." Calvin Coolidge was justified in his complacent statement that the election revealed "a state of contentment seldom before seen."

Election of 1928

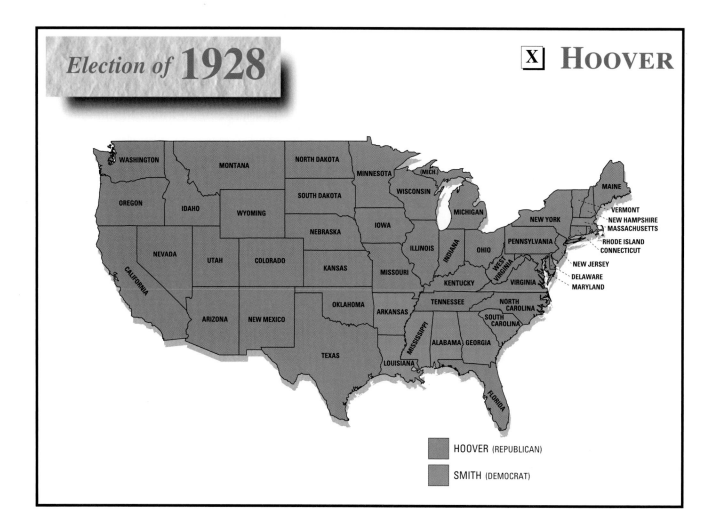

[X] HOOVER

HOOVER (REPUBLICAN)

SMITH (DEMOCRAT)

States	Electoral Votes	Hoover	Smith	States	Electoral Votes	Hoover	Smith
Alabama	(12)	-	12	Nebraska	(8)	8	-
Arizona	(3)	3	-	Nevada	(3)	3	-
Arkansas	(9)	-	9	New Hampshire	(4)	4	-
California	(13)	13	-	New Jersey	(14)	14	-
Colorado	(6)	6	-	New Mexico	(3)	3	-
Connecticut	(7)	7	-	New York	(45)	45	-
Delaware	(3)	3	-	North Carolina	(12)	12	-
Florida	(6)	6	-	North Dakota	(5)	5	-
Georgia	(14)	-	14	Ohio	(24)	24	-
Idaho	(4)	4	-	Oklahoma	(10)	10	-
Illinois	(29)	29	-	Oregon	(5)	5	-
Indiana	(15)	15	-	Pennsylvania	(38)	38	-
Iowa	(13)	13	-	Rhode Island	(5)	-	5
Kansas	(10)	10	-	South Carolina	(9)	-	9
Kentucky	(13)	13	-	South Dakota	(5)	5	-
Louisiana	(10)	-	10	Tennessee	(12)	12	-
Maine	(6)	6	-	Texas	(20)	20	-
Maryland	(8)	8	-	Utah	(4)	4	-
Massachusetts	(18)	-	18	Vermont	(4)	4	-
Michigan	(15)	15	-	Virginia	(12)	12	-
Minnesota	(12)	12	-	Washington	(7)	7	-
Mississippi	(10)	-	10	West Virginia	(8)	8	-
Missouri	(18)	18	-	Wisconsin	(13)	13	-
Montana	(4)	4	-	Wyoming	(3)	3	-
				Totals	**(531)**	**444**	**87**

E L E C T O R A L   V O T E

Election of 1928

STATE	TOTAL VOTE	HERBERT C. HOOVER (Republican)		ALFRED E. SMITH (Democrat)		NORMAN M. THOMAS (Socialist)		WILLIAM Z. FOSTER (Communist)		OTHER		PLURALITY	
		Votes	%	Votes	%	Votes	%	Votes	%	Votes	%		
Alabama	248,981	120,725	48.5	127,796	51.3	460	0.2	—		—		7,071	D
Arizona	91,254	52,533	57.6	38,537	42.2	—		184	0.2	—		13,996	R
Arkansas	197,726	77,784	39.3	119,196	60.3	429	0.2	317	0.2	—		41,412	D
California	1,796,656	1,162,323	64.7	614,365	34.2	19,595	1.1	—		373		547,958	R
Colorado	392,242	253,872	64.7	133,131	33.9	3,472	0.9	675	0.2	1,092	0.3	120,741	R
Connecticut	553,118	296,641	53.6	252,085	45.6	3,029	0.5	738	0.1	625	0.1	44,556	R
Delaware	104,602	68,860	65.8	35,354	33.8	329	0.3	59	0.1	—		33,506	R
Florida	252,068	145,860	57.9	101,764	40.4	2,284	0.9	2,160	0.9	—		44,096	R
Georgia	231,592	101,800	44.0	129,604	56.0	124	0.1	64		—		27,804	D
Idaho	151,541	97,322	64.2	52,926	34.9	1,293	0.9	—		—		44,396	R
Illinois	3,107,489	1,769,141	56.9	1,313,817	42.3	19,138	0.6	3,581	0.1	1,812	0.1	455,324	R
Indiana	1,421,314	848,290	59.7	562,691	39.6	3,871	0.3	321		6,141	0.4	285,599	R
Iowa	1,009,189	623,570	61.8	379,011	37.6	2,960	0.3	328		3,320	0.3	244,559	R
Kansas	713,200	513,672	72.0	193,003	27.1	6,205	0.9	320		—		320,669	R
Kentucky	940,521	558,064	59.3	381,070	40.5	783	0.1	288		316		176,994	R
Louisiana	215,833	51,160	23.7	164,655	76.3	—		—		18		113,495	D
Maine	262,170	179,923	68.6	81,179	31.0	1,068	0.4	—		—		98,744	R
Maryland	528,348	301,479	57.1	223,626	42.3	1,701	0.3	636	0.1	906	0.2	77,853	R
Massachusetts	1,577,823	775,566	49.2	792,758	50.2	6,262	0.4	2,461	0.2	776		17,192	D
Michigan	1,372,082	965,396	70.4	396,762	28.9	3,516	0.3	2,881	0.2	3,527	0.3	568,634	R
Minnesota	970,976	560,977	57.8	396,451	40.8	6,774	0.7	4,853	0.5	1,921	0.2	164,526	R
Mississippi	151,568	27,030	17.8	124,538	82.2	—		—		—		97,508	D
Missouri	1,500,845	834,080	55.6	662,684	44.2	3,739	0.2	—		342		171,396	R
Montana	194,108	113,300	58.4	78,578	40.5	1,667	0.9	563	0.3	—		34,722	R
Nebraska	547,128	345,745	63.2	197,950	36.2	3,433	0.6	—		—		147,795	R
Nevada	32,417	18,327	56.5	14,090	43.5	—		—		—		4,237	R
New Hampshire	196,757	115,404	58.7	80,715	41.0	465	0.2	173	0.1	—		34,689	R
New Jersey	1,549,381	926,050	59.8	616,517	39.8	4,897	0.3	1,257	0.1	660		309,533	R
New Mexico	118,077	69,708	59.0	48,211	40.8	—		158	0.1	—		21,497	R
New York	4,405,626	2,193,344	47.4	2,089,863	47.4	107,332	2.4	10,876	0.2	4,211	0.1	103,481	R
North Carolina	635,150	348,923	54.9	286,227	45.1	—		—		—		62,696	R
North Dakota	239,845	131,419	54.8	106,648	44.5	936	0.4	842	0.4	—		24,771	R
Ohio	2,508,346	1,627,546	64.9	864,210	34.5	8,683	0.3	2,836	0.1	5,071	0.2	763,336	R
Oklahoma	618,427	394,046	63.7	219,174	35.4	3,924	0.6	—		1,283	0.2	174,872	R
Oregon	319,942	205,341	64.2	109,223	34.1	2,720	0.9	1,094	0.3	1,564	0.5	96,118	R
Pennsylvania	3,150,612	2,055,382	65.2	1,067,586	33.9	18,647	0.6	4,726	0.2	4,271	0.1	987,796	R
Rhode Island	237,194	117,522	49.5	118,973	50.2	—		283	0.1	416	0.2	1,451	D
South Carolina	68,605	5,858	8.5	62,700	91.4	47	0.1	—		—		56,842	D
South Dakota	261,857	157,603	60.2	102,660	39.2	443	0.2	224	0.1	927	0.4	54,943	R
Tennessee	353,192	195,388	55.3	157,143	44.5	567	0.2	94		—		38,245	R
Texas	717,733	372,324	51.9	344,542	48.0	658	0.1	209		—		27,782	R
Utah	176,603	94,618	53.6	80,985	45.9	954	0.5	46		—		13,633	R
Vermont	135,191	90,404	66.9	44,440	32.9	—		—		347	0.3	45,964	R
Virginia	305,364	164,609	53.9	140,146	45.9	249	0.1	179	0.1	181	0.1	24,463	R
Washington	500,840	335,844	67.1	156,772	31.3	2,615	0.5	1,541	0.3	4,068	0.8	179,072	R
West Virginia	642,752	375,551	58.4	263,784	41.0	1,313	0.2	401	0.1	1,703	0.3	111,767	R
Wisconsin	1,016,831	544,205	53.5	450,259	44.3	18,213	1.8	1,528	0.2	2,626	0.3	93,946	R
Wyoming	82,835	52,748	63.7	29,299	35.4	788	1.0	—		—		23,449	R
Totals	**36,805,951**	**21,437,277**	**58.2**	**15,007,698**	**40.8**	**265,583**	**0.7**	**46,896**	**0.1**	**48,497**	**0.1**	**6,429,579**	**R**

POPULAR VOTE

The Republican Party took the credit for the economic growth that led to the prosperity of 1928. Sales on the New York Stock Exchange jumped from 236 million shares in 1923 to more than 1 billion in 1928. Automobile manufacturing ranked number one in terms of product value. Almost 2.5 million passenger cars were manufactured in that year. The output of tires and inner tubes doubled from 1920 to 1928, and gasoline production increased fourfold. Although religion and Prohibition played large roles in the campaign, the election itself was about the booming economy. The 1928 campaign stressed the differences between the candidates: Secretary of Commerce Herbert Hoover of California and Governor Alfred E. Smith of New York. Although their backgrounds were as different as one could imagine, their positions on the political issues were often similar.

On 2 August 1927, exactly four years after his initial oath of office, Calvin Coolidge announced: "I do not choose to run for President in 1928." Coolidge, at the height of his popularity, never gave his reasons for not seeking re-election. The Republican Party met in Kansas City, Missouri, on 12 June 1928, and six names were placed in nomination. Former Illinois Governor Frank O. Lowden withdrew, and Herbert Hoover was nominated on the first ballot. Hoover had gained fame as an able war administrator and as an effective secretary of commerce in the administrations of Warren G. Harding and Calvin Coolidge. Senator Charles Curtis of Kansas received the nomination for vice president. It was a relatively uneventful convention, highlighted by the speech of Senator George Moses of New Hampshire. Moses said: "Bring on the Tammany Tiger and we will bury him. We welcome him with hospitable hands to a bloody grave."

The Democrats met in Houston, Texas, in late June. Franklin D. Roosevelt again placed Alfred E. Smith's name in nomination and, after some vote switching, Smith was nominated on the first ballot. He was the first Catholic to be nominated for the presidency by a major party. He had risen in New York politics through his loyalty to the Tammany Hall political machine. As governor, Smith supported progressive social reforms and became the spokesman for the new urban masses. Smith faced an impossible fight at a time when the prejudices of the Ku Klux Klan were very powerful. Senate Minority Leader Joseph T. Robinson of Arkansas was nominated for vice president. Robinson, a "dry" Protestant from the South, balanced the ticket. However, neither vice presidential candidate had any real impact on the election.

The Republican platform pledged the "vigorous enforcement" of the Eighteenth Amendment (Prohibition). Hoover called it a "social and economic experiment, noble in motive." The Democrats pledged "the party and its nominees to an honest effort to enforce" Prohibition. However, Smith sent a telegraph to the Democratic Convention, saying that he refused to accept the Eighteenth Amendment.

In 1787, Thomas Jefferson wrote: "When we get piled upon one another in large cities, we shall become as corrupt as in Europe, and go to eating one another as they do there." By 1920, half the population of the United States lived in cities. Rural Americans distrusted cities and those who lived in them. The city came to symbolize corruption, saloons, the Catholic Church, a place where bankers lived, and home to immigrants who did not understand traditional American values. Between 1890 and 1920, 15 million immigrants arrived in the United States. Four out of five immigrants settled in the industrial cities of the Northeast and Midwest, where economic opportunities were the best. By 1900, more than one-third of Chicago's population was foreign-born. New York City had more foreign born residents than any city in the world. It had as many Italians as Naples, as many Germans as Hamburg, and twice as many Irish as Dublin.

Alfred E. Smith was born in a tenement in New York City's Lower East Side. His father, a Civil War veteran, was the son of a German mother and an Italian father. His mother was born in the same neighborhood to Irish parents. At age 14, a month before completing eighth grade, he had to leave school to work for $3 a week. Smith developed an interest in local politics. He ran errands for the local Democratic leaders, and he gradually worked his way into their inner circle. Early in 1895, at age 22, Smith was appointed to the political position of process server for the Commissioner of Jurors. In 1903, as a reward for his faithful service to the local ward boss, Smith won election to the New York State Assembly at the age of 30. Smith, untrained in law or in parliamentary procedure, rapidly developed a reputation as a hardworking, progressive legislator. He supported many efforts to help the "plain people": a bill to protect purchasers of coal against false weight; regulations for ventilating factories; a bill to install washrooms and eating places in factories; a bill to limit employment of women after childbirth; and legislation to force employers to grant rest periods to female workers. Smith introduced legislation to prohibit smoking near open gas jets in factories and a bill to establish worker's compensation for injuries sustained in the workplace. According to Republican Senator Elihu Root, Smith was the best-informed man in the state on legislative matters.

Smith always remained a faithful supporter of the Tammany Hall political machine. In 1916, Tammany leaders helped elect him sheriff of New York County. This post controlled political jobs and had very little to do with law enforcement. Through his skillful use of patronage, Smith built a loyal personal political organization. His salary as sheriff was about $60,000 a year in fees, a great sum of money for the time. In 1918, Smith was elected governor of New York. Defeated in the Harding landslide of 1920, he was reelected in 1922, 1924, and 1926. Smith's administrations continued his social legislative agenda. He surrounded himself with superb advisers regardless of their gender or religion, and many of his advisers went on to major positions in Franklin D. Roosevelt's presidential administrations.

Herbert Hoover was born in West Branch, Iowa, the son of a blacksmith. He and his family produced their own vegetables, baked the bread they ate, and made the soap they used. In the fall, jars and barrels filled the cellar which Hoover called in his memoirs "social security itself." His father died when he was 6; his mother died when he was 10. West Branch was a Quaker town, and the characteristic Quaker traits of self-reliance and individualism became deeply ingrained in his core beliefs. At age 11, Hoover was sent to live with an uncle and aunt in Oregon. In his autobiography, he recalled growing to love fishing in the mountain streams, using a "willow pole with a butcher's string-line, fixed with hooks ten for a dime." He wrote of the swimming holes and of trapping rabbits.

Hoover worked his way through Stanford University, where he majored in geology. After graduating, Hoover worked as a mining engineer throughout the world and was a millionaire by the age of 30. When the United States declared war on Germany in April 1917, President Woodrow Wilson asked him to become director of the U.S. Food Administration. At the end of the war, Wilson named

Hoover to administer food relief to starving Europeans. Hoover was, as his nominee had noted at the Republican Convention, "engineer, practical scientist, minister of mercy to the hungry, administrator, executive, statesman, beneficent American, kindly neighbor, wholesome human being."

Both Hoover and Smith were self-made men and were proud of it. During the 1928 campaign, Hoover stressed prosperity—"a chicken in every pot and two cars in every garage." Smith became the spokesman for city dwellers, most of whom had immigrant and Catholic backgrounds. Traditional southern Democrats supported Prohibition, believed in fundamental Protestantism, and saw Smith as the enemy. During the campaign, Smith crossed the Mississippi River for the first time. As he campaigned in Oklahoma, the Ku Klux Klan kept a burning cross, a symbol of the Klan, always in his sight. Smith became the embodiment of everything that aroused rural and small-town suspicions.

During the campaign, Hoover said, "My ancestors (Quakers) were persecuted for their beliefs . . . I stand for religious tolerance both in act and spirit." In spite of that, the Republican Party waged an ugly anti-Catholic campaign. Republican speakers claimed that the Catholic Church would rule the United States if Smith won. Abusive and insulting pamphlets slandered him for his religious convictions. However, it was neither religion nor Prohibition nor the personality differences between the candidates that decided the election. Eight years of Republican administrations had brought prosperity. Real wages had gone up, and unemployment was at a record low. There were more voters than ever before—almost 37 million. Hoover won the election with 21,437,277 votes (58.2 percent) to Smith's 15,007,698 (40.8 percent), taking the Electoral College by the decisive margin of 444 to 87. Smith won fewer electoral votes than had any Democrat since Horace Greeley in 1872. For the first time since Reconstruction, the Republicans split the Solid South. On the other hand, Smith came close to carrying most of the nation's 12 largest cities, and he carried two states—Massachusetts and Rhode Island—in the traditionally Republican Northeast. Smith's appeal to the new mix of voters in cities helped make the Democratic Party the urban party in America for the future.

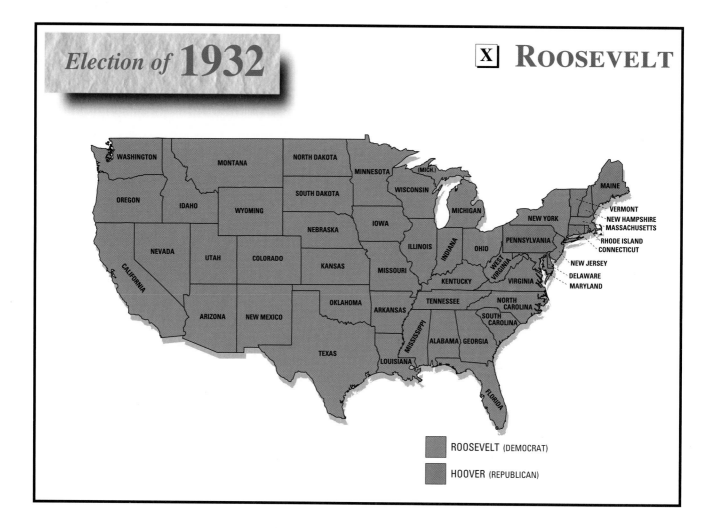

Election of 1932

X **ROOSEVELT**

States	Electoral Votes	Roosevelt	Hoover		States	Electoral Votes	Roosevelt	Hoover
Alabama	(11)	11	-		Nebraska	(7)	7	-
Arizona	(3)	3	-		Nevada	(3)	3	-
Arkansas	(9)	9	-		New Hampshire	(4)	-	4
California	(22)	22	-		New Jersey	(16)	16	-
Colorado	(6)	6	-		New Mexico	(3)	3	-
Connecticut	(8)	-	8		New York	(47)	47	-
Delaware	(3)	-	3		North Carolina	(13)	13	-
Florida	(7)	7	-		North Dakota	(4)	4	-
Georgia	(12)	12	-		Ohio	(26)	26	-
Idaho	(4)	4	-		Oklahoma	(11)	11	-
Illinois	(29)	29	-		Oregon	(5)	5	-
Indiana	(14)	14	-		Pennsylvania	(36)	-	36
Iowa	(11)	11	-		Rhode Island	(4)	4	-
Kansas	(9)	9	-		South Carolina	(8)	8	-
Kentucky	(11)	11	-		South Dakota	(4)	4	-
Louisiana	(10)	10	-		Tennessee	(11)	11	-
Maine	(5)	-	5		Texas	(23)	23	-
Maryland	(8)	8	-		Utah	(4)	4	-
Massachusetts	(17)	17	-		Vermont	(3)	-	3
Michigan	(19)	19	-		Virginia	(11)	11	-
Minnesota	(11)	11	-		Washington	(8)	8	-
Mississippi	(9)	9	-		West Virginia	(8)	8	-
Missouri	(15)	15	-		Wisconsin	(12)	12	-
Montana	(4)	4	-		Wyoming	(3)	3	-
					Totals	**(531)**	**472**	**59**

ELECTORAL VOTE

Election of 1932

STATE	TOTAL VOTE	FRANKLIN D. ROOSEVELT (Democrat)		HERBERT C. HOOVER (Republican)		NORMAN M. THOMAS (Socialist)		WILLIAM Z. FOSTER (Communist)		OTHER		PLURALITY	
		Votes	%	Votes	%	Votes	%	Votes	%	Votes	%		
Alabama	245,303	207,910	84.8	34,675	14.1	2,030	0.8	675	0.3	13		173,235	D
Arizona	118,251	79,264	67.0	36,104	30.5	2,618	2.2	256	0.2	9		43,160	D
Arkansas	216,569	186,829	86.3	27,465	12.7	1,166	0.5	157	0.1	952	0.4	159,364	D
California	2,266,972	1,324,157	58.4	847,902	37.4	63,299	2.8	1,023		30,591	1.3	476,255	D
Colorado	457,696	250,877	54.8	189,617	41.4	13,591	3.0	787	0.2	2,824	0.6	61,260	D
Connecticut	594,183	281,632	47.4	288,420	48.5	20,480	3.4	1,364	0.2	2,287	0.4	6,788	R
Delaware	112,901	54,319	48.1	57,073	50.6	1,376	1.2	133	0.1	—		2,754	R
Florida	276,943	206,307	74.5	69,170	25.0	775	0.3	—		691	0.2	137,137	D
Georgia	255,590	234,118	91.6	19,863	7.8	461	0.2	23		1,125	0.4	214,255	D
Idaho	186,520	109,479	58.7	71,312	38.2	526	0.3	491	0.3	4,712	2.5	38,167	D
Illinois	3,407,926	1,882,304	55.2	1,432,756	42.0	67,258	2.0	15,582	0.5	10,026	0.3	449,548	D
Indiana	1,576,927	862,054	54.7	677,184	42.9	21,388	1.4	2,187	0.1	14,114	0.9	184,870	D
Iowa	1,036,687	598,019	57.7	414,433	40.0	20,467	2.0	559	0.1	3,209	0.3	183,586	D
Kansas	791,978	424,204	53.6	349,498	44.1	18,276	2.3	—		—		74,706	D
Kentucky	983,059	580,574	59.1	394,716	40.2	3,853	0.4	271		3,645	0.4	185,858	D
Louisiana	268,804	249,418	92.8	18,853	7.0	—		—		533	0.2	230,565	D
Maine	298,444	128,907	43.2	166,631	55.8	2,489	0.8	162	0.1	255	0.1	37,724	R
Maryland	511,054	314,314	61.5	184,184	36.0	10,489	2.1	1,031	0.2	1,036	0.2	130,130	D
Massachusetts	1,580,114	800,148	50.6	736,959	46.6	34,305	2.2	4,821	0.3	3,881	0.2	63,189	D
Michigan	1,664,765	871,700	52.4	739,894	44.4	39,205	2.4	9,318	0.6	4,648	0.3	131,806	D
Minnesota	1,002,843	600,806	59.9	363,959	36.3	25,476	2.5	6,101	0.6	6,501	0.6	236,847	D
Mississippi	146,034	140,168	96.0	5,180	3.5	686	0.5	—		—		134,988	D
Missouri	1,609,894	1,025,406	63.7	564,713	35.1	16,374	1.0	568		2,833	0.2	460,693	D
Montana	216,479	127,286	58.8	78,078	36.1	7,891	3.6	1,775	0.8	1,449	0.7	49,208	D
Nebraska	570,135	359,082	63.0	201,177	35.3	9,876	1.7	—		—		157,905	D
Nevada	41,430	28,756	69.4	12,674	30.6	—		—		—		16,082	D
New Hampshire	205,520	100,680	49.0	103,629	50.4	947	0.5	264	0.1	—		2,949	R
New Jersey	1,630,063	806,630	49.5	775,684	47.6	42,998	2.6	2,915	0.2	1,836	0.1	30,946	D
New Mexico	151,606	95,089	62.7	54,217	35.8	1,776	1.2	135	0.1	389	0.3	40,872	D
New York	4,688,614	2,534,959	54.1	1,937,963	41.3	177,397	3.8	27,956	0.6	10,339	0.2	596,996	D
North Carolina	711,498	497,566	69.9	208,344	29.3	5,588	0.8	—		—		289,222	D
North Dakota	256,290	178,350	69.6	71,772	28.0	3,521	1.4	830	0.3	1,817	0.7	106,578	D
Ohio	2,609,728	1,301,695	49.9	1,227,319	47.0	64,094	2.5	7,231	0.3	9,389	0.4	74,376	D
Oklahoma	704,633	516,468	73.3	188,165	26.7	—		—		—		328,303	D
Oregon	368,751	213,871	58.0	136,019	36.9	15,450	4.2	1,681	0.5	1,730	0.5	77,852	D
Pennsylvania	2,859,021	1,295,948	45.3	1,453,540	50.8	91,119	3.2	5,658	0.2	12,756	0.4	157,592	R
Rhode Island	266,170	146,604	55.1	115,266	43.3	3,138	1.2	546	0.2	616	0.2	31,338	D
South Carolina	104,407	102,347	98.0	1,978	1.9	82	0.1	—		—		100,369	D
South Dakota	288,438	183,515	63.6	99,212	34.4	1,551	0.5	364	0.1	3,796	1.3	84,303	D
Tennessee	390,273	259,473	66.5	126,752	32.5	1,796	0.5	254	0.1	1,998	0.5	132,721	D
Texas	874,382	771,109	88.2	98,218	11.2	4,414	0.5	207		434		672,891	D
Utah	206,578	116,750	56.5	84,795	41.0	4,087	2.0	946	0.5	—		31,955	D
Vermont	136,980	56,266	41.1	78,984	57.7	1,533	1.1	195	0.1	2		22,718	R
Virginia	297,942	203,979	68.5	89,637	30.1	2,382	0.8	86		1,858	0.6	114,342	D
Washington	614,814	353,260	57.5	208,645	33.9	17,080	2.8	2,972	0.5	32,857	5.3	144,615	D
West Virginia	743,774	405,124	54.5	330,731	44.5	5,133	0.7	444	0.1	2,342	0.3	74,393	D
Wisconsin	1,114,814	707,410	63.5	347,741	31.2	53,379	4.8	3,105	0.3	3,179	0.3	359,669	D
Wyoming	96,962	54,370	56.1	39,583	40.8	2,829	2.9	180	0.2	—		14,787	D
Totals	39,758,759	22,829,501	57.4	15,760,684	39.6	884,649	2.2	103,253	0.3	180,672	0.5	7,068,817	D

P O P U L A R   V O T E

The 1932 presidential election came in the third year of the greatest economic depression ever experienced by the American people. The descent from the height of prosperity of the late 1920s had been rapid, bringing fear and uncertainty. During the 1920s, the United States was the most prosperous country in the world. American factories produced millions of automobiles, refrigerators, radios, phonographs, vacuum cleaners, and all sorts of manufactured goods. Wages were the highest in history.

In 1926, the president of the New York Stock Exchange declared that the average employee could become wealthy through stock investments: "The benefits of the capitalistic system are becoming practically universal," he boasted. It seemed as though everyone was trying to get rich quick. Between 1923 and 1929, common stock prices rose about 200 percent. In his 1929 inaugural address, President Herbert Hoover had declared: "I have no fear for the future of our country. It is bright with hope." Less than eight months later, on Black Monday, 29 October 1929, stock prices at the New York Stock Exchange fell in the most disastrous day in the history of the market. This sharp downward plunge of the market triggered a terrible contraction in the economy. Stocks and bonds, ironically called securities, declined steadily for the next three and one-half years. Thousands of speculators, large and small, were wiped out. Between 1929 and 1932, thousands of manufacturers closed plants or reduced their work forces. On the average, 100,000 workers were fired each week. The number of unemployed stood at 2 million in 1929; by 1932, it had risen to 12 million. Over 5,000 banks went bankrupt and 9 million savings accounts were wiped out. Tens of thousands of mortgages were foreclosed.

There are many reasons for the economic collapse and the ensuing period known as the Great Depression. Democrats blamed it on Republican economic policies, such as the high protective tariff. Hoover argued that the European banking crises of 1931 prevented the United States from coming out of the depression without serious hardships. He described the 17 months from October 1929 to April 1931 as "a period of a comparatively mild domestic readjustment such as the country had experienced before." The *Washington Post,* which supported Hoover, denounced the Democrats for trying to make the economic situation a political issue. When "we give freedom to individuals and business," the newspaper editorialized, "we shouldn't blame the government if that

freedom brings mistakes and depression and trouble." Former Senator James A. Reed of Missouri replied bitingly that the Republican Party had maintained for 40 years that "it was the producer of prosperity, and now if it says it has no control over financial and economic conditions, it has perpetrated a 40-year fraud upon the American people and has gained and kept office by false pretenses."

By 1932, the great automobile plants of Detroit were operating at only 20 percent of capacity. Henry Ford attributed this to "mass laziness." The huge steel plants of Pittsburgh were working at 12 percent of capacity. On 11 December 1930, the Bank of the United States, a private bank with 60 offices and 400,000 depositors, went bankrupt. Day after day, week after week, the unemployed faced locked factories. Deaths due to starvation became a new category for the New York City Board of Health. A million or more Americans wandered aimlessly through the country in search of work. A popular song, "Brother, Can you spare a dime?" was a sign of how common a sight begging had become. "No one can live and work in New York this winter without a profound sense of uneasiness," economist Rexford G. Tugwell recorded in his diary. Tugwell noted: "Never in modern times, I think, has there been so widespread unemployment and such moving distress from sheer hunger and cold."

Hoover, the "great humanitarian" of the war years, became the symbol of heartlessness. His statements attempting to minimize the extent of the human crisis hurt his image even more. The way he responded to the 1932 Bonus Army wiped out any chance of reelection he may have had. Some 17,000 jobless veterans of World War I had marched to Washington in hopes of persuading Congress to vote a bonus for them. On Hoover's orders, the marchers were driven from the city by army units. The Chief of Staff, General Douglas MacArthur, went further than Hoover had intended, using tear gas and bayonets. Hoover's contention that the bonus seekers were infiltrated by "communists and other persons with criminal records" carried little weight with the voters.

The dispirited Republican Convention opened in Chicago on 14 June 1932. "There is not a single soul thus far I have met, stand-pat, Progressive or otherwise, who believes Hoover can be elected," Senator Hiram Johnson of California wrote. A few Republicans tried to start a movement to draft Calvin Coolidge but the former president firmly ended such talk. The delegates, according to a reporter for *The Nation,* seemed to take little interest in the huge economic problems facing the country and focused on whether or not the Prohibition Amendment should be repealed. They adopted a plank which both defended prohibition and also asserted the right of the people to repeal it.

Hoover was renominated on the first ballot. Speakers praised him as a leader who had saved the nation from communism and who "knows the burden of the heat of the day." The delegates paraded up and down the aisles for half an hour and balloons drifted down from the rafters. There was no opportunity for the national radio audience to hear any dissent. The convention adjourned after selecting Charles Curtis of Kansas for vice president. They left the task of saving the party from impending disaster in the President's hands.

The Democrats began their convention in Chicago on 27 June confident of victory. The leading candidates were Franklin D. Roosevelt, governor of New York, Alfred E. Smith, the former governor of New York, and John Nance Garner, Speaker of the House of Representatives. Fearing a deadlocked convention, Garner threw his support to Roosevelt who won the nomination on the fourth ballot. Garner was chosen for vice president. Roosevelt's pre-convention campaign was managed by journalist Louis Howe and James A. Farley, the New York Democratic chairman. Roosevelt had cleverly bridged the gulf between the urban and rural Democrats. He was ready to emphasize economic issues and ignore the earlier divisions over prohibition and religion. Breaking precedent, the 50-year-old governor flew to Chicago from Albany to deliver his acceptance address before the convention. He was unable to walk even a short distance without canes and leg braces because of an attack of polio in 1921, and he wanted to silence the doubts about his health. "I pledge you," he told the delegates, "I pledge myself to a new deal for the American people." Thus, the Roosevelt program acquired a name before the electorate had the haziest notion of what that program might be.

Roosevelt toured the nation talking about economic reforms. He declared his total support for the system of capitalism but insisted that changes were needed to prevent dangerous revolutionary movements from developing out of the economic collapse. Hoover, on the other hand, opposed proposals for additional federal controls. Hoover wrote every word of his speeches. They were long and boring and warned of great disasters if the people abandoned his wise leadership for the radicalism of Roosevelt and his advisers. He stressed his belief that the voluntary cooperation of individuals would restore prosperity. Only a monumental mistake by the Democrats or a spectacular improvement in the economy could save the Republicans from defeat. Neither event occurred.

On Election Day, the nation gave Roosevelt a smashing victory. He received almost 23 million votes (57.4 percent) to less than 16 million votes for Hoover (39.6 percent). Hoover carried only six states, losing the electoral vote 472 to 59. The Democrats elected heavy majorities to both houses of Congress. The election also marked the first time since 1876 that a majority of voters cast their presidential ballot for the Democratic nominee.

"This is the greatest night of my life!" Roosevelt declared on hearing the election results. Later that evening, as his son James helped him into bed, the president-elect told his son that fire was the only thing he had ever been afraid of. He said, "Tonight I think I'm afraid of something else . . . I'm afraid that I may not have the strength to do this job." He then asked his son to pray for him.

The people looked to Roosevelt for leadership but they had only a vague notion of the direction in which he intended to lead them. "I have looked into the faces of thousands of Americans," Roosevelt told a friend during the campaign. "They have the frightened look of lost children . . . They are saying 'We're caught in something we don't understand; perhaps this fellow can help us out.'" The voters wanted a change, and they had placed their faith in Franklin Delano Roosevelt.

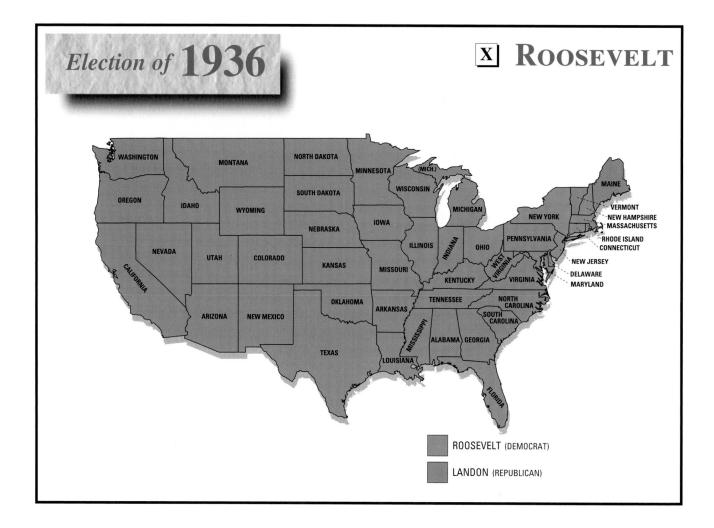

Election of 1936

☒ **ROOSEVELT**

ROOSEVELT (DEMOCRAT)

LANDON (REPUBLICAN)

States	Electoral Votes	Roosevelt	Landon	States	Electoral Votes	Roosevelt	Landon
Alabama	(11)	11	-	Nebraska	(7)	7	-
Arizona	(3)	3	-	Nevada	(3)	3	-
Arkansas	(9)	9	-	New Hampshire	(4)	4	-
California	(22)	22	-	New Jersey	(16)	16	-
Colorado	(6)	6	-	New Mexico	(3)	3	-
Connecticut	(8)	8	-	New York	(47)	47	-
Delaware	(3)	3	-	North Carolina	(13)	13	-
Florida	(7)	7	-	North Dakota	(4)	4	-
Georgia	(12)	12	-	Ohio	(26)	26	-
Idaho	(4)	4	-	Oklahoma	(11)	11	-
Illinois	(29)	29	-	Oregon	(5)	5	-
Indiana	(14)	14	-	Pennsylvania	(36)	36	-
Iowa	(11)	11	-	Rhode Island	(4)	4	-
Kansas	(9)	9	-	South Carolina	(8)	8	-
Kentucky	(11)	11	-	South Dakota	(4)	4	-
Louisiana	(10)	10	-	Tennessee	(11)	11	-
Maine	(5)	-	5	Texas	(23)	23	-
Maryland	(8)	8	-	Utah	(4)	4	-
Massachusetts	(17)	17	-	Vermont	(3)	-	3
Michigan	(19)	19	-	Virginia	(11)	11	-
Minnesota	(11)	11	-	Washington	(8)	8	-
Mississippi	(9)	9	-	West Virginia	(8)	8	-
Missouri	(15)	15	-	Wisconsin	(12)	12	-
Montana	(4)	4	-	Wyoming	(3)	3	-
				Totals	**(531)**	**523**	**8**

ELECTORAL VOTE

Election of 1936

STATE	TOTAL VOTE	FRANKLIN D. ROOSEVELT (Democrat)		ALFRED M. LANDON (Republican)		WILLIAM LEMKE (Union)		NORMAN M. THOMAS (Socialist)		OTHER		PLURALITY	
		Votes	%	Votes	%	Votes	%	Votes	%	Votes	%		
Alabama	275,744	238,196	86.4	35,358	12.8	551	0.2	242	0.1	1,397	0.5	202,838	D
Arizona	124,163	86,722	69.8	33,433	26.9	3,307	2.7	317	0.3	384	0.3	53,289	D
Arkansas	179,431	146,765	81.8	32,049	17.9	4		446	0.2	167	0.1	114,716	D
California	2,638,882	1,766,836	67.0	836,431	31.7	—		11,331	0.4	24,284	0.9	930,405	D
Colorado	488,685	295,021	60.4	181,267	37.1	9,962	2.0	1,594	0.3	841	0.2	113,754	D
Connecticut	690,723	382,129	55.3	278,685	40.3	21,805	3.2	5,683	0.8	2,421	0.4	103,444	D
Delaware	127,603	69,702	54.6	57,236	44.9	442	0.3	172	0.1	51		12,466	D
Florida	327,436	249,117	76.1	78,248	23.9	—		—		71		170,869	D
Georgia	293,170	255,363	87.1	36,943	12.6	136		68		660	0.2	218,420	D
Idaho	199,617	125,683	63.0	66,256	33.2	7,678	3.8	—		—		59,427	D
Illinois	3,956,522	2,282,999	57.7	1,570,393	39.7	89,439	2.3	7,530	0.2	6,161	0.2	712,606	D
Indiana	1,650,897	934,974	56.6	691,570	41.9	19,407	1.2	3,856	0.2	1,090	0.1	243,404	D
Iowa	1,142,737	621,756	54.4	487,977	42.7	29,687	2.6	1,373	0.1	1,944	0.2	133,779	D
Kansas	865,507	464,520	53.7	397,727	46.0	494	0.1	2,766	0.3	—		66,793	D
Kentucky	926,214	541,944	58.5	369,702	39.9	12,501	1.3	627	0.1	1,440	0.2	172,242	D
Louisiana	329,778	292,894	88.8	36,791	11.2	—		—		93		256,103	D
Maine	304,240	126,333	41.5	168,823	55.5	7,581	2.5	783	0.3	720	0.2	42,490	R
Maryland	624,896	389,612	62.3	231,435	37.0	—		1,629	0.3	2,220	0.4	158,177	D
Massachusetts	1,840,357	942,716	51.2	768,613	41.8	118,639	6.4	5,111	0.3	5,278	0.3	174,103	D
Michigan	1,805,098	1,016,794	56.3	699,733	38.8	75,795	4.2	8,208	0.5	4,568	0.3	317,061	D
Minnesota	1,129,975	698,811	61.8	350,461	31.0	74,296	6.6	2,872	0.3	3,535	0.3	348,350	D
Mississippi	162,142	157,333	97.0	4,467	2.8	—		342	0.2	—		152,866	D
Missouri	1,828,635	1,111,043	60.8	697,891	38.2	14,630	0.8	3,454	0.2	1,617	0.1	413,152	D
Montana	230,502	159,690	69.3	63,598	27.6	5,539	2.4	1,066	0.5	609	0.3	96,092	D
Nebraska	608,023	347,445	57.1	247,731	40.7	12,847	2.1	—		—		99,714	D
Nevada	43,848	31,925	72.8	11,923	27.2	—		—		—		20,002	D
New Hampshire	218,114	108,460	49.7	104,642	48.0	4,819	2.2	—		193	0.1	3,818	D
New Jersey	1,820,437	1,083,850	59.5	720,322	39.6	9,407	0.5	3,931	0.2	2,927	0.2	363,528	D
New Mexico	169,135	106,037	62.7	61,727	36.5	924	0.5	343	0.2	104	0.1	44,310	D
New York	5,596,398	3,293,222	58.8	2,180,670	39.0	—		86,897	1.6	35,609	0.6	1,112,552	D
North Carolina	839,475	616,141	73.4	223,294	26.6	2		21		17		392,847	D
North Dakota	273,716	163,148	59.6	72,751	26.6	36,708	13.4	552	0.2	557	0.2	90,397	D
Ohio	3,012,660	1,747,140	58.0	1,127,855	37.4	132,212	4.4	167		5,286	0.2	619,285	D
Oklahoma	749,740	501,069	66.8	245,122	32.7	—		2,221	0.3	1,328	0.2	255,947	D
Oregon	414,021	266,733	64.4	122,706	29.6	21,831	5.3	2,143	0.5	608	0.1	144,027	D
Pennsylvania	4,138,105	2,353,788	56.9	1,690,300	40.8	67,467	1.6	14,375	0.3	12,175	0.3	663,488	D
Rhode Island	310,278	164,338	53.0	125,031	40.3	19,569	6.3	—		1,340	0.4	39,307	D
South Carolina	115,437	113,791	98.6	1,646	1.4	—		—		—		112,145	D
South Dakota	296,452	160,137	54.0	125,977	42.5	10,338	3.5	—		—		34,160	D
Tennessee	477,086	328,083	68.8	147,055	30.8	296	0.1	692	0.1	960	0.2	181,028	D
Texas	849,701	739,952	87.1	104,661	12.3	3,187	0.4	1,122	0.1	779	0.1	635,291	D
Utah	216,679	150,248	69.3	64,555	29.8	1,121	0.5	432	0.2	323	0.1	85,693	D
Vermont	143,689	62,124	43.2	81,023	56.4	—		—		542	0.4	18,899	R
Virginia	334,590	234,980	70.2	98,336	29.4	233	0.1	313	0.1	728	0.2	136,644	D
Washington	692,338	459,579	66.4	206,892	29.9	17,463	2.5	3,496	0.5	4,908	0.7	252,687	D
West Virginia	829,945	502,582	60.6	325,358	39.2	—		832	0.1	1,173	0.1	177,224	D
Wisconsin	1,258,560	802,984	63.8	380,828	30.3	60,297	4.8	10,626	0.8	3,825	0.3	422,156	D
Wyoming	103,382	62,624	60.6	38,739	37.5	1,653	1.6	200	0.2	166	0.2	23,885	D
Totals	45,654,763	27,757,333	60.8	16,684,231	36.5	892,267	2.0	187,833	0.4	133,099	0.3	11,073,102	D

P O P U L A R   V O T E

More important legislation was passed during Franklin D. Roosevelt's first term than in any other four years in U.S. history. Roosevelt and his advisers believed that immediate federal action was needed to restore confidence in the economic system. Their goal was to maintain capitalism but, at the same time, to reform not destroy the economic system that had brought hardships to so many. Roosevelt was at the height of his popularity in 1936. His vigorous reform policies and his attack on the conditions brought on by the depression had made him a sure winner for a second term. The Republicans, however, attacked every aspect of his programs. "America is in peril," their 1936 platform began. "We invite all Americans, irrespective of party to join us in defense of American institutions." The President also faced the objections of radicals who thought the capitalist system should be replaced.

The President's optimism and self-assurance were conveyed in a series of very successful radio addresses which came to be known as "the fireside chats." There were about 30 such broadcasts during his 12 years in office. "My friends," he would begin, and then, in simple but eloquent language, he would explain a new program or policy. Eleanor Roosevelt later wrote that, after her husband's death, people would stop her on the street to say, "He used to talk to me about my government." The first fireside chat, a few days after he took office, dealt with the banking and financial crisis. After discussing his program, which included a four-day national banking holiday, Roosevelt asked the public to share their views with him. The White House received thousands of letters from ordinary people who were convinced that the President was willing to listen. And he did.

A bewildering number of laws had been passed under the New Deal, and dozens of agencies had been created to meet the problems of relief, recovery, and reform. Although these policies did not completely alleviate depression conditions, they did return hope to the United States. Unemployment was reduced and the government's vast relief programs cared for millions still without work. Farm prices rose dramatically. In 1936, corn sold at $1.26 a bushel compared to 24 cents in 1933. The price of wheat reached $1.51 a bushel; it had been 47 cents four years earlier. Weekly factory wages increased an estimated 65 percent. The New Deal programs quickly made Roosevelt the hero of the working class.

One of Roosevelt's favorite programs was the Civilian Conservation Corps (CCC). Between 1933 and 1941, the CCC hired some 2.7 million men between the ages of 18 and 25. They were put to work on erosion control, planting trees, fighting forest fires, dam construction, and other such projects. The young men were recruited mainly from the cities where it was almost impossible to find a job and lived in camps built by the War Department. Of the $30 a month in wages received, $22 was sent home to the young man's family. Young people were also assisted by the National Youth Administration (NYA). The agency paid small stipends to more than 500,000 college students to do part-time work, in libraries or as research aides. Another 1.5 million high school students received similar aid. The aim of both the CCC and the NYA, in addition to helping young people, was to try to prevent them from adding to the ranks of the unemployed.

In 1935, most relief programs—that is, programs to help the unemployed—had been combined under a new agency, the Works Progress Administration (WPA). The WPA attempted to make use of an individual's skill, whether it be sewing or translating books into Braille. At its peak in November 1938, nearly 3.3 million persons were on its payroll. When the WPA ended in 1941, it had provided work for a total of 8 million people. Among its 250,000 projects, the WPA had built or improved more than 2,500 hospitals, 5,900 school buildings, 1,000 airports, and nearly 13,000 playgrounds. The WPA also gave employment to artists, musicians, actors, singers, and writers. Critics called these make-work programs a "boondoggle"— a waste of money. However, they put people back to work. Their salaries, besides giving them the ability to buy things, also helped to stimulate the depressed economy.

There were dozens of these "alphabet agencies" which affected agriculture, banking, housing, finance, and electric power. Though Roosevelt vastly expanded presidential involvement in the process of government, the balance of power with the legislative and judicial branches survived. The economic system of capitalism remained. No industry was nationalized and the profit motive still prevailed. In the 1934 congressional elections, the Democrats had won overwhelming victories, swelling their majorities in both the House and the Senate. This Democratic landslide could only be interpreted as a ringing endorsement for Roosevelt's policies.

But where did the money come from for these programs? In 1933, Roosevelt took the nation permanently off the gold standard. The government now could issue paper currency without gold backing as "legal tender for all debts, public and private." Conservatives were horrified. Banker Winthrop Aldrich told a congressional committee that nobody could possibly propose a rejection of the gold contract written on every bank and every piece of Federal Reserve currency. Financier Bernard Baruch, a Democrat, reacted with indignation: "The crowd has seized the seat of government and is trying to seize the wealth." In addition, the Wealth Tax Cut of 1935 increased the income tax surcharge on the upper brackets to the highest rates in history. The President, for his part, missed few opportunities to point out, with puckish delight, that the rich and well-born detested him.

The Republicans nominated Alfred M. Landon, the governor of Kansas, for president, and Colonel Frank Knox for vice president. Knox, the owner-publisher of the Chicago *Daily News,* had served as a Rough Rider under Theodore Roosevelt. Landon's supporters described him as an administrator who could be humane without being wasteful. Landon was an excellent choice for the party. He had been a successful independent oil operator who favored a balanced budget and a return to the gold standard. Although he had pledged to support many New Deal programs, such as Social Security, he opposed a strong central government with its increased bureaucracy. In November 1935, he summed up his middle-of-the-road political philosophy: "I think four more years of the same polices that we have had will wreck our parliamentary government and four years of the old policies will do the job also."

A poor public speaker, especially when compared to Roosevelt, Landon's earthy small-town manner made him an appealing candidate. He was promoted as a "liberal Coolidge." Eleanor Medill "Cissy" Patterson, publisher of the Washington *Herald,* said on leaving the governor's office: "I thought of Lincoln." Some leading Democrats bitterly criticized Roosevelt's advisers as well as Roosevelt himself for the enormous authority he had assumed. John W. Davis and Alfred E. Smith, the Democratic presidential candidates in 1924 and 1928, endorsed Landon.

Roosevelt was at the height of his political powers in 1936. He electrified more than 100,000 people who came to hear his acceptance speech at the Democratic Convention at rain-soaked Franklin Field in Philadelphia. He then embarked on a triumphal trip across the United States, speaking to crowds of unprecedented size. Wherever he spoke, Roosevelt boasted of the economic gains his administration had made. He contrasted the United States in 1936 and in 1932. From the rear platform of a train in Colorado Springs on 12 October, he said, "You know, there has been a good deal of difference in tourists. In 1932, when I came out through here, there were a lot of tourists—but they were riding in box cars. This year there are more of them—and they are riding in Pullmans." The enthusiastic responses of the crowds to Roosevelt startled most veterans of previous campaigns. People carried homemade signs: "He gave me a job;" "He restored my dignity." Huge crowds greeted him everywhere he went.

Landon told a reporter 20 years later: "Shortly after I was nominated in June, I sent for Mr. Benjamin Anderson of the Chase National Bank and Colonel Ayres of the Cleveland Trust Company. I asked them what business conditions would be like from June to November. They advised me each month would be better than the succeeding month. I realized then the campaign was pretty hopeless."

Roosevelt received the greatest landslide in U.S. history up to that time. He received 60.8 percent of the popular votes to Landon's 36.5 percent. Roosevelt won by more than 11 million votes, carrying every state except Maine and Vermont. He received 523 electoral votes to Landon's 8. The staunchly Republican states of Pennsylvania, Delaware, and Connecticut had gone Democratic for the first time since 1856. Landon's popular percentage was the smallest for any Republican nominee since Taft, when the party divided in 1912. The 1936 election demonstrated that the New Deal had created a new coalition that included farmers, union members, and the poor. African Americans switched en masse from the party of Lincoln to the party of Roosevelt. The voters had the opportunity to reject the growth of big government but instead they gave it a rousing endorsement.

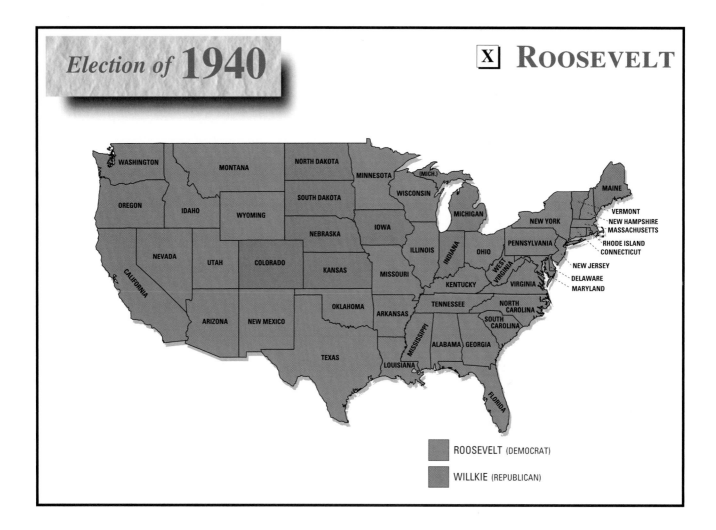

Election of **1940**

X ROOSEVELT

ROOSEVELT (DEMOCRAT)

WILLKIE (REPUBLICAN)

States	Electoral Votes	Roosevelt	Willkie	States	Electoral Votes	Roosevelt	Willkie
Alabama	(11)	11	-	Nebraska	(7)	-	7
Arizona	(3)	3	-	Nevada	(3)	3	-
Arkansas	(9)	9	-	New Hampshire	(4)	4	-
California	(22)	22	-	New Jersey	(16)	16	-
Colorado	(6)	-	6	New Mexico	(3)	3	-
Connecticut	(8)	8	-	New York	(47)	47	-
Delaware	(3)	3	-	North Carolina	(13)	13	-
Florida	(7)	7	-	North Dakota	(4)	-	4
Georgia	(12)	12	-	Ohio	(26)	26	-
Idaho	(4)	4	-	Oklahoma	(11)	11	-
Illinois	(29)	29	-	Oregon	(5)	5	-
Indiana	(14)	-	14	Pennsylvania	(36)	36	-
Iowa	(11)	-	11	Rhode Island	(4)	4	-
Kansas	(9)	-	9	South Carolina	(8)	8	-
Kentucky	(11)	11	-	South Dakota	(4)	-	4
Louisiana	(10)	10	-	Tennessee	(11)	11	-
Maine	(5)	-	5	Texas	(23)	23	-
Maryland	(8)	8	-	Utah	(4)	4	-
Massachusetts	(17)	17	-	Vermont	(3)	-	3
Michigan	(19)	-	19	Virginia	(11)	11	-
Minnesota	(11)	11	-	Washington	(8)	8	-
Mississippi	(9)	9	-	West Virginia	(8)	8	-
Missouri	(15)	15	-	Wisconsin	(12)	12	-
Montana	(4)	4	-	Wyoming	(3)	3	-
				Totals	**(531)**	**449**	**82**

ELECTORAL VOTE

Election of 1940

STATE	TOTAL VOTE	FRANKLIN D. ROOSEVELT (Democrat)		WENDELL WILLKIE (Republican)		NORMAN M. THOMAS (Socialist)		ROGER W. BABSON (Prohibition)		OTHER		PLURALITY	
		Votes	%	Votes	%	Votes	%	Votes	%	Votes	%		
Alabama	294,219	250,726	85.2	42,184	14.3	100		700	0.2	509	0.2	208,542	D
Arizona	150,039	95,267	63.5	54,030	36.0	—		742	0.5	—		41,237	D
Arkansas	200,429	157,213	78.4	42,122	21.0	301	0.2	793	0.4	—		115,091	D
California	3,268,791	1,877,618	57.4	1,351,419	41.3	16,506	0.5	9,400	0.3	13,848	0.4	526,199	D
Colorado	549,004	265,554	48.4	279,576	50.9	1,899	0.3	1,597	0.3	378	0.1	14,022	R
Connecticut	781,502	417,621	53.4	361,819	46.3	—		—		2,062	0.3	55,802	D
Delaware	136,374	74,599	54.7	61,440	45.1	115	0.1	220	0.2	—		13,159	D
Florida	485,640	359,334	74.0	126,158	26.0	—		—		148		233,176	D
Georgia	312,686	265,194	84.8	46,495	14.9	—		983	0.3	14		218,699	D
Idaho	235,168	127,842	54.4	106,553	45.3	497	0.2	—		276	0.1	21,289	D
Illinois	4,217,935	2,149,934	51.0	2,047,240	48.5	10,914	0.3	9,190	0.2	657		102,694	D
Indiana	1,782,747	874,063	49.0	899,466	50.5	2,075	0.1	6,437	0.4	706		25,403	R
Iowa	1,215,432	578,802	47.6	632,370	52.0	—		2,284	0.2	1,976	0.2	53,568	R
Kansas	860,297	364,725	42.4	489,169	56.9	2,347	0.3	4,056	0.5	—		124,444	R
Kentucky	970,163	557,322	57.4	410,384	42.3	1,014	0.1	1,443	0.1	—		146,938	D
Louisiana	372,305	319,751	85.9	52,446	14.1	—		—		108		267,305	D
Maine	320,840	156,478	48.8	163,951	51.1	—		—		411	0.1	7,473	R
Maryland	660,104	384,546	58.3	269,534	40.8	4,093	0.6	—		1,931	0.3	115,012	D
Massachusetts	2,026,993	1,076,522	53.1	939,700	46.4	4,091	0.2	1,370	0.1	5,310	0.3	136,822	D
Michigan	2,085,929	1,032,991	49.5	1,039,917	49.9	7,593	0.4	1,795	0.1	3,633	0.2	6,926	R
Minnesota	1,251,188	644,196	51.5	596,274	47.7	5,454	0.4	—		5,264	0.4	47,922	D
Mississippi	175,824	168,267	95.7	7,364	4.2	193	0.1	—		—		160,903	D
Missouri	1,833,729	958,476	52.3	871,009	47.5	2,226	0.1	1,809	0.1	209		87,467	D
Montana	247,873	145,698	58.8	99,579	40.2	1,443	0.6	664	0.3	489	0.2	46,119	D
Nebraska	615,878	263,677	42.8	352,201	57.2	—		—		—		88,524	R
Nevada	53,174	31,945	60.1	21,229	39.9	—		—		—		10,716	D
New Hampshire	235,419	125,292	53.2	110,127	46.8	—		—		—		15,165	D
New Jersey	1,972,552	1,016,808	51.5	945,475	47.9	2,433	0.1	873		6,963	0.4	71,333	D
New Mexico	183,258	103,699	56.6	79,315	43.3	144	0.1	100	0.1	—		24,384	D
New York	6,301,596	3,251,918	51.6	3,027,478	48.0	18,950	0.3	3,250	0.1	—		224,440	D
North Carolina	822,648	609,015	74.0	213,633	26.0	—		—		—		395,382	D
North Dakota	280,775	124,036	44.2	154,590	55.1	1,279	0.5	325	0.1	545	0.2	30,554	R
Ohio	3,319,912	1,733,139	52.2	1,586,773	47.8	—		—		—		146,366	D
Oklahoma	826,212	474,313	57.4	348,872	42.2	—		3,027	0.4	—		125,441	D
Oregon	481,240	258,415	53.7	219,555	45.6	398	0.1	154		2,718	0.6	38,860	D
Pennsylvania	4,078,714	2,171,035	53.2	1,889,848	46.3	10,967	0.3	—		6,864	0.2	281,187	D
Rhode Island	321,152	182,181	56.7	138,654	43.2	—		74		243	0.1	43,527	D
South Carolina	99,830	95,470	95.6	4,360	4.4	—		—		—		91,110	D
South Dakota	308,427	131,362	42.6	177,065	57.4	—		—		—		45,703	R
Tennessee	522,823	351,601	67.3	169,153	32.4	463	0.1	1,606	0.3	—		182,448	D
Texas	1,124,437	909,974	80.9	212,692	18.9	628	0.1	928	0.1	215		697,282	D
Utah	247,819	154,277	62.3	93,151	37.6	200	0.1	—		191	0.1	61,126	D
Vermont	143,062	64,269	44.9	78,371	54.8	—		—		422	0.3	14,102	R
Virginia	346,608	235,961	68.1	109,363	31.6	282	0.1	882	0.3	120		126,598	D
Washington	793,833	462,145	58.2	322,123	40.6	4,586	0.6	1,686	0.2	3,293	0.4	140,022	D
West Virginia	868,076	495,662	57.1	372,414	42.9	—		—		—		123,248	D
Wisconsin	1,405,522	704,821	50.1	679,206	48.3	15,071	1.1	2,148	0.2	4,276	0.3	25,615	D
Wyoming	112,240	59,287	52.8	52,633	46.9	148	0.1	172	0.2	—		6,654	D
Totals	49,900,418	27,313,041	54.7	22,348,480	44.8	116,410	0.2	58,708	0.1	63,779	0.1	4,964,561	D

P O P U L A R   V O T E

Thomas Jefferson stated that the presidency could be turned into an undemocratic lifetime position without a fixed limit. Franklin D. Roosevelt decided to break precedent and seek a third term in 1940. He argued that the tradition of the two-term limit was less important than keeping his experienced leadership as another world war threatened to involve the United States.

Throughout the 1930s, the United States had clung to an isolationist foreign policy. However, events in Europe, climaxing with the German invasion of Poland in 1939, convinced many Americans that their own interests were seriously threatened. According to a Gallup Poll, 82 percent of the people in the United States favored an Allied victory and only 2 percent supported Nazi Germany. Nevertheless, there was an almost unanimous feeling that the United States must avoid any involvement in another European war. Sensing the divided mood of the country, Roosevelt tried to balance the desire to stay out of the war against the wish to help the Allies—Great Britain and France—defeat Germany. "Even a neutral," said Roosevelt, "cannot be asked to close his mind or his conscience."

Roosevelt urged Congress to repeal a ban begun after World War I on sales of munitions to foreign countries. A new "cash-and-carry" program allowed warring nations to buy war material in the United States, but the buyers had to pay cash and carry away the material in their own ships. The law clearly favored Great Britain and France, who controlled the major sea routes. Between September 1939 and August 1940, 44 percent of all American exports went to the British Empire. In the spring of 1940, Germany conquered Denmark, Norway, Holland, Luxembourg, Belgium, and France. Horrified by the rapid German victories, the United States rushed to aid Great Britain. In September 1940, Roosevelt issued a daring executive order called "lend-lease." The United States exchanged destroyers with Great Britain for long-term leases to several British naval bases extending from Newfoundland to British Guiana (now Guyana). Congress also passed the first peacetime draft in U.S. history and voted to increase spending for the nation's defenses.

Roosevelt seemed to have decided to run for reelection sometime toward the end of May 1940. He believed that he alone, of all the Democrats, could be certain of election and that it was imperative for the world that his foreign policy continue. Roosevelt did not tell his decision to anyone except his wife, Eleanor. He refused to appear to do anything to win the nomination and he dismissed all talk about a third term. In fact, Roosevelt sent a message to the Democratic Convention, meeting in Chicago in mid-July, that he would not run again. However, he and his supporters had carefully orchestrated the appearance of a draft, and he was renominated on the first ballot. The President selected Secretary of Agriculture Henry A. Wallace as his new running mate, replacing Vice President John Nance Garner.

After Wallace's nomination, the President addressed the convention by radio. In a calm, paternal voice, he told the delegates that, "Lying awake, as I have, on many nights, I have asked myself whether I have the right as Commander-in-Chief of the Army and Navy to call on men and women to serve their country . . . and, at the same time, decline to serve in my own personal capacity." He said that, "my conscience will not let me turn my back upon a call to service."

The three leading candidates for the Republican Party's nomination were Thomas E. Dewey, Robert A. Taft, and Arthur H. Vandenberg. They were all isolationists in varying degrees, almost out of tune with the rapidly changing world situation and the potential peril it presented to the United States. The Republican Convention chose Wendell L. Willkie, whom most of the country had never heard of at the beginning of 1940. Between 1933 and 1939, Willkie had personified the frustrated business executive who fought a long, losing struggle against the Tennessee Valley Administration (TVA), a major New Deal project. He did not question the New Deal's underlying policies but found fault with its extravagances and inefficiency. Willkie had the devoted support of a group of Republican dissenters who also favored an internationalist foreign policy.

Willkie's rapid rise to win the Republican presidential nomination in late June 1940 coincided with events in Europe. On 7 May, on the eve of the German invasion of the Netherlands, Willkie had the support of only 3 percent of respondents to a Gallup Poll. On 12 June, as Hitler's armies invaded France, Willkie's popularity jumped to 17 percent. The opening of the Republican Convention took place at the same time as the imminent surrender of France, by which time Willkie had the support of 29 percent of those polled. Although Willkie did not have a single delegate pledged to him at the beginning of June, the tactics of his supporters and rapidly changing events in Europe helped them to capture the convention. Willkie was nominated on the sixth ballot.

In his acceptance speech on 17 August, Willkie described himself as "a liberal Democrat who changed his party affiliation because he found democracy in the Republican party rather than the New Deal party." He endorsed Roosevelt's defense policies, and pledged himself to the principle of selective service, as well as to the fullest possible aid to Great Britain. He endorsed a long list of New Deal programs and promised to make them more efficient. The issue, therefore, was the third term. Willkie challenged Roosevelt to meet him in a series of debates in different parts of the country to discuss "fundamental issues." The President did not respond.

During the summer of 1940, foreign policy and defense matters preoccupied Roosevelt. The President and Prime Minister Winston Churchill had negotiated the transfer of 50 old U.S. destroyers to Great Britain. In return, the United States acquired the right to 99-year leases on naval and air force bases on British territory stretching from Newfoundland to the Caribbean. Roosevelt tried to obtain Willkie's support for his destroyers for bases deal while it was being negotiated, but Willkie declined. When the President announced the "deal" to Congress, Willkie, at first, approved of it. Then, after consultation with isolationist Republicans, he changed his position. He now called it "the most arbitrary and dictatorial action ever taken by any President in the history of the United States."

Willkie began an extensive campaign trip in mid-September that continued until the eve of the election. His speeches became more critical of Roosevelt's foreign policy. On 11 October, in Boston, he promised: "We shall not undertake to fight anybody else's war. Our boys shall stay out of European wars." At the Hollywood Bowl, he told a cheering crowd of 75,000 that Roosevelt had promised in 1932 to cut government costs by a quarter and that the 1940 Democratic platform pledged that the United States would not get involved in a European war. "I hope and pray," said Willkie, "that he remembers the pledge of the 1940 platform better than he did the one of 1932. If he does not, you better

get ready to get on the transports." By mid-October, Gallup polls found that midwestern voters were returning to the Republican Party.

Roosevelt announced that he would deliver a series of five major political speeches to respond to the "systematic and deliberate falsification of the facts." Drafted by adviser Samuel Rosenman and playwright Robert E. Sherwood and retouched by Roosevelt, these speeches were highly effective. In Philadelphia, New York, Boston, Brooklyn, and Cleveland, Roosevelt defended his record and attacked the Republican isolationists, never mentioning Willkie by name. Sherwood wrote: "That man would be one of the best actors on our stage with his fine sense of timing and the way he can modulate his voice and change his expression."

On 28 October, Roosevelt made the major speech at the traditional Democratic pre-election rally at Madison Square Garden in New York City. Earlier in the day, more than 2 million New Yorkers saw him make a strenuous 58-mile tour of the city's streets. The President linked Willkie with isolationist Republicanism in a brilliantly timed phrase "Martin, Barton and Fish." The reference was to Republican National Chairman Joseph W. Martin, Jr. and Congressmen Hamilton Fish and Bruce Barton. The crowd howled with delight and repeated the three names with him in a chorus with uproarious pleasure.

Almost 50 million Americans voted. Roosevelt was elected to a third term with 27,313,041 votes (54.7 percent) to Willkie's 22,348,480 (44.8 percent). Willkie received a larger number of votes than had been given to any previous Republican candidate, giving Roosevelt his narrowest margin of victory so far. The electoral vote was more decisive. Roosevelt finished with 449 to Willkie's 82. Willkie carried only 10 states. His backers claimed he could have won if he had paid more attention to the Republican conservative wing. However, he ran against one of the great campaigners in U.S. history, and memories of the Great Depression were still too fresh for a Republican victory. The people had placed their faith in Roosevelt to avoid war—even if it meant breaking with the tradition of the president serving only two terms.

Election of 1944

X ROOSEVELT

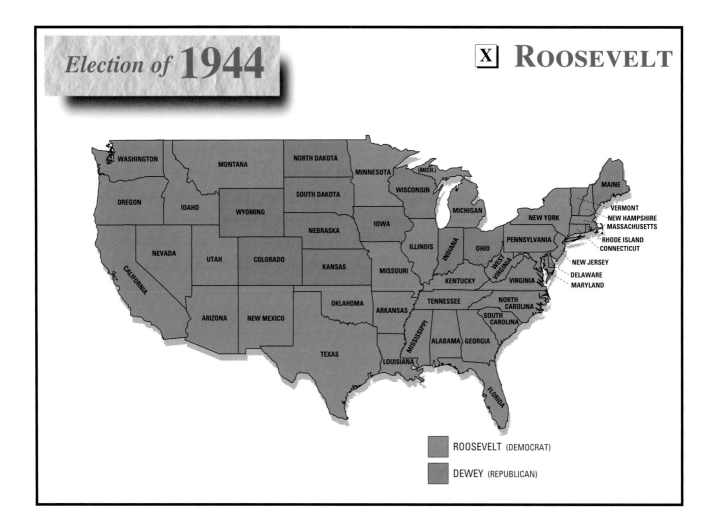

ROOSEVELT (DEMOCRAT)

DEWEY (REPUBLICAN)

States	Electoral Votes	Roosevelt	Dewey	States	Electoral Votes	Roosevelt	Dewey
Alabama	(11)	11	–	Nebraska	(6)	–	6
Arizona	(4)	4	–	Nevada	(3)	3	–
Arkansas	(9)	9	–	New Hampshire	(4)	4	–
California	(25)	25	–	New Jersey	(16)	16	–
Colorado	(6)	–	6	New Mexico	(4)	4	–
Connecticut	(8)	8	–	New York	(47)	47	–
Delaware	(3)	3	–	North Carolina	(14)	14	–
Florida	(8)	8	–	North Dakota	(4)	–	4
Georgia	(12)	12	–	Ohio	(25)	–	25
Idaho	(4)	4	–	Oklahoma	(10)	10	–
Illinois	(28)	28	–	Oregon	(6)	6	–
Indiana	(13)	–	13	Pennsylvania	(35)	35	–
Iowa	(10)	–	10	Rhode Island	(4)	4	–
Kansas	(8)	–	8	South Carolina	(8)	8	–
Kentucky	(11)	11	–	South Dakota	(4)	–	4
Louisiana	(10)	10	–	Tennessee	(12)	12	–
Maine	(5)	–	5	Texas	(23)	23	–
Maryland	(8)	8	–	Utah	(4)	4	–
Massachusetts	(16)	16	–	Vermont	(3)	–	3
Michigan	(19)	19	–	Virginia	(11)	11	–
Minnesota	(11)	11	–	Washington	(8)	8	–
Mississippi	(9)	9	–	West Virginia	(8)	8	–
Missouri	(15)	15	–	Wisconsin	(12)	–	12
Montana	(4)	4	–	Wyoming	(3)	–	3
				Totals	**(531)**	**432**	**99**

ELECTORAL VOTE

Election of 1944

STATE	TOTAL VOTE	FRANKLIN D. ROOSEVELT (Democrat)		THOMAS E. DEWEY (Republican)		NORMAN M. THOMAS (Socialist)		CLAUDE A. WATSON (Prohibition)		OTHER		PLURALITY	
		Votes	%	Votes	%	Votes	%	Votes	%	Votes	%		
Alabama	244,743	198,918	81.3	44,540	18.2	190	0.1	1,095	0.4	—		154,378	D
Arizona	137,634	80,926	58.8	56,287	40.9	—		421	0.3	—		24,639	D
Arkansas	212,954	148,965	70.0	63,551	29.8	438	0.2	—		—		85,414	D
California	3,520,875	1,988,564	56.5	1,512,965	43.0	2,515	0.1	14,770	0.4	2,061	0.1	475,599	D
Colorado	505,039	234,331	46.4	268,731	53.2	1,977	0.4	—		—		34,400	R
Connecticut	831,990	435,146	52.3	390,527	46.9	5,097	0.6	—		1,220	0.1	44,619	D
Delaware	125,361	68,166	54.4	56,747	45.3	154	0.1	294	0.2	—		11,419	D
Florida	482,803	339,377	70.3	143,215	29.7	—		—		211		196,162	D
Georgia	328,129	268,187	81.7	59,900	18.3	6		36		—		208,287	D
Idaho	208,321	107,399	51.6	100,137	48.1	282	0.1	503	0.2	—		7,262	D
Illinois	4,036,061	2,079,479	51.5	1,939,314	48.0	180		7,411	0.2	9,677	0.2	140,165	D
Indiana	1,672,091	781,403	46.7	875,891	52.4	2,223	0.1	12,574	0.8	—		94,488	R
Iowa	1,052,599	499,876	47.5	547,267	52.0	1,511	0.1	3,752	0.4	193		47,391	R
Kansas	733,776	287,458	39.2	442,096	60.2	1,613	0.2	2,609	0.4	—		154,638	R
Kentucky	867,924	472,589	54.5	392,448	45.2	535	0.1	2,023	0.2	329		80,141	D
Louisiana	349,383	281,564	80.6	67,750	19.4	—		—		69		213,814	D
Maine	296,400	140,631	47.4	155,434	52.4	—		—		335	0.1	14,803	R
Maryland	608,439	315,490	51.9	292,949	48.1	—		—		—		22,541	D
Massachusetts	1,960,665	1,035,296	52.8	921,350	47.0	—		973		3,046	0.2	113,946	D
Michigan	2,205,223	1,106,899	50.2	1,084,423	49.2	4,598	0.2	6,503	0.3	2,800	0.1	22,476	D
Minnesota	1,125,504	589,864	52.4	527,416	46.9	5,048	0.4	—		3,176	0.3	62,448	D
Mississippi	180,234	168,621	93.6	11,613	6.4	—		—		—		157,008	D
Missouri	1,571,697	807,356	51.4	761,175	48.4	1,751	0.1	1,195	0.1	220		46,181	D
Montana	207,355	112,556	54.3	93,163	44.9	1,296	0.6	340	0.2	—		19,393	D
Nebraska	563,126	233,246	41.4	329,880	58.6	—		—		—		96,634	R
Nevada	54,234	29,623	54.6	24,611	45.4	—		—		—		5,012	D
New Hampshire	229,625	119,663	52.1	109,916	47.9	46		—		—		9,747	D
New Jersey	1,963,761	987,874	50.3	961,335	49.0	3,358	0.2	4,255	0.2	6,939	0.4	26,539	D
New Mexico	152,225	81,389	53.5	70,688	46.4	—		148	0.1	—		10,701	D
New York	6,316,790	3,304,238	52.3	2,987,647	47.3	10,553	0.2	—		14,352	0.2	316,591	D
North Carolina	790,554	527,399	66.7	263,155	33.3	—		—		—		264,244	D
North Dakota	220,182	100,144	45.5	118,535	53.8	954	0.4	549	0.2	—		18,391	R
Ohio	3,153,056	1,570,763	49.8	1,582,293	50.2	—		—		—		11,530	R
Oklahoma	722,636	401,549	55.6	319,424	44.2	—		1,663	0.2	—		82,125	D
Oregon	480,147	248,635	51.8	225,365	46.9	3,785	0.8	2,362	0.5	—		23,270	D
Pennsylvania	3,794,793	1,940,479	51.1	1,835,054	48.4	11,721	0.3	5,750	0.2	1,789		105,425	D
Rhode Island	299,276	175,356	58.6	123,487	41.3	—		433	0.1	—		51,869	D
South Carolina	103,382	90,601	87.6	4,617	4.5	—		365	0.4	7,799	7.5	82,802	D
South Dakota	232,076	96,711	41.7	135,365	58.3	—		—		—		38,654	R
Tennessee	510,692	308,707	60.4	200,311	39.2	792	0.2	882	0.2	—		108,396	D
Texas	1,150,334	821,605	71.4	191,423	16.6	594	0.1	1,018	0.1	135,694	11.8	630,182	D
Utah	248,319	150,088	60.4	97,891	39.4	340	0.1	—		—		52,197	D
Vermont	125,361	53,820	42.9	71,527	57.1	—		—		14		17,707	R
Virginia	388,485	242,276	62.4	145,243	37.4	417	0.1	459	0.1	90		97,033	D
Washington	856,328	486,774	56.8	361,689	42.2	3,824	0.4	2,396	0.3	1,645	0.2	125,085	D
West Virginia	715,596	392,777	54.9	322,819	45.1	—		—		—		69,958	D
Wisconsin	1,339,152	650,413	48.6	674,532	50.4	13,205	1.0	—		1,002	0.1	24,119	R
Wyoming	101,340	49,419	48.8	51,921	51.2	—		—		—		2,502	R
Totals	47,976,670	25,612,610	53.4	22,017,617	45.9	79,003	0.2	74,779	0.2	192,661	0.4	3,594,993	D

P O P U L A R   V O T E

The 1944 election was the first time since 1864 that the voters chose a president in the midst of a major war. Franklin D. Roosevelt ran for an unprecedented fourth term. While many domestic problems remained unresolved, the President now had to devote almost all of his time and energy to winning the war. He assumed direction of the armed forces with the same determination that characterized his New Deal leadership. His first priority, obviously, was a military victory.

Conservatives saw the war as an opportunity to end the New Deal; some liberals regarded it as a favorable time to fulfill Woodrow Wilson's ideals and to establish a global New Deal. The Republicans, as the minority party, did not criticize the conduct of the war nor the war objectives, but they did accuse the Roosevelt administration of inefficiency. The price of food increased sharply and inflation became a problem. As a result, the pressure from labor for wage increases became stronger. In the 1942 congressional election, the Republicans won an additional 46 seats in the House and 9 in the Senate. The Democrats, however, retained control of both houses.

Roosevelt spent most of 1943 and 1944 attending to his duties as commander in chief. Roosevelt and Prime Minister Winston Churchill met at Casablanca, Morocco, in 1943 and declared that the Axis powers must surrender without any conditions. This policy, explained the President, "does not mean the destruction of the population of Germany, Italy, and Japan, but it does mean the destruction of the philosophies in those countries which are based on conquest and the subjugation of other people."

Wendell Willkie had been the chief Republican spokesman during the war. His worldwide travels and his book, *Our World,* kept his name before the public. He harshly condemned Roosevelt's "one-man rule" and his "inept" administration. However, Old Guard Republicans detested Willkie, the former Democrat whom they considered an outsider. Nevertheless, he entered the Republican primary in Wisconsin and spent two weeks speaking to groups in six or seven towns a day. Although no other candidate campaigned, the regular Republican machine supported a slate of delegates pledged to Governor Thomas E. Dewey of New York. Republican voters in Wisconsin did not elect a single Willkie delegate, and he withdrew from the race the next day. *Newsweek* commented: "By Wednesday, 5 April, the day after

the primary, it was apparent that Wisconsin voters had not merely administered an unprecedented defeat to Willkie, they had virtually chosen the next Republican presidential nominee in the person of Dewey, three months in advance of the GOP national convention."

Some extreme Roosevelt haters could not accept Dewey because he had pledged to keep most of the New Deal programs. Supported by the Chicago *Tribune* and the Hearst Press, they attacked Roosevelt's basic strategic decision of first defeating the enemy in Europe. Conservative Republicans wanted complete victory in the Pacific first. They supported General Douglas MacArthur for the presidential nomination. MacArthur had spoken out against communism and had routed the bonus marchers, whom he called radicals, in 1932. He disliked Roosevelt and the New Dealers, especially their desire for an international organization as the best means to guarantee peace. MacArthur favored a strong American military deterrent. At first, the General encouraged the movement to draft him for the presidential nomination. Representative A. L. Miller of Nebraska wrote to MacArthur in September 1943, " I am certain that unless this New Deal can be stopped in time, our American way of life is doomed. You owe it to civilization and the children yet unborn to accept the nomination." MacArthur replied: "I do not anticipate in any way your flattering predictions, but I do unreservedly agree with the complete wisdom and statesmanship of your comments." By May 1944, MacArthur realized that only a fringe group of Republicans supported him and he withdrew.

Thomas E. Dewey won the Republican nomination before he announced his candidacy. The 42-year-old governor had gained a national reputation, first as an outstanding special prosecutor, and then as a crime-busting district attorney of New York County. In 1940, he had been a major contender for the presidential nomination. Elected governor in 1942, Dewey had a strong political base in New York, then the nation's most populous state. The 15 April 1944 Gallup Poll showed 50.3 percent of Republicans nationwide supported him, compared to 9.3 percent for Willkie. On 23 June, the Republican Convention nominated Dewey on the first ballot, choosing John W. Bricker, the governor of Ohio, for vice president.

It was a foregone conclusion that Roosevelt would run for a fourth term. Public opinion polls showed that voters of both parties wanted him to continue as the wartime commander. Labor leaders, Democratic politicians, and spokesmen for veterans made statements that only Roosevelt could complete the New Deal domestically and obtain a just peace. On 11 July 1944, a week before the Democratic Convention met in Chicago, Roosevelt released a letter to the Democratic National Committee Chairman saying that he would "reluctantly" run and continue to serve "as a good soldier" if "so ordered by the Commander-in-Chief of us all, the sovereign people of the United States. The vice presidential nomination became an extremely important issue for the party leaders. Although the President's physicians reported him "to be fit as a fiddle" and in "good condition for a man of his age [62]," we now know that the hardening of his arteries as well as other ailments from which Roosevelt was suffering were much more serious than admitted. Those closest to him observed that he was not well and was visibly aging. They observed the dark circles under his eyes, his emaciated neck, and the shakiness of his hands when he lit a cigarette.

The vice presidency was discussed at a meeting between the Democratic leaders and Roosevelt on 11 July 1944, a week before the nominating convention. Vice President Henry Wallace was too radical; Senator James Byrnes of South Carolina was too southern; Senator Alben Barkley of Kentucky was too old; and Supreme Court Justice William Douglas was too liberal. Gradually, they agreed that Senator Harry S. Truman would be the least harmful addition to the ticket. Truman came from Missouri, a border state. He had fought in World War I and was sympathetic to veterans' problems. Although he was a protégé of the Kansas City Pendergast political machine, he had never been involved in any of its scandals. Truman's votes in the Senate on labor were good; and at the same time, conservatives supported him. During World War II, he achieved national prominence as chairman of the Senate Committee to Investigate the National Defense Program. At the end of the meeting, Roosevelt remarked to Robert Hannegan, chairman of the Democratic National Committee: "Bob, I think you and everyone else here want Truman."

While the Democratic Convention met, Roosevelt began a lengthy trip, by train to San Diego and then by ship to Hawaii, for a conference with the Pacific area admirals and generals. MacArthur recorded that the President looked terrible but that his voice was strong and his mind as quick as ever. He then traveled to the Aleutian Islands to inspect naval installations. The President returned to Seattle on 12 August and delivered a nationwide radio address from the deck of a destroyer. He seemed unsure of himself, and we now know he suffered sharp chest pains which caused him to lose his concentration. Public opinion polls reported an increase in support for Dewey after this speech. At the same time, the Republican Party circulated news photographs of the President showing him to be stooping forward and looking thin and gaunt.

Roosevelt bounced back with one of the greatest speeches of his career on 25 September. Speaking before officials of the Teamsters Union, Roosevelt lashed out at the Republicans in mock anger over some remarks made about his dog, Fala. The speech was carried on nationwide radio. He followed this triumph with a strenuous campaign to Chicago and then throughout the East. His campaign climaxed with a day-long drive in an open car through New York City in a soaking rain.

The 1944 election results were almost exactly the same as in 1940. The war had not undermined the basic Democratic alliance of labor union members, big city political machines, African Americans in the North, and the Solid South. Dewey carried 12 states. The final electoral count was 432 for Roosevelt to 99 for Dewey. In the popular vote, Dewey cut Roosevelt's victory margin to 3.6 million, the closet of all four of his presidential elections. However, 53.4 percent had voted for Roosevelt and 45.9 percent for Dewey. Roosevelt received more than 53 percent of the votes in each of his four presidential victories.

Roosevelt's evaluation of his last campaign appears in a letter he wrote to a friend a few weeks after the election. She had knitted a new pair of socks for the President at the time of his previous inauguration. She had asked him what color socks he now wanted, "I would suggest either black or blue," he wrote "because that is a little bit the way I felt after going through *the dirtiest campaign in all history.*"

Election of 1948

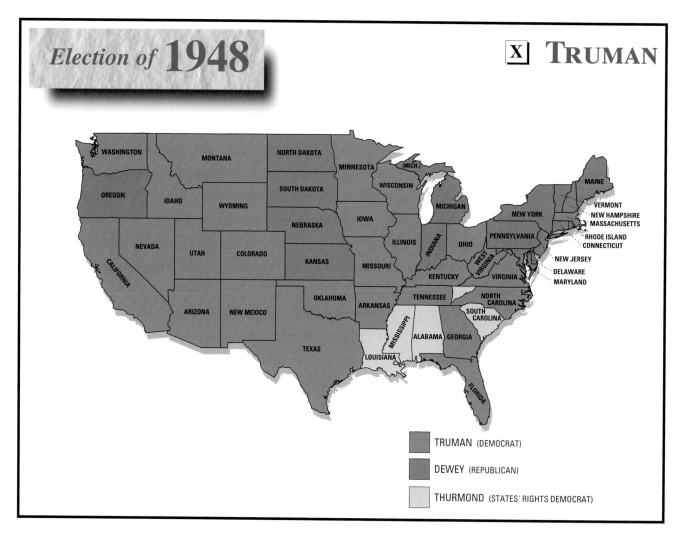

TRUMAN (DEMOCRAT)

DEWEY (REPUBLICAN)

THURMOND (STATES' RIGHTS DEMOCRAT)

States	Electoral Votes	Truman	Dewey	Thurmond	States	Electoral Votes	Truman	Dewey	Thurmond
Alabama	(11)	-	-	11	Nebraska	(6)	-	6	-
Arizona	(4)	4	-	-	Nevada	(3)	3	-	-
Arkansas	(9)	9	-	-	New Hampshire	(4)	-	4	-
California	(25)	25	-	-	New Jersey	(16)	-	16	-
Colorado	(6)	6	-	-	New Mexico	(4)	4	-	-
Connecticut	(8)	-	8	-	New York	(47)	-	47	-
Delaware	(3)	-	3	-	North Carolina	(14)	14	-	-
Florida	(8)	8	-	-	North Dakota	(4)	-	4	-
Georgia	(12)	12	-	-	Ohio	(25)	25	-	-
Idaho	(4)	4	-	-	Oklahoma	(10)	10	-	-
Illinois	(28)	28	-	-	Oregon	(6)	-	6	-
Indiana	(13)	-	13	-	Pennsylvania	(35)	-	35	-
Iowa	(10)	10	-	-	Rhode Island	(4)	4	-	-
Kansas	(8)	-	8	-	South Carolina	(8)	-	-	8
Kentucky	(11)	11	-	-	South Dakota	(4)	-	4	-
Louisiana	(10)	-	-	10	Tennessee	(12)	11	-	1
Maine	(5)	-	5	-	Texas	(23)	23	-	-
Maryland	(8)	-	8	-	Utah	(4)	4	-	-
Massachusetts	(16)	16	-	-	Vermont	(3)	-	3	-
Michigan	(19)	-	19	-	Virginia	(11)	11	-	-
Minnesota	(11)	11	-	-	Washington	(8)	8	-	-
Mississippi	(9)	-	-	9	West Virginia	(8)	8	-	-
Missouri	(15)	15	-	-	Wisconsin	(12)	12	-	-
Montana	(4)	4	-	-	Wyoming	(3)	3	-	-
					Totals	**(531)**	**303**	**189**	**39**

E L E C T O R A L   V O T E

Election of 1948

STATE	TOTAL VOTE	HARRY S. TRUMAN (Democrat)		THOMAS E. DEWEY (Republican)		J. STROM THURMOND (States' Rights Democrat)		HENRY A. WALLACE (Progressive)		OTHER		PLURALITY	
		Votes	%	Votes	%	Votes	%	Votes	%	Votes	%		
Alabama	214,980	—		40,930	19.0	171,443	79.7	1,522	0.7	1,085	0.5	130,513	SR
Arizona	177,065	95,251	53.8	77,597	43.8	—		3,310	1.9	907	0.5	17,654	D
Arkansas	242,475	149,659	61.7	50,959	21.0	40,068	16.5	751	0.3	1,038	0.4	98,700	D
California	4,021,538	1,913,134	47.6	1,895,269	47.1	1,228		190,381	4.7	21,526	0.5	17,865	D
Colorado	515,237	267,288	51.9	239,714	46.5	—		6,115	1.2	2,120	0.4	27,574	D
Connecticut	883,518	423,297	47.9	437,754	49.5	—		13,713	1.6	8,754	1.0	14,457	R
Delaware	139,073	67,813	48.8	69,588	50.0	—		1,050	0.8	622	0.4	1,775	R
Florida	577,643	281,988	48.8	194,280	33.6	89,755	15.5	11,620	2.0	—		87,708	D
Georgia	418,844	254,646	60.8	76,691	18.3	85,135	20.3	1,636	0.4	736	0.2	169,511	D
Idaho	214,816	107,370	50.0	101,514	47.3	—		4,972	2.3	960	0.4	5,856	D
Illinois	3,984,046	1,994,715	50.1	1,961,103	49.2	—		—		28,228	0.7	33,612	D
Indiana	1,656,212	807,831	48.8	821,079	49.6	—		9,649	0.6	17,653	1.1	13,248	R
Iowa	1,038,264	522,380	50.3	494,018	47.6	—		12,125	1.2	9,741	0.9	28,362	D
Kansas	788,819	351,902	44.6	423,039	53.6	—		4,603	0.6	9,275	1.2	71,137	R
Kentucky	822,658	466,756	56.7	341,210	41.5	10,411	1.3	1,567	0.2	2,714	0.3	125,546	D
Louisiana	416,336	136,344	32.7	72,657	17.5	204,290	49.1	3,035	0.7	10		67,946	SR
Maine	264,787	111,916	42.3	150,234	56.7	—		1,884	0.7	753	0.3	38,318	R
Maryland	596,748	286,521	48.0	294,814	49.4	2,489	0.4	9,983	1.7	2,941	0.5	8,293	R
Massachusetts	2,107,146	1,151,788	54.7	909,370	43.2	—		38,157	1.8	7,831	0.4	242,418	D
Michigan	2,109,609	1,003,448	47.6	1,038,595	49.2	—		46,515	2.2	21,051	1.0	35,147	R
Minnesota	1,212,226	692,966	57.2	483,617	39.9	—		27,866	2.3	7,777	0.6	209,349	D
Mississippi	192,190	19,384	10.1	5,043	2.6	167,538	87.2	225	0.1	—		148,154	SR
Missouri	1,578,628	917,315	58.1	655,039	41.5	—		3,998	0.3	2,276	0.1	262,276	D
Montana	224,278	119,071	53.1	96,770	43.1	—		7,313	3.3	1,124	0.5	22,301	D
Nebraska	488,940	224,165	45.8	264,774	54.2	—		—		1		40,609	R
Nevada	62,117	31,291	50.4	29,357	47.3	—		1,469	2.4	—		1,934	D
New Hampshire	231,440	107,995	46.7	121,299	52.4	7		1,970	0.9	169	0.1	13,304	R
New Jersey	1,949,555	895,455	45.9	981,124	50.3	—		42,683	2.2	30,293	1.6	85,669	R
New Mexico	187,063	105,464	56.4	80,303	42.9	—		1,037	0.6	259	0.1	25,161	D
New York	6,177,337	2,780,204	45.0	2,841,163	46.0	—		509,559	8.2	46,411	0.8	60,959	R
North Carolina	791,209	459,070	58.0	258,572	32.7	69,652	8.8	3,915	0.5	—		200,498	D
North Dakota	220,716	95,812	43.4	115,139	52.2	374	0.2	8,391	3.8	1,000	0.5	19,327	R
Ohio	2,936,071	1,452,791	49.5	1,445,684	49.2	—		37,596	1.3	—		7,107	D
Oklahoma	721,599	452,782	62.7	268,817	37.3	—		—		—		183,965	D
Oregon	524,080	243,147	46.4	260,904	49.8	—		14,978	2.9	5,051	1.0	17,757	R
Pennsylvania	3,735,348	1,752,426	46.9	1,902,197	50.9	—		55,161	1.5	25,564	0.7	149,771	R
Rhode Island	327,702	188,736	57.6	135,787	41.4	—		2,619	0.8	560	0.2	52,949	D
South Carolina	142,571	34,423	24.1	5,386	3.8	102,607	72.0	154	0.1	1		68,184	SR
South Dakota	250,105	117,653	47.0	129,651	51.8	—		2,801	1.1	—		11,998	R
Tennessee	550,283	270,402	49.1	202,914	36.9	73,815	13.4	1,864	0.3	1,288	0.2	67,488	D
Texas	1,249,577	824,235	66.0	303,467	24.3	113,920	9.1	3,918	0.3	4,037	0.3	520,768	D
Utah	276,306	149,151	54.0	124,402	45.0	—		2,679	1.0	74		24,749	D
Vermont	123,382	45,557	36.9	75,926	61.5	—		1,279	1.0	620	0.5	30,369	R
Virginia	419,256	200,786	47.9	172,070	41.0	43,393	10.4	2,047	0.5	960	0.2	28,716	D
Washington	905,058	476,165	52.6	386,314	42.7	—		31,692	3.5	10,887	1.2	89,851	D
West Virginia	748,750	429,188	57.3	316,251	42.2	—		3,311	0.4	—		112,937	D
Wisconsin	1,276,800	647,310	50.7	590,959	46.3	—		25,282	2.0	13,249	1.0	56,351	D
Wyoming	101,425	52,354	51.6	47,947	47.3	—		931	0.9	193	0.2	4,407	D
Totals	48,793,826	24,179,345	49.6	21,991,291	45.1	1,176,125	2.4	1,157,326	2.4	289,739	0.6	2,188,054	D

P O P U L A R V O T E

The 1948 election is especially interesting because almost every political commentator and public opinion analyst agreed that President Harry S. Truman had little chance for election. President Franklin D. Roosevelt had died on 12 April 1945. Truman told reporters the next day, "When they told me yesterday what had happened, I felt like the moon, the stars, and all the planets had fallen on me." He tried to maintain and to expand the social and economic domestic reforms of the New Deal. In foreign policy, the idealistic post-war world envisioned by Roosevelt had been suspended by a "cold war" with the Soviet Union. During Truman's eleven-and-one-half-week service as vice president, Roosevelt had not kept him informed about the many important international decisions that were taking place. Largely unprepared for the presidency, Truman faced the momentous problems of post-war America and set out, as he said, to "do my darndest."

Truman, Soviet Premier Joseph Stalin, and British Prime Minister Clement Attlee met at Potsdam, near Berlin, in July 1945. They agreed on arrangements for a joint occupation of Germany, and they also demanded that Japan surrender unconditionally. When Japan refused, Truman, in perhaps the most agonizing decision of modern history, ordered an atomic bomb dropped on the industrial city of Hiroshima. Three days later, another bomb wiped out Nagasaki. The two blasts killed about 80,000 people. Japan accepted the Potsdam terms, and General Douglas MacArthur presided over the formal surrender ceremonies on 2 September.

The first and most urgent task on the domestic front was to convert from a wartime to a peacetime economy. Veterans had little difficulty in finding work, and unemployment remained low. The rate of inflation became alarmingly high. Americans were earning money at unprecedented rates and trying to spend it as never before. The demand for consumer goods seemed insatiable and shortages developed. In 1945, razor blades, nylon stockings, electrical appliances, automobiles, and cigarettes were unobtainable and the supply of meat had reached a new low. Living costs rose 33 percent between 1941 and 1945. There were widespread disputes between labor and management as workers sought to preserve their wartime gains in earnings. Industry, on the other hand, pressed for relief from scores of federal wartime controls. Through all the conflicts of converting to a peacetime economy, Truman's political strength steadily declined. On

5 November 1946, the Republicans won control of both houses of Congress for the first time since 1930.

Truman's instincts led him to sympathize with the liberal principles of Roosevelt even though the temper of the country was becoming increasingly conservative. In several messages to Congress, Truman proposed additional aid for housing, aid to education, and a fair employment practices law to prohibit discrimination based on race, religion, or national origin. However, the President was often at odds with Congress, especially with southern Democrats and most Republicans who claimed that Truman's programs would create a welfare state.

The sharpest conflict between the President and Congress occurred over labor legislation. Influenced by the fact that more than 4.7 million workers went on strike in 1946, the Republican dominated Eightieth Congress passed a strong labor bill over the President's veto. Labor organizations bitterly denounced the act (the Taft-Hartley Labor-Management Relations Act). Among other things, it banned secondary boycotts and required unions to file complete financial statements with the Department of Labor. Unions labeled it the "slave labor act" and pledged to defeat all who had supported it. The Taft-Hartley Act was one of the major issues in the 1948 presidential election.

The Republican Convention opened in Philadelphia on 21 June 1948. A feeling of victory was in the air. The Gallup Poll showed Truman's approval rating at 36 percent, down from 60 percent a year before. Congresswoman Clare Boothe Luce told the cheering delegates that Truman was a "gone goose." When a group of Republicans endorsed General Dwight D. Eisenhower, he declared: "It is my conviction that the necessary and wise subordination of the military to civil power will be best sustained . . . when lifelong professional soldiers . . . abstain from seeking political office." Thomas E. Dewey, governor of New York, was nominated on the third ballot. This was the first time in the party's history that they had renominated a defeated candidate. Dewey chose Earl Warren, governor of California, for his running mate. *Time* and *Newsweek* agreed that only a miracle could save Truman from an overwhelming defeat by two popular, youthful, progressive governors from two crucial states that were needed for victory.

Truman's chances for nomination and election seemed slim as the Democratic Convention began its sessions in

Philadelphia on 12 July. Many delegates stayed home and, on opening day, the galleries were largely empty. "You could cut the gloom with a corn knife," recalled Senator Alben W. Barkley. "The very air smelled of defeat."

The Eightieth Congress had blocked most of Truman's legislative proposals, and it seemed as if the Democratic Party was coming apart. Conservative southern Democrats were furious with Truman over his growing concern with civil rights for African Americans. The extreme left-wing of the party had broken with Truman because of his Cold War policies. Their hero, former Vice President Henry A. Wallace, had vowed in December 1947 that he definitely would run for president on a third-party ticket. Old line New Deal liberals, led by Minneapolis Mayor Hubert Humphrey, had formed Americans for Democratic Action (ADA), a non-communist response to the Wallace movement. They backed Eisenhower, now president of Columbia University, who had become the favorite candidate of many Democrats as well as Republicans. When Eisenhower again made it unmistakably clear that he would not run, the ADA announced its support for Supreme Court Justice William O. Douglas.

On 14 July, the day scheduled for Truman's nominating and acceptance speech, the convention divided bitterly over the civil rights plank in the platform. Humphrey and his supporters prevailed, causing many southern delegates to walk out of the convention. They obtained a platform pledged to a federal anti-lynching law; a federal anti-poll tax law; legislation guaranteeing fair employment regardless of race; and an end to segregation in the armed forces. Finally, at nearly midnight, Truman received the presidential nomination and 71-year-old Alben Barkley was chosen for vice president.

Truman delivered his acceptance speech at 2 A.M. Speaking without notes, he emphatically declared: "Senator Barkley and I will win this election and make those Republicans like it—don't you forget that." Then the President announced that he was calling the Republican dominated Congress into special session with the challenge that they enact the social and economic planks of their platform into law. *The New York Times* said that he had "set the convention on fire."

Three days later, some 300 conservative southern Democrats assembled in Birmingham, Alabama, for a convention of States' Rights Democrats (Dixiecrats). They named Governor J. Strom Thurmond of South Carolina for president. Their platform denounced the civil rights plank of the Democratic platform and affirmed their belief in "the segregation of the races." If Thurmond and his running mate, Governor Fielding L. Wright of Mississippi, could obtain all of the South's electoral votes, they might deny both Truman and Dewey an electoral majority. This would put the election into the U.S. House of Representatives, placing the South in a strong position, and perhaps capable of electing their candidates. Thurmond was asked why he was breaking up the Democratic Party now when Roosevelt had made similar promises on civil rights. Thurmond replied: "But Truman really means it."

More than 3,000 delegates attended a fourth convention in Philadelphia on 23 July. The Progressive Party nominated Henry A. Wallace and Senator Glenn Taylor of Idaho by acclamation. The newly formed party called for an "an understanding between the Soviet Union and the United States;" removal from power of "the war-producing elite;" a repudiation of the Marshall Plan; the destruction of all atomic bombs; better housing; lower food prices; and an immediate end to segregation. The Wallace "movement" was labeled as being communist dominated, and it was already in decline before the convention met.

Several presidential candidates have had to cope with splits within their parties, but Truman faced a situation unprecedented in political history. He waged an aggressive campaign, relentlessly attacking the record of the Republican Party and reaffirming the principles of the New Deal. He defied the Dixiecrats and held on to the African American vote in northern cities. He countered Wallace's attack with an aggressive defense of his foreign policy. Dewey, on the other hand, never caught the imagination of the voters. Truman, aware of the fight he had to make, campaigned across the country denouncing "the do-nothing, good-for-nothing Eightieth Congress."

When the ballots were counted, Truman had pulled off the greatest upset in U.S. political history, winning 24,179,345 popular votes and 303 electoral votes to Dewey's 21,991,291 and 189. Thurmond carried only four in the Deep South and Wallace carried no states at all, although each received 2.4 percent of the popular vote. The Democrats recaptured control of both houses of Congress and also won 21 out of 33 contests for governor.

Election of 1952

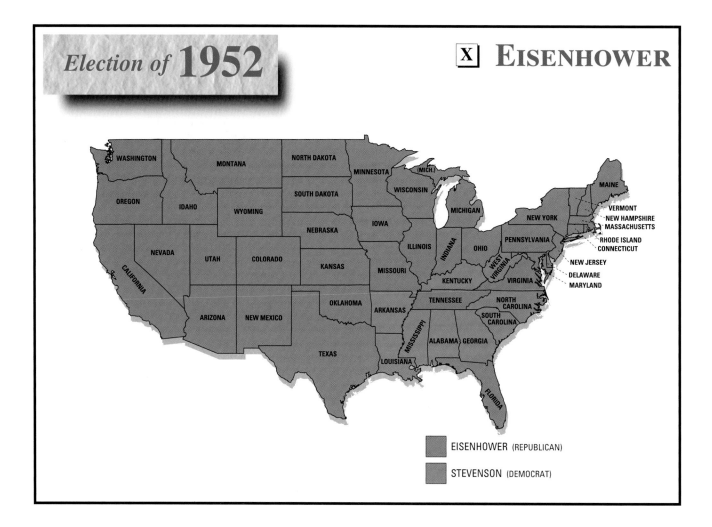

X EISENHOWER

EISENHOWER (REPUBLICAN)

STEVENSON (DEMOCRAT)

States	Electoral Votes	Eisenhower	Stevenson	States	Electoral Votes	Eisenhower	Stevenson
Alabama	(11)	-	11	Nebraska	(6)	6	-
Arizona	(4)	4	-	Nevada	(3)	3	-
Arkansas	(8)	-	8	New Hampshire	(4)	4	-
California	(32)	32	-	New Jersey	(16)	16	-
Colorado	(6)	6	-	New Mexico	(4)	4	-
Connecticut	(8)	8	-	New York	(45)	45	-
Delaware	(3)	3	-	North Carolina	(14)	-	14
Florida	(10)	10	-	North Dakota	(4)	4	-
Georgia	(12)	-	12	Ohio	(25)	25	-
Idaho	(4)	4	-	Oklahoma	(8)	8	-
Illinois	(27)	27	-	Oregon	(6)	6	-
Indiana	(13)	13	-	Pennsylvania	(32)	32	-
Iowa	(10)	10	-	Rhode Island	(4)	4	-
Kansas	(8)	8	-	South Carolina	(8)	-	8
Kentucky	(10)	-	10	South Dakota	(4)	4	-
Louisiana	(10)	-	10	Tennessee	(11)	11	-
Maine	(5)	5	-	Texas	(24)	24	-
Maryland	(9)	9	-	Utah	(4)	4	-
Massachusetts	(16)	16	-	Vermont	(3)	3	-
Michigan	(20)	20	-	Virginia	(12)	12	-
Minnesota	(11)	11	-	Washington	(9)	9	-
Mississippi	(8)	-	8	West Virginia	(8)	-	8
Missouri	(13)	13	-	Wisconsin	(12)	12	-
Montana	(4)	4	-	Wyoming	(3)	3	-
				Totals	**(531)**	**442**	**89**

ELECTORAL VOTE

Election of 1952

STATE	TOTAL VOTE	DWIGHT D. EISENHOWER (Republican)		ADLAI E. STEVENSON (Democrat)		VINCENT HALLINAN (Progressive)		STUART HAMBLEN (Prohibition)		OTHER		PLURALITY	
		Votes	%	Votes	%	Votes	%	Votes	%	Votes	%		
Alabama	426,120	149,231	35.0	275,075	64.6	—		1,814	0.4	—		125,844	D
Arizona	260,570	152,042	58.3	108,528	41.7	—		—		—		43,514	R
Arkansas	404,800	177,155	43.8	226,300	55.9	—		886	0.2	459	0.1	49,145	D
California	5,141,849	2,897,310	56.3	2,197,548	42.7	24,106	0.5	15,653	0.3	7,232	0.1	699,762	R
Colorado	630,103	379,782	60.3	245,504	39.0	1,919	0.3	—		2,898	0.5	134,278	R
Connecticut	1,096,911	611,012	55.7	481,649	43.9	1,466	0.1	—		2,784	0.3	129,363	R
Delaware	174,025	90,059	51.8	83,315	47.9	155	0.1	234	0.1	262	0.2	6,744	R
Florida	989,337	544,036	55.0	444,950	45.0	—		—		351		99,086	R
Georgia	655,785	198,961	30.3	456,823	69.7	—		—		1		257,862	D
Idaho	276,254	180,707	65.4	95,081	34.4	443	0.2	—		23		85,626	R
Illinois	4,481,058	2,457,327	54.8	2,013,920	44.9	—		—		9,811	0.2	443,407	R
Indiana	1,955,049	1,136,259	58.1	801,530	41.0	1,085	0.1	15,335	0.8	840		334,729	R
Iowa	1,268,773	808,906	63.8	451,513	35.6	5,085	0.4	2,882	0.2	387		357,393	R
Kansas	896,166	616,302	68.8	273,296	30.5	—		6,038	0.7	530	0.1	343,006	R
Kentucky	993,148	495,029	49.8	495,729	49.9	336		1,161	0.1	893	0.1	700	D
Louisiana	651,952	306,925	47.1	345,027	52.9	—		—		—		38,102	D
Maine	351,786	232,353	66.0	118,806	33.8	332	0.1	—		295	0.1	113,547	R
Maryland	902,074	499,424	55.4	395,337	43.8	7,313	0.8	—		—		104,087	R
Massachusetts	2,383,398	1,292,325	54.2	1,083,525	45.5	4,636	0.2	886		2,026	0.1	208,800	R
Michigan	2,798,592	1,551,529	55.4	1,230,657	44.0	3,922	0.1	10,331	0.4	2,153	0.1	320,872	R
Minnesota	1,379,483	763,211	55.3	608,458	44.1	2,666	0.2	2,147	0.2	3,001	0.2	154,753	R
Mississippi	285,532	112,966	39.6	172,566	60.4	—		—		—		59,600	D
Missouri	1,892,062	959,429	50.7	929,830	49.1	987	0.1	885		931		29,599	R
Montana	265,037	157,394	59.4	106,213	40.1	723	0.3	548	0.2	159	0.1	51,181	R
Nebraska	609,660	421,603	69.2	188,057	30.8	—		—		—		233,546	R
Nevada	82,190	50,502	61.4	31,688	38.6	—		—		—		18,814	R
New Hampshire	272,950	166,287	60.9	106,663	39.1	—		—		—		59,624	R
New Jersey	2,418,554	1,373,613	56.8	1,015,902	42.0	5,589	0.2	989		22,461	0.9	357,711	R
New Mexico	238,608	132,170	55.4	105,661	44.3	225	0.1	297	0.1	255	0.1	26,509	R
New York	7,128,239	3,952,813	55.5	3,104,601	43.6	64,211	0.9	—		6,614	0.1	848,212	R
North Carolina	1,210,910	558,107	46.1	652,803	53.9	—		—		—		94,696	D
North Dakota	270,127	191,712	71.0	76,694	28.4	344	0.1	302	0.1	1,075	0.4	115,018	R
Ohio	3,700,758	2,100,391	56.8	1,600,367	43.2	—		—		—		500,024	R
Oklahoma	948,984	518,045	54.6	430,939	45.4	—		—		—		87,106	R
Oregon	695,059	420,815	60.5	270,579	38.9	3,665	0.5	—		—		150,236	R
Pennsylvania	4,580,969	2,415,789	52.7	2,146,269	46.9	4,222	0.1	8,951	0.2	5,738	0.1	269,520	R
Rhode Island	414,498	210,935	50.9	203,293	49.0	187		—		83		7,642	R
South Carolina	341,087	168,082	49.3	173,004	50.7	—		1		—		4,922	D
South Dakota	294,283	203,857	69.3	90,426	30.7	—		—		—		113,431	R
Tennessee	892,553	446,147	50.0	443,710	49.7	885	0.1	1,432	0.2	379		2,437	R
Texas	2,075,946	1,102,878	53.1	969,228	46.7	294		1,983	0.1	1,563	0.1	133,650	R
Utah	329,554	194,190	58.9	135,364	41.1	—		—		—		58,826	R
Vermont	153,557	109,717	71.5	43,355	28.2	282	0.2	—		203	0.1	66,362	R
Virginia	619,689	349,037	56.3	268,677	43.4	311	0.1	—		1,664	0.3	80,360	R
Washington	1,102,708	599,107	54.3	492,845	44.7	2,460	0.2	—		8,296	0.8	106,262	R
West Virginia	873,548	419,970	48.1	453,578	51.9	—		—		—		33,608	D
Wisconsin	1,607,370	979,744	61.0	622,175	38.7	2,174	0.1	—		3,277	0.2	357,569	R
Wyoming	129,253	81,049	62.7	47,934	37.1	—		194	0.2	76	0.1	33,115	R
Totals	61,550,918	33,936,234	55.1	27,314,992	44.4	140,023	0.2	72,949	0.1	86,720	0.1	6,621,242	R

POPULAR VOTE

In the 1952 presidential election, voters were ready for a change from 20 years of Democratic administrations. Disillusionment, anxiety, and frustration gripped the American people in the midst of prosperity. Prices were high; the Soviet Union had developed an atomic bomb; there were suggestions of disloyalty in the government; the State Department had "lost" China to the communists; and the war in Korea was at a stalemate. The major issues were called K1C2—Korea, communism, and corruption. The voters turned to Dwight D. Eisenhower to provide the leadership to deal with these problems.

The Korean War (1950–1953) destroyed President Harry S. Truman's administration. The war had begun on 25 June 1950. China entered the war on 7 October and there was a stalemate. By mid-1952, the United States had suffered more than 100,000 casualties, including some 22,000 combat deaths. Republicans blamed Truman for having failed to define the "line of containment" against communist expansion. They especially blamed Secretary of State Dean Acheson for having stated in January 1950 that Korea was not essential to U.S. security. Senator Joseph McCarthy of Wisconsin charged that Truman had advisers who were pro-Russian and even Russian spies.

Although foreign events dominated Truman's second administration, Americans were also concerned about domestic legislation. On 5 January 1949, the President announced that "every segment of our economy and every individual has a right to expect from our Government a fair deal." He then outlined a program which extended New Deal measures. Congress passed federal low-rent housing and slum-clearance bills. Legislation raised the minimum hourly wage from 40 cents to 75 cents an hour. Rent control was broadened and an extension of the Social Security Act brought approximately 10 million new persons under coverage. However, the administration failed to obtain repeal of the Taft-Hartley Labor-Management Relations Act or enact a strong civil rights bill because of a congressional alliance between southern Democrats and conservative Republicans. The charge of communists in government became a major issue during Truman's second administration. In February 1950, McCarthy charged that "the State Department is infested with Communists" who had "handed over" China to the Soviet Union. A Senate special committee found no truth in McCarthy's brash charges, but he continued to make them. His smear campaigns against many prominent individuals created a general atmosphere of distrust and suspicion.

On 10 July 1952, the Republicans chose Dwight D. Eisenhower, popular wartime hero, former chief of staff, and NATO (North Atlantic Treaty Organization) commander, as their presidential candidate. Conservative Republicans supported Senator Robert A. Taft of Ohio for the nomination, but the liberal faction managed to defeat him at the convention after a bitter primary fight that almost split the party. Eisenhower chose Senator Richard M. Nixon of California as his running mate. Nixon, a dynamic young conservative from an important state, had demonstrated his zeal in exploiting the issue of "subversion" in the government.

After Truman lost the New Hampshire primary to Senator Estes Kefauver of Tennessee, he announced that he would not run again. The Democrats were faced with choosing a candidate acceptable to the dissident groups in the party but not too closely identified with the Truman administration. At Truman's urging, they nominated Governor Adlai E. Stevenson of Illinois on the third ballot. Truman did not approve of the other candidates, including Vice President Alben Barkley, who was then 74 years old. Although Stevenson did not wish to run against the very popular Eisenhower, he accepted the nomination. Stevenson was the grandson of President Grover Cleveland's vice president. He had served as an assistant to Secretary of the Navy Frank Knox and Secretary of State Edward Stettinius. He helped plan the United Nations, and he had served as an adviser to the U.S. delegation at the first session of the United Nations. Stevenson was a progressive governor of a major industrial state. He could count on the support of the President, of organized labor, and of the intellectuals within the party who admired the Governor for his intelligence and eloquence. In an appeal for southern support, Senator John J. Sparkman of Alabama was chosen as his running mate. Sparkman was progressive and liberal on almost every issue except racial equality.

Between 1945 and 1952, the number of television stations had grown from 23 to 108. The Republicans used this growing new media to their advantage. They hired a major advertising firm for overall management of their campaign, and they targeted the approximately 45 million eligible voters who had stayed home in the 1948 election. The advertising company reasoned that, in television, drama and images were as important as ideas and substance. Eisenhower's 30-minute television specials, for example, were completely different from those of the radio era. They were carefully sculpted productions. There were also 30-second television spots featuring Eisenhower giving informed answers to the questions that were on the minds of the voters. Simple slogans were used for television commercials: "Eisenhower, man of peace" and "I like Ike." Eisenhower once protested when it was suggested that makeup be used to remove some of the shine from his head. He said, "Why don't you get an actor? That's what you really want." Harlan Cleveland, executive editor of *Reader's Digest,* commented that Eisenhower was being sold like toothpaste.

On the other hand, Stevenson had difficulty using television. He read his speeches as though he was on the radio, and he often did not finish them before time ran out. He began the campaign determined to make it a high-level debate of the issues. However, he was forced to defend the record of the Truman administration. He could never shed the "egghead" label that suggested he was an intellectual out of touch with the real world of average Americans. Stevenson despised Nixon who questioned his loyalty by calling him, "Adlai the appeaser." Nixon asked on a nationwide broadcast, "Can such a man as Stevenson be trusted to lead our crusade against Communism?" Stevenson's articulate responses to charges made by Nixon and McCarthy were lost in the heat of the campaign.

The most dramatic incident of the campaign occurred in mid-September. A group of California businessmen had created a fund to pay for Nixon's travel and other expenses. Newspapers hostile to Nixon seized upon the story. "Secret Nixon Fund" read the 15 September headline of the liberal *New York Post.* Eisenhower held a press briefing in which he asked rhetorically: "Of what avail is it for us to carry on this crusade against this business of what has been going on in Washington if we ourselves aren't clean as a hound's tooth?" William Knowland, an influential Republican senator from California, was alerted to be ready to replace Nixon on the ticket.

On 23 September, Nixon seized the initiative with a 30-minute television speech. It was known as the Checkers speech because of a reference to the family dog, received as

a gift. Some 58 million people saw an earnest young man state that he was not guilty of anything. He explained the difficulties of raising two young children and maintaining a middle-class standard of living on a senator's salary. Telegrams of support poured into Republican national headquarters. Eisenhower appeared before the press later that evening and said that he had seen many brave young men in tough situations but, "I have never seen anyone come through in better fashion than Senator Nixon did tonight." Nixon had saved his position on the ticket but Eisenhower never fully trusted him again.

The polls showed Eisenhower well in the lead. The polls also showed that the stalemate in Korea worried most voters. On 24 October, in a nationally televised address, Eisenhower blamed the Democrats for the "blunders" in Korea. He called Korea "the burial ground for twenty-thousand American dead," and he promised to end the war. If elected, Eisenhower declared dramatically, "I shall go to Korea." It was an electrifying announcement, and the response was enthusiastic. His pledge was a dramatic way to use his prestige and experience to win votes while retaining flexibility.

The Eisenhower victory was overwhelming. He carried 39 states, including Stevenson's Illinois and Truman's Missouri, and received 442 electoral votes. Stevenson's 89 electoral votes came from either southern or border states. However, Eisenhower carried Florida, Tennessee, Texas, and Virginia. For the first time since Herbert Hoover's election in 1928, a Republican candidate split the solid Democratic South. Throughout the nation, Eisenhower consistently ran ahead of his party. He received 55.1 percent of the popular vote; Stevenson received 44.4 percent. Despite the landslide proportion of Eisenhower's victory, the Republicans barely won control of Congress. The dissatisfaction with the policies of the Truman administration, especially in Korea, is only a partial explanation of election results. Essentially, the victory was the personal success of Eisenhower rather than his party. Eisenhower was the most admired public figure in the nation. With no background in politics, he caught the mood of the American people who thought his leadership skills could solve the complex problems confronting the nation, particularly the war in Korea.

Election of 1956

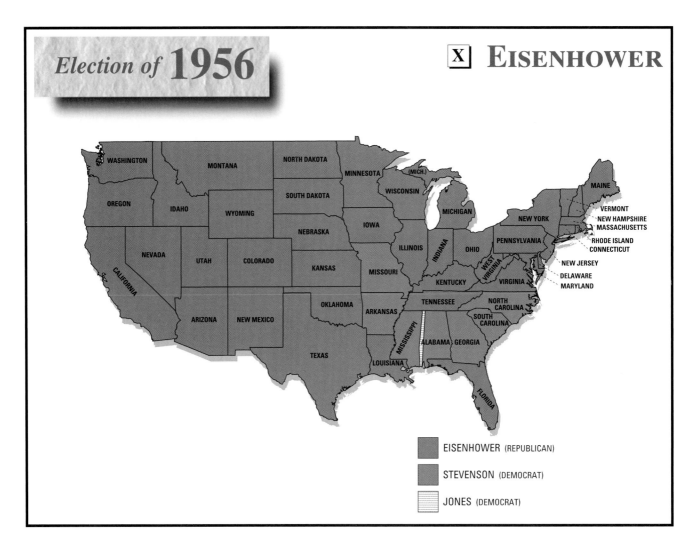

☒ **EISENHOWER**

EISENHOWER (REPUBLICAN)

STEVENSON (DEMOCRAT)

JONES (DEMOCRAT)

States	Electoral Votes	Eisenhower	Stevenson	Jones	States	Electoral Votes	Eisenhower	Stevenson	Jones
Alabama	(11)	-	10	1	Nebraska	(6)	6	-	-
Arizona	(4)	4	-	-	Nevada	(3)	3	-	-
Arkansas	(8)	-	8	-	New Hampshire	(4)	4	-	-
California	(32)	32	-	-	New Jersey	(16)	16	-	-
Colorado	(6)	6	-	-	New Mexico	(4)	4	-	-
Connecticut	(8)	8	-	-	New York	(45)	45	-	-
Delaware	(3)	3	-	-	North Carolina	(14)	-	14	-
Florida	(10)	10	-	-	North Dakota	(4)	4	-	-
Georgia	(12)	-	12	-	Ohio	(25)	25	-	-
Idaho	(4)	4	-	-	Oklahoma	(8)	8	-	-
Illinois	(27)	27	-	-	Oregon	(6)	6	-	-
Indiana	(13)	13	-	-	Pennsylvania	(32)	32	-	-
Iowa	(10)	10	-	-	Rhode Island	(4)	4	-	-
Kansas	(8)	8	-	-	South Carolina	(8)	-	8	-
Kentucky	(10)	10	-	-	South Dakota	(4)	4	-	-
Louisiana	(10)	10	-	-	Tennessee	(11)	11	-	-
Maine	(5)	5	-	-	Texas	(24)	24	-	-
Maryland	(9)	9	-	-	Utah	(4)	4	-	-
Massachusetts	(16)	16	-	-	Vermont	(3)	3	-	-
Michigan	(20)	20	-	-	Virginia	(12)	12	-	-
Minnesota	(11)	11	-	-	Washington	(9)	9	-	-
Mississippi	(8)	-	8	-	West Virginia	(8)	8	-	-
Missouri	(13)	-	13	-	Wisconsin	(12)	12	-	-
Montana	(4)	4	-	-	Wyoming	(3)	3	-	-
					Totals	**(531)**	**457**	**73**	**1**

ELECTORAL VOTE

Election of 1956

STATE	TOTAL VOTE	DWIGHT D. EISENHOWER (Republican)		ADLAI E. STEVENSON (Democrat)		T. COLEMAN ANDREWS (Constitution)		ERIC HASS (Socialist Labor)		OTHER		PLURALITY	
		Votes	%	Votes	%	Votes	%	Votes	%	Votes	%		
Alabama	496,861	195,694	39.4	280,844	56.5	—		—		20,323	4.1	85,150	D
Arizona	290,173	176,990	61.0	112,880	38.9	303	0.1	—		—		64,110	R
Arkansas	406,572	186,287	45.8	213,277	52.5	7,008	1.7	—		—		26,990	D
California	5,466,355	3,027,668	55.4	2,420,135	44.3	6,087	0.1	300		12,165	0.2	607,533	R
Colorado	657,074	394,479	60.0	257,997	39.3	759	0.1	3,308	0.5	531	0.1	136,482	R
Connecticut	1,117,121	711,837	63.7	405,079	36.3	—		—		205		306,758	R
Delaware	177,988	98,057	55.1	79,421	44.6	—		110	0.1	400	0.2	18,636	R
Florida	1,125,762	643,849	57.2	480,371	42.7	—		—		1,542	0.1	163,478	R
Georgia	669,655	222,778	33.3	444,688	66.4	2,096	0.3	—		93		221,910	D
Idaho	272,989	166,979	61.2	105,868	38.8	126		—		16		61,111	R
Illinois	4,407,407	2,623,327	59.5	1,775,682	40.3	—		8,342	0.2	56		847,645	R
Indiana	1,974,607	1,182,811	59.9	783,908	39.7	—		1,334	0.1	6,554	0.3	398,903	R
Iowa	1,234,564	729,187	59.1	501,858	40.7	3,202	0.3	125		192		227,329	R
Kansas	866,243	566,878	65.4	296,317	34.2	—		—		3,048	0.4	270,561	R
Kentucky	1,053,805	572,192	54.3	476,453	45.2	—		358		4,802	0.5	95,739	R
Louisiana	617,544	329,047	53.3	243,977	39.5	—		—		44,520	7.2	85,070	R
Maine	351,706	249,238	70.9	102,468	29.1	—		—		—		146,770	R
Maryland	932,827	559,738	60.0	372,613	39.9	—		—		476	0.1	187,125	R
Massachusetts	2,348,506	1,393,197	59.3	948,190	40.4	—		5,573	0.2	1,546	0.1	445,007	R
Michigan	3,080,468	1,713,647	55.6	1,359,898	44.1	—		—		6,923	0.2	353,749	R
Minnesota	1,340,005	719,302	53.7	617,525	46.1	—		2,080	0.2	1,098	0.1	101,777	R
Mississippi	248,104	60,685	24.5	144,453	58.2	—		—		42,966	17.3	83,768	D
Missouri	1,832,562	914,289	49.9	918,273	50.1	—		—		—		3,984	D
Montana	271,171	154,933	57.1	116,238	42.9	—		—		—		38,695	R
Nebraska	577,137	378,108	65.5	199,029	34.5	—		—		—		179,079	R
Nevada	96,689	56,049	58.0	40,640	42.0	—		—		—		15,409	R
New Hampshire	266,994	176,519	66.1	90,364	33.8	111		—		—		86,155	R
New Jersey	2,484,312	1,606,942	64.7	850,337	34.2	5,317	0.2	6,736	0.3	14,980	0.6	756,605	R
New Mexico	253,926	146,788	57.8	106,098	41.8	364	0.1	69		607	0.2	40,690	R
New York	7,095,971	4,345,506	61.2	2,747,944	38.7	1,027		150		1,344		1,597,562	R
North Carolina	1,165,592	575,062	49.3	590,530	50.7	—		—		—		15,468	D
North Dakota	253,991	156,766	61.7	96,742	38.1	483	0.2	—		—		60,024	R
Ohio	3,702,265	2,262,610	61.1	1,439,655	38.9	—		—		—		822,955	R
Oklahoma	859,350	473,769	55.1	385,581	44.9	—		—		—		88,188	R
Oregon	736,132	406,393	55.2	329,204	44.7	—		—		535	0.1	77,189	R
Pennsylvania	4,576,503	2,585,252	56.5	1,981,769	43.3	—		7,447	0.2	2,035		603,483	R
Rhode Island	387,609	225,819	58.3	161,790	41.7	—		—		—		64,029	R
South Carolina	300,583	75,700	25.2	136,372	45.4	2		—		88,509	29.4	47,863	D
South Dakota	293,857	171,569	58.4	122,288	41.6	—		—		—		49,281	R
Tennessee	939,404	462,288	49.2	456,507	48.6	19,820	2.1	—		789	0.1	5,781	R
Texas	1,955,168	1,080,619	55.3	859,958	44.0	14,591	0.7	—		—		220,661	R
Utah	333,995	215,631	64.6	118,364	35.4	—		—		—		97,267	R
Vermont	152,978	110,390	72.2	42,549	27.8	—		—		39		67,841	R
Virginia	697,978	386,459	55.4	267,760	38.4	42,964	6.2	351	0.1	444	0.1	118,699	R
Washington	1,150,889	620,430	53.9	523,002	45.4	—		7,457	0.6	—		97,428	R
West Virginia	830,831	449,297	54.1	381,534	45.9	—		—		—		67,763	R
Wisconsin	1,550,558	954,844	61.6	586,768	37.8	6,918	0.4	710		1,318	0.1	368,076	R
Wyoming	124,127	74,573	60.1	49,554	39.9	—		—		—		25,019	R
Totals	62,026,908	35,590,472	57.4	26,022,752	42.0	111,178	0.2	44,450	0.1	258,056	0.4	9,567,720	R

Dwight D. Eisenhower was one of the most popular leaders in U.S. history. British Field Marshal Bernard L. Montgomery said of his wartime colleague, "He merely has to smile at you and you trust him at once." The most famous American general of World War II, Eisenhower had become a symbol of the hopes for a better world. He had won an overwhelming victory in the 1952 election, and he had gone to Korea, as he had promised. An armistice in Korea had begun in July 1953. As the 1956 presidential election approached, there was little doubt that Eisenhower could be easily reelected. The doubt was whether he would again accept nomination by the Republican Party.

On 24 September 1955, the President suffered his first heart attack. The news was not made public until Saturday afternoon, almost 12 hours after the attack. That Monday morning, the stock market took its worst plunge since the Great Panic of 1929. The nation anxiously waited for the medical bulletins coming from Fitzsimons Hospital, an army facility near Denver. Gradually, the outlook changed from cautious to guarded optimism. No one, including Eisenhower, seriously thought at that time that he would run again in 1956. Eisenhower's recovery, however, was remarkable. He was back in the White House less than three weeks later and resumed a full schedule by mid-January 1956. In February, Dr. Paul Dudley White, the President's cardiologist, said that Eisenhower was healthy enough to serve another term, and he would vote for him if he ran again. On 1 March, Eisenhower announced that he would seek reelection "if the Republican Convention . . . wants me."

In June 1956, Eisenhower had emergency surgery for chronic ileitis at Walter Reed Hospital in Washington. Again, there was speculation that he would not run again. Never before had the health of a president been so candidly discussed. On 10 July, Eisenhower again stated that he would run and two days later, spokesmen made it clear that Richard M. Nixon would be his running mate. Nixon had outraged Democrats and offended liberal Republicans by his strident abuse of the issue of communists in government. However, Republican strategists regarded him as an important link between the moderate and conservative wings of the party. Eisenhower was renominated unanimously on 22 August at the Republican Convention in San Francisco. Harold Stassen, who had sought the Republican nomination for president on nine different occasions, tried to have Nixon replaced on the ticket with Governor Christian Herter of Massachusetts, but his attempt failed. The Republican slogan was "Peace, Prosperity, and Progress."

Eisenhower described himself as "President of 160 million Americans." He preferred to stand above partisan politics. On several occasions, he expressed his dislike for arguing with Congress. The President was essentially a practical man, and he made no major changes in domestic policy during his first administration. Many of Eisenhower's advisers, especially his initial cabinet appointments, came from the business world. They brought to their offices a philosophy perhaps summed up by Charles E. Wilson, the former president of General Motors. At his confirmation hearings for secretary of defense, Wilson stated his belief that "what was good for the country was good for General Motors, and vice versa."

Eisenhower was a symbol of stability and patience. The motto on his desk translated as "Gentle in manner, strong in deed." On several occasions, he repeated that Congress had every right to dispose of his legislative proposals as its members saw fit. As a party leader, he tolerated opposition within Republican ranks but, at the same time, he also gave the impression that opposition did not exist. He refused to criticize Republican legislators who voted against his programs, or cabinet members who openly disagreed with his policies. Although the Democrats regained control of Congress in the 1954 elections, Gallup polls showed that approximately 65 percent of the public approved of the way Eisenhower handled his job as president. It was taken for granted that he would win a second term.

The Democratic Convention met in Chicago and renominated Adlai E. Stevenson on the first ballot. However, he did not win the second nomination without a struggle. Senator Estes Kefauver of Tennessee challenged Stevenson in several primaries. Kefauver was a southern liberal whose national reputation was based largely upon his televised crime investigations. Although Kefauver won some early primaries, he withdrew after losing to Stevenson in the Florida and California primaries. Stevenson had another challenger—Governor W. Averell Harriman of New York. Former President Harry S. Truman supported Harriman as the true heir of the New Deal–Fair Deal. The former President called Stevenson a "hesitant man" now aligned with the "conservative and reactionaries" of the Democratic Party. However, Truman's support was too little and too late. Stevenson defeated Harriman on the first ballot.

In a surprise move, Stevenson gave the convention free choice to select the vice presidential candidate. There was a mad scramble for delegates on the convention floor as several younger hopefuls competed for the nomination—notably Senators Hubert Humphrey of Minnesota, Albert Gore, Sr. of Tennessee, and John F. Kennedy of Massachusetts. Kefauver also entered the contest which became a Kefauver-Kennedy duel. Kefauver won on the second ballot.

The second Eisenhower-Stevenson campaign was a dull one. Charges that the President's health posed a problem made little impact with the voters. Attempts to make Vice President Nixon an issue also failed. Unemployment remained fairly low. Civil rights seemed to be a liability for the Democrats in 1956 as southern Democratic governors tried to prevent racial integration. The bus boycott in Montgomery, Alabama started the great struggle against racial injustice which spread throughout the South. Early in 1956, the Democratic governors of South Carolina, Georgia, Mississippi, and Virginia called on all southern legislatures to declare that the federal government, including the Supreme Court, had no power to prohibit segregation and to "protest in appropriate language, against the encroachment of the central government upon the sovereignty of the several states and their people." South Carolina, Georgia, Mississippi, and Virginia passed resolutions of interposition, while several other southern state legislatures considered such action. Eisenhower chose to stay out of the civil rights struggle and expressed his desire that southern governors would do what was best.

Most Americans apparently believed that Eisenhower's experienced leadership was necessary now that a major conflict with the Soviet Union seemed possible. Two major international crises occurred in October 1956, during the last days of the campaign. Gamal Abdel Nasser, the president of Egypt, nationalized the Suez Canal. In response to this action, Great Britain, France, and Israel attacked Egypt. Eisenhower used his influence to achieve a cease-fire. The second crisis was in Hungary where the people tried to overthrow their communist government. The Soviet Union intervened and sent in troops to support the dictatorship. Eisenhower resisted the efforts of many Republicans, including Nixon, to challenge the Soviet Union in their own sphere of influence. Eisenhower's actions during both crises increased the voters' confidence in him.

Also in October, Stevenson injected some controversy into the campaign. He made two controversial proposals: that the selective service system be discontinued and the army rely on a small corps of highly trained professionals; and that the United States suspend hydrogen bomb tests as a practical step towards disarmament. Eisenhower dismissed both proposals as "a theatrical gesture" and Nixon accused Stevenson of "playing dangerous politics with American security." In raising national defense issues, Stevenson challenged the one area in which voters believed Eisenhower to have the greatest competence.

There was probably little that Stevenson might have said or done that would have affected the outcome. He campaigned vigorously and once again inspired almost fanatical devotion in his followers. The Eisenhower landslide was of staggering proportion. He carried 41 states with 457 electoral votes. Stevenson won only 7 states (Missouri plus 6 states of the Deep South) with 73 electoral votes. Eisenhower received almost 10 million votes more than Stevenson: 57.4 percent of the popular vote compared to Stevenson's 42 percent. It was the most one-sided victory since Franklin D. Roosevelt had defeated Alfred M. Landon in 1936. The extent of Eisenhower's landslide was astonishing. He won New York State, for example, by more than 1.5 million votes, and ran unusually strong in African American districts—a first in both instances for a Republican candidate. Given the magnitude of Eisenhower's victory, the congressional results were striking and without precedent. Eisenhower led the Republican congressional ticket by more than 6.5 million votes, and the Democrats carried both houses of Congress. Never before in a two-way presidential race had a party won control of Congress while losing the presidency. The race was between Eisenhower, the person, and the Democratic Party. The outcome of the election was again a personal tribute to Eisenhower.

The election results also indicate that a national Democratic majority survived except for the presidency. However, no Democrat commanded the affection and devotion that Eisenhower aroused. But, precisely because Eisenhower chose to stand above political parties, he was unable to transfer his prestige to anyone, not even to his vice president.

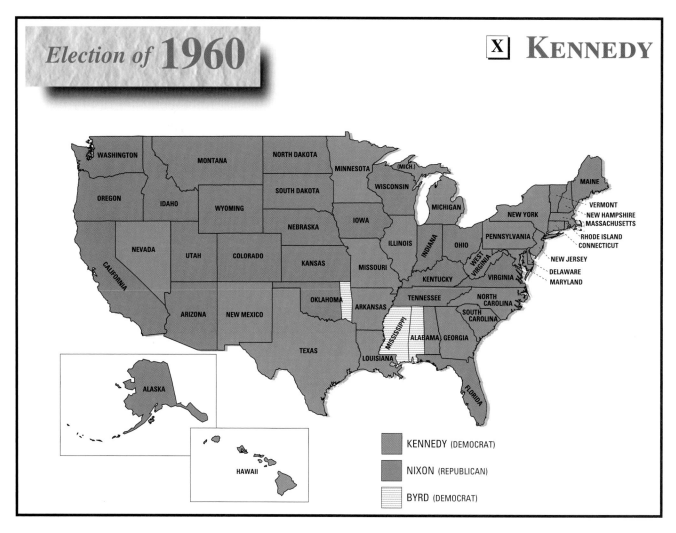

KENNEDY (DEMOCRAT)

NIXON (REPUBLICAN)

BYRD (DEMOCRAT)

States	Electoral Votes	Kennedy	Nixon	Byrd	States	Electoral Votes	Kennedy	Nixon	Byrd
Alabama	(11)	5	-	6	Montana	(4)	-	4	-
Alaska	(3)	-	3	-	Nebraska	(6)	-	6	-
Arizona	(4)	-	4	-	Nevada	(3)	3	-	-
Arkansas	(8)	8	-	-	New Hampshire	(4)	-	4	-
California	(32)	-	32	-	New Jersey	(16)	16	-	-
Colorado	(6)	-	6	-	New Mexico	(4)	4	-	-
Connecticut	(8)	8	-	-	New York	(45)	45	-	-
Delaware	(3)	3	-	-	North Carolina	(14)	14	-	-
Florida	(10)	-	10	-	North Dakota	(4)	-	4	-
Georgia	(12)	12	-	-	Ohio	(25)	-	25	-
Hawaii	(3)	3	-	-	Oklahoma	(8)	-	7	1
Idaho	(4)	-	4	-	Oregon	(6)	-	6	-
Illinois	(27)	27	-	-	Pennsylvania	(32)	32	-	-
Indiana	(13)	-	13	-	Rhode Island	(4)	4	-	-
Iowa	(10)	-	10	-	South Carolina	(8)	8	-	-
Kansas	(8)	-	8	-	South Dakota	(4)	-	4	-
Kentucky	(10)	-	10	-	Tennessee	(11)	-	11	-
Louisiana	(10)	10	-	-	Texas	(24)	24	-	-
Maine	(5)	-	5	-	Utah	(4)	-	4	-
Maryland	(9)	9	-	-	Vermont	(3)	-	3	-
Massachusetts	(16)	16	-	-	Virginia	(12)	-	12	-
Michigan	(20)	20	-	-	Washington	(9)	-	9	-
Minnesota	(11)	11	-	-	West Virginia	(8)	8	-	-
Mississippi	(8)	-	-	8	Wisconsin	(12)	-	12	-
Missouri	(13)	13	-	-	Wyoming	(3)	-	3	-
					Totals	**(537)**	**303**	**219**	**15**

ELECTORAL VOTE

Election of 1960

STATE	TOTAL VOTE	JOHN F. KENNEDY (Democrat)		RICHARD M. NIXON (Republican)		ERIC HASS (Socialist Labor)		UNPLEDGED		OTHER		PLURALITY	
		Votes	%	Votes	%	Votes	%	Votes	%	Votes	%		
Alabama	570,225	324,050	56.8	237,981	41.7	—		—		8,194	1.4	86,069	D
Alaska	60,762	29,809	49.1	30,953	50.9	—		—		—		1,144	R
Arizona	398,491	176,781	44.4	221,241	55.5	469	0.1	—		—		44,460	R
Arkansas	428,509	215,049	50.2	184,508	43.1	—		—		28,952	6.8	30,541	D
California	6,506,578	3,224,099	49.6	3,259,722	50.1	1,051		—		21,706	0.3	35,623	R
Colorado	736,236	330,629	44.9	402,242	54.6	2,803	0.4	—		562	0.1	71,613	R
Connecticut	1,222,883	657,055	53.7	565,813	46.3	—		—		15		91,242	D
Delaware	196,683	99,590	50.6	96,373	49.0	82		—		638	0.3	3,217	D
Florida	1,544,176	748,700	48.5	795,476	51.5	—		—		—		46,776	R
Georgia	733,349	458,638	62.5	274,472	37.4	—		—		239		184,166	D
Hawaii	184,705	92,410	50.0	92,295	50.0	—		—		—		115	D
Idaho	300,450	138,853	46.2	161,597	53.8	—		—		—		22,744	R
Illinois	4,757,409	2,377,846	50.0	2,368,988	49.8	10,560	0.2	—		15		8,858	D
Indiana	2,135,360	952,358	44.6	1,175,120	55.0	1,136	0.1	—		6,746	0.3	222,762	R
Iowa	1,273,810	550,565	43.2	722,381	56.7	230		—		634		171,816	R
Kansas	928,825	363,213	39.1	561,474	60.4	—		—		4,138	0.4	198,261	R
Kentucky	1,124,462	521,855	46.4	602,607	53.6	—		—		—		80,752	R
Louisiana	807,891	407,339	50.4	230,980	28.6	—		—		169,572	21.0	176,359	D
Maine	421,767	181,159	43.0	240,608	57.0	—		—		—		59,449	R
Maryland	1,055,349	565,808	53.6	489,538	46.4	—		—		3		76,270	D
Massachusetts	2,469,480	1,487,174	60.2	976,750	39.6	3,892	0.2	—		1,664	0.1	510,424	D
Michigan	3,318,097	1,687,269	50.9	1,620,428	48.8	1,718	0.1	—		8,682	0.3	66,841	D
Minnesota	1,541,887	779,933	50.6	757,915	49.2	962	0.1	—		3,077	0.2	22,018	D
Mississippi	298,171	108,362	36.3	73,561	24.7	—		116,248	39.0	—		7,886	U
Missouri	1,934,422	972,201	50.3	962,221	49.7	—		—		—		9,980	D
Montana	277,579	134,891	48.6	141,841	51.1	—		—		847	0.3	6,950	R
Nebraska	613,095	232,542	37.9	380,553	62.1	—		—		—		148,011	R
Nevada	107,267	54,880	51.2	52,387	48.8	—		—		—		2,493	D
New Hampshire	295,761	137,772	46.6	157,989	53.4	—		—		—		20,217	R
New Jersey	2,773,111	1,385,415	50.0	1,363,324	49.2	4,262	0.2	—		20,110	0.7	22,091	D
New Mexico	311,107	156,027	50.2	153,733	49.4	570	0.2	—		777	0.2	2,294	D
New York	7,291,079	3,830,085	52.5	3,446,419	47.3	—		—		14,575	0.2	383,666	D
North Carolina	1,368,556	713,136	52.1	655,420	47.9	—		—		—		57,716	D
North Dakota	278,431	123,963	44.5	154,310	55.4	—		—		158	0.1	30,347	R
Ohio	4,161,859	1,944,248	46.7	2,217,611	53.3	—		—		—		273,363	R
Oklahoma	903,150	370,111	41.0	533,039	59.0	—		—		—		162,928	R
Oregon	776,421	367,402	47.3	408,060	52.6	—		—		959	0.1	40,658	R
Pennsylvania	5,006,541	2,556,282	51.1	2,439,956	48.7	7,185	0.1	—		3,118	0.1	116,326	D
Rhode Island	405,535	258,032	63.6	147,502	36.4	—		—		1		110,530	D
South Carolina	386,688	198,129	51.2	188,558	48.8	—		—		1		9,571	D
South Dakota	306,487	128,070	41.8	178,417	58.2	—		—		—		50,347	R
Tennessee	1,051,792	481,453	45.8	556,577	52.9	—		—		13,762	1.3	75,124	R
Texas	2,311,084	1,167,567	50.5	1,121,310	48.5	—		—		22,207	1.0	46,257	D
Utah	374,709	169,248	45.2	205,361	54.8	—		—		100		36,113	R
Vermont	167,324	69,186	41.3	98,131	58.6	—		—		7		28,945	R
Virginia	771,449	362,327	47.0	404,521	52.4	397	0.1	—		4,204	0.5	42,194	R
Washington	1,241,572	599,298	48.3	629,273	50.7	10,895	0.9	—		2,106	0.2	29,975	R
West Virginia	837,781	441,786	52.7	395,995	47.3	—		—		—		45,791	D
Wisconsin	1,729,082	830,805	48.0	895,175	51.8	1,310	0.1	—		1,792	0.1	64,370	R
Wyoming	140,782	63,331	45.0	77,451	55.0	—		—		—		14,120	R
Totals	68,838,219	34,226,731	49.7	34,108,157	49.5	47,522	0.1	116,248	0.2	339,561	0.5	118,574	D

P O P U L A R   V O T E

The 1960 presidential election ranks as a turning point in U.S. political history. Dwight D. Eisenhower, the oldest man to serve in the presidency up to then, was succeeded by the youngest man ever elected to it. The nation chose its first Catholic president. It also was the first time that a major party had nominated two incumbent senators for president and vice president—John F. Kennedy and Lyndon B. Johnson.

Kennedy had won election to the House of Representatives from Massachusetts in 1946 and to the Senate in 1952 on his good looks, his father's wealth, and his World War II record. Although he remained an outsider in Congress, he had come within a few votes of winning the vice presidential nomination at the 1956 Democratic Convention. At that time, Kennedy set his sights on the 1960 election. He criss-crossed the country several times, meeting local politicians and charming audiences. After being reelected to the Senate in 1958, Kennedy and his family began to put together a very effective national political organization. He emerged as the leading Democratic candidate after primary victories in New Hampshire, Wisconsin, and West Virginia over Senator Hubert Humphrey of Minnesota. At the Los Angeles convention, Kennedy won the nomination on the first ballot. He received unanimous support from New England delegates, from those in primary states which he had won, and the backing of all the larger northern states and half the votes from western states. However, Kennedy received only 13 votes from the southern delegates. In a maneuver that surprised nearly everyone, Kennedy offered the vice presidential spot to Senator Lyndon B. Johnson of Texas, and Johnson accepted. This decision would shape U.S. presidential politics for the rest of the decade.

There was no major struggle within the Republican Party. It had been clear for months that Richard M. Nixon enjoyed overwhelming support from party regulars in all sections of the country. Nixon, only 47 years old, had served as a congressman, senator, and, for eight years, as vice president. He had Eisenhower's backing although it seemed hesitant at times. Nixon was nominated on the first ballot, and he chose Henry Cabot Lodge, Jr., ambassador to the United Nations and former senator from Massachusetts, as his running mate.

Nixon, far better known than Kennedy, repeatedly stressed that he was more qualified for the task of national leadership than his youthful, inexperienced opponent. The two candidates were internationalists and moderate progressives. They agreed on most basic issues although their programs differed in detail and emphasis. Kennedy's theme was the need for positive leadership and bold efforts to "get America moving again." In his acceptance speech at the Democratic Convention, he had stated: "We stand today on the edge of a New Frontier—the frontier of the 1960s—a frontier of unknown opportunities and perils—a frontier of unfulfilled hopes and threats." Nixon defended the Eisenhower record and denied that the military and economic situations were as grave as his opponent claimed. Nixon continued to enjoy a substantial lead in the late summer public opinion polls.

Throughout the 1960 presidential campaign, tensions between the Soviet Union and the United States increased dramatically. In May, the Soviets announced that an American reconnaissance plane, a U-2, had been shot down deep in Russian territory. Eisenhower believed that the pilot was dead so he said that the plane was doing weather research and had gotten lost. However, the pilot had been captured alive, and he confessed to being a CIA agent. Within days, the headlines became increasingly alarmist. "Khrushchev warns of Rocket Attack on Bases Used by U.S. Spying Planes," *The New York Times* announced on 10 May. The Russian leader used the U-2 incident to break up the May Paris Summit Conference and to cancel Eisenhower's scheduled visit to the Soviet Union. As the election approached, Cuban Prime Minister Fidel Castro was causing alarm and confusion in the Caribbean. Neither Eisenhower nor his advisers could decide if Castro was a communist. In the President's view, the worst possibility would be if Castro allowed Khrushchev to use Cuba as a base for Soviet strategic forces. At the same time, Khrushchev was making trouble in the Congo where Eisenhower feared a communist take-over. In southeast Asia, communist military forces had gained new strength and boldness. Eisenhower's intense concern was the security of the United States, and he did not think Kennedy was mature enough for the presidency. "I will do almost anything to avoid turning over my chair and the country to Kennedy," he told a confidant on 19 August.

The turning point of the campaign was a series of four televised debates between Nixon and Kennedy. The largest television audience in U.S. history—estimated at 70 million adults—watched the candidates confront each other in the first debate on 26 September. Kennedy, rested and well-briefed, seemed forceful and at ease in answering questions posed by a panel of newsmen. Nixon looked pale and tired and seemed to be hesitant and defensive. Until then, the lesser-known Kennedy had been the underdog. Journalist Theodore H. White wrote: "There was, first and above all, the crude, overwhelming impression that side by side the two seemed evenly matched— and this even matching in the popular imagination was for Kennedy a major victory." More important though, the first debate strengthened Kennedy's support in the Democratic Party, quieting talk of Democratic defections.

Kennedy emerged from the debates as a celebrity. His crowds grew larger and more enthusiastic. The economy showed signs of faltering and this was good news for Kennedy. Unemployment rose in October and Kennedy proclaimed "the third Republican recession in six years." Kennedy aide Theodore Sorensen wrote later: "The votes of newly unemployed workers alone in Illinois, New Jersey, Michigan, Minnesota, Missouri, and South Carolina were greater than Kennedy's margin in those states."

During the last week of October, a Georgia judge sentenced Reverend Martin Luther King, Jr. to four months in jail on a legal technicality. It seemed entirely probable that King would not get out alive from this prison in rural Georgia. Eisenhower ignored Nixon's urging that the White House announce that the Justice Department would look into the matter. Kennedy telephoned the distraught and pregnant Mrs. King on 26 October and promised to help. Robert Kennedy, the Senator's brother, called the judge on King's behalf, and King was released the following day. Dr. King's father announced that he had intended to vote against Kennedy on religious grounds but had changed his mind. "Imagine Martin Luther King having a bigot for a father," Kennedy said privately. King himself did not endorse either candidate. However, he stated that "It took a lot of courage for Senator Kennedy to do this especially in Georgia . . . I am convinced he will seek to exercise the power of his office to fully implement the civil rights plank of his party's platform." On the Sunday before Election Day, the Democrats distributed 2 million copies of a pamphlet outside

African American churches. The pamphlet quoted various King family members praising Kennedy for his decisive action. The election ended in a virtual dead heat. Kennedy had a winning margin of only 118,574 votes out of a record 68.8 million votes cast. He won by two-tenths of 1 percent of the popular vote for a total of 49.7 percent to Nixon's 49.5 percent. Kennedy won 12 states, including Illinois, with less than 2 percent of the two-party vote. He lost 6 states, including California, by an equally close margin. Kennedy received 303 electoral votes to Nixon's 219. Kennedy's electoral vote count was the same as Truman's in 1948, but the winner-take-all electoral system magnified Kennedy's tiny popular vote margin into a more comfortable electoral vote. Six of Alabama's 11 Democratic electors and all 8 of Mississippi's were "unpledged." These electors, together with a defecting Republican elector in Oklahoma, strongly disagreed with both the Republican and Democratic Party planks on civil rights and cast their votes for Senator Harry F. Byrd of Virginia.

Kennedy narrowly carried both Illinois and Texas, where Republicans doubted that there had been honest vote counts. Mayor Richard J. Daley of Chicago told Kennedy on election night "with a little bit of luck and the help of a few close friends, you're going to carry Illinois." In one Chicago ward, there were only 22 registered voters but 74 votes were cast for Kennedy and 3 for Nixon. Indeed, to judge by the available evidence, Daley probably did steal Cook County and the state for Kennedy. Mass voter confusion and irregularities also took place in Texas. If both Illinois and Texas had gone for Nixon, he would have been elected president.

The most important issue in the campaign was Kennedy's religion. Democratic Protestant defectors cost Kennedy at least two states—Tennessee and Oklahoma. However, the Catholic vote for the Democratic candidate increased from about 63 percent in 1956 to almost 80 percent in 1960. While Kennedy lost Protestant Democrats in important northern states, the outpouring of Catholic support offset this loss. In short, Kennedy's religion hurt him in the popular vote but helped him in the electoral vote.

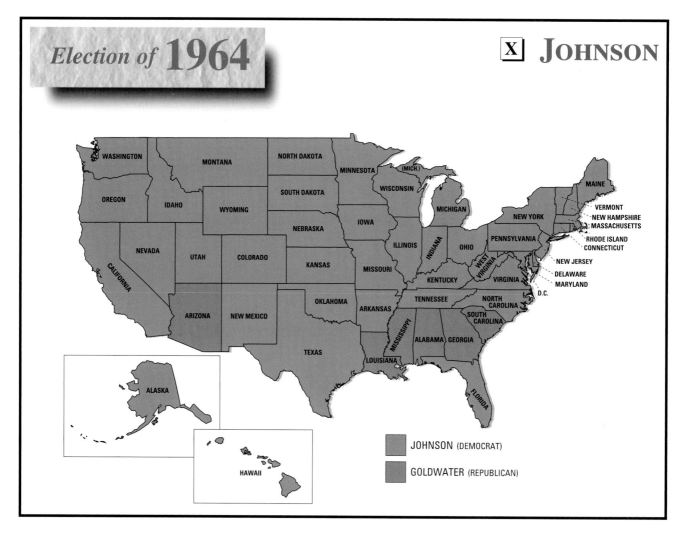

Election of 1964

JOHNSON (DEMOCRAT)

GOLDWATER (REPUBLICAN)

States	Electoral Votes	Johnson	Goldwater	States	Electoral Votes	Johnson	Goldwater
Alabama	(10)	-	10	Montana	(4)	4	-
Alaska	(3)	3	-	Nebraska	(5)	5	-
Arizona	(5)	-	5	Nevada	(3)	3	-
Arkansas	(6)	6	-	New Hampshire	(4)	4	-
California	(40)	40	-	New Jersey	(17)	17	-
Colorado	(6)	6	-	New Mexico	(4)	4	-
Connecticut	(8)	8	-	New York	(43)	43	-
Delaware	(3)	3	-	North Carolina	(13)	13	-
District of Columbia	(3)	3	-	North Dakota	(4)	4	-
Florida	(14)	14	-	Ohio	(26)	26	-
Georgia	(12)	-	12	Oklahoma	(8)	8	-
Hawaii	(4)	4	-	Oregon	(6)	6	-
Idaho	(4)	4	-	Pennsylvania	(29)	29	-
Illinois	(26)	26	-	Rhode Island	(4)	4	-
Indiana	(13)	13	-	South Carolina	(8)	-	8
Iowa	(9)	9	-	South Dakota	(4)	4	-
Kansas	(7)	7	-	Tennessee	(11)	11	-
Kentucky	(9)	9	-	Texas	(25)	25	-
Louisiana	(10)	-	10	Utah	(4)	4	-
Maine	(4)	4	-	Vermont	(3)	3	-
Maryland	(10)	10	-	Virginia	(12)	12	-
Massachusetts	(14)	14	-	Washington	(9)	9	-
Michigan	(21)	21	-	West Virginia	(7)	7	-
Minnesota	(10)	10	-	Wisconsin	(12)	12	-
Mississippi	(7)	-	7	Wyoming	(3)	3	-
Missouri	(12)	12	-	**Totals**	**(538)**	**486**	**52**

ELECTORAL VOTE

Election of 1964

STATE	TOTAL VOTE	LYNDON B. JOHNSON (Democrat)		BARRY M. GOLDWATER (Republican)		ERIC HASS (Socialist Labor)		CLIFTON DeBERRY (Socialist Workers)		OTHER		PLURALITY	
		Votes	%	Votes	%	Votes	%	Votes	%	Votes	%		
Alabama	689,818	—		479,085	69.5	—		—		210,733	30.5	268,353	R
Alaska	67,259	44,329	65.9	22,930	34.1	—		—		—		21,399	D
Arizona	480,770	237,753	49.5	242,535	50.4	482	0.1	—		—		4,782	R
Arkansas	560,426	314,197	56.1	243,264	43.4	—		—		2,965	0.5	70,933	D
California	7,057,586	4,171,877	59.1	2,879,108	40.8	489		378		5,734	0.1	1,292,769	D
Colorado	776,986	476,024	61.3	296,767	38.2	302		2,537	0.3	1,356	0.2	179,257	D
Connecticut	1,218,578	826,269	67.8	390,996	32.1	—		—		1,313	0.1	435,273	D
Delaware	201,320	122,704	60.9	78,078	38.8	113	0.1	—		425	0.2	44,626	D
Florida	1,854,481	948,540	51.1	905,941	48.9	—		—		—		42,599	D
Georgia	1,139,335	522,556	45.9	616,584	54.1	—		—		195		94,028	R
Hawaii	207,271	163,249	78.8	44,022	21.2	—		—		—		119,227	D
Idaho	292,477	148,920	50.9	143,557	49.1	—		—		—		5,363	D
Illinois	4,702,841	2,796,833	59.5	1,905,946	40.5	—		—		62		890,887	D
Indiana	2,091,606	1,170,848	56.0	911,118	43.6	1,374	0.1	—		8,266	0.4	259,730	D
Iowa	1,184,539	733,030	61.9	449,148	37.9	182		159		2,020	0.2	283,882	D
Kansas	857,901	464,028	54.1	386,579	45.1	1,901	0.2	—		5,393	0.6	77,449	D
Kentucky	1,046,105	669,659	64.0	372,977	35.7	—		—		3,469	0.3	296,682	D
Louisiana	896,293	387,068	43.2	509,225	56.8	—		—		—		122,157	R
Maine	380,965	262,264	68.8	118,701	31.2	—		—		—		143,563	D
Maryland	1,116,457	730,912	65.5	385,495	34.5	—		—		50		345,417	D
Massachusetts	2,344,798	1,786,422	76.2	549,727	23.4	4,755	0.2	—		3,894	0.2	1,236,695	D
Michigan	3,203,102	2,136,615	66.7	1,060,152	33.1	1,704	0.1	3,817	0.1	814		1,076,463	D
Minnesota	1,554,462	991,117	63.8	559,624	36.0	2,544	0.2	1,177	0.1	—		431,493	D
Mississippi	409,146	52,618	12.9	356,528	87.1	—		—		—		303,910	R
Missouri	1,817,879	1,164,344	64.0	653,535	36.0	—		—		—		510,809	D
Montana	278,628	164,246	58.9	113,032	40.6	—		332	0.1	1,018	0.4	51,214	D
Nebraska	584,154	307,307	52.6	276,847	47.4	—		—		—		30,460	D
Nevada	135,433	79,339	58.6	56,094	41.4	—		—		—		23,245	D
New Hampshire	288,093	184,064	63.9	104,029	36.1	—		—		—		80,035	D
New Jersey	2,847,663	1,868,231	65.6	964,174	33.9	7,075	0.2	8,183	0.3	—		904,057	D
New Mexico	328,645	194,015	59.0	132,838	40.4	1,217	0.4	—		575	0.2	61,177	D
New York	7,166,275	4,913,102	68.6	2,243,559	31.3	6,118	0.1	3,228		268		2,669,543	D
North Carolina	1,424,983	800,139	56.2	624,844	43.8	—		—		—		175,295	D
North Dakota	258,389	149,784	58.0	108,207	41.9	—		224	0.1	174	0.1	41,577	D
Ohio	3,969,196	2,498,331	62.9	1,470,865	37.1	—		—		—		1,027,466	D
Oklahoma	932,499	519,834	55.7	412,665	44.3	—		—		—		107,169	D
Oregon	786,305	501,017	63.7	282,779	36.0	—		—		2,509	0.3	218,238	D
Pennsylvania	4,822,690	3,130,954	64.9	1,673,657	34.7	5,092	0.1	10,456	0.2	2,531	0.1	1,457,297	D
Rhode Island	390,091	315,463	80.9	74,615	19.1	—		—		13		240,848	D
South Carolina	524,779	215,723	41.1	309,048	58.9	—		—		8		93,325	R
South Dakota	293,118	163,010	55.6	130,108	44.4	—		—		—		32,902	D
Tennessee	1,143,946	634,947	55.5	508,965	44.5	—		—		34		125,982	D
Texas	2,626,811	1,663,185	63.3	958,566	36.5	—		—		5,060	0.2	704,619	D
Utah	401,413	219,628	54.7	181,785	45.3	—		—		—		37,843	D
Vermont	163,089	108,127	66.3	54,942	33.7	—		—		20		53,185	D
Virginia	1,042,267	558,038	53.5	481,334	46.2	2,895	0.3	—		—		76,704	D
Washington	1,258,556	779,881	62.0	470,366	37.4	7,772	0.6	537		—		309,515	D
West Virginia	792,040	538,087	67.9	253,953	32.1	—		—		—		284,134	D
Wisconsin	1,691,815	1,050,424	62.1	638,495	37.7	1,204	0.1	1,692	0.1	—		411,929	D
Wyoming	142,716	80,718	56.6	61,998	43.4	—		—		—		18,720	D
Dist. of Col.	198,597	169,796	85.5	28,801	14.5	—		—		—		140,995	D
Totals	70,644,592	43,129,566	61.1	27,178,188	38.5	45,219	0.1	32,720		258,899	0.4	15,951,378	D

P O P U L A R   V O T E

In the 1964 election, Lyndon B. Johnson won the highest percentage of the popular vote in any presidential contest in U.S. history. He received 61.1 percent as compared with Franklin D. Roosevelt's previous record of 60.8 percent in 1936. Many voters, still shocked by President John F. Kennedy's assassination in November 1963, voted for Johnson as a tribute to the slain president. Many also voted less for Johnson than against his Republican opponent, Senator Barry M. Goldwater of Arizona. Goldwater and the right wing movement of the Republican Party had frightened many voters. The great Goldwater crusade of 1964, which was a minority faction of the minority party, had begun with a proud slogan: "In your heart you know he's right." The Democrats responded: "In Your Guts You Know He's Nuts."

Throughout the twentieth century, the Republican Party has been split along ideological lines, progressive versus conservative. The progressives, for example, accepted most New Deal legislation and reluctantly agreed with the vast authority assumed by the federal government. Conservative Republicans generally had rejected almost all New Deal programs as an unwarranted interference with state responsibilities. In 1952, in a bitter convention fight, the conservatives backed Senator Robert A. Taft while the progressives supported Dwight D. Eisenhower. For eight years, President Eisenhower refused to become involved in the arguing that simmered beneath the illusion of party unity. In 1960, the "true" conservative, Richard M. Nixon, had compromised unnecessarily with the progressives. Nixon's defeat was caused by his attempt to appeal to both wings of the party and pleasing neither. His defeat renewed the bitter feud within the Republican Party.

By 1964, Goldwater had become the star of the most conservative faction within the Republican Party. He was an outgoing man who seemed to embody the rugged values about which he spoke. Goldwater disliked Roosevelt's New Deal and Johnson's War on Poverty. He opposed minimum wage laws as well as social security, the Tennessee Valley Authority, unions, school desegregation, subsidies to farmers, funding for urban renewal, the income tax, and federal aid to education. He favored replacing the Supreme Court with a "court of the union" composed of 50 state chief justices. He wanted the United States out of the United Nations and the United Nations out of the United States. He opposed disarmament negotiations, foreign aid, and decolonialization of European overseas empires. He supported a stronger military, a stronger CIA and FBI, and an expanded national security system. He favored an assault on Fidel Castro's Cuba, and he wanted to drop a "low-yield" nuclear bomb on Chinese supply lines in North Vietnam. He stood firmly for states' rights, siding with the segregationists. According to Goldwater, the threat to the United States came from the "radical left." He had been one of the most loyal supporters of Senator Joseph McCarthy and voted against his 1954 censure by the Senate. At the 1960 Republican Convention, Goldwater protested Nixon's "capitulation to the liberals" and urged conservatives to "take this party back."

Goldwater announced his candidacy in January 1964. His principal opponents were Governor Nelson A. Rockefeller of New York and Governor William W. Scranton of Pennsylvania, both progressive Republicans. The Goldwater forces won control of Republican state organizations throughout the South. After a defeat in the New Hampshire primary, they chose to compete in those states where their organizational skills would bring out the most conservative Republican voters. Following this strategy, Goldwater won the Texas primary with 75.3 percent of the vote; the Indiana primary with 67 percent; and the Illinois presidential preference poll with 62 percent. Rockefeller and Scranton seemed no match for Goldwater, whose supporters were on a crusade.

The Republican Convention nominated Goldwater on the first ballot. His supporters made it clear that they wanted a total ideological victory. They booed the moderate Rockefeller with savage fury when he attempted to address the convention. They repeatedly directed a chorus of jeers at the press and television reporters whom they accused of liberal bias. Goldwater, refusing any compromises to heal party wounds, chose as his running mate William Miller, an obscure New York congressman, whose views paralleled his own. In his acceptance speech, Goldwater defiantly ended any possibility of party unity. "I would remind you that extremism in the defense of liberty is no vice!" he told the cheering delegates. "And let me remind you also that moderation in the pursuit of justice is no virtue!" In a subsequent press conference, Goldwater called President Johnson "the greatest faker in the United States."

Goldwater's views placed him as far outside the national consensus as was the movement which claimed him as one of their own. Conservative publications like William F. Buckley, Jr.'s *National Review* had outlined a "southern strategy" for him which would appeal to conservatives. It was suggested that Goldwater run as the states' rights candidate, sweeping the South and border states, with perhaps 165 electoral votes. The votes in Republican strongholds elsewhere added to them would result in a clear electoral majority. It was also suggested that the dimensions of a Goldwater victory would be greater if he stirred up feelings against African Americans in the North, especially among ethnic White voters—"the silent majority." Hopes of profiting from this White backlash rose when riots erupted in African American areas of northern cities during the summer of 1964. Goldwater also expected to obtain the votes of George Wallace supporters. Wallace, the segregationist governor of Alabama, had dropped out of the Democratic primaries, but he had won 34 percent of the vote in Wisconsin, 30 percent in Indiana, and 43 percent in Maryland. What was needed, conservatives maintained, was "a choice, not an echo."

Lyndon B. Johnson, Kennedy's successor, had guided the nation through a difficult year. The former Texas senator and Senate majority leader had been a loyal vice president. He had come to the office with greater knowledge and mastery of the national political process than any man before him. His task, he announced, would be to complete the Kennedy program. "Let us begin," he said. And Congress passed just about every item of legislation he requested including the sweeping Civil Rights Act of 1964. "We have talked long enough about equal rights," said Johnson. It was now time to "write it in the book of laws."

Johnson asked Congress to declare a "war on poverty" in the United States. They assented by appropriating nearly $1 billion for 10 separate anti-poverty programs to be supervised by the new office of Economic Opportunity. "There were times in those days," recalled Bill Moyers, the President's press secretary, "when he thought the poor are poor because the economy is mismanaged against them, but most of the time he thought the problems could be solved if the poor were managed better—train them for some better jobs, help them to see a doctor, move them to a better place." That was the premise on which the Great Society operated. The President eagerly anticipated the 1964 presidential election. He wanted a massive triumph which would make him president in his own right. The

Democratic Convention nominated Johnson by acclamation. He chose Senator Hubert H. Humphrey of Minnesota, an old friend and firm liberal, as his running mate. Johnson called the Democrats "a party for all Americans," and Humphrey urged Republicans to join them because their party had been captured by men "of stridency, of unrestrained passion, of extreme and radical language." The delegates enthusiastically ratified the Great Society programs to fight poverty, discrimination, unemployment, pollution, and all other ills confronting the nation.

Goldwater had hoped the campaign would be a debate about major issues, especially civil rights. He had hoped to educate the nation about the evils of a centralized government. However, the Democrats circulated statements which Goldwater had made on dozens of issues through the years. His own words made Goldwater seem confused, even dangerous. In November 1963 and again in February 1964, for example, he said that the NATO commander in Europe should have authority to use tactical nuclear weapons without waiting "while the White House calls a conference." Seizing upon this statement, the Democrats ran a one-minute television commercial showing a young girl plucking petals from a daisy as a voice counted down, "ten, nine, eight. . ." The film faded to an atomic cloud at "zero." Johnson's voice said: "These are the stakes . . . we must love each other or we must die." He did not have to mention Goldwater's name. The ad was so controversial that it was only shown once by the Democrats. Johnson shrewdly conducted a restrained personal campaign as dramatic events abroad diverted the nation's attention from politics. In mid-October, Soviet Premier Nikita Khrushchev was ousted from power in Moscow, and China exploded its first nuclear bomb. Both occurrences worked in Johnson's favor.

Johnson's victory was a landslide. He received 486 electoral votes. Goldwater won only 6 states with 52 electoral votes. Johnson received almost 16 million more votes than did Goldwater. He carried with him the most heavily Democratic Congress since 1936. The sweeping Democratic triumph cut deeply into Republican strength at all levels of government across the nation. Voters had overwhelmingly affirmed their allegiance to the progressive tradition in U.S. politics. Johnson had received a mandate to continue with his Great Society programs.

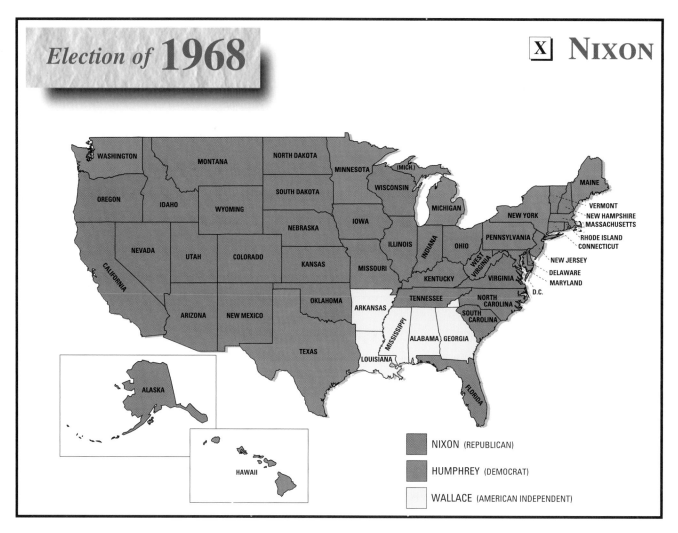

Election of 1968

NIXON (REPUBLICAN)

HUMPHREY (DEMOCRAT)

WALLACE (AMERICAN INDEPENDENT)

States	Electoral Votes	Nixon	Humphrey	Wallace	States	Electoral Votes	Nixon	Humphrey	Wallace
Alabama	(10)	-	-	10	Montana	(4)	4	-	-
Alaska	(3)	3	-	-	Nebraska	(5)	5	-	-
Arizona	(5)	5	-	-	Nevada	(3)	3	-	-
Arkansas	(6)	-	-	6	New Hampshire	(4)	4	-	-
California	(40)	40	-	-	New Jersey	(17)	17	-	-
Colorado	(6)	6	-	-	New Mexico	(4)	4	-	-
Connecticut	(8)	-	8	-	New York	(43)	-	43	-
Delaware	(3)	3	-	-	North Carolina	(13)	12	-	1
District of Columbia	(3)	-	3	-	North Dakota	(4)	4	-	-
Florida	(14)	14	-	-	Ohio	(26)	26	-	-
Georgia	(12)	-	-	12	Oklahoma	(8)	8	-	-
Hawaii	(4)	-	4	-	Oregon	(6)	6	-	-
Idaho	(4)	4	-	-	Pennsylvania	(29)	-	29	-
Illinois	(26)	26	-	-	Rhode Island	(4)	-	4	-
Indiana	(13)	13	-	-	South Carolina	(8)	8	-	-
Iowa	(9)	9	-	-	South Dakota	(4)	4	-	-
Kansas	(7)	7	-	-	Tennessee	(11)	11	-	-
Kentucky	(9)	9	-	-	Texas	(25)	-	25	-
Louisiana	(10)	-	-	10	Utah	(4)	4	-	-
Maine	(4)	-	4	-	Vermont	(3)	3	-	-
Maryland	(10)	-	10	-	Virginia	(12)	12	-	-
Massachusetts	(14)	-	14	-	Washington	(9)	-	9	-
Michigan	(21)	-	21	-	West Virginia	(7)	-	7	-
Minnesota	(10)	-	10	-	Wisconsin	(12)	12	-	-
Mississippi	(7)	-	-	7	Wyoming	(3)	3	-	-
Missouri	(12)	12	-	-	**Totals**	**(538)**	**301**	**191**	**46**

ELECTORAL VOTE

Election of 1968

STATE	TOTAL VOTE	RICHARD M. NIXON (Republican)		HUBERT H. HUMPHREY (Democrat)		GEORGE C. WALLACE (American Independent)		HENNING A. BLOMEN (Socialist Labor)		OTHER		PLURALITY	
		Votes	%	Votes	%	Votes	%	Votes	%	Votes	%		
Alabama	1,049,922	146,923	14.0	196,579	18.7	691,425	65.9	—		14,995	1.4	494,846	A
Alaska	83,035	37,600	45.3	35,411	42.6	10,024	12.1	—		—		2,189	R
Arizona	486,936	266,721	54.8	170,514	35.0	46,573	9.6	75		3,053	0.6	96,207	R
Arkansas	619,969	190,759	30.8	188,228	30.4	240,982	38.9	—		—		50,223	A
California	7,251,587	3,467,664	47.8	3,244,318	44.7	487,270	6.7	341		51,994	0.7	223,346	R
Colorado	811,199	409,345	50.5	335,174	41.3	60,813	7.5	3,016	0.4	2,851	0.4	74,171	R
Connecticut	1,256,232	556,721	44.3	621,561	49.5	76,650	6.1	—		1,300	0.1	64,840	D
Delaware	214,367	96,714	45.1	89,194	41.6	28,459	13.3	—		—		7,520	R
Florida	2,187,805	886,804	40.5	676,794	30.9	624,207	28.5	—		—		210,010	R
Georgia	1,250,266	380,111	30.4	334,440	26.7	535,550	42.8	—		165		155,439	A
Hawaii	236,218	91,425	38.7	141,324	59.8	3,469	1.5	—		—		49,899	D
Idaho	291,183	165,369	56.8	89,273	30.7	36,541	12.5	—		—		76,096	R
Illinois	4,619,749	2,174,774	47.1	2,039,814	44.2	390,958	8.5	13,878	0.3	325		134,960	R
Indiana	2,123,597	1,067,885	50.3	806,659	38.0	243,108	11.4	—		5,945	0.3	261,226	R
Iowa	1,167,931	619,106	53.0	476,699	40.8	66,422	5.7	241		5,463	0.5	142,407	R
Kansas	872,783	478,674	54.8	302,996	34.7	88,921	10.2	—		2,192	0.3	175,678	R
Kentucky	1,055,893	462,411	43.8	397,541	37.6	193,098	18.3	—		2,843	0.3	64,870	R
Louisiana	1,097,450	257,535	23.5	309,615	28.2	530,300	48.3	—		—		220,685	A
Maine	392,936	169,254	43.1	217,312	55.3	6,370	1.6	—		—		48,058	D
Maryland	1,235,039	517,995	41.9	538,310	43.6	178,734	14.5	—		—		20,315	D
Massachusetts	2,331,752	766,844	32.9	1,469,218	63.0	87,088	3.7	6,180	0.3	2,422	0.1	702,374	D
Michigan	3,306,250	1,370,665	41.5	1,593,082	48.2	331,968	10.0	1,762	0.1	8,773	0.3	222,417	D
Minnesota	1,588,506	658,643	41.5	857,738	54.0	68,931	4.3	285		2,909	0.2	199,095	D
Mississippi	654,509	88,516	13.5	150,644	23.0	415,349	63.5	—		—		264,705	A
Missouri	1,809,502	811,932	44.9	791,444	43.7	206,126	11.4	—		—		20,488	R
Montana	274,404	138,835	50.6	114,117	41.6	20,015	7.3	—		1,437	0.5	24,718	R
Nebraska	536,851	321,163	59.8	170,784	31.8	44,904	8.4	—		—		150,379	R
Nevada	154,218	73,188	47.5	60,598	39.3	20,432	13.2	—		—		12,590	R
New Hampshire	297,298	154,903	52.1	130,589	43.9	11,173	3.8	—		633	0.2	24,314	R
New Jersey	2,875,395	1,325,467	46.1	1,264,206	44.0	262,187	9.1	6,784	0.2	16,751	0.6	61,261	R
New Mexico	327,350	169,692	51.8	130,081	39.7	25,737	7.9	—		1,840	0.6	39,611	R
New York	6,791,688	3,007,932	44.3	3,378,470	49.7	358,864	5.3	8,432	0.1	37,990	0.6	370,538	D
North Carolina	1,587,493	627,192	39.5	464,113	29.2	496,188	31.3	—		—		131,004	R
North Dakota	247,882	138,669	55.9	94,769	38.2	14,244	5.7	—		200	0.1	43,900	R
Ohio	3,959,698	1,791,014	45.2	1,700,586	42.9	467,495	11.8	120		483		90,428	R
Oklahoma	943,086	449,697	47.7	301,658	32.0	191,731	20.3	—		—		148,039	R
Oregon	819,622	408,433	49.8	358,866	43.8	49,683	6.1	—		2,640	0.3	49,567	R
Pennsylvania	4,747,928	2,090,017	44.0	2,259,405	47.6	378,582	8.0	4,977	0.1	14,947	0.3	169,388	D
Rhode Island	385,000	122,359	31.8	246,518	64.0	15,678	4.1	—		445	0.1	124,159	D
South Carolina	666,978	254,062	38.1	197,486	29.6	215,430	32.3	—		—		38,632	R
South Dakota	281,264	149,841	53.3	118,023	42.0	13,400	4.8	—		—		31,818	R
Tennessee	1,248,617	472,592	37.8	351,233	28.1	424,792	34.0	—		—		47,800	R
Texas	3,079,216	1,227,844	39.9	1,266,804	41.1	584,269	19.0	—		299		38,960	D
Utah	422,568	238,728	56.5	156,665	37.1	26,906	6.4	—		269	0.1	82,063	R
Vermont	161,404	85,142	52.8	70,255	43.5	5,104	3.2	—		903	0.6	14,887	R
Virginia	1,361,491	590,319	43.4	442,387	32.5	321,833	23.6	4,671	0.3	2,281	0.2	147,932	R
Washington	1,304,281	588,510	45.1	616,037	47.2	96,990	7.4	488		2,256	0.2	27,527	D
West Virginia	754,206	307,555	40.8	374,091	49.6	72,560	9.6	—		—		66,536	D
Wisconsin	1,691,538	809,997	47.9	748,804	44.3	127,835	7.6	1,338	0.1	3,564	0.2	61,193	R
Wyoming	127,205	70,927	55.8	45,173	35.5	11,105	8.7	—		—		25,754	R
Dist. of Col.	170,578	31,012	18.2	139,566	81.8	—		—		—		108,554	D
Totals	73,211,875	31,785,480	43.4	31,275,166	42.7	9,906,473	13.5	52,588	0.1	192,168	0.3	510,314	R

P O P U L A R   V O T E

The 1968 presidential campaign raised profound concern over the viability of the U.S. political system. By the time the year had run its course, a president had been toppled from office, a presidential candidate and a prominent civil rights leader had been murdered, and a party convention was disrupted by riots and bloodshed. Journalist James Reston observed: "The main crisis is not Vietnam itself, or in the cities, but in the feeling that the political system for dealing with these things has broken down."

On 3 January 1968, Senator Eugene McCarthy of Minnesota, a passionate critic of the administration's Vietnam policy, announced his plans to take the Democratic presidential nomination from Lyndon B. Johnson. In late January, polling data showed that McCarthy had the support of only 8 percent of Democratic voters in New Hampshire. On 29 January, the situation changed dramatically when North Vietnam launched the Tet Offensive, the turning point of the Vietnam War. Many Americans now became convinced that U.S. military leaders had badly underestimated the military capacity of the North Vietnamese. The offensive had created mistrust in government evaluations and confusion over the administration's goals in pursuing the war.

President Johnson resisted demands from hawks who wanted to use atomic weapons to end the war and from doves who wanted an unconditional cease-fire and immediate negotiations. Instead, the President committed additional ground troops. By April 1968, the number of U.S. forces in Vietnam soared to 543,000 and U.S. deaths in combat had reached 23,000. The Gallup Poll reported a major shift in public opinion. In February 1968, self-described hawks had outnumbered doves 60 percent to 24 percent. A month later, 42 percent described themselves as doves compared to 41 percent as hawks.

On 2 March 1968, McCarthy's performance in the New Hampshire Democratic primary electrified the country. Some 3,000 student volunteers, 1 for every 25 Democratic voters, had saturated the small state in a massive grass-roots operation to explain their doubts about the wisdom and morality of the Vietnam War. McCarthy received 42.4 percent of the popular vote to President Johnson's 49.5 percent. When Republican write-ins were added, Johnson's margin of victory in New Hampshire fell to less than 1 percent. On 31 March, Johnson announced he would not seek reelection. It had taken the McCarthy forces less than 3 months to bring

down a president. On 27 April, Vice President Hubert H. Humphrey, praising Johnson's "dramatic leadership," became a candidate.

A few days after the New Hampshire primary, Senator Robert F. Kennedy of New York announced he was entering the race. "I run," he told a press conference, "to seek new policies, policies to end the bloodshed in Vietnam and in our cities, policies to close the gap . . . between black and white, between rich and poor." Kennedy drew large and enthusiastic audiences on an extensive speaking tour but his decision divided the anti-war movement. However, pro-administration Democrats, including leaders of organized labor and northern city bosses, remained hawkish on Vietnam. They were suspicious of Kennedy and uncomfortable with McCarthy.

The assassination of civil rights leader Dr. Martin Luther King, Jr. on 4 April in Memphis, Tennessee, shocked the United States. Rioting, looting, and arson engulfed the nation. The major spring primaries lost their significance. Kennedy narrowly beat McCarthy in the Indiana and Nebraska primaries in early May. However, on 28 May, McCarthy defeated Kennedy in the Oregon primary. It was the first time any Kennedy had ever lost an election. The final showdown between the two men came in early June in California, where Kennedy won 174 delegates and the clear leadership in the fight to deny Humphrey the Democratic nomination. A few minutes after addressing his supporters, Kennedy was assassinated.

Hubert Humphrey's nomination by the Democrats was never in doubt after Kennedy's death. The convention chose him on the first ballot. Humphrey selected Senator Edmund Muskie of Maine as his running mate. However, the party was deeply divided over what to do in Vietnam. A bitter platform dispute between proponents of "peace" and supporters of "pro-administration" Vietnam planks resulted in adoption of the latter, which praised the President's efforts to end the war. A raging battle took place outside the Chicago amphitheater where the convention was held. Downtown Chicago swarmed with police, federal agents, and more than 5,000 Illinois National Guardsmen who tried to keep order among the anti-war demonstrators assembled in the city. The inevitable bloody confrontation between this security force and the protesters was seen by millions who watched the drama unfold on television. Humphrey accepted the nomination of a party wracked by internal discord. He urged the Democrats to "take heart" and "make this moment of crisis . . . a moment of creation." But the Vice President told confidants that he knew that he emerged from the convention a beaten man. McCarthy refused to appear with him at the traditional reconciliation scene of losers with the winner. All pretense of party unity was shattered.

Richard M. Nixon made a remarkable comeback at the Republican Convention. Although defeated in the 1962 California gubernatorial election, he had campaigned for Republican candidates both in 1964 and 1966. Two-thirds of those for whom he campaigned in 1966 won their races. Attempts by both Governor Nelson A. Rockefeller of New York and Governor Ronald Reagan of California to deny him the nomination failed. Nixon won the nomination on the first ballot and strengthened his "southern strategy" by choosing the little known Governor Spiro T. Agnew of Maryland as his running mate. Nixon delivered an acceptance address aimed at the "forgotten Americans," the workers and taxpayers who were angered by the Vietnam War, domestic violence, and the rising rate of inflation. He promised them "new leadership" which would bring "an honorable end to the war in Vietnam."

In private conversations before and during the convention, Nixon clarified his position on issues of particular concern to southern Republicans. Nixon told the hawkish Senator J. Strom Thurmond of South Carolina, for example, that the way to get the North Vietnamese to settle the war was to make it clear that drastic consequences would result if they did not agree to negotiations. He spoke in favor of an expanded missile program. Nixon disliked federal intervention in local school affairs and opposed mandatory school bussing. He promised Southerners that he would appoint "strict Constitutionalists" to the Supreme Court and that he would not "ram anything down your throats."

Nixon's positions took supporters away from George Wallace, the segregationist governor of Alabama, who was running as a third party candidate. The Governor delighted his audience with his assaults on "scummy anarchists" and "pseudointellectuals" who catered to criminals. Wallace was by no means a sectional candidate. He was well financed, and his name appeared on all 50 state ballots. Wallace pledged deliverance from African Americans, radicals, bureaucrats, peace demonstrators, hippies, integrationists,

do-gooders, and "pointy headed professors" whose fuzzy thinking had caused the nation's problems.

Humphrey's campaign was a disaster. He and his staff had devoted little time or thought to a coherent strategy. Anti-war hecklers interrupted his speeches, causing him to depart from his prepared texts. Before September ended, the Vice President had contradicted himself on the administration's Vietnam policy. He seemed to endorse an immediate halt in the bombing and said "we can start to remove some of the American forces in early 1969 or late 1968." But a furious Johnson corrected him. "No one can predict" he angrily said, when Americans would begin to leave Vietnam. Humphrey could not disengage himself from Johnson's policy.

Nixon was heavily favored. While Wallace divided voters and Humphrey seemed disorganized, Nixon promised to heed the "quiet voice of the great majority of Americans . . . the non-shooters, the non-demonstrators." He made it into an "us versus them" contest, the "us" being middle America—the White, comfortable, patriotic "forgotten Americans." While Humphrey's compassion began to come through as the campaign ended, his attempt to adopt a Vietnam policy independent of Johnson failed. Nixon carried 32 states with 301 electoral votes (he lost 1 electoral vote when a North Carolina Nixon elector cast his ballot for Wallace.) In the popular vote, Nixon received 43.4 percent, the lowest for a winning candidate since Woodrow Wilson in the three-way election of 1912. White backlash did take place, validating Nixon's strategy. Of the 13 states in the once solid Democratic South, Humphrey carried only Texas. Five southern states went to Wallace and 7 to Nixon. While 95 percent of African American voters cast their ballots for Humphrey, less than 35 percent of Whites did so. Three out of 10 White Johnson voters in 1964 cast their vote for either Nixon or Wallace in 1968.

Wallace held the balance of power in the election. Neither Nixon nor Humphrey was able to win a clear majority in 25 states. A shift of approximately 45,000 votes would have denied Nixon an electoral majority and given Wallace the bargaining position he sought if the election were to be decided by the U.S. House of Representatives.

In Nixon's own analysis, he stressed that 57 percent of the voters had chosen either him or Wallace, meaning that a majority of voters wanted a change. However, the type of change wanted by the American people remained unclear.

Election of 1972

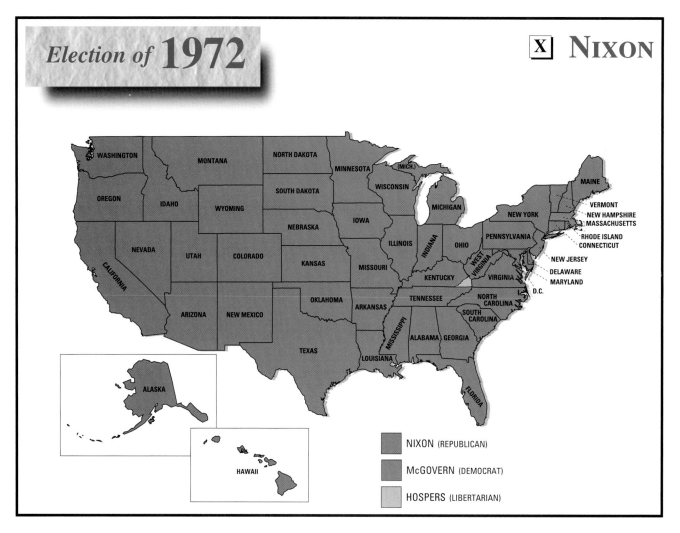

NIXON (REPUBLICAN)

McGOVERN (DEMOCRAT)

HOSPERS (LIBERTARIAN)

States	Electoral Votes	Nixon	McGovern	Hospers	States	Electoral Votes	Nixon	McGovern	Hospers
Alabama	(9)	9	-	-	Montana	(4)	4	-	-
Alaska	(3)	3	-	-	Nebraska	(5)	5	-	-
Arizona	(6)	6	-	-	Nevada	(3)	3	-	-
Arkansas	(6)	6	-	-	New Hampshire	(4)	4	-	-
California	(45)	45	-	-	New Jersey	(17)	17	-	-
Colorado	(7)	7	-	-	New Mexico	(4)	4	-	-
Connecticut	(8)	8	-	-	New York	(41)	41	-	-
Delaware	(3)	3	-	-	North Carolina	(13)	13	-	-
District of Columbia	(3)	-	3	-	North Dakota	(3)	3	-	-
Florida	(17)	17	-	-	Ohio	(25)	25	-	-
Georgia	(12)	12	-	-	Oklahoma	(8)	8	-	-
Hawaii	(4)	4	-	-	Oregon	(6)	6	-	-
Idaho	(4)	4	-	-	Pennsylvania	(27)	27	-	-
Illinois	(26)	26	-	-	Rhode Island	(4)	4	-	-
Indiana	(13)	13	-	-	South Carolina	(8)	8	-	-
Iowa	(8)	8	-	-	South Dakota	(4)	4	-	-
Kansas	(7)	7	-	-	Tennessee	(10)	10	-	-
Kentucky	(9)	9	-	-	Texas	(26)	26	-	-
Louisiana	(10)	10	-	-	Utah	(4)	4	-	-
Maine	(4)	4	-	-	Vermont	(3)	3	-	-
Maryland	(10)	10	-	-	Virginia [1]	(12)	11	-	1
Massachusetts	(14)	-	14	-	Washington	(9)	9	-	-
Michigan	(21)	21	-	-	West Virginia	(6)	6	-	-
Minnesota	(10)	10	-	-	Wisconsin	(11)	11	-	-
Mississippi	(7)	7	-	-	Wyoming	(3)	3	-	-
Missouri	(12)	12	-	-	**Totals**	**(538)**	**520**	**17**	**1**

ELECTORAL VOTE

Election of 1972

STATE	TOTAL VOTE	RICHARD M. NIXON (Republican)		GEORGE S. McGOVERN (Democrat)		JOHN G. SCHMITZ (American)		BENJAMIN SPOCK (People's)		OTHER		PLURALITY	
		Votes	%	Votes	%	Votes	%	Votes	%	Votes	%		
Alabama	1,006,111	728,701	72.4	256,923	25.5	11,928	1.2	—		8,559	0.9	471,778	R
Alaska	95,219	55,349	58.1	32,967	34.6	6,903	7.2	—		—		22,382	R
Arizona	622,926	402,812	64.7	198,540	31.9	21,208	3.4	—		366	0.1	204,272	R
Arkansas	651,320	448,541	68.9	199,892	30.7	2,887	0.4	—		—		248,649	R
California	8,367,862	4,602,096	55.0	3,475,847	41.5	232,554	2.8	55,167	0.7	2,198		1,126,249	R
Colorado	953,884	597,189	62.6	329,980	34.6	17,269	1.8	2,403	0.3	7,043	0.7	267,209	R
Connecticut	1,384,277	810,763	58.6	555,498	40.1	17,239	1.2	—		777	0.1	255,265	R
Delaware	235,516	140,357	59.6	92,283	39.2	2,638	1.1	—		238	0.1	48,074	R
Florida	2,583,283	1,857,759	71.9	718,117	27.8	—		—		7,407	0.3	1,139,642	R
Georgia	1,174,772	881,496	75.0	289,529	24.6	812	0.1	—		2,935	0.2	591,967	R
Hawaii	270,274	168,865	62.5	101,409	37.5	—		—		—		67,456	R
Idaho	310,379	199,384	64.2	80,826	26.0	28,869	9.3	903	0.3	397	0.1	118,558	R
Illinois	4,723,236	2,788,179	59.0	1,913,472	40.5	2,471	0.1	—		19,114	0.4	874,707	R
Indiana	2,125,529	1,405,154	66.1	708,568	33.3	—		4,544	0.2	7,263	0.3	696,586	R
Iowa	1,225,944	706,207	57.6	496,206	40.5	22,056	1.8	—		1,475	0.1	210,001	R
Kansas	916,095	619,812	67.7	270,287	29.5	21,808	2.4	—		4,188	0.5	349,525	R
Kentucky	1,067,499	676,446	63.4	371,159	34.8	17,627	1.7	1,118	0.1	1,149	0.1	305,287	R
Louisiana	1,051,491	686,852	65.3	298,142	28.4	52,099	5.0	—		14,398	1.4	388,710	R
Maine	417,042	256,458	61.5	160,584	38.5	—		—		—		95,874	R
Maryland	1,353,812	829,305	61.3	505,781	37.4	18,726	1.4	—		—		323,524	R
Massachusetts	2,458,756	1,112,078	45.2	1,332,540	54.2	2,877	0.1	101		11,160	0.5	220,462	D
Michigan	3,489,727	1,961,721	56.2	1,459,435	41.8	63,321	1.8	—		5,250	0.2	502,286	R
Minnesota	1,741,652	898,269	51.6	802,346	46.1	31,407	1.8	2,805	0.2	6,825	0.4	95,923	R
Mississippi	645,963	505,125	78.2	126,782	19.6	11,598	1.8	—		2,458	0.4	378,343	R
Missouri	1,855,803	1,153,852	62.2	697,147	37.6	—		—		4,804	0.3	456,705	R
Montana	317,603	183,976	57.9	120,197	37.8	13,430	4.2	—		—		63,779	R
Nebraska	576,289	406,298	70.5	169,991	29.5	—		—		—		236,307	R
Nevada	181,766	115,750	63.7	66,016	36.3	—		—		—		49,734	R
New Hampshire	334,055	213,724	64.0	116,435	34.9	3,386	1.0	—		510	0.2	97,289	R
New Jersey	2,997,229	1,845,502	61.6	1,102,211	36.8	34,378	1.1	5,355	0.2	9,783	0.3	743,291	R
New Mexico	386,241	235,606	61.0	141,084	36.5	8,767	2.3	—		784	0.2	94,522	R
New York	7,165,919	4,192,778	58.5	2,951,084	41.2	—		—		22,057	0.3	1,241,694	R
North Carolina	1,518,612	1,054,889	69.5	438,705	28.9	25,018	1.6	—		—		616,184	R
North Dakota	280,514	174,109	62.1	100,384	35.8	5,646	2.0	—		375	0.1	73,725	R
Ohio	4,094,787	2,441,827	59.6	1,558,889	38.1	80,067	2.0	—		14,004	0.3	882,938	R
Oklahoma	1,029,900	759,025	73.7	247,147	24.0	23,728	2.3	—		—		511,878	R
Oregon	927,946	486,686	52.4	392,760	42.3	46,211	5.0	—		2,289	0.2	93,926	R
Pennsylvania	4,592,106	2,714,521	59.1	1,796,951	39.1	70,593	1.5	—		10,041	0.2	917,570	R
Rhode Island	415,808	220,383	53.0	194,645	46.8	25		5		750	0.2	25,738	R
South Carolina	673,960	477,044	70.8	186,824	27.7	10,075	1.5	—		17		290,220	R
South Dakota	307,415	166,476	54.2	139,945	45.5	—		—		994	0.3	26,531	R
Tennessee	1,201,182	813,147	67.7	357,293	29.7	30,373	2.5	—		369		455,854	R
Texas	3,471,281	2,298,896	66.2	1,154,289	33.3	6,039	0.2	—		12,057	0.3	1,144,607	R
Utah	478,476	323,643	67.6	126,284	26.4	28,549	6.0	—		—		197,359	R
Vermont	186,947	117,149	62.7	68,174	36.5	—		1,010	0.5	614	0.3	48,975	R
Virginia	1,457,019	988,493	67.8	438,887	30.1	19,721	1.4	—		9,918	0.7	549,606	R
Washington	1,470,847	837,135	56.9	568,334	38.6	58,906	4.0	2,644	0.2	3,828	0.3	268,801	R
West Virginia	762,399	484,964	63.6	277,435	36.4	—		—		—		207,529	R
Wisconsin	1,852,890	989,430	53.4	810,174	43.7	47,525	2.6	2,701	0.1	3,060	0.2	179,256	R
Wyoming	145,570	100,464	69.0	44,358	30.5	748	0.5	—		—		56,106	R
Dist. of Col.	163,421	35,226	21.6	127,627	78.1	—		—		568	0.3	92,401	D
Totals	77,718,554	47,169,911	60.7	29,170,383	37.5	1,099,482	1.4	78,756	0.1	200,022	0.3	17,999,528	R

P O P U L A R   V O T E

The 1972 campaign was filled with dramatic surprises: the Democratic front-runner, Edmund Muskie, faltered early; George Wallace, also a Democratic contender, was critically wounded; and Thomas Eagleton, the Democratic vice presidential nominee, withdrew when it was revealed that he had undergone psychiatric treatment. Above all, a massive criminal cover-up during the campaign would lead to the resignation of President Richard M. Nixon two years later.

In August, Nixon and Vice President Spiro T. Agnew were renominated at the Republican Convention in Miami Beach. With the aid of his chief political adviser, Attorney General John Mitchell, Nixon had devised a reelection plan which was aimed at the "real majority" in the United States, the "unyoung, unblack, and unpoor"—the mature, White, middle-class citizen who was disgusted with campus protests, school integration, street crime, and rising health care costs. In particular, they planned to win over those who had voted for George Wallace in 1968 and hoped to establish a permanent Republican majority by also appealing to blue-collar workers in northern cities. To achieve these goals, Nixon decided to run his reelection campaign independent of the Republican Party. His staff set up the Committee to Reelect the President. To his annoyance, it became known as CREEP instead of CRP. Nixon located CREEP headquarters down the street from the White House and staffed it with people loyal to him. The Committee directed the campaign, raised the needed money, and had easy access to the President.

Nixon was far more interested in his Democratic opponents than in any campaign issue. The opponents Nixon most feared were Senator Edmund Muskie of Maine and Governor George Wallace of Alabama. He hoped that the Democrats would nominate George McGovern, the liberal senator from South Dakota. Nixon later wrote: "If by some miracle [McGovern] would be nominated, I had no doubt that he would be the easiest Democrat to beat." Using CREEP, Nixon set out to manipulate the Democratic Party into nominating its weakest candidate. The political goal of Nixon's racial policies was to outflank George Wallace, the Alabama segregationist. Wallace would deprive Nixon of the crucial support of discontented White voters if he ran as a third party candidate. School desegregation had proceeded throughout the South until 1971, when the President warned federal officials to stop pressing for school desegregation

through "forced bussing." He threatened to seek legislation, even a constitutional amendment, to prevent federal courts from promoting racial balance through bussing. He also declared that efforts to compel integration in northern suburbs were "counterproductive, and not in the interest of better race relations."

When Wallace decided to seek the presidency through the Democratic primaries, Democratic Party chairman Larry O'Brien immediately disavowed his candidacy. Labor leader George Meany called Wallace a "bigot and racist." Nixon kept his reaction to himself. Throughout the spring, Wallace swept the southern Democratic primaries. He finished a strong second in Pennsylvania and Indiana. He appealed to lower-middle-class White voters who opposed integration. An early March Gallup Poll of Democrats showed Wallace with a 15 percent approval rating, running third in a list of 11 potential nominees. Then, on 15 May, Wallace was shot five times at point-blank range at a political rally in Prince Georges County, Maryland. The following day, he easily won the Maryland and Michigan primaries. But the Governor was paralyzed and too ill to continue the race. Wallace's withdrawal assured Nixon of a November victory.

At the beginning of 1972, Senator Edmund Muskie of Maine was the leading contender for the Democratic nomination. He had solid financial backing, a large and experienced staff, and the endorsement of the party's leading figures. Muskie planned to enter every primary so he could establish what he called "credibility." His supporters felt that Muskie had won the nomination even before the first primary in New Hampshire. The *Manchester Union Leader* was the daily newspaper read by 40 percent of New Hampshire's population. In late February, it published a phony letter saying that Muskie's wife, Jane, noted that Maine did not have a Black problem but it did have "Cannocks," a derogatory term for French-Canadian Americans. A week before the primary, Muskie cried while defending his wife. The evening news showed that moment as well as a triumphant Nixon with Prime Minister Chou En-lai on the President's historic visit to China. The contrast between the two images was very unfortunate for Muskie. He won the New Hampshire primary with 46.4 percent of the vote to McGovern's 37 percent. However, this was less than the clear majority he needed in a state where he was well known. Muskie's campaign all but ended. A year later, the nation learned that CREEP, as part of its "dirty tricks" operation, with Nixon's approval, had been responsible for the incident which triggered Muskie's emotional outburst.

To Nixon's relief, the Democratic Party now turned not to its center but to its left faction. Senator George McGovern was chiefly known for his long record of outspoken opposition to the Vietnam War. Following the disorderly 1968 Democratic Convention, the party appointed a commission to make future delegate selection more inclusive of young people, women, and minorities. McGovern chaired the commission form 1969 to 1971. In a flush of enthusiasm, assisted by the newly ratified Twenty-sixth Amendment which lowered the voting age to 18, young people registered in record numbers. They provided McGovern with his margin of victory in the key primary states of New York and California.

The New Left's participation in national politics peaked at the Democratic Convention in Miami Beach on 10 July. Speakers for gay rights, Black Power, and other counterculture causes dragged out the nomination process. McGovern did not speak until almost 3:00 A.M., by which time most of the television audience had gone to bed. McGovern pledged himself to advancing the rights of minorities, expanding social welfare legislation, and to closing high-income tax loopholes. He proposed giving $1,000 each year to everyone "from the poorest migrant workers to the Rockefellers," to tax it back from the rich and redistribute it to the needy. McGovern favored amnesty for Vietnam draft evaders and a woman's right to choose abortion, and he proposed removing criminal penalties for marijuana use. He promised an immediate end to the bombing in Vietnam and vowed that within 90 days of his inauguration every American prisoner would be out of Vietnam. McGovern chose Senator Thomas Eagleton of Missouri as his running mate. Almost immediately it was learned that Eagleton had undergone psychiatric treatment for depression, which had included several hospitalizations and electroshock therapy. After saying that he continued to support Eagleton, McGovern replaced him with Sargent Shriver, a brother-in-law of the Kennedy's and the first director of the Peace Corps. The McGovern campaign never recovered.

Nixon had an insurmountable lead. He became the favorite not only of Republicans but of many Democrats and independents. During the primaries, McGovern's uncompromising stands won him support from the left wing of the Democratic Party. During the campaign, however, he lost the center which he desperately needed. The AFL-CIO refused to endorse him. Even former President Lyndon B. Johnson turned on him, giving campaign advice to Nixon. Nixon hardly campaigned, content with the strength of his record. Two weeks before the election, Secretary of State Henry Kissinger announced, "Peace is at hand!" Two-thirds of those polled thought Nixon would be "better able to move the world closer to peace." Nixon carried every state except Massachusetts and the District of Columbia, receiving a total of 520 electoral votes to McGovern's 17. Nixon received 60.7 percent of the popular vote which is second only to Lyndon B. Johnson's record-breaking 61.1 percent in the landslide of 1964. Nixon swept the Solid South, completely capturing the Wallace vote. Nixon noted in his diary, however, that he was overcome by "a curious feeling, perhaps a foreboding that muted my enjoyment of this triumphal moment."

The 1972 election cannot be fully explained without mentioning the Watergate scandal, the most important event of the year. It occurred in Washington, D.C. on 17 June 1972 at the hotel and office complex known as the Watergate. Seven men, including two former White House aides and a member of CREEP, were apprehended and indicted for breaking into the headquarters of the Democratic National Committee. They were later tried and convicted. They seem to have been trying to place a bug in the telephone of Larry O'Brien, chairman of the Democratic Party. Nixon apparently wanted to know how much O'Brien knew about the President's dealings with billionaire Howard Hughes, a contributor to Nixon's campaign and a friend of O'Brien. The criminals badly bungled the job and were caught. It seemed far-fetched that the Republican Party, much less the President of the United States, had anything to do with this illegal act. Administration officials dismissed the Watergate break-in as a "caper" and a "third-rate burglary attempt" of no significance. "I can say categorically," the President stated on 29 August, "that . . . investigations indicate that no one in the White House staff, no one in this administration, presently employed, was involved in this very bizarre incident." However, the President was lying; he had authorized the burglary. This botched illegal entry led to the unraveling of Nixon's presidency —and to his resignation in the face of imminent impeachment by Congress.

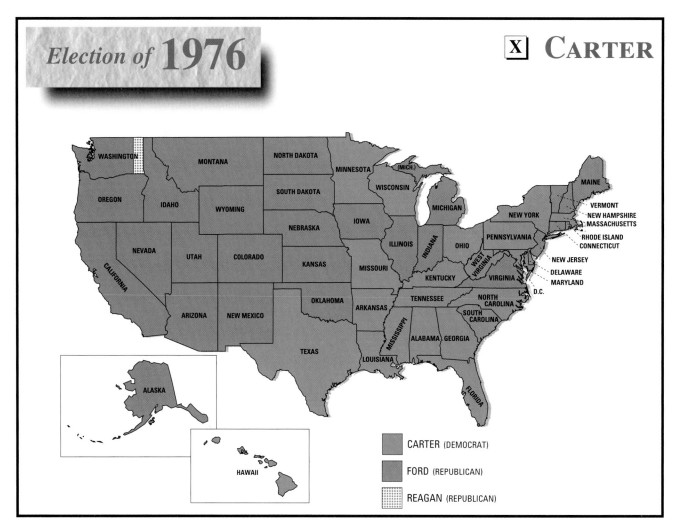

Election of 1976

X CARTER

CARTER (DEMOCRAT)

FORD (REPUBLICAN)

REAGAN (REPUBLICAN)

States	Electoral Votes	Carter	Ford	Reagan
Alabama	(9)	9	-	-
Alaska	(3)	-	3	-
Arizona	(6)	-	6	-
Arkansas	(6)	6	-	-
California	(45)	-	45	-
Colorado	(7)	-	7	-
Connecticut	(8)	-	8	-
Delaware	(3)	3	-	-
District of Columbia	(3)	3	-	-
Florida	(17)	17	-	-
Georgia	(12)	12	-	-
Hawaii	(4)	4	-	-
Idaho	(4)	-	4	-
Illinois	(26)	-	26	-
Indiana	(13)	-	13	-
Iowa	(8)	-	8	-
Kansas	(7)	-	7	-
Kentucky	(9)	9	-	-
Louisiana	(10)	10	-	-
Maine	(4)	-	4	-
Maryland	(10)	10	-	-
Massachusetts	(14)	14	-	-
Michigan	(21)	-	21	-
Minnesota	(10)	10	-	-
Mississippi	(7)	7	-	-
Missouri	(12)	12	-	-

States	Electoral Votes	Carter	Ford	Reagan
Montana	(4)	-	4	-
Nebraska	(5)	-	5	-
Nevada	(3)	-	3	-
New Hampshire	(4)	-	4	-
New Jersey	(17)	-	17	-
New Mexico	(4)	-	4	-
New York	(41)	41	-	-
North Carolina	(13)	13	-	-
North Dakota	(3)	-	3	-
Ohio	(25)	25	-	-
Oklahoma	(8)	-	8	-
Oregon	(6)	-	6	-
Pennsylvania	(27)	27	-	-
Rhode Island	(4)	4	-	-
South Carolina	(8)	8	-	-
South Dakota	(4)	-	4	-
Tennessee	(10)	10	-	-
Texas	(26)	26	-	-
Utah	(4)	-	4	-
Vermont	(3)	-	3	-
Virginia	(12)	-	12	-
Washington	(9)	-	8	1
West Virginia	(6)	6	-	-
Wisconsin	(11)	11	-	-
Wyoming	(3)	-	3	-
Totals	**(538)**	**297**	**240**	**1**

ELECTORAL VOTE

Election of 1976

STATE	TOTAL VOTE	JIMMY CARTER (Democrat)		GERALD R. FORD (Republican)		EUGENE J. McCARTHY (Independent)		ROGER MacBRIDE (Libertarian)		OTHER		PLURALITY	
		Votes	%	Votes	%	Votes	%	Votes	%	Votes	%		
Alabama	1,182,850	659,170	55.7	504,070	42.6	99		1,481	0.1	18,030	1.5	155,100	D
Alaska	123,574	44,058	35.7	71,555	57.9	—		6,785	5.5	1,176	1.0	27,497	R
Arizona	742,719	295,602	39.8	418,642	56.4	19,229	2.6	7,647	1.0	1,599	0.2	123,040	R
Arkansas	767,535	498,604	65.0	267,903	34.9	639	0.1	—		389	0.1	230,701	D
California	7,867,117	3,742,284	47.6	3,882,244	49.3	58,412	0.7	56,388	0.7	127,789	1.6	139,960	R
Colorado	1,081,554	460,353	42.6	584,367	54.0	26,107	2.4	5,330	0.5	5,397	0.5	124,014	R
Connecticut	1,381,526	647,895	46.9	719,261	52.1	3,759	0.3	209		10,402	0.8	71,366	R
Delaware	235,834	122,596	52.0	109,831	46.6	2,437	1.0	—		970	0.4	12,765	D
Florida	3,150,631	1,636,000	51.9	1,469,531	46.6	23,643	0.8	103		21,354	0.7	166,469	D
Georgia	1,467,458	979,409	66.7	483,743	33.0	991	0.1	175		3,140	0.2	495,666	D
Hawaii	291,301	147,375	50.6	140,003	48.1	—		3,923	1.3	—		7,372	D
Idaho	344,071	126,549	36.8	204,151	59.3	1,194	0.3	3,558	1.0	8,619	2.5	77,602	R
Illinois	4,718,914	2,271,295	48.1	2,364,269	50.1	55,939	1.2	8,057	0.2	19,354	0.4	92,974	R
Indiana	2,220,362	1,014,714	45.7	1,183,958	53.3	—		—		21,690	1.0	169,244	R
Iowa	1,279,306	619,931	48.5	632,863	49.5	20,051	1.6	1,452	0.1	5,009	0.4	12,932	R
Kansas	957,845	430,421	44.9	502,752	52.5	13,185	1.4	3,242	0.3	8,245	0.9	72,331	R
Kentucky	1,167,142	615,717	52.8	531,852	45.6	6,837	0.6	814	0.1	11,922	1.0	83,865	D
Louisiana	1,278,439	661,365	51.7	587,446	46.0	6,588	0.5	3,325	0.3	19,715	1.5	73,919	D
Maine	483,216	232,279	48.1	236,320	48.9	10,874	2.3	11		3,732	0.8	4,041	R
Maryland	1,439,897	759,612	52.8	672,661	46.7	4,541	0.3	255		2,828	0.2	86,951	D
Massachusetts	2,547,558	1,429,475	56.1	1,030,276	40.4	65,637	2.6	135		22,035	0.9	399,199	D
Michigan	3,653,749	1,696,714	46.4	1,893,742	51.8	47,905	1.3	5,406	0.1	9,982	0.3	197,028	R
Minnesota	1,949,931	1,070,440	54.9	819,395	42.0	35,490	1.8	3,529	0.2	21,077	1.1	251,045	D
Mississippi	769,361	381,309	49.6	366,846	47.7	4,074	0.5	2,788	0.4	14,344	1.9	14,463	D
Missouri	1,953,600	998,387	51.1	927,443	47.5	24,029	1.2	—		3,741	0.2	70,944	D
Montana	328,734	149,259	45.4	173,703	52.8	—		—		5,772	1.8	24,444	R
Nebraska	607,668	233,692	38.5	359,705	59.2	9,409	1.5	1,482	0.2	3,380	0.6	126,013	R
Nevada	201,876	92,479	45.8	101,273	50.2	—		1,519	0.8	6,605	3.3	8,794	R
New Hampshire	339,618	147,635	43.5	185,935	54.7	4,095	1.2	936	0.3	1,017	0.3	38,300	R
New Jersey	3,014,472	1,444,653	47.9	1,509,688	50.1	32,717	1.1	9,449	0.3	17,965	0.6	65,035	R
New Mexico	418,409	201,148	48.1	211,419	50.5	1,161	0.3	1,110	0.3	3,571	0.9	10,271	R
New York	6,534,170	3,389,558	51.9	3,100,791	47.5	4,303	0.1	12,197	0.2	27,321	0.4	288,767	D
North Carolina	1,678,914	927,365	55.2	741,960	44.2	780		2,219	0.1	6,590	0.4	185,405	D
North Dakota	297,188	136,078	45.8	153,470	51.6	2,952	1.0	253	0.1	4,435	1.5	17,392	R
Ohio	4,111,873	2,011,621	48.9	2,000,505	48.7	58,258	1.4	8,961	0.2	32,528	0.8	11,116	D
Oklahoma	1,092,251	532,442	48.7	545,708	50.0	14,101	1.3	—		—		13,266	R
Oregon	1,029,876	490,407	47.6	492,120	47.8	40,207	3.9	—		7,142	0.7	1,713	R
Pennsylvania	4,620,787	2,328,677	50.4	2,205,604	47.7	50,584	1.1	—		35,922	0.8	123,073	D
Rhode Island	411,170	227,636	55.4	181,249	44.1	479	0.1	715	0.2	1,091	0.3	46,387	D
South Carolina	802,583	450,807	56.2	346,149	43.1	289		53		5,285	0.7	104,658	D
South Dakota	300,678	147,068	48.9	151,505	50.4	—		1,619	0.5	486	0.2	4,437	R
Tennessee	1,476,345	825,879	55.9	633,969	42.9	5,004	0.3	1,375	0.1	10,118	0.7	191,910	D
Texas	4,071,884	2,082,319	51.1	1,953,300	48.0	20,118	0.5	189		15,958	0.4	129,019	D
Utah	541,198	182,110	33.6	337,908	62.4	3,907	0.7	2,438	0.5	14,835	2.7	155,798	R
Vermont	187,765	80,954	43.1	102,085	54.4	4,001	2.1	—		725	0.4	21,131	R
Virginia	1,697,094	813,896	48.0	836,554	49.3	—		4,648	0.3	41,996	2.5	22,658	R
Washington	1,555,534	717,323	46.1	777,732	50.0	36,986	2.4	5,042	0.3	18,451	1.2	60,409	R
West Virginia	750,964	435,914	58.0	314,760	41.9	113		16		161		121,154	D
Wisconsin	2,104,175	1,040,232	49.4	1,004,987	47.8	34,943	1.7	3,814	0.2	20,199	1.0	35,245	D
Wyoming	156,343	62,239	39.8	92,717	59.3	624	0.4	89	0.1	674	0.4	30,478	R
Dist. of Col.	168,830	137,818	81.6	27,873	16.5	—		274	0.2	2,865	1.7	109,945	D
Totals	81,555,889	40,830,763	50.1	39,147,793	48.0	756,691	0.9	173,011	0.2	647,631	0.8	1,682,970	D

P O P U L A R   V O T E

The 1976 election was the first in which the government subsidized a campaign. A new federal law provided for public funds derived from a check off on the federal income tax form. The law was intended to attract office-seekers who otherwise could not afford to get involved in presidential politics. The Democratic Party also mandated that each state implement a plan of "affirmative action" to ensure that a state's convention delegation be representative of the population-at-large. As a result, many more states now conducted primaries, thereby reducing the power of party leaders and union officials. Seventy percent of the delegates at the 1976 Democratic Convention were chosen under these new procedures. However, the most striking feature of the 1976 election was the turnout—the lowest proportion of eligible voters since 1948. Alienated from the political process by Watergate and distrustful of both candidates, 72 million registered voters made their feelings known on Election Day by staying home.

On 23 September 1974, Senator Edward M. Kennedy of Massachusetts, the leading favorite for the Democratic nomination, announced that under no circumstances would he be a candidate for president in 1976. Within months, at least 12 Democrats declared their presidential aspirations. Among them was former Georgia Governor Jimmy Carter, a man with a reputation for administrative efficiency. Carter, a graduate of the United States Naval Academy, had returned to Plains, Georgia in 1953 to manage the family's peanut farm. He served in the Georgia Senate and was elected governor in 1970.

Carter won the Democratic nomination because he had a superb grasp of the complex rules of the new primary system. He sensed the mood of the nation's disillusionment which was caused by the Vietnam War and by the Watergate scandal. The very fact that the public had little perception of what Carter was really like enabled him to shape his image to meet the demands of the new political realities. Carter built his own organization in key states with little money and only a handful of aides. He decided to base his campaign in his hometown of Plains, Georgia, allowing reporters to see for themselves the virtues of a friendly small, rural southern town. By June 1975, he had traveled some 50,000 miles, visited 37 states, delivered over 200 speeches and appeared on about 100 radio and television shows. However, less than 1 percent of Democrats favored him for the 1976

nomination. He spoke about his Christian faith and described himself as a new kind of political leader who could heal the country's wounds. He carried his own luggage, washed his own clothes in hotel rooms, and made his own bed when he stayed in private homes. Columnist Marquis Childs wrote on 16 December 1975: "Visionary as it seems, I believe Carter at the present moment has a better chance than any of the others to win the nomination." It seemed inconceivable that the Democrats would choose someone who held no current office, had no power base, and came from the Deep South.

In January, Carter won the caucuses in Iowa with 27.6 percent of those who designated a candidate. "None of the above" received just less than 30 percent. Nevertheless, UPI (United Press International) and *Time* called him the front-runner. In New Hampshire the following month, he defeated the five other candidates in the race, receiving 28.4 percent of the total vote. Carter swept the southern primaries and, after receiving 37 percent of the vote in the Pennsylvania primary in April, he proclaimed that he had won the nomination. (A *Washington Post* exit poll showed that 46 percent would have preferred former Vice President Hubert Humphrey had he been a candidate.) His task now, he said, was to unify the party. "I have been accused of being an outsider," Carter asserted. "I plead guilty. Unfortunately, the vast majority of Americans are also outsiders." His strategy of representing those outside the establishment worked and the "Anyone but Carter" effort by labor leaders and political professionals failed. Carter won the nomination on the first ballot at the Democratic Convention. He chose Senator Walter F. Mondale of Minnesota as his running mate.

Facing imminent impeachment by Congress because of his role in the Watergate affair, President Richard M. Nixon had resigned from office on 9 August 1974. As vice president by appointment, Gerald R. Ford became president. Ford had been appointed vice president by Nixon after the resignation of Spiro T. Agnew in 1973. Ford had the overwhelming support of the American people when he took office, but he squandered that support within a month by granting Nixon an unconditional pardon. Most Americans did not approve and believed that there had been some sort of deal between Ford and Nixon.

Many of Ford's policies also lessened his popularity. He vetoed a wide range of legislation—federal aid to education, health care, a school lunch program, control of strip mining, among others. In one year, he vetoed 39 bills, more than President Herbert Hoover's 37 in a full four-year term. Ford also had the bad luck to inherit a recession which had begun in 1973. By March 1975, unemployment had reached 9 percent, the highest since 1941. Stock prices had dropped sharply. New York, the nation's largest city, teetered on bankruptcy. In November 1974, three months after Ford entered the White House, the Democrats won their biggest congressional victory in a decade.

Ronald Reagan had decided to run for the 1976 Republican nomination in the spring of 1974 while Nixon was still in office. Reagan had captured the hearts of the Republican right with a nationally televised campaign address supporting Barry Goldwater in 1964. His attacks on welfare cheats, crime, student radicals, and communism had made him a conservative hero. Elected governor of California in 1966, this former movie actor had gained national recognition through his many television appearances, radio shows, newspaper columns, and public speeches. Reagan frequently criticized Ford for choosing Nelson A. Rockefeller, the liberal former governor of New York, as his vice president and for compromising principles for practical political gains. Ford won the Republican nomination at the August convention by the razor thin margin of 1,187 votes to 1,070 for Reagan. Rockefeller, under attack by party conservatives, said that he would not run again, and Ford chose Senator Robert (Bob) Dole of Kansas as his running mate.

Carter led Ford by about 15 points in early September and seemed unbeatable. Ford's strategy consisted of trying to act presidential, making almost daily announcements against the backdrop of the White House Rose Garden or the Oval Office. Carter presented himself as an outsider and told voters, "I'll never tell a lie." So shallow were Carter's speeches that he left himself open to Ford's charge that "he wavers, he wanders, he wiggles, and he waffles." Three televised debates between Ford and Carter occurred between 23 September and 22 October. These were the first debates since the Nixon-Kennedy encounters of 1960. Carter appeared wooden, nervous, and decidedly "unpresidential." Ford seemed equally uncomfortable and had trouble communicating effectively. In the second debate, Ford hurt his chances for election when he inexplicably blurted out,

"There is no Soviet domination of Eastern Europe." This obvious misstatement added to the comic reputation of a man ungenerously characterized by Lyndon B. Johnson as not having the intellectual capacity to "walk and chew gum at the same time."

Perhaps the most interesting event of an otherwise lack-luster campaign occurred in late September. Carter had given an interview to *Playboy* and the contents became known days before the first debate. He compared himself to past presidents. "But I don't think I would ever take on the same frame of mind that Nixon or Johnson did, lying, cheating, and distorting the truth," he said. What attracted the most attention, however, was Carter's comment that he often looked at women with "lust in his heart." Many Americans were startled by this deeply religious man saying such a thing. His comment had opened him to ridicule and Christian conservatives reacted swiftly. Seventeen politically independent Baptist ministers reprimanded Carter for having "brought reproach to the Christian faith." A CBS correspondent declared: "The campaign is dying right under our feet."

By Election Day, it was not clear who would win. The unfocused campaign had bored many voters. Carter appeared to be above reproach during the primaries, but he seemed too perfect. After the nomination, he emerged as an ordinary politician, making deals and promises to hold his campaign together. In the Electoral College, Carter won by a narrow margin, 297 to 240. (One Washington state elector pledged to Ford cast his ballot for Reagan.) This was the closest victory since Woodrow Wilson's 1916 victory over Charles Evans Hughes. Carter received 50.1 percent of the popular vote to Ford's 48 percent. Ironically, Carter, the outsider, won with the traditional Democratic vote: 82 percent of registered Democrats voted for him as did 85 percent of nonwhites; 63 percent of union families; 58 percent of manual laborers; and 57 percent of the Catholic vote. African Americans contributed to his winning electoral vote in New York, Louisiana, Mississippi, and Texas. Democrats swept congressional races, giving them a two-thirds control of the House and a 62-38 margin in the Senate. Americans looked forward to a fresh beginning and the end of the political bickering between the President and Congress, so characteristic of the Nixon-Ford administrations. They also looked forward to watching their anti-establishment president deal with the greatest of establishment jobs.

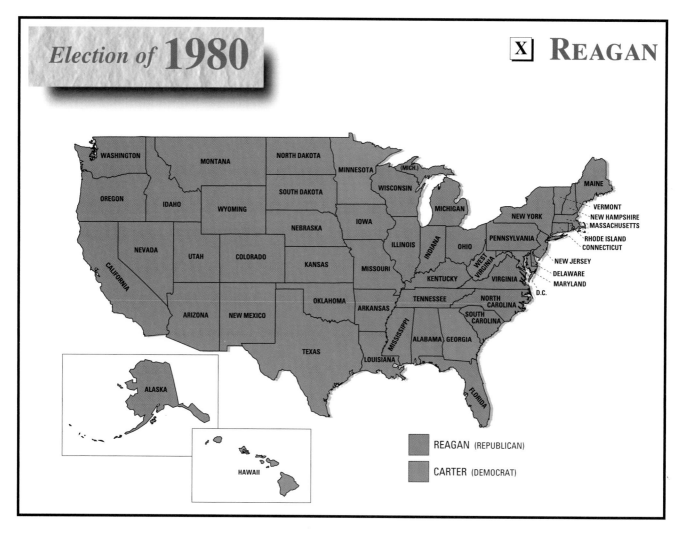

Election of **1980**

REAGAN (REPUBLICAN)

CARTER (DEMOCRAT)

States	Electoral Votes	Reagan	Carter	States	Electoral Votes	Reagan	Carter
Alabama	(9)	9	-	Montana	(4)	4	-
Alaska	(3)	3	-	Nebraska	(5)	5	-
Arizona	(6)	6	-	Nevada	(3)	3	-
Arkansas	(6)	6	-	New Hampshire	(4)	4	-
California	(45)	45	-	New Jersey	(17)	17	-
Colorado	(7)	7	-	New Mexico	(4)	4	-
Connecticut	(8)	8	-	New York	(41)	41	-
Delaware	(3)	3	-	North Carolina	(13)	13	-
District of Columbia	(3)	-	3	North Dakota	(3)	3	-
Florida	(17)	17	-	Ohio	(25)	25	-
Georgia	(12)	-	12	Oklahoma	(8)	8	-
Hawaii	(4)	-	4	Oregon	(6)	6	-
Idaho	(4)	4	-	Pennsylvania	(27)	27	-
Illinois	(26)	26	-	Rhode Island	(4)	-	4
Indiana	(13)	13	-	South Carolina	(8)	8	-
Iowa	(8)	8	-	South Dakota	(4)	4	-
Kansas	(7)	7	-	Tennessee	(10)	10	-
Kentucky	(9)	9	-	Texas	(26)	26	-
Louisiana	(10)	10	-	Utah	(4)	4	-
Maine	(4)	4	-	Vermont	(3)	3	-
Maryland	(10)	-	10	Virginia	(12)	12	-
Massachusetts	(14)	14	-	Washington	(9)	9	-
Michigan	(21)	21	-	West Virginia	(6)	-	6
Minnesota	(10)	-	10	Wisconsin	(11)	11	-
Mississippi	(7)	7	-	Wyoming	(3)	3	-
Missouri	(12)	12	-	**Totals**	**(538)**	**489**	**49**

ELECTORAL VOTE

Election of 1980

STATE	TOTAL VOTE	RONALD REAGAN (Republican)		JIMMY CARTER (Democrat)		JOHN B. ANDERSON (Independent)		ED CLARK (Libertarian)		OTHER		PLURALITY	
		Votes	%	Votes	%	Votes	%	Votes	%	Votes	%		
Alabama	1,341,929	654,192	48.8	636,730	47.4	16,481	1.2	13,318	1.0	21,208	1.6	17,462	R
Alaska	158,445	86,112	54.3	41,842	26.4	11,155	7.0	18,479	11.7	857	0.5	44,270	R
Arizona	873,945	529,688	60.6	246,843	28.2	76,952	8.8	18,784	2.1	1,678	0.2	282,845	R
Arkansas	837,582	403,164	48.1	398,041	47.5	22,468	2.7	8,970	1.1	4,939	0.6	5,123	R
California	8,587,063	4,524,858	52.7	3,083,661	35.9	739,833	8.6	148,434	1.7	90,277	1.1	1,441,197	R
Colorado	1,184,415	652,264	55.1	367,973	31.1	130,633	11.0	25,744	2.2	7,801	0.7	284,291	R
Connecticut	1,406,285	677,210	48.2	541,732	38.5	171,807	12.2	8,570	0.6	6,966	0.5	135,478	R
Delaware	235,900	111,252	47.2	105,754	44.8	16,288	6.9	1,974	0.8	632	0.3	5,498	R
Florida	3,686,930	2,046,951	55.5	1,419,475	38.5	189,692	5.1	30,524	0.8	288		627,476	R
Georgia	1,596,695	654,168	41.0	890,733	55.8	36,055	2.3	15,627	1.0	112		236,565	D
Hawaii	303,287	130,112	42.9	135,879	44.8	32,021	10.6	3,269	1.1	2,006	0.7	5,767	D
Idaho	437,431	290,699	66.5	110,192	25.2	27,058	6.2	8,425	1.9	1,057	0.2	180,507	R
Illinois	4,749,721	2,358,049	49.6	1,981,413	41.7	346,754	7.3	38,939	0.8	24,566	0.5	376,636	R
Indiana	2,242,033	1,255,656	56.0	844,197	37.7	111,639	5.0	19,627	0.9	10,914	0.5	411,459	R
Iowa	1,317,661	676,026	51.3	508,672	38.6	115,633	8.8	13,123	1.0	4,207	0.3	167,354	R
Kansas	979,795	566,812	57.9	326,150	33.3	68,231	7.0	14,470	1.5	4,132	0.4	240,662	R
Kentucky	1,294,627	635,274	49.1	616,417	47.6	31,127	2.4	5,531	0.4	6,278	0.5	18,857	R
Louisiana	1,548,591	792,853	51.2	708,453	45.7	26,345	1.7	8,240	0.5	12,700	0.8	84,400	R
Maine	523,011	238,522	45.6	220,974	42.3	53,327	10.2	5,119	1.0	5,069	1.0	17,548	R
Maryland	1,540,496	680,606	44.2	726,161	47.1	119,537	7.8	14,192	0.9	—		45,555	D
Massachusetts	2,524,298	1,057,631	41.9	1,053,802	41.7	382,539	15.2	22,038	0.9	8,288	0.3	3,829	R
Michigan	3,909,725	1,915,225	49.0	1,661,532	42.5	275,223	7.0	41,597	1.1	16,148	0.4	253,693	R
Minnesota	2,051,980	873,268	42.6	954,174	46.5	174,990	8.5	31,592	1.5	17,956	0.9	80,906	D
Mississippi	892,620	441,089	49.4	429,281	48.1	12,036	1.3	5,465	0.6	4,749	0.5	11,808	R
Missouri	2,099,824	1,074,181	51.2	931,182	44.3	77,920	3.7	14,422	0.7	2,119	0.1	142,999	R
Montana	363,952	206,814	56.8	118,032	32.4	29,281	8.0	9,825	2.7	—		88,782	R
Nebraska	640,854	419,937	65.5	166,851	26.0	44,993	7.0	9,073	1.4	—		253,086	R
Nevada	247,885	155,017	62.5	66,666	26.9	17,651	7.1	4,358	1.8	4,193	1.7	88,351	R
New Hampshire	383,990	221,705	57.7	108,864	28.4	49,693	12.9	2,064	0.5	1,664	0.4	112,841	R
New Jersey	2,975,684	1,546,557	52.0	1,147,364	38.6	234,632	7.9	20,652	0.7	26,479	0.9	399,193	R
New Mexico	456,971	250,779	54.9	167,826	36.7	29,459	6.4	4,365	1.0	4,542	1.0	82,953	R
New York	6,201,959	2,893,831	46.7	2,728,372	44.0	467,801	7.5	52,648	0.8	59,307	1.0	165,459	R
North Carolina	1,855,614	915,018	49.3	875,635	47.2	52,800	2.8	9,677	0.5	2,703	0.1	39,383	R
North Dakota	301,545	193,695	64.2	79,189	26.3	23,640	7.8	3,743	1.2	1,278	0.4	114,506	R
Ohio	4,283,603	2,206,545	51.5	1,752,414	40.9	254,472	5.9	49,033	1.1	21,139	0.5	454,131	R
Oklahoma	1,149,708	695,570	60.5	402,026	35.0	38,284	3.3	13,828	1.2	—		293,544	R
Oregon	1,181,516	571,044	48.3	456,890	38.7	112,389	9.5	25,838	2.2	15,355	1.3	114,154	R
Pennsylvania	4,561,501	2,261,872	49.6	1,937,540	42.5	292,921	6.4	33,263	0.7	35,905	0.8	324,332	R
Rhode Island	416,072	154,793	37.2	198,342	47.7	59,819	14.4	2,458	0.6	660	0.2	43,549	D
South Carolina	894,071	441,841	49.4	430,385	48.1	14,153	1.6	5,139	0.6	2,553	0.3	11,456	R
South Dakota	327,703	198,343	60.5	103,855	31.7	21,431	6.5	3,824	1.2	250	0.1	94,488	R
Tennessee	1,617,616	787,761	48.7	783,051	48.4	35,991	2.2	7,116	0.4	3,697	0.2	4,710	R
Texas	4,541,636	2,510,705	55.3	1,881,147	41.4	111,613	2.5	37,643	0.8	528		629,558	R
Utah	604,222	439,687	72.8	124,266	20.6	30,284	5.0	7,226	1.2	2,759	0.5	315,421	R
Vermont	213,299	94,628	44.4	81,952	38.4	31,761	14.9	1,900	0.9	3,058	1.4	12,676	R
Virginia	1,866,032	989,609	53.0	752,174	40.3	95,418	5.1	12,821	0.7	16,010	0.9	237,435	R
Washington	1,742,394	865,244	49.7	650,193	37.3	185,073	10.6	29,213	1.7	12,671	0.7	215,051	R
West Virginia	737,715	334,206	45.3	367,462	49.8	31,691	4.3	4,356	0.6	—		33,256	D
Wisconsin	2,273,221	1,088,845	47.9	981,584	43.2	160,657	7.1	29,135	1.3	13,000	0.6	107,261	R
Wyoming	176,713	110,700	62.6	49,427	28.0	12,072	6.8	4,514	2.6	—		61,273	R
Dist. of Col.	175,237	23,545	13.4	131,113	74.8	16,337	9.3	1,114	0.6	3,128	1.8	107,568	D
Totals	86,515,221	43,904,153	50.7	35,483,883	41.0	5,720,060	6.6	921,299	1.1	485,826	0.6	8,420,270	R

P O P U L A R   V O T E

The election of 1980 was a stinging rejection of the administration of Jimmy Carter. A January 1980 Gallup Poll found that 78 percent of Americans thought Carter was "a man of high moral principles" but only 29 percent considered him "a person of exceptional abilities." Dissatisfaction with Carter's handling of both foreign and domestic issues gave the Republicans the opportunity to become the nation's majority party again. In 1976, Carter had declared: "The insiders have had their chance, and they have not delivered. Their time has run out." His Republican opponent in 1980 said essentially the same thing.

Carter had pledged that he would be a chief executive in touch with the people. He and his wife, Rosalynn, had walked down Pennsylvania Avenue to the White House after his inauguration in 1976 as a symbolic rejection of the "imperial presidency" of President Richard M. Nixon. In his first months in office, Carter attempted to keep his campaign promises. However, by the summer of 1978, his popularity had fallen to a lower level than any of the five previous presidents at the same time in their presidencies. By the time the 1980 presidential campaign began, he faced angry voters who were disappointed in his failures in domestic and foreign policy.

When Carter attempted to eliminate a series of expensive pork-barrel water projects, Democratic leaders revolted—and the President retreated. His efforts to restore confidence in government failed with disclosures of wide-spread congressional corruption. More than 100 congressmen had received bribes from the South Korean Government (a situation known as Koreagate). Others accepted bribes from federal agents posing as Arabs (Abscam). Carter nominated his good friend, Bert Lance, to be director of the Office of Management and Budget, and he stood by him long after Lance's shady banking practices became known.

The failure of the Carter presidency was his inability to stop inflation. His efforts to stimulate the economy, reduce unemployment, and balance the budget had failed. The President rejected wage and price controls in favor of voluntary guidelines, but the inflation rate continued to soar. By the end of 1979, the annual rate of inflation stood at 13.3 percent—the highest since the Korean War and nearly double the 7.2 percent Carter had inherited from Gerald R. Ford's administration. The prime lending rate had risen to 16 percent, the highest in many years. Mortgage money vir-

tually disappeared. The number of new houses being built declined while older homes went unsold. The dollar grew weaker against foreign currencies, and the price of gold skyrocketed. In 1980, the country experienced the second consecutive year of double-digit inflation for the first time since World War I.

Events in Iran and Afghanistan caused great political damage to Carter. In January 1979, Islamic fundamentalists overthrew the Shah of Iran. In November, a mob of young Iranians stormed the U.S. embassy in Tehran and took more than 50 American hostages. They demanded the return of the Shah, who had entered the United States for medical treatment. An attempt to rescue the hostages through a military operation (Desert One) failed, and it added to Carter's image as incompetent. The spectacle of "America Held Hostage" shown on television every night left many Americans feeling angry and frustrated. In July 1980, Carter's approval rating dropped to 21 percent, the lowest recorded for a president since the Gallup Poll initiated this measurement in 1938.

Carter had asked Congress for power to impose national gasoline rationing, but the House, in a humiliating defeat for the President, voted down his proposal. The 1979 Iranian Revolution had brought Iranian oil production to a halt. OPEC (Organization of Oil Exporting Countries) began another round of oil price hikes that increased energy costs almost 60 percent. Serious shortages developed, and automobiles lined up for long waits at gasoline stations. By the summer of 1979, most Americans were angered by the failure of the administration's efforts to end the crisis. Carter now said the oil shortage was a real one and Americans would just have to use less gasoline. However, a May poll by the Associated Press (AP) and the National Broadcasting Company (NBC) reported that 54 percent thought that the shortage was a hoax perpetrated by oil companies to boost prices. Only 32 percent believed Carter's message that a shortage actually existed. Although the crisis lifted by the fall of 1979, credibility in Carter's competence had been all but lost. In December, the Soviet Union sent troops into Afghanistan to support a Marxist government. They stayed there in spite of Carter's efforts, including a boycott of the 1980 Summer Olympics in Moscow.

Senator Edward M. Kennedy challenged Carter for the 1980 Democratic nomination, and early polls showed he led Carter by better than 2 to 1 as the choice of Democrats. However, Kennedy seemed to have a drinking problem, and he could not adequately explain an automobile accident in 1967 on the island of Chappaquidick in Massachusetts in which a young woman was killed. Carter declared that he would not campaign because of the crisis in Iran. The strategy worked, and Carter defeated Kennedy in two-thirds of the primaries. When the Democratic Convention opened in New York on 11 August, Carter had more than a majority of the delegates and was renominated, as was Vice President Walter F. Mondale.

The Republicans entered the 1980 campaign with confidence, encouraged by President Carter's sharp decline in popularity. The clear choice of the party's rank and file was 69-year-old Ronald Reagan. Reagan had developed a superb, well-financed organization. His principal backers considered themselves part of the New Right—a broad, loose coalition of conservative ideologues and fundamental Christians. They strongly disapproved of the social and economic excesses of the 1960s and 1970s, and they hoped to reverse them. Reagan's support also came from neoconservatives. These former liberals were repelled by President Richard M. Nixon's détente (easing of tensions) with the Soviet Union which was continued by the administrations of Ford and Carter. They charged that the United States had allowed the Soviets to become a dangerous adversary which now had superiority in both conventional and nuclear arms. This superiority had encouraged the Soviets to engage in reckless adventures such as their support of worldwide terrorism and the invasion of Afghanistan.

Reagan had begun his political life in the 1930s as a New Deal Democrat. However, the growth in Soviet power after World War II had left him disillusioned with liberalism. By the 1950s, Reagan had become an ardent anti-communist. He gained a conservative reputation as a popular public speaker and as a corporate spokesman for General Electric. In 1966, he was elected governor of California and served for eight years. Although he spoke of reducing state programs, spending jumped sharply during his two terms in office. Similarly, he spoke about family values although he was divorced and was estranged from some of his children. Reagan easily won most of the Republican primaries. The Republican Convention nominated him on the first ballot. For a brief time, Reagan considered choosing former

President Gerald R. Ford as his vice presidential nominee in an effort to unify the party. However, when Ford used the word "co-presidency" in an interview, talk of the "dream ticket" ended. Reagan then chose George Bush, former director of the Central Intelligence Agency, as his running mate. Republican liberals, discontented with both Reagan and Bush, joined Representative John Anderson of Illinois in a third party. Carter felt that he could draw Anderson's moderate supporters to him by ignoring him and by portraying Reagan as an extremist.

Ronald Reagan and Jimmy Carter had very different campaign themes. Reagan successfully exploited domestic economic distress and international instability. Reagan favored huge increases in military spending, massive tax cuts, and the transfer of many federal social programs to state and local governments. He opposed the Strategic Arms Limitation Treaty (SALT) and any national health insurance or other new social program. Reagan promised to restore the nation's power and credibility. Carter was clearly to the left of Reagan. Carter supported SALT and modest increases in both domestic and military spending. He tried to divert attention from his own record by emphasizing Reagan's right-wing background. He warned that Reagan's election would be a threat to peace. Reagan scored the most decisive point in the campaign by ending a televised debate with Carter with two brilliant questions: "Ask yourself, are you better off than you were four years ago?" and "Is America as respected throughout the world as it was four years ago?" "The election," said a Carter adviser, "ended up becoming exactly the referendum on unhappiness we had been trying to avoid."

The results were decisive. Reagan won the popular vote by almost a 10-point margin, 50.7 percent to 41 percent. Anderson received almost 6 million votes, 6.6 percent. Democratic support declined from 1976 in every state. Reagan carried all the states that Ford had won in 1976 plus 17 others that had previously gone to Carter. Reagan received 489 electoral votes to Carter's 49. The Republicans gained 34 seats in the House, their largest gain since 1966, and increased their strength in the Senate by 12 seats, giving them a majority for the first time since 1954. Conservatives interpreted Reagan's victory as a mandate for their policies. Liberals argued that the results were a personal rejection of Jimmy Carter for his failure of leadership.

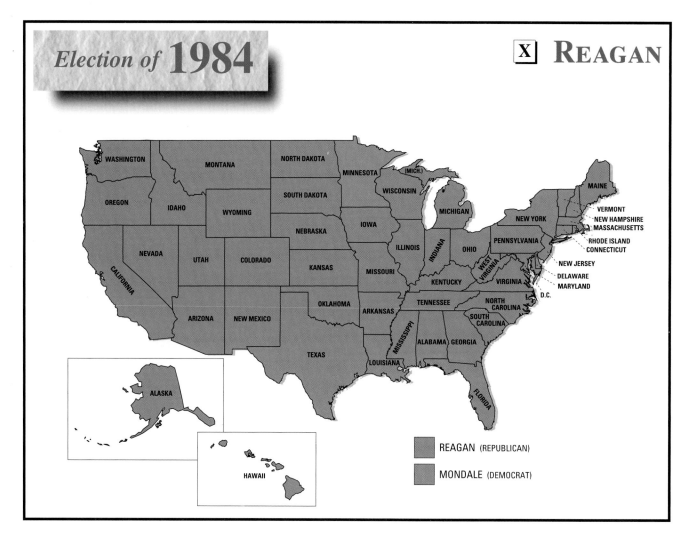

Election of 1984

REAGAN (REPUBLICAN)

MONDALE (DEMOCRAT)

States	Electoral Votes	Reagan	Mondale	States	Electoral Votes	Reagan	Mondale
Alabama	(9)	9	-	Montana	(4)	4	-
Alaska	(3)	3	-	Nebraska	(5)	5	-
Arizona	(7)	7	-	Nevada	(4)	4	-
Arkansas	(6)	6	-	New Hampshire	(4)	4	-
California	(47)	47	-	New Jersey	(16)	16	-
Colorado	(8)	8	-	New Mexico	(5)	5	-
Connecticut	(8)	8	-	New York	(36)	36	-
Delaware	(3)	3	-	North Carolina	(13)	13	-
District of Columbia	(3)	-	3	North Dakota	(3)	3	-
Florida	(21)	21	-	Ohio	(23)	23	-
Georgia	(12)	12	-	Oklahoma	(8)	8	-
Hawaii	(4)	4	-	Oregon	(7)	7	-
Idaho	(4)	4	-	Pennsylvania	(25)	25	-
Illinois	(24)	24	-	Rhode Island	(4)	4	-
Indiana	(12)	12	-	South Carolina	(8)	8	-
Iowa	(8)	8	-	South Dakota	(3)	3	-
Kansas	(7)	7	-	Tennessee	(11)	11	-
Kentucky	(9)	9	-	Texas	(29)	29	-
Louisiana	(10)	10	-	Utah	(5)	5	-
Maine	(4)	4	-	Vermont	(3)	3	-
Maryland	(10)	10	-	Virginia	(12)	12	-
Massachusetts	(13)	13	-	Washington	(10)	10	-
Michigan	(20)	20	-	West Virginia	(6)	6	-
Minnesota	(10)	-	10	Wisconsin	(11)	11	-
Mississippi	(7)	7	-	Wyoming	(3)	3	-
Missouri	(11)	11	-	**Totals**	**(538)**	**525**	**13**

ELECTORAL VOTE

Election of 1984

STATE	TOTAL VOTE	RONALD REAGAN (Republican)		WALTER F. MONDALE (Democrat)		DAVID BERGLAND (Libertarian)		LYNDON H. LaROUCHE JR. (Independent)		OTHER		PLURALITY	
		Votes	%	Votes	%	Votes	%	Votes	%	Votes	%		
Alabama	1,441,713	872,849	60.5	551,899	38.3	9,504	0.7	—		7,461	0.5	320,950	R
Alaska	207,605	138,377	66.7	62,007	29.9	6,378	3.1	—		843	0.4	76,370	R
Arizona	1,025,897	681,416	66.4	333,854	32.5	10,585	1.0	—		42		347,562	R
Arkansas	884,406	534,774	60.5	338,646	38.3	2,221	0.3	1,890	0.2	6,875	0.8	196,128	R
California	9,505,423	5,467,009	57.5	3,922,519	41.3	49,951	0.5	—		65,944	0.7	1,544,490	R
Colorado	1,295,380	821,817	63.4	454,975	35.1	11,257	0.9	4,662	0.4	2,669	0.2	366,842	R
Connecticut	1,466,900	890,877	60.7	569,597	38.8	204		—		6,222	0.4	321,280	R
Delaware	254,572	152,190	59.8	101,656	39.9	268	0.1	—		458	0.2	50,534	R
Florida	4,180,051	2,730,350	65.3	1,448,816	34.7	754		—		131		1,281,534	R
Georgia	1,776,120	1,068,722	60.2	706,628	39.8	152		34		584		362,094	R
Hawaii	335,846	185,050	55.1	147,154	43.8	2,167	0.6	654	0.2	821	0.2	37,896	R
Idaho	411,144	297,523	72.4	108,510	26.4	2,823	0.7	—		2,288	0.6	189,013	R
Illinois	4,819,088	2,707,103	56.2	2,086,499	43.3	10,086	0.2	—		15,400	0.3	620,604	R
Indiana	2,233,069	1,377,230	61.7	841,481	37.7	6,741	0.3	—		7,617	0.3	535,749	R
Iowa	1,319,805	703,088	53.3	605,620	45.9	1,844	0.1	6,248	0.5	3,005	0.2	97,468	R
Kansas	1,021,991	677,296	66.3	333,149	32.6	3,329	0.3	—		8,217	0.8	344,147	R
Kentucky	1,369,345	821,702	60.0	539,539	39.4	—		1,776	0.1	6,328	0.5	282,163	R
Louisiana	1,706,822	1,037,299	60.8	651,586	38.2	1,876	0.1	3,552	0.2	12,509	0.7	385,713	R
Maine	553,144	336,500	60.8	214,515	38.8	—		—		2,129	0.4	121,985	R
Maryland	1,675,873	879,918	52.5	787,935	47.0	5,721	0.3	—		2,299	0.1	91,983	R
Massachusetts	2,559,453	1,310,936	51.2	1,239,606	48.4	—		—		8,911	0.3	71,330	R
Michigan	3,801,658	2,251,571	59.2	1,529,638	40.2	10,055	0.3	3,862	0.1	6,532	0.2	721,933	R
Minnesota	2,084,449	1,032,603	49.5	1,036,364	49.7	2,996	0.1	3,865	0.2	8,621	0.4	3,761	D
Mississippi	941,104	582,377	61.9	352,192	37.4	2,336	0.2	1,001	0.1	3,198	0.3	230,185	R
Missouri	2,122,783	1,274,188	60.0	848,583	40.0	—		—		12		425,605	R
Montana	384,377	232,450	60.5	146,742	38.2	5,185	1.3	—		—		85,708	R
Nebraska	652,090	460,054	70.6	187,866	28.8	2,079	0.3	—		2,091	0.3	272,188	R
Nevada	286,667	188,770	65.8	91,655	32.0	2,292	0.8	—		3,950	1.4	97,115	R
New Hampshire	389,066	267,051	68.6	120,395	30.9	735	0.2	467	0.1	418	0.1	146,656	R
New Jersey	3,217,862	1,933,630	60.1	1,261,323	39.2	6,416	0.2	—		16,493	0.5	672,307	R
New Mexico	514,370	307,101	59.7	201,769	39.2	4,459	0.9	—		1,041	0.2	105,332	R
New York	6,806,810	3,664,763	53.8	3,119,609	45.8	11,949	0.2	—		10,489	0.2	545,154	R
North Carolina	2,175,361	1,346,481	61.9	824,287	37.9	3,794	0.2	—		799		522,194	R
North Dakota	308,971	200,336	64.8	104,429	33.8	703	0.2	1,278	0.4	2,225	0.7	95,907	R
Ohio	4,547,619	2,678,560	58.9	1,825,440	40.1	5,886	0.1	10,693	0.2	27,040	0.6	853,120	R
Oklahoma	1,255,676	861,530	68.6	385,080	30.7	9,066	0.7	—		—		476,450	R
Oregon	1,226,527	685,700	55.9	536,479	43.7	—		—		4,348	0.4	149,221	R
Pennsylvania	4,844,903	2,584,323	53.3	2,228,131	46.0	6,982	0.1	—		25,467	0.5	356,192	R
Rhode Island	410,492	212,080	51.7	197,106	48.0	277	0.1	—		1,029	0.3	14,974	R
South Carolina	968,529	615,539	63.6	344,459	35.6	4,359	0.5	—		4,172	0.4	271,080	R
South Dakota	317,867	200,267	63.0	116,113	36.5	—		—		1,487	0.5	84,154	R
Tennessee	1,711,994	990,212	57.8	711,714	41.6	3,072	0.2	1,852	0.1	5,144	0.3	278,498	R
Texas	5,397,571	3,433,428	63.6	1,949,276	36.1	—		14,613	0.3	254		1,484,152	R
Utah	629,656	469,105	74.5	155,369	24.7	2,447	0.4	—		2,735	0.4	313,736	R
Vermont	234,561	135,865	57.9	95,730	40.8	1,002	0.4	423	0.2	1,541	0.7	40,135	R
Virginia	2,146,635	1,337,078	62.3	796,250	37.1	—		13,307	0.6	—		540,828	R
Washington	1,883,910	1,051,670	55.8	807,352	42.9	8,844	0.5	4,712	0.3	11,332	0.6	244,318	R
West Virginia	735,742	405,483	55.1	328,125	44.6	—		—		2,134	0.3	77,358	R
Wisconsin	2,211,689	1,198,584	54.2	995,740	45.0	4,883	0.2	3,791	0.2	8,691	0.4	202,844	R
Wyoming	188,968	133,241	70.5	53,370	28.2	2,357	1.2	—		—		79,871	R
Dist. of Col.	211,288	29,009	13.7	180,408	85.4	279	0.1	127	0.1	1,465	0.7	151,399	D
Totals	92,652,842	54,455,075	58.8	37,577,185	40.6	228,314	0.2	78,807	0.1	313,461	0.3	16,877,890	R

POPULAR VOTE

The nation seemed prosperous as the 1984 campaign began. Inflation and unemployment remained low. Interest rates had dropped, and taxes had been reduced. No matter how loudly Ronald Reagan's critics complained, the President remained very popular with the American people. The Republican campaign slogan—"It's Morning in America"—reflected the optimistic mood of the country, and Reagan seemed to be virtually unbeatable.

Reagan's political strength was personal. Reagan often distanced himself in public from his own administration and stayed above the internal bickering of his appointees. Reagan exuded confidence, and his charm, good humor, and positive approach to life made him popular even among Democrats. There were endless stories and jokes about his casual and relaxed approach to the presidency, his frequent naps and vacations, his delegation of enormous power to senior aides, his forgetfulness, and his unfamiliarity with details, even the main issues in key disputes. However, the public liked Reagan and seemed serenely confident with his style of leadership. They remembered his attitude after being shot on 30 March 1981. Although a bullet was lodged dangerously near his heart, he was still able to comment, "I forgot to duck." On the operating table, he joked with the surgeons, saying, "Please tell me you're Republicans." Reports of his good sprits pushed his popularity ratings to extraordinary heights during his recuperation.

Eight Democrats struggled for their party's nomination through exhausting and divisive primaries which began on 20 January and ended on 6 June. The leading candidate was Walter F. Mondale, who had been vice president in the administration of Jimmy Carter. Mondale had strong liberal credentials in Minnesota politics and as a U.S. senator. He was challenged by Senator Edward M. Kennedy of Massachusetts; Senator John Glenn of Ohio; the Reverend Jesse Jackson, the first African American to make a serious run for the nomination of a major party; Senator Gary Hart of Colorado; Senator Alan Cranston of California; Senator Ernest Hollings of South Carolina; and Governor Reuben Askew of Florida. The results of the Democratic primaries were very close. After 18 million votes had been cast, fewer than 450,000 votes separated Mondale from his closest rival, Gary Hart. More than one in five voters had chosen a third candidate, Jesse Jackson. Jackson had won the primaries in South Carolina, Louisiana, and the District of Columbia.

He also carried several large cities, including Philadelphia. The seemingly endless charges and countercharges plus negative campaign ads weakened all the candidates. A winner did not emerge until Mondale won the New Jersey primary on 5 June.

Mondale had made a bold and dramatic move by announcing Representative Geraldine A. Ferraro of New York as his running mate before the Democratic Convention convened in San Francisco in July. She became the first woman to run for vice president on a major ticket. Mondale believed that this historic choice would help him with women, Catholics, ethnic groups, and in New York, a state essential to the Democrats. Ferraro was a Roman Catholic born to immigrant parents. Married for 24 years and the mother of three children, she had served three terms representing a racially and ethnically diverse congressional district in New York City. She held her own in debates with Vice President George Bush, but she was hit with several misfortunate events. The first involved her family finances and tax records and centered on some questionable real estate activities of her husband. The second was a bitter verbal battle with New York's Archbishop John J. O'Connor over her pro-choice position. Both of these events hurt the Democratic campaign. Mondale proposed a tax increase at the convention, saying, "He (Reagan) won't tell you. I just did." He used charts and statistics to show how he would raise taxes on corporations and families earning more than $25,000 a year in order to reduce the deficit. Mondale's speeches were boring and his staff mismanaged his campaign.

During the 1980 Republican primaries, Reagan had promised to reduce taxes and increase defense spending while balancing the budget. His critics said this was impossible to achieve. George Bush, later to become Reagan's vice president, had called it "voodoo economics." However, Congress enacted Reagan's programs. In 1982, however, the nation entered a recession, the worst economic decline since the Great Depression. Unemployment exceeded 10 percent of the work force, a figure not seen since before World War II. Business bankruptcies reached a 50-year high. Reagan's job approval rating dropped dramatically, and commentators began to talk about a one-term presidency. Reagan refused to change course. By the end of 1983, the economy was booming again because of a sharp drop in international oil prices and because of lower interest rates imposed by the Federal Reserve Board. Reagan's popularity shot up—and his vision of an America revived both economically and militarily seemed to have been achieved. In January 1984, at age 73, already the oldest man to serve as president, he announced he would seek another term.

The Republican Convention met in Dallas, Texas, and nominated Reagan and Bush in an unusual joint roll call. The Republicans were strong and united in their attacks on Carter-Mondale policies. In an attempt to counter the Ferraro candidacy, they had a "ladies' night" featuring four women speakers, including Jeane J. Kirkpatrick, former ambassador to the United Nations. She delivered a foreign policy speech highly critical of her fellow Democrats. Reagan, standing before a convention of his party for the last time as a candidate for president, said, "The choices this year are not just between two different personalities or between two political parties. They are between two different visions of the future, two fundamentally different ways of governing—their government of pessimism, fear, and limits . . . or ours of hope, confidence, and growth."

Television emphasized the differences between the candidates. Reagan was experienced and telegenic, and Mondale was stiff and uncomfortable. Reagan repeated the same message endless times using different words and different settings. He was against government controls, and he was fiercely opposed to communism. He spoke about his youth and of small-town rural values where he learned patriotism, self-help, hard work, religious faith, family values, and a love for the American flag. With great oratorical skill, he talked about the lives of senior citizens and how their dreams and future hopes could be fulfilled without government restraints and regulations. The press referred to him as the "Great Communicator."

Although Reagan was a likable person with many positive personal traits, his domestic programs were a disaster for the American poor. He said that the federal government was the root of problems, and he promised to "get government off the backs of the people." His proposals signaled a sharp retreat from the New Deal and Great Society traditions. His budget requests called for cutbacks in social programs. The objective, he said, was to eliminate services and benefits for those who should be able to make it on their own. The 1982 appropriations bill had slashed over $35 billion in domestic

expenditures from the proposed Carter budget. Reagan succeeded in dismantling many anti-poverty programs while promising a "safety net" for the "truly needy." He obtained cuts in both federal welfare and food stamp programs. Federal aid to various educational programs were reduced by almost 50 percent. Likewise, sharp cuts affected federal support for the arts, subsidized housing, child nutrition programs, and student loans. Only public pressure forced Reagan to retreat on his planned proposals for reduction in Social Security benefits and public assistance to the elderly.

Reagan considered the Soviet Union an "evil empire" with "aggressive impulses," responsible for causing unrest and revolutions throughout the world. Any reduction in Cold War tensions, he believed, had to be linked to demonstrated improvement in Soviet behavior. Reagan proceeded with a massive military buildup. He was convinced that Soviet leaders understood only force. By 1984, defense spending had reached $284 billion. The President insisted that the intermediate-range Pershing 2 and cruise missiles be deployed in Western Europe. These missiles could reach targets far within the Soviet Union. Protests throughout NATO (North Atlantic Treaty Organization) nations modified the President's decision. However, Reagan never retreated from his conviction that the United States had a moral obligation to encourage anti-communist movements throughout the world. His critics claimed that his administration had confused nationalistic uprisings against right-wing dictatorships with Soviet-backed revolutions.

Reagan's campaign theme was confidence and optimism. The President and his media experts repeated the same message, saying the words: "We think in America every day is the Fourth of July. Our opponents think every day is April 15!" On Election Day, Reagan achieved one of the greatest personal triumphs in U.S. political history. He carried 49 states, losing only Mondale's home state of Minnesota and the District of Columbia. His popular vote of 58.8 percent to Mondale's 40.6 percent placed him close behind Warren G. Harding, Franklin D. Roosevelt, Lyndon B. Johnson, and Richard M. Nixon as landslide winners. The economic recovery plus the President's charm won him support from large numbers of traditional Democrats, especially Southerners and blue-collar workers. He even won 57 percent of the women's vote. Reagan hailed the results as an endorsement of his economic and foreign policies.

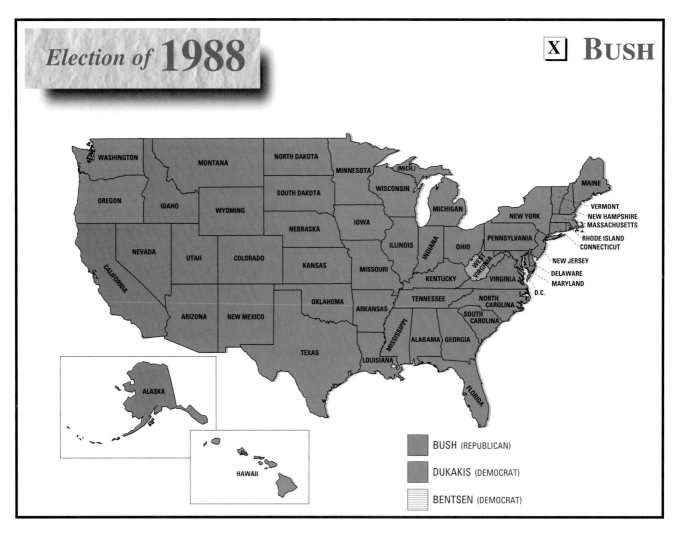

Election of 1988

BUSH (REPUBLICAN)

DUKAKIS (DEMOCRAT)

BENTSEN (DEMOCRAT)

States	Electoral Votes	Bush	Dukakis	Bentsen	States	Electoral Votes	Bush	Dukakis	Bentsen
Alabama	(9)	9	-	-	Montana	(4)	4	-	-
Alaska	(3)	3	-	-	Nebraska	(5)	5	-	-
Arizona	(7)	7	-	-	Nevada	(4)	4	-	-
Arkansas	(6)	6	-	-	New Hampshire	(4)	4	-	-
California	(47)	47	-	-	New Jersey	(16)	16	-	-
Colorado	(8)	8	-	-	New Mexico	(5)	5	-	-
Connecticut	(8)	8	-	-	New York	(36)	-	36	-
Delaware	(3)	3	-	-	North Carolina	(13)	13	-	-
District of Columbia	(3)	-	3	-	North Dakota	(3)	3	-	-
Florida	(21)	21	-	-	Ohio	(23)	23	-	-
Georgia	(12)	12	-	-	Oklahoma	(8)	8	-	-
Hawaii	(4)	-	4	-	Oregon	(7)	-	7	-
Idaho	(4)	4	-	-	Pennsylvania	(25)	25	-	-
Illinois	(24)	24	-	-	Rhode Island	(4)	-	4	-
Indiana	(12)	12	-	-	South Carolina	(8)	8	-	-
Iowa	(8)	-	8	-	South Dakota	(3)	3	-	-
Kansas	(7)	7	-	-	Tennessee	(11)	11	-	-
Kentucky	(9)	9	-	-	Texas	(29)	29	-	-
Louisiana	(10)	10	-	-	Utah	(5)	5	-	-
Maine	(4)	4	-	-	Vermont	(3)	3	-	-
Maryland	(10)	10	-	-	Virginia	(12)	12	-	-
Massachusetts	(13)	-	13	-	Washington	(10)	-	10	-
Michigan	(20)	20	-	-	West Virginia	(6)	-	5	1
Minnesota	(10)	-	10	-	Wisconsin	(11)	-	11	-
Mississippi	(7)	7	-	-	Wyoming	(3)	3	-	-
Missouri	(11)	11	-	-	**Totals**	**(538)**	**426**	**111**	**1**

ELECTORAL VOTE

Election of 1988

STATE	TOTAL VOTE	GEORGE BUSH (Republican)		MICHAEL S. DUKAKIS (Democrat)		RON PAUL (Libertarian)		LENORA B. FULANI (New Alliance)		OTHER		PLURALITY	
		Votes	%	Votes	%	Votes	%	Votes	%	Votes	%		
Alabama	1,378,476	815,576	59.2	549,506	39.9	8,460	0.6	3,311	0.2	1,623	0.1	266,070	R
Alaska	200,116	119,251	59.6	72,584	36.3	5,484	2.7	1,024	0.5	1,773	0.9	46,667	R
Arizona	1,171,873	702,541	60.0	454,029	38.7	13,351	1.1	1,662	0.1	290		248,512	R
Arkansas	827,738	466,578	56.4	349,237	42.2	3,297	0.4	2,161	0.3	6,465	0.8	117,341	R
California	9,887,065	5,054,917	51.1	4,702,233	47.6	70,105	0.7	31,181	0.3	28,629	0.3	352,684	R
Colorado	1,372,394	728,177	53.1	621,453	45.3	15,482	1.1	2,539	0.2	4,743	0.3	106,724	R
Connecticut	1,443,394	750,241	52.0	676,584	46.9	14,071	1.0	2,491	0.2	7		73,657	R
Delaware	249,891	139,639	55.9	108,647	43.5	1,162	0.5	443	0.2	—		30,992	R
Florida	4,302,313	2,618,885	60.9	1,656,701	38.5	19,796	0.5	6,655	0.2	276		962,184	R
Georgia	1,809,672	1,081,331	59.8	714,792	39.5	8,435	0.5	5,099	0.3	15		366,539	R
Hawaii	354,461	158,625	44.8	192,364	54.3	1,999	0.6	1,003	0.3	470	0.1	33,739	D
Idaho	408,968	253,881	62.1	147,272	36.0	5,313	1.3	2,502	0.6	—		106,609	R
Illinois	4,559,120	2,310,939	50.7	2,215,940	48.6	14,944	0.3	10,276	0.2	7,021	0.2	94,999	R
Indiana	2,168,621	1,297,763	59.8	860,643	39.7	—		10,215	0.5	—		437,120	R
Iowa	1,225,614	545,355	44.5	670,557	54.7	2,494	0.2	540		6,668	0.5	125,202	D
Kansas	993,044	554,049	55.8	422,636	42.6	12,553	1.3	3,806	0.4	—		131,413	R
Kentucky	1,322,517	734,281	55.5	580,368	43.9	2,118	0.2	1,256	0.1	4,494	0.3	153,913	R
Louisiana	1,628,202	883,702	54.3	717,460	44.1	4,115	0.3	2,355	0.1	20,570	1.3	166,242	R
Maine	555,035	307,131	55.3	243,569	43.9	2,700	0.5	1,405	0.3	230		63,562	R
Maryland	1,714,358	876,167	51.1	826,304	48.2	6,748	0.4	5,115	0.3	24		49,863	R
Massachusetts	2,632,805	1,194,635	45.4	1,401,415	53.2	24,251	0.9	9,561	0.4	2,943	0.1	206,780	D
Michigan	3,669,163	1,965,486	53.6	1,675,783	45.7	18,336	0.5	2,513	0.1	7,045	0.2	289,703	R
Minnesota	2,096,790	962,337	45.9	1,109,471	52.9	5,109	0.2	1,734	0.1	18,139	0.9	147,134	D
Mississippi	931,527	557,890	59.9	363,921	39.1	3,329	0.4	2,155	0.2	4,232	0.5	193,969	R
Missouri	2,093,713	1,084,953	51.8	1,001,619	47.8	434		6,656	0.3	51		83,334	R
Montana	365,674	190,412	52.1	168,936	46.2	5,047	1.4	1,279	0.3	—		21,476	R
Nebraska	661,465	397,956	60.2	259,235	39.2	2,534	0.4	1,740	0.3	—		138,721	R
Nevada	350,067	206,040	58.9	132,738	37.9	3,520	1.0	835	0.2	6,934	2.0	73,302	R
New Hampshire	451,074	281,537	62.4	163,696	36.3	4,502	1.0	790	0.2	549	0.1	117,841	R
New Jersey	3,099,553	1,743,192	56.2	1,320,352	42.6	8,421	0.3	5,139	0.2	22,449	0.7	422,840	R
New Mexico	521,287	270,341	51.9	244,497	46.9	3,268	0.6	2,237	0.4	944	0.2	25,844	R
New York	6,485,683	3,081,871	47.5	3,347,882	51.6	12,109	0.2	15,845	0.2	27,976	0.4	266,011	D
North Carolina	2,134,370	1,237,258	58.0	890,167	41.7	1,263	0.1	5,682	0.3	—		347,091	R
North Dakota	297,261	166,559	56.0	127,739	43.0	1,315	0.4	396	0.1	1,252	0.4	38,820	R
Ohio	4,393,699	2,416,549	55.0	1,939,629	44.1	11,989	0.3	12,017	0.3	13,515	0.3	476,920	R
Oklahoma	1,171,036	678,367	57.9	483,423	41.3	6,261	0.5	2,985	0.3	—		194,944	R
Oregon	1,201,694	560,126	46.6	616,206	51.3	14,811	1.2	6,487	0.5	4,064	0.3	56,080	D
Pennsylvania	4,536,251	2,300,087	50.7	2,194,944	48.4	12,051	0.3	4,379	0.1	24,790	0.5	105,143	R
Rhode Island	404,620	177,761	43.9	225,123	55.6	825	0.2	280	0.1	631	0.2	47,362	D
South Carolina	986,009	606,443	61.5	370,554	37.6	4,935	0.5	4,077	0.4	—		235,889	R
South Dakota	312,991	165,415	52.8	145,560	46.5	1,060	0.3	730	0.2	226	0.1	19,855	R
Tennessee	1,636,250	947,233	57.9	679,794	41.5	2,041	0.1	1,334	0.1	5,848	0.4	267,439	R
Texas	5,427,410	3,036,829	56.0	2,352,748	43.3	30,355	0.6	7,208	0.1	270		684,081	R
Utah	647,008	428,442	66.2	207,343	32.0	7,473	1.2	455	0.1	3,295	0.5	221,099	R
Vermont	243,328	124,331	51.1	115,775	47.6	1,000	0.4	205	0.1	2,017	0.8	8,556	R
Virginia	2,191,609	1,309,162	59.7	859,799	39.2	8,336	0.4	14,312	0.7	—		449,363	R
Washington	1,865,253	903,835	48.5	933,516	50.0	17,240	0.9	3,520	0.2	7,142	0.4	29,681	D
West Virginia	653,311	310,065	47.5	341,016	52.2	—		2,230	0.3	—		30,951	D
Wisconsin	2,191,608	1,047,499	47.8	1,126,794	51.4	5,157	0.2	1,953	0.1	10,205	0.5	79,295	D
Wyoming	176,551	106,867	60.5	67,113	38.0	2,026	1.1	545	0.3	—		39,754	R
Dist. of Col.	192,877	27,590	14.3	159,407	82.6	554	0.3	2,901	1.5	2,425	1.3	131,817	D
Totals	91,594,809	48,886,097	53.4	41,809,074	45.6	432,179	0.5	217,219	0.2	250,240	0.3	7,077,023	R

P O P U L A R   V O T E

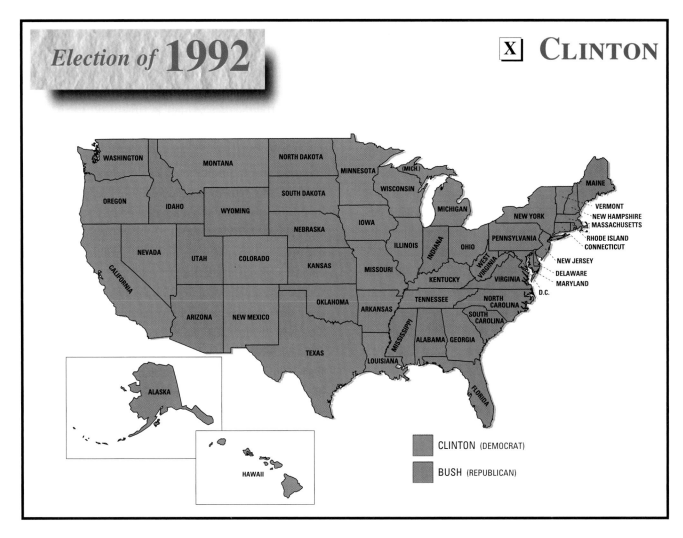

Election of 1992

☒ CLINTON

CLINTON (DEMOCRAT)

BUSH (REPUBLICAN)

States	Electoral Votes	Clinton	Bush	States	Electoral Votes	Clinton	Bush
Alabama	(9)	-	9	Montana	(3)	3	-
Alaska	(3)	-	3	Nebraska	(5)	-	5
Arizona	(8)	-	8	Nevada	(4)	4	-
Arkansas	(6)	6	-	New Hampshire	(4)	4	-
California	(54)	54	-	New Jersey	(15)	15	-
Colorado	(8)	8	-	New Mexico	(5)	5	-
Connecticut	(8)	8	-	New York	(33)	33	-
Delaware	(3)	3	-	North Carolina	(14)	-	14
District of Columbia	(3)	3	-	North Dakota	(3)	-	3
Florida	(25)	-	25	Ohio	(21)	21	-
Georgia	(13)	13	-	Oklahoma	(8)	-	8
Hawaii	(4)	4	-	Oregon	(7)	7	-
Idaho	(4)	-	4	Pennsylvania	(23)	23	-
Illinois	(22)	22	-	Rhode Island	(4)	4	-
Indiana	(12)	-	12	South Carolina	(8)	-	8
Iowa	(7)	7	-	South Dakota	(3)	-	3
Kansas	(6)	-	6	Tennessee	(11)	11	-
Kentucky	(8)	8	-	Texas	(32)	-	32
Louisiana	(9)	9	-	Utah	(5)	-	5
Maine	(4)	4	-	Vermont	(3)	3	-
Maryland	(10)	10	-	Virginia	(13)	-	13
Massachusetts	(12)	12	-	Washington	(11)	11	-
Michigan	(18)	18	-	West Virginia	(5)	5	-
Minnesota	(10)	10	-	Wisconsin	(11)	11	-
Mississippi	(7)	-	7	Wyoming	(3)	-	3
Missouri	(11)	11	-	**Totals**	**(538)**	**370**	**168**

ELECTORAL VOTE

Election of 1992

STATE	TOTAL VOTE	BILL CLINTON (Democrat)		GEORGE BUSH (Republican)		ROSS PEROT (Independent)		ANDRE V. MARROU (Libertarian)		OTHER ¹		PLURALITY	
		Votes	%	Votes	%	Votes	%	Votes	%	Votes	%		
Alabama	1,688,060	690,080	40.9	804,283	47.6	183,109	10.8	5,737	0.3	4,851	0.3	114,203	R
Alaska	258,506	78,294	30.3	102,000	39.5	73,481	28.4	1,378	0.5	3,353	1.3	23,706	R
Arizona	1,486,975	543,050	36.5	572,086	38.5	353,741	23.8	6,759	0.5	11,339	0.8	29,036	R
Arkansas	950,653	505,823	53.2	337,324	35.5	99,132	10.4	1,261	0.1	7,113	0.7	168,499	D
California	11,131,721	5,121,325	46.0	3,630,574	32.6	2,296,006	20.6	48,139	0.4	35,677	0.3	1,490,751	D
Colorado	1,569,180	629,681	40.1	562,850	35.9	366,010	23.3	8,669	0.6	1,970	0.1	66,831	D
Connecticut	1,616,332	682,318	42.2	578,313	35.8	348,771	21.6	5,391	0.3	1,539	0.1	104,005	D
Delaware	289,735	126,054	43.5	102,313	35.3	59,213	20.4	935	0.3	1,220	0.4	23,741	D
Florida	5,314,392	2,072,698	39.0	2,173,310	40.9	1,053,067	19.8	15,079	0.3	238		100,612	R
Georgia	2,321,125	1,008,966	43.5	995,252	42.9	309,657	13.3	7,110	0.3	140		13,714	D
Hawaii	372,842	179,310	48.1	136,822	36.7	53,003	14.2	1,119	0.3	2,588	0.7	42,488	D
Idaho	482,142	137,013	28.4	202,645	42.0	130,395	27.0	1,167	0.2	10,922	2.3	65,632	R
Illinois	5,050,157	2,453,350	48.6	1,734,096	34.3	840,515	16.6	9,218	0.2	12,978	0.3	719,254	D
Indiana	2,305,871	848,420	36.8	989,375	42.9	455,934	19.8	7,936	0.3	4,206	0.2	140,955	R
Iowa	1,354,607	586,353	43.3	504,891	37.3	253,468	18.7	1,076	0.1	8,819	0.7	81,462	D
Kansas	1,157,335	390,434	33.7	449,951	38.9	312,358	27.0	4,314	0.4	278		59,517	R
Kentucky	1,492,900	665,104	44.6	617,178	41.3	203,944	13.7	4,513	0.3	2,161	0.1	47,926	D
Louisiana	1,790,017	815,971	45.6	733,386	41.0	211,478	11.8	3,155	0.2	26,027	1.5	82,585	D
Maine	679,499	263,420	38.8	206,504	30.4	206,820	30.4	1,681	0.2	1,074	0.2	56,600	D
Maryland	1,985,046	988,571	49.8	707,094	35.6	281,414	14.2	4,715	0.2	3,252	0.2	281,477	D
Massachusetts	2,773,700	1,318,662	47.5	805,049	29.0	630,731	22.7	9,024	0.3	10,234	0.4	513,613	D
Michigan	4,274,673	1,871,182	43.8	1,554,940	36.4	824,813	19.3	10,175	0.2	13,563	0.3	316,242	D
Minnesota	2,347,948	1,020,997	43.5	747,841	31.9	562,506	24.0	3,374	0.1	13,230	0.6	273,156	D
Mississippi	981,793	400,258	40.8	487,793	49.7	85,626	8.7	2,154	0.2	5,962	0.6	87,535	R
Missouri	2,391,565	1,053,873	44.1	811,159	33.9	518,741	21.7	7,497	0.3	295		242,714	D
Montana	410,611	154,507	37.6	144,207	35.1	107,225	26.1	986	0.2	3,686	0.9	10,300	D
Nebraska	737,546	216,864	29.4	343,678	46.6	174,104	23.6	1,340	0.2	1,560	0.2	126,814	R
Nevada	506,318	189,148	37.4	175,828	34.7	132,580	26.2	1,835	0.4	6,927	1.4	13,320	D
New Hampshire	537,943	209,040	38.9	202,484	37.6	121,337	22.6	3,548	0.7	1,534	0.3	6,556	D
New Jersey	3,343,594	1,436,206	43.0	1,356,865	40.6	521,829	15.6	6,822	0.2	21,872	0.7	79,341	D
New Mexico	569,986	261,617	45.9	212,824	37.3	91,895	16.1	1,615	0.3	2,035	0.4	48,793	D
New York	6,926,925	3,444,450	49.7	2,346,649	33.9	1,090,721	15.7	13,451	0.2	31,654	0.5	1,097,801	D
North Carolina	2,611,850	1,114,042	42.7	1,134,661	43.4	357,864	13.7	5,171	0.2	112		20,619	R
North Dakota	308,133	99,168	32.2	136,244	44.2	71,084	23.1	416	0.1	1,221	0.4	37,076	R
Ohio	4,939,967	1,984,942	40.2	1,894,310	38.3	1,036,426	21.0	7,252	0.1	17,037	0.3	90,632	D
Oklahoma	1,390,359	473,066	34.0	592,929	42.6	319,878	23.0	4,486	0.3	—		119,863	R
Oregon	1,462,643	621,314	42.5	475,757	32.5	354,091	24.2	4,277	0.3	7,204	0.5	145,557	D
Pennsylvania	4,959,810	2,239,164	45.1	1,791,841	36.1	902,667	18.2	21,477	0.4	4,661	0.1	447,323	D
Rhode Island	453,477	213,299	47.0	131,601	29.0	105,045	23.2	571	0.1	2,961	0.7	81,698	D
South Carolina	1,202,527	479,514	39.9	577,507	48.0	138,872	11.5	2,719	0.2	3,915	0.3	97,993	R
South Dakota	336,254	124,888	37.1	136,718	40.7	73,295	21.8	814	0.2	539	0.2	11,830	R
Tennessee	1,982,638	933,521	47.1	841,300	42.4	199,968	10.1	1,847	0.1	6,002	0.3	92,221	D
Texas	6,154,018	2,281,815	37.1	2,496,071	40.6	1,354,781	22.0	19,699	0.3	1,652		214,256	R
Utah	743,999	183,429	24.7	322,632	43.4	203,400	27.3	1,900	0.3	32,638	4.4	119,232	R
Vermont	289,701	133,592	46.1	88,122	30.4	65,991	22.8	501	0.2	1,495	0.5	45,470	D
Virginia	2,558,665	1,038,650	40.6	1,150,517	45.0	348,639	13.6	5,730	0.2	15,129	0.6	111,867	R
Washington	2,288,230	993,037	43.4	731,234	32.0	541,780	23.7	7,533	0.3	14,646	0.6	261,803	D
West Virginia	683,762	331,001	48.4	241,974	35.4	108,829	15.9	1,873	0.3	85		89,027	D
Wisconsin	2,531,114	1,041,066	41.1	930,855	36.8	544,479	21.5	2,877	0.1	11,837	0.5	110,211	D
Wyoming	200,598	68,160	34.0	79,347	39.6	51,263	25.6	844	0.4	984	0.5	11,187	R
Dist. of Col.	227,572	192,619	84.6	20,698	9.1	9,681	4.3	467	0.2	4,107	1.8	171,921	D
Totals	104,425,014	44,909,326	43.0	39,103,882	37.4	19,741,657	18.9	291,627	0.3	378,522	0.4	5,805,444	D

POPULAR VOTE

The 1992 presidential election concentrated more on issues and less on personalities than recent elections. During the campaign, President George Bush's job approval rating plunged from a historic all-time high of 89 percent in early March 1991 to 29 percent at the end of July 1992. The Democratic candidate was nearly destroyed by scandal, and a billionaire independent waged the strongest third-party challenge since 1912. Candidates found new means to reach voters by using television talk shows, radio call-in programs, and electronic bulletin boards.

The 1991 Gulf War was the most important event of the Bush presidency. On 2 August 1990, Saddam Hussein, the military ruler of Iraq, invaded the neighboring Kingdom of Kuwait, believing that the United States would not respond. However, President Bush feared the war could spread to oil-rich Saudi Arabia, a U.S. ally since the 1940s, and he acted decisively. He believed that the world's price of oil—and the world economy—would be endangered. "This will not stand," the President declared. "What is at stake is more than one small country; it is a big idea—a new world order." Bush obtained a congressional authorization for war and mobilized the United Nations to resist Iraqi forces. On 27 February 1991, after a month of bombing, 550,000 United States and United Nations forces unleashed Operation DESERT STORM. In 100 hours, Kuwait had been liberated and southern Iraq was occupied. According to a Gallup Poll, nearly 80 percent approved of the way Bush handled foreign policy. Most analysts agreed that he was guaranteed renomination and an easy reelection.

In mid February 1991, 10 days before Operation DESERT STORM had begun, the Gallup Poll asked registered Democrats whom they would like to see as their party's nominee for president in 1992. On a list of 13 possible candidates, Bill Clinton ranked 12th with 2 percent. Two months later, his support had dwindled to 1 percent. In an extensive Gallup survey conducted in early November, a month after Clinton had officially entered the race, 42 percent of registered Democrats replied that they had never heard of him. Of those who had heard of him, only 6 percent said they would like him as the party's nominee. Exactly one year later, Bill Clinton was elected president of the United States.

William Jefferson Clinton, who chose to go by the more familiar name Bill, was born in the small town of Hope,

Arkansas, just two months after his father had died in an automobile accident. His mother was a chronic gambler, and his stepfather was an abusive alcoholic. In 1963, Clinton met President John F. Kennedy in the Rose Garden when he was attending the Washington, D.C. national convention of Boys' Nation, a leadership organization for high school students. The Clinton campaign in 1992 made prominent use of pictures showing him shaking hands with Kennedy. Clinton graduated from Georgetown University and won a Rhodes Scholarship for two years of study at Oxford University. In 1974, a year after graduating from Yale Law School, Clinton ran unsuccessfully for a congressional seat in Arkansas. In 1978, at age 32, Clinton became the nation's youngest governor. Defeated in 1980, he was reelected in 1982 and held that office for the next decade. Although his critics within the state were numerous, other governors considered Clinton one of the nation's most effective chief executives.

In October 1991, Clinton entered the race for the Democratic nomination. None of the major Democratic candidates entered the primaries because they did not believe that Bush could be beaten. Clinton quickly moved from little-known candidate to front-runner over former Senator Paul Tsongas of Massachusetts, Senator Tom Harkin of Iowa, and former Governor Edmund (Jerry) Brown of California. By early April, Clinton had won the nomination. Throughout the primaries, he came under attack for extramarital affairs, for having smoked marijuana, and for charges that he was a draft dodger during the Vietnam War. However, Clinton focused on the economy. Privately, his strategists used the slogan, "It's the economy, stupid," to remind themselves of the main campaign issue. Clinton was nominated at the July Democratic Convention and chose as his running mate Senator Albert Gore, Jr. of Tennessee, a fellow moderate Southerner.

Patrick (Pat) J. Buchanan, a conservative columnist and television commentator, challenged President Bush in the New Hampshire primary in February and, surprisingly, obtained 37.4 percent of the vote. Buchanan stressed family value issues, opposed the North American Free Trade Agreement (NAFTA), and supported a Constitutional amendment outlawing abortion. He remained in the race through the August convention, receiving a total of 22.8 percent of all votes cast in 35 Republican primaries.

Buchanan delivered a strident speech at the convention. He told the delegates, "You can't be a Christian and a Democrat." Buchanan's speech, delivered on television during prime time, left the impression that the Republican Party was controlled by right-wing advocates. Bush and Quayle were renominated on the first ballot.

H. Ross Perot, a Texas billionaire with no political experience, was a major figure in the 1992 presidential election. His campaign began in mid September 1991 with a group of well-financed "volunteers." Perot officially launched his third party on a national televised talk show in February 1992. The crew-cut, plain-talking Perot captured people's imagination. In an early June Gallup Poll, Perot held a significant lead among registered voters in test elections against President Bush and Bill Clinton. Thirty-eight percent of voters named him as the candidate most able to bring about the changes the country needed, while 24 percent named Clinton and 20 percent named Bush. Analysts at the Gallup Poll observed that Perot supporters did not care where he stood on issues as long as they perceived him as an agent of change. There was much speculation that Perot could carry enough states to force the election to be decided by the U.S. House of Representatives.

President Bush had devoted most of his attention to foreign policy during his first term. The Berlin Wall had been torn down in November 1989, leading to the reunification of Germany; U.S. troops had invaded Panama in January 1990 to arrest its drug-trafficking president; the Soviet Union had formally dissolved in December 1991, effectively ending the Cold War; and U.S.-led forces had defeated Iraq in February 1991. These events had kept the President's approval rating high. However, domestic issues, especially the economy, were first and foremost on voters' minds in the 1992 campaign.

In January 1990, Bush agreed to raise taxes, breaking the pledge that he had made at the 1988 Republican Convention. Under pressure from congressional Democrats, the President decided to stimulate the economy by reducing the budget deficit through a payroll tax increase. In June, he requested additional tax increases, ending up with the second-largest tax increase in U.S. history. Conservative Republicans were stunned by the President breaking his vow. William Kristol, the conservative writer, noted: "It was not so much breaking it, but the way he broke it, the almost cavalier way he

announced it . . . It seemed to reveal, perhaps unfairly, that there was no core of belief there . . . He doesn't stand for anybody." Bush defended his decision: "I've got to see the country go forward, and I've got to take the heat. And I think in the final analysis the American people will understand that." But they did not. The President's decision to raise taxes probably cost him the election.

The three candidates avoided the tradition of facing the disciplined questioners of Sunday-morning interview programs. They preferred to discuss politics on early-morning or late-evening talk shows. Bush made 16 appearances on these programs; Perot, 39; and Clinton, 45. In an appeal to younger voters, Clinton put on his sunglasses, got out his saxophone, and played "Heartbreak Hotel" on the Arsenio Hall late-night program. The musical portion of his appearance was brief, but it was repeated endlessly on news programs.

Bush's campaign was disorganized and harsh, and he seemed tired and distracted. During a debate with Clinton and Perot, he checked his watch several times as if he were bored. Bush unveiled a new economic plan but quickly put it aside. He spoke about traditional family values, religious faith, and patriotism. He discussed his support for stiffer criminal penalties and his opposition to abortion, pornography, and welfare cheats. Clinton was better organized. He appealed to the post–World War II generation and newer constituencies—single mothers, working women, welfare recipients, gays, and MTV viewers. He spoke about urban renewal, the right to choose an abortion, job training, gun control, family medical leave, the new information technology, welfare reform, and a comprehensive health program.

Perot did not carry a single state on Election Day. He finished with 18.9 percent of the popular vote, a protest vote expressing dissatisfaction with both major political parties. Perot probably affected the outcome only in Ohio, which might have gone to Bush instead of Clinton had he not been running. President Bush received 37.4 percent of the popular vote, a lower vote than that cast for any Republican since Herbert Hoover in 1932. Bill Clinton won 43 percent, about the same percentage as Richard M. Nixon in 1968. In the Electoral College, Clinton received 370 votes to Bush's 168. It was a good campaign in which the candidates competed by discussing their specific positions on the major issues confronting the country.

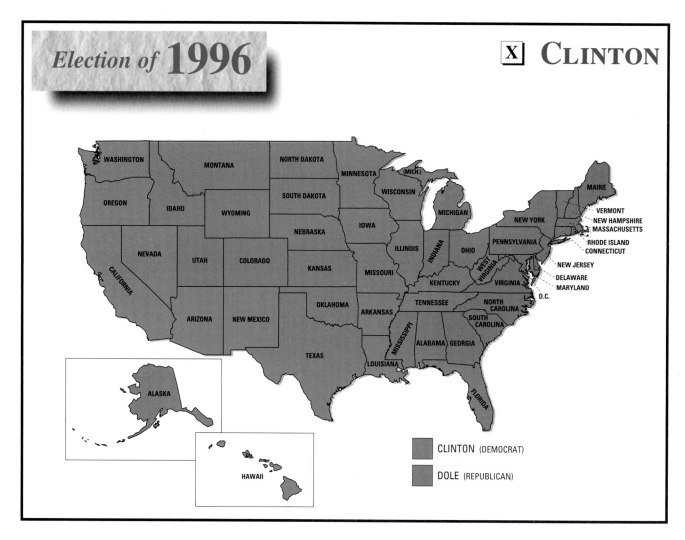

Election of 1996

X CLINTON

CLINTON (DEMOCRAT)

DOLE (REPUBLICAN)

States	Electoral Votes	Clinton	Dole	States	Electoral Votes	Clinton	Dole
Alabama	(9)	-	9	Montana	(3)	-	3
Alaska	(3)	-	3	Nebraska	(5)	-	5
Arizona	(8)	8	-	Nevada	(4)	4	-
Arkansas	(6)	6	-	New Hampshire	(4)	4	-
California	(54)	54	-	New Jersey	(15)	15	-
Colorado	(8)	-	8	New Mexico	(5)	5	-
Connecticut	(8)	8	-	New York	(33)	33	-
Delaware	(3)	3	-	North Carolina	(14)	-	14
District of Columbia	(3)	3	-	North Dakota	(3)	-	3
Florida	(25)	25	-	Ohio	(21)	21	-
Georgia	(13)	-	13	Oklahoma	(8)	-	8
Hawaii	(4)	4	-	Oregon	(7)	7	-
Idaho	(4)	-	4	Pennsylvania	(23)	23	-
Illinois	(22)	22	-	Rhode Island	(4)	4	-
Indiana	(12)	-	12	South Carolina	(8)	-	8
Iowa	(7)	7	-	South Dakota	(3)	-	3
Kansas	(6)	-	6	Tennessee	(11)	11	-
Kentucky	(8)	8	-	Texas	(32)	-	32
Louisiana	(9)	9	-	Utah	(5)	-	5
Maine	(4)	4	-	Vermont	(3)	3	-
Maryland	(10)	10	-	Virginia	(13)	-	13
Massachusetts	(12)	12	-	Washington	(11)	11	-
Michigan	(18)	18	-	West Virginia	(5)	5	-
Minnesota	(10)	10	-	Wisconsin	(11)	11	-
Mississippi	(7)	-	7	Wyoming	(3)	-	3
Missouri	(11)	11	-	**Totals**	**(538)**	**379**	**159**

ELECTORAL VOTE

Election of 1996

STATE	TOTAL VOTE	BILL CLINTON (Democrat)		ROBERT DOLE (Republican)		ROSS PEROT (Reform Party)		OTHER		PLURALITY	
		Votes	%	Votes	%	Votes	%	Votes	%		
Alabama	1,534,349	662,165	43.2	769,044	50.1	92,149	6.0	10,991	0.7	106,879	R
Alaska	241,620	80,380	33.3	122,746	50.8	26,333	10.9	12,161	5.0	42,366	R
Arizona	1,404,405	653,288	46.5	622,073	44.3	112,072	8.0	16,972	1.2	31,215	D
Arkansas	884,262	475,171	53.7	325,416	36.8	69,884	7.9	13,791	1.6	149,755	D
California	10,019,484	5,119,835	51.1	3,828,380	38.2	697,847	7.0	373,422	3.7	1,291,455	D
Colorado	1,510,704	671,152	44.4	691,848	45.8	99,629	6.6	48,075	3.2	20,696	R
Connecticut	1,392,614	735,740	52.8	483,109	34.7	139,523	10.0	34,242	2.5	252,631	D
Delaware	270,810	140,355	51.8	99,062	36.6	28,719	10.6	2,674	1.0	41,293	D
Dist. of Col.	185,726	158,220	85.2	17,339	9.3	3,611	1.9	6,556	3.5	140,881	D
Florida	5,300,927	2,545,968	48.0	2,243,324	42.3	483,776	9.1	27,859	0.5	302,644	D
Georgia	2,298,899	1,053,849	45.8	1,080,843	47.0	146,337	6.4	17,870	0.8	26,994	R
Hawaii	360,120	205,012	56.9	113,943	31.6	27,358	7.6	13,807	3.8	91,069	D
Idaho	491,711	165,443	33.6	256,595	52.2	62,518	12.7	7,155	1.5	91,152	R
Illinois	4,311,391	2,341,744	54.3	1,587,021	36.8	346,408	8.0	36,218	0.8	754,723	D
Indiana	2,135,431	887,424	41.6	1,006,693	47.1	224,299	10.5	17,015	0.8	119,269	R
Iowa	1,234,075	620,258	50.3	492,644	39.9	105,159	8.5	16,014	1.3	127,614	D
Kansas	1,074,300	387,659	36.1	583,245	54.3	92,639	8.6	10,757	1.0	195,586	R
Kentucky	1,388,707	636,614	45.8	623,283	44.9	120,396	8.7	8,414	0.6	13,331	D
Louisiana	1,783,959	927,837	52.0	712,586	39.9	123,293	6.9	20,243	1.1	215,251	D
Maine	605,897	312,788	51.6	186,378	30.8	85,970	14.2	20,761	3.4	126,410	D
Maryland	1,780,870	966,207	54.3	681,530	38.3	115,812	6.5	17,321	1.0	284,677	D
Massachusetts	2,556,459	1,571,509	61.5	718,058	28.1	227,206	8.9	39,686	1.6	853,451	D
Michigan	3,848,844	1,989,653	51.7	1,481,212	38.5	336,670	8.7	41,309	1.1	508,441	D
Minnesota	2,192,640	1,120,438	51.1	766,476	35.0	257,704	11.8	48,022	2.2	353,962	D
Mississippi	893,857	394,022	44.1	439,838	49.2	52,222	5.8	7,775	0.9	45,816	R
Missouri	2,158,065	1,025,935	47.5	890,016	41.2	217,188	10.1	24,926	1.2	135,919	D
Montana	407,083	167,922	41.3	179,652	44.1	55,229	13.6	4,280	1.1	11,730	R
Nebraska	677,415	236,761	35.0	363,467	53.7	71,278	10.5	5,909	0.9	126,706	R
Nevada	464,279	203,974	43.9	199,244	42.9	43,986	9.5	17,075	3.7	4,730	D
New Hampshire	499,053	246,166	49.3	196,486	39.4	48,387	9.7	8,014	1.6	49,680	D
New Jersey	3,075,860	1,652,361	53.7	1,103,099	35.9	262,134	8.5	58,266	1.9	549,262	D
New Mexico	556,074	273,495	49.2	232,751	41.9	32,257	5.8	17,571	3.2	40,744	D
New York	6,316,129	3,756,177	59.5	1,933,492	30.6	503,458	8.0	123,002	1.9	1,822,685	D
North Carolina	2,515,807	1,107,849	44.0	1,225,938	48.7	168,059	6.7	13,961	0.6	118,089	R
North Dakota	266,411	106,905	40.1	125,050	46.9	32,515	12.2	1,941	0.7	18,145	R
Ohio	4,534,434	2,148,222	47.4	1,859,883	41.0	483,207	10.7	43,122	1.0	288,339	D
Oklahoma	1,206,713	488,105	40.4	582,315	48.3	130,788	10.8	5,505	0.5	94,210	R
Oregon	1,377,760	649,641	47.2	538,152	39.1	121,221	8.8	68,746	5.0	111,489	D
Pennsylvania	4,506,118	2,215,819	49.2	1,801,169	40.0	430,984	9.6	58,146	1.3	414,650	D
Rhode Island	390,247	233,050	59.7	104,683	26.8	43,723	11.2	8,791	2.3	128,367	D
South Carolina	1,151,422	506,152	44.0	573,339	49.8	64,377	5.6	7,554	0.7	67,187	R
South Dakota	323,826	139,333	43.0	150,543	46.5	31,250	9.7	2,700	0.8	11,210	R
Tennessee	1,894,105	909,146	48.0	863,530	45.6	105,918	5.6	15,511	0.8	45,616	D
Texas	5,611,644	2,459,683	43.8	2,736,167	48.8	378,537	6.7	37,257	0.7	276,484	R
Utah	665,629	221,633	33.3	361,911	54.4	66,461	10.0	15,624	2.3	140,278	R
Vermont	258,449	137,894	53.4	80,352	31.1	31,024	12.0	9,179	3.6	57,542	D
Virginia	2,416,642	1,091,060	45.1	1,138,350	47.1	159,861	6.6	27,371	1.1	47,290	R
Washington	2,253,837	1,123,323	49.8	840,712	37.3	201,003	8.9	88,799	3.9	282,611	D
West Virginia	636,459	327,812	51.5	233,946	36.8	71,639	11.3	3,062	0.5	93,866	D
Wisconsin	2,196,169	1,071,971	48.8	845,029	38.5	227,339	10.4	51,830	2.4	226,942	D
Wyoming	211,571	77,934	36.8	105,388	49.8	25,928	12.3	2,321	1.1	27,454	R
	96,273,262	47,401,054	49.2	39,197,350	40.7	8,085,285	8.4	1,589,573	1.7	8,203,704	D

(Based on reports from the secretaries of state for the 50 states and the District of Columbia)

P O P U L A R V O T E

The economy was again the major issue in the 1996 presidential election. Voters asked themselves which candidate was best for their pocketbook. President Bill Clinton started the campaign ahead of any Republican opponent, and he stayed in front. He became the first Democrat since Franklin D. Roosevelt to be elected to a second term.

In July 1996, a record 43 percent of register voters rated national economic conditions as excellent or good compared to 11 percent just prior to the 1992 presidential election. Forty-three percent also thought that economic conditions as a whole were getting better. The unemployment rate had dropped to a six-year low of 5.3 percent in June, and the annual rate of inflation was below 3 percent. Applications for mortgages soared, and home sales neared a five-year high. Consumer spending was high and the economy was growing at a vigorous annual rate of 4.2 percent during the spring. The President proudly pointed to the fact that he had reduced the deficit in each of the four years of his first term.

Less than two years before, in the 1994 mid-term elections, enough middle-income voters had turned against the Democrats to give the Republicans control of Congress for the first time since 1956. Speaker of the House Newt Gingrich proposed a "Contract with America," but he had misread the mood of the voters who soon tired of his talking about a "Republican revolution." President Clinton regained his political footing by vetoing Republican measures to cut taxes and curb social programs and by portraying himself as the defender of Social Security and Medicare. The President shrewdly adopted the Republican promise to balance the budget early in the next century. In fact, he stressed his support of traditional values—fighting tobacco companies for selling cigarettes to minors, endorsing wearing school uniforms, and putting more police on the streets. He also endorsed the death penalty, a victims' rights bill, and a ban on assault weapons.

The President refused to sign budgets which would cut environmental and educational programs and sharply reduce health care and welfare benefits. As a result, the federal government shut down twice. Most voters blamed the Republican-controlled Congress for the shutdowns and supported Clinton for standing up to them. At the same time, he seemed to abandon many liberal themes. In July 1996, for example, Clinton signed a sweeping Republican welfare bill. He defied leaders in his own party as he ended a 61-year Democratic promise of federal aid to the nation's poor. However, he fulfilled a 1992 campaign pledge to "end welfare as we know it." This was the ultimate example of Clinton's new political strategy—achieving a balance between too-liberal Democrats and too-conservative Republicans. *The New York Times* wrote: "He is a moderate who cannot suppress his liberal impulses, a liberal who cannot escape his moderating instincts. He confounds his friends, who think he has agreed with them, only to find he had not. He confuses his enemies, who think they can work with him only to find they cannot." Clinton positioned himself to run for reelection as both a protector of the middle class and a defender of fiscal responsibility.

Senator Robert (Bob) Dole of Kansas had become the runaway choice among Republicans for their party's nomination by the beginning of March 1996. He suffered a narrow loss in New Hampshire to Patrick (Pat) Buchanan, a conservative journalist and former speech writer for Presidents Richard M. Nixon and Ronald Reagan. Although Dole won every Republican primary after that, he seemed unable to articulate why he wanted to be president and what his party stood for. Dole appeared old and dull, and his speeches were disjointed and rambling. He received the blame for Republican disunity over positions on abortion, tax cutting, affirmative action, and economic priorities. Conservative writers and commentators suggested that Dole step aside, but there was no stronger candidate. Dole tried to bring the issue of character into the campaign, but the voters seemed uninterested. He talked about building a bridge to the past, reminding voters of his record as a World War II hero and his 36 years of service in Congress. Clinton responded by saying that what was needed was a bridge to the twenty-first century.

A "gender gap" haunted Dole. In every Gallup Poll between mid-January and mid-July 1996, registered women voters' support for Clinton over Dole held steady in the high 50 and the low 60 percentages. This was because of Dole's ambiguous stand on abortion and the perceived Republican bashing of the President's wife, Hillary Rodham. Many women were bothered by the tone of the Republican "revolutionaries" and by the content of their programs. Historically, women have taken Medicare very seriously and also have been more sympathetic to social spending, especially on education and programs for children.

"Here in San Diego, the real race begins," said Bob Dole as the Republican Convention convened on 12 August. The nearly 2,000 delegates were overwhelmingly White, male, wealthy, and 40 years and older. They adopted a rigidly conservative party platform which supported a constitutional amendment outlawing abortion under any circumstances. They endorsed a constitutional amendment which would declare that children born in the United States of parents "who are not legally present in the United States or who are long-term residents are not automatically citizens." In addition, the platform opposed affirmative action but promised to enforce laws against "discrimination based on sex, race, age, creed, or national origin." The next sentence stated: "We reject the distortion of those laws to cover sexual preferences." Dole said he had not read the platform and did not feel bound by it.

Dole chose Jack Kemp as his running mate. Kemp was a former congressman from New York and had been secretary of housing and urban development in the administration of George Bush. Dole delivered his acceptance speech before a television audience estimated between 25 to 30 million. He seized this prime-time opportunity to present his plan to cut taxes by 15 percent and to balance the federal budget. Few voters believed that he could accomplish both. Dole depicted the Clinton administration as a "corps of elite who never grew up, never did anything real, never sacrificed, never suffered, and never learned." He resigned from the U.S. Senate, where he was majority leader, to devote full time to the campaign.

On 11 August, H. Ross Perot, the Texas billionaire businessman, told the newly created Reform Party: "I want to be your president." In 1992, Perot, running as an independent, had won 18.9 percent of the popular vote. Once again, he entered a presidential election using a third party which he created and financed. Dole took Perot seriously enough to urge voters to ignore the Texan because the Republican Party "is the real Reform Party."

The Democratic Convention began its sessions in Chicago on 26 August. Bill Clinton and Vice President Al Gore were renominated by acclamation. Many delegates were worried about the President's tendency to compromise, and they were disturbed by the questions about his character and the potential scandals surrounding his first term. However, the President continued to hold sizable leads in the polls. An overwhelming 95 percent said that they supported Clinton's renomination. His approval rating soared to 60 percent, the highest of his presidency. Politicians from both parties agreed the odds favored him in the November election.

The campaign consisted of dull speeches, news conferences, and the televised debates in search of issues which truly separated the candidates. Dole proposed cutting Medicare by $26 billion; Clinton proposed cutting it $19 billion. Dole spoke against the use of marijuana; Clinton spoke against tobacco. Dole insisted that Clinton was committed to liberalism; the President denied he was a liberal, a denial which caused many Democrats to flinch. He had sent troops to Haiti and Bosnia, and the interventions had not ended in disasters, as many had predicted. His deployment of naval forces seemed to end a Chinese threat to Taiwan. The Middle East remained relatively calm, and Boris Yeltsin, whom he supported, was reelected president of Russia. While untested in a major crisis, Clinton had kept the peace during his first term, and Americans were not fighting in a foreign war.

The election results seemed almost predictable. Some 92 million voters, roughly 50 percent of those eligible, cast a ballot. It was proportionately the lowest voter turnout since 1924. Clinton won 49.2 percent of the popular vote to Dole's 40.7 percent and Perot's 8.4 percent. The President won with 6.2 percentage points more of the popular vote, and 9 more electoral votes, than in 1992. Dole carried only the broad band of Great Plains and Mountain states stretching from the Canadian border to Texas, most of the Deep South, and Indiana, a Republican island in the Democratic sea which covered the whole northeastern quadrant. The fundraising scandals which had emerged during the final days of the campaign probably cost Clinton support from Republicans and independents who were prepared to cross over to the Democratic ticket.

When the results of the election were final, Clinton spoke to the crowd gathered outside the Old State House in Little Rock, Arkansas. He said, "Now we've got a bridge to build, and I'm ready if you are." For the first time in U.S. history, a Democrat had been elected to the White House with a Congress controlled by the opposition. The voters had elected a moderate Democratic president to carry out moderate Republican agendas.

SUGGESTED READING

General

History of American Presidential Elections, 1789–1968 (Chelsea House Publishers, 1971), edited by Arthur M. Schlesinger, Jr. and Fred L. Israel, is a four-volume work. Written by prominent historians and political scientists, it provides a comprehensive history. A fifth volume covering elections through 1984 followed in 1986. Arthur M. Schlesinger, Jr. is also Editor of *Running for President: The Candidates and Their Images* (Simon & Schuster, 1994). The Associate Editors are Fred L. Israel and David J. Frent. This is a two-volume collection of original essays on each election through 1992. It is a beautiful reference work in four colors, and it contains thousands of illustrations. Israel states that the contributors were given two assignments: "to analyze an election and to focus, wherever possible, on the diverse styles, tactics, and techniques used by presidential candidates and their parties to woo the electorate."

Encyclopedia of the American Presidency (Simon & Schuster, 1994), edited by Leonard W. Levy and Louis Fisher, is an excellent reference work in four volumes. The second volume contains articles on all the presidential elections through 1992. *The Presidents* (Grolier Educational, 1997) is an eight-volume work edited by Fred L. Israel. It is intended for middle and high school readers. *A History of Presidential Elections: From George Washington to Richard M. Nixon* (Eugene H. Roseboom, Macmillan, 3rd ed., 1970) covers "not only the elections themselves, but the developments in each administration that influenced the work of party conventions, and determined the character and outcome of campaigns." It includes sketches of winners, losers, also-rans, and pre-convention hopefuls. *A Statistical History of the American Presidential Elections* (Svend Peterson, Frederick Ungar Publishing Co., 1963) gives a complete statistical analysis for every presidential election from 1789 to 1960. Congressional Quarterly's *Guide to the Presidency* (Michael Nelson, 2nd ed., 1996) is a comprehensive reference on the origins, evolution, and contemporary workings of the U.S. presidency. It is an invaluable treasury of facts and figures. *Selecting the President from 1789 to 1996* (Congressional Quarterly Books, 1997) is a briefer paperback drawn from *Guide to the Presidency*.

Presidential Elections, 1789–1996 (Congressional Quarterly Books, 1997) traces the electoral process, describing the functions of party nominating conventions. It lists the candidates nominated by all parties since 1831 and includes an appendix of presidential and vice presidential biographies. *The American Voter* (Angus Campbell, Philip E. Converse, Warren E. Miller, and Donald E. Stokes, John Wiley & Sons, 1960) uses survey research to analyze and explain what leads the American voter to decision at the polls. *The Presidency, A to Z* (Congressional Quarterly Books, 1994) examines the history, processes, and people of the U.S. presidency. Charts, tables, and illustrations enhance over 300 alphabetical entries. *The American Party Systems* (William N. Chambers and Walter Dean Burnham, eds., Oxford University Press, 1975) applies novel conceptual approaches to the history of political parties. Walter Dean Burnham presents statistical compilations in *Presidential Ballots, 1836–1892* (2nd ed., Ayer Co. Pubs. Inc., 1976). Sidney Warren gives lively popular accounts of 10 key elections in *The Battle for the Presidency* (Lippincott, 1968).

Campaigns and Campaign Strategy

Presidential Elections in American Politics: The Techniques of Modern Election Campaigns (Herbert Asher, 5th ed., The Dorsey Press, 1992) compares the conduct of campaigns. It examines what they have in common and how they differ. *The Political Persuaders: The Techniques of Modern Election Campaigns* (Dan Nimmo, Prentice-Hall, Inc., 1970) describes and assesses the "impact of the rapid changes taking place in the technology of modern political campaigning." *Over the Wire and On TV: CBS and UPI in Campaign '80* (Michael J. Robinson and Margaret A. Sheehan, Russell Sage Foundation, 1983) draws on almost 6,000 news stories and dozens of interviews with writers and reporters to "measure the level of objectivity, fairness, seriousness, and criticism displayed by CBS News and United Press International" in covering the 1980 campaign.

What It Takes: The Way to the White House (Richard B. Cramer, Random House, 1993) examines eight contenders (George Bush, Robert Dole, Michael Dukakis, Gary Hart, Richard Gephardt, and Joseph Biden) in the election of 1988. *The Road to the White House: The Politics of Presidential Elections* (Stephen J. Wayne, 4th ed., St. Martin's Press, 1992) provides a concise, behind-the-scenes guide for anyone who has an interest in presidential elections. *Packaging the Presidency: A History and Criticism of Presidential Campaign Advertising* (Kathleen Hall Jamieson, Oxford University Press, 1984) "traces the origins and evolution of presidential advertising from the earliest days of banners and broadsides to the advent of broadcasts." She examines the elections from 1952 through 1980 in detail. It contains an excellent bibliography.

Electoral College and Reform

Reform and Continuity: The Electoral College, the Convention, and the Party System (Alexander M. Bickel, Harper Colophon Books, 1971) explores the Electoral College, national party conventions, and minority parties in light of the congressional action on electoral reform during the late 1960s. This book is a revised and expanded version of Bickel's original work *The New Age of Political Reform* (Harper & Row, 1968). *The Politics of Electoral College Reform* (Lawrence D. Longley and Alan G. Braun, Yale University Press, 1972) discusses the establishment of the Electoral College system and how it works, while carefully reconstructing the events surrounding electoral reform activities in the late 1960s. The authors describe and assess the various reform proposals and come out in favor of the direct vote plan. *Voting for President: The Electoral College and the American Political System* (Wallace S. Sayre and Judith H. Parris, The Brookings Institution, 1970) presents a comprehensive analysis of the existing electoral system and compares its results with the likely impact of four leading alternatives: the direct vote, the automatic plan, the district plan, and the proportional plan. *The Electoral College* (Lucius Wilmerding, Jr., Rutgers University Press, 1958) discusses the history of the Electoral College while analyzing and examining three plans of electoral reform: the national plebiscite system, the proportional voting system, and the district system.

Presidential Primaries

Presidential Primaries and Nominations (William Crotty and John S. Jackson III, Congressional Quarterly Books, 1985) analyzes the presidential nominating system, examining in detail the prenomination process and participants. This book focuses on how the nominating system has changed in recent decades and what the consequences of the changes have been. *The Invisible Primary* (Arthur T. Hadley, Prentice-Hall, Inc., 1976) examines the period of political time between the election of one president and the start of the first state primary to determine the next presidential candidates. It deals with the people, winners and losers, and politics of presidential selection from 1973 through December 1975. *Quiet Revolution: The Struggle for the Democratic Party and the Shaping of Post-Reform Politics* (Byron E. Shafer, Russell Sage Foundation, 1983) provides a definitive account of the struggle for reform within the Democratic Party from 1968 to 1972. The author uses candid interviews with numerous key participants and extensive archival material.

Nominating Presidential Candidates

Presidential Elections: Strategies of American Electoral Politics (Nelson W. Polsby and Aaron Wildavsky, 9th ed., Chatham House, 1995) is a highly acclaimed guide to the process of electing an American president. The authors describe and analyze all the participants in the electoral process, the resources available to parties and candidates, and the process itself. *National Party Conventions, 1831–1992* (Congressional Quarterly Books, 1995) traces the development of the political party convention, beginning with a detailed description of the pre-convention nominating process from 1789 to 1828. It discusses the delegate-selection process, party convention rules, and communication with the media. *Convention Decisions and Voting Records* (Richard C. Bain and Judith H. Parris, 2nd ed., Books on Demand, 1960) deals with presidential convention deliberations, controversies, and decisions.

Third Parties and Third-Party Candidates

Encyclopedia of Third Parties in the United States (Earl R. Krushke, ABC-CLIO, 1991) is intended for the general reader and student. Krushke notes that "it should be viewed as a source to which such persons can turn in order to begin their study of third parties." *Third Parties in Presidential Elections* (Daniel A. Mazmanian, The Brookings Institution, 1974) examines the leading third-party movements in the U.S. political system and finds that they are an integral part of the party system in the United States. *Third Parties in America: Citizen Response to Major Party Failure* (Steven J. Rosenstone, Roy L. Behr, and Edward H. Lazarus, Princeton University Press, 1984) explains why and when the two-party system deteriorates and third parties flourish. *The Other Candidates: Third Parties in Presidential Elections* (Frank Smallwood, University Press of New England, 1983) points out that over 200 third-party candidates have run since 1860, yet only 8 have managed to capture more than 1 million popular votes. This book is a series of interviews with each of the third-party candidates who ran in two or more states in 1980.

INDEX